MW01073190

Advance Praise for *Wo*...

"Wherever there is space in Hebrew Scripture, Lucky for modern readers she is. Lots of place... voices, perspective, and contributions of women have been silenced or ... male biblical writers themselves and centuries of ensuing (largely male) commentary. Inspired by the tradition of rabbinic sages to provide explanatory comments, expansive additions, illustrative anecdotes, and legendary stories to interpret texts fraught with silence, Gafney deftly deploys what she refers to uniquely as a womanist midrash (combining seriously impressive scholarship, a black womanist reading lens, and the inspiration of midrashic sages) to question and, best of all, fill in blanks to read women back into Scripture as divine agents who resisted, persisted, subverted, disrupted, and reconstituted the biblical (and the modern!) world order. Sure, every interpretation of biblical texts is a combination of the stories themselves and the location, interests, and biases of the person or groups reading the stories. In light of the social and political times in which we live, with exceptional skill in *Womanist Midrash* Wil Gafney makes certain that women's voices in Hebrew Scripture are not erased, are heard, and are reckoned with in fact and that the lived experiences of black women (and other marginalized communities) get equal time around the hermeneutical table."

—Dr. Renita J. Weems, author of *Just a Sister Away: A Womanist Vision
of Women's Relationships in the Bible*

"*Womanist Midrash* is a page-turner. Womanist questions about power and marginalization epitomize Gafney's fearless honesty, such as on texts allowing women and girls to be held in sexual slavery by Israelites: 'the truth of these passages is the truth of the world in which they originated.' Gafney's deep involvement in the Jewish community and in Jewish ways of reading enables her to use the ancient rabbinic method to fill in gaps in the biblical text through textually informed imagination for an audience of Christians, Jews, and others. Maybe Rachel did not want to marry Jacob. Why did Abraham not give an inheritance to his children by Keturah? How did Michal's mother respond when King David abandoned her daughter, his wife? As a preacher and a liturgist, Gafney wonders whether Laban's charge to Jacob not to abuse his daughters Leah and Rachel could become part of a wedding ceremony. In short, through eye-opening imagination Gafney shows her love for those who read and live by the Bible."

—Dr. Bernadette J. Brooten, editor of *Beyond Slavery: Overcoming Its Religious and
Sexual Legacies* and Robert and Myra Kraft and Jacob Hiatt
Professor of Christian Studies, Brandeis University

"*Womanist Midrash* is a masterful tapestry of many threads, at once three dimensional in scope, fastidious in attention to translation and hermeneutics, and dedicated to stimulating our curiosity regarding named and unnamed women of the Torah and throne. The volume incarnates Professor Wil Gafney's rich, complex journey to create a rabbinic pedagogy and vision that responds to contemporary problems, constructs new stories, and makes connections between new life realities and unchanging biblical texts. Gafney provides historical and traditional interpretations from a womanist perspective, mindful of oppression arising from gender, class, and, where appropriate, ethnicity. *Womanist Midrash* is a must-read for academician and believer alike who dare to take these texts seriously, particularly if one is willing to see and listen, with their own 'sanctified imagination,' as they study the instruction, revelation, and sometimes law of Torah."

—Dr. Cheryl A. Kirk-Duggan, Professor of Religion,
Shaw University Divinity School

"Gafney's groundbreaking work, *Womanist Midrash*, weaves together womanist biblical hermeneutics and Jewish midrashic interpretive strategies to offer stunning new perspectives on biblical narratives about women in the Hebrew Bible. Gafney grounds her 'sacred imagination' in classical biblical scholarship while designating the articulations of black women's experiences as authoritative and central. She draws inspiration from midrash, which fills in the untold stories behind the stories. On almost every page of this book, Gafney offers fresh, womanish, and proudly audacious interpretations and questions. This is one of those rare commentaries that speaks to Jewish and Christian readers alike. *Womanist Midrash* will be required reading for my rabbinical students alongside the classic male-stream Bible commentaries."

—Dr. S. Tamar Kamionkowski, Professor of Bible,
Reconstructionist Rabbinical College

"As a black woman bearing the history of two interwoven strands of subjugation in her own embodied memory, along with love for the Bible and its women, Gafney shows us in unexampled detail how biblical society—struggling to be sacred, yet entwined with the subjugation of women—works out in their intimate lives. The result is 'sacred subversion'—a lover's wrestle within the Bible, against the Bible, for the sake of God and the Bible. I greet with admiration a sister in that painful, joyful Wrestle, and I encourage readers to join with her in the painful, joyful adventure."

—Rabbi Arthur Waskow, director of The Shalom Center and
author of *Godwrestling—Round 2*

"Using her scholarly expertise and her inspired, sanctified imagination, Wil Gafney offers brilliant new readings of Scripture while also retrieving the ancient wisdom of women from the biblical world. Gafney's lyrical prose expresses passionate advocacy for marginalized and oppressed individuals found in the biblical text, the ancient world, and our own society. In this volume, the reader encounters the liberative power of wrestling with sacred texts."

—Dr. Joy A. Schroeder, Bergener Professor of Theology and Religion at Capital
University and Trinity Lutheran Seminary and author of *Deborah's Daughters:
Gender Politics and Biblical Interpretation*

"Wil Gafney's brilliant fusion of womanist poetics and the 'sanctified imagination' of the black church allows us to experience the oft-overlooked women in Torah narratives and those selectively recounted in the annals of the Israelite monarchy as multidimensional figures central to the Hebrew Bible. Gafney invites us to deploy the riches of African American women's wisdom traditions in our engagement of Scripture and to appreciate how such usage—inclusive of philological inquiry and attentiveness to the art of translation—has the capacity to positively transform the ways we read, think, and live. Her interpretations are original, highly nuanced, and compelling. This exceptional compendium is a must-read for all interested in the forms, creative potentialities, and applications of midrash, both ancient and modern."

—(The Rev. Canon) Dr. Hugh R. Page Jr., Vice President, Associate Provost,
Dean—First Year of Studies, and Professor of Theology
and Africana Studies University of Notre Dame

"Dr. Gafney's close reading of the text is profound while remaining accessible; her creative writing, like the best of classical midrash, stays true to the text and its context. I have learned much from her insightful readings of Torah, which now take their rightful place on the pulpit as well as in educational venues. Dr. Gafney gives Torah-acquainted readers the gift of womanist perspectives—which it behooves us Jews, among others, to grasp—while giving wider audiences the benefit of a midrashic approach. I cannot recommend her work highly enough."

—Rabbi Fred Scherlinder Dobb, Adat Shalom Reconstructionist Congregation,
Bethesda, Maryland

Womanist Midrash

© 2017 Wilda C. Gafney

First edition
Published by Westminster John Knox Press
Louisville, Kentucky

17 18 19 20 21 22 23 24 25 26—10 9 8 7 6 5 4 3 2 1

All rights reserved. No part of this book may be reproduced or transmitted in any form or by any means, electronic or mechanical, including photocopying, recording, or by any information storage or retrieval system, without permission in writing from the publisher. For information, address Westminster John Knox Press, 100 Witherspoon Street, Louisville, Kentucky 40202-1396. Or contact us online at www.wjkbooks.com.

Unless otherwise indicated, Scripture quotations are the author's own translation.

Scripture quotations marked NRSV are from the New Revised Standard Version of the Bible, copyright © 1989 by the Division of Christian Education of the National Council of the Churches of Christ in the U.S.A., and are used by permission.

Scripture quotations marked JPS are from *The TANAKH: The New JPS Translation according to the Traditional Hebrew Text.* Copyright 1985 by the Jewish Publication Society. Used by permission.

Scripture quotations marked NIV are from *The Holy Bible, New International Version.* Copyright © 1973, 1978, 1984, 2011 by Biblica, Inc.® Used by permission. All rights reserved worldwide.

Book design by Sharon Adams
Cover design by Allison Taylor
Cover art: Miriam, 2006, Laura James, laurajamesart.com

Library of Congress Cataloging-in-Publication Data

Names: Gafney, Wilda, 1966– author.
Title: Womanist Midrash : a reintroduction to the women of the Torah and the throne / Wilda C. Gafney.
Description: First edition. | Louisville, KY : Westminster John Knox Press, 2017. | Includes index. |
Identifiers: LCCN 2017005498 (print) | LCCN 2017026716 (ebook) | ISBN 9781611648126 (ebk.) | ISBN 9780664239039 (pbk. : alk. paper)
Subjects: LCSH: Women in the Bible. | Bible. Old Testament—Feminist criticism. | Womanism—Religious aspects—Judaism. | Womanist theology.
Classification: LCC BS1181.8 (ebook) | LCC BS1181.8 .G34 2017 (print) | DDC 221.9/22082—dc23
LC record available at https://lccn.loc.gov/2017005498

♾ The paper used in this publication meets the minimum requirements of the American National Standard for Information Sciences—Permanence of Paper for Printed Library Materials, ANSI Z39.48-1992.

Most Westminster John Knox Press books are available at special quantity discounts when purchased in bulk by corporations, organizations, and special-interest groups. For more information, please e-mail SpecialSales@wjkbooks.com.

Womanist Midrash

A Reintroduction to the Women
of the Torah and the Throne

Wilda C. Gafney

WESTMINSTER
JOHN KNOX PRESS
LOUISVILLE · KENTUCKY

Contents

APPENDIXES

Acknowledgments

I am most deeply indebted to the scholarship of Renita Weems and Alice Laffey. This project is in many ways a descendant of their flowering (preferable to the standard masculinist adjective, "seminal") work: *Just a Sister Away: A Womanist Vision of Women's Relationships in the Bible* (Weems, LuraMedia, 1988) and *An Introduction to the Old Testament: A Feminist Perspective* (Laffey, Fortress Press, 1988). I was introduced to both by Dr. Alice Ogden Bellis while a seminarian at the Howard University School of Divinity.

The scholarship of Renita Weems has provided ongoing companionship, illumination, and inspiration in my journey from seminarian to ordained clergywoman, congregational pastor and Army chaplain, graduate student in biblical studies, seminary professor, and published author in biblical studies. Weems's *I Asked for Intimacy* (1993) modeled a womanist exegetical practice drawn from her scholarly acumen as well as interpretive practices within black Christian communities. It was the first time I had seen black feminist biblical scholarship that emerged from and validated the faith community in which I was formed. Weems's subsequent texts, *Battered Love* (Fortress, 1995), *Listening for God* (Simon & Schuster, 1999), *Showing Mary* (Walk Worthy Press, 2002), and *What Matters Most* (Walk Worthy Press, 2005), each modeled the possibilities of womanist and black feminist biblical scholarship for the academy and church, while speaking honestly about the struggle of being located in two such seemingly contradictory institutions.

Laffey's collection of texts was familiar and unfamiliar to me; they focused on narratives with female characters and those implicated in the construction of gendered roles and behaviors under her rubrics "texts from a feminist perspective" and "themes from a feminist perspective." Her work helped the

Bible come alive to me as a woman, as a feminist, and as a scholar. Her questions and observations answered some of my questions and invited others.

This volume is a descendant of—if not Weems's and Laffey's own work—my experiences of their work. The classical feminist principle that shapes this text from Laffey's scholarship and its ideological context is the *fundamental equality of women and men*. In this work, that principle means that women and men in the Bible are worthy objects of study and inquiry, and that women's questions and observations about the text, particularly those of black women, are essential to understanding the text.

Elisabeth Schüssler Fiorenza's four paradigms (religious-theological-scriptural, critical-scientific-modern, cultural-hermeneutic-postmodern, and emancipatory-radical democratic) in *Democratizing Biblical Studies* (Westminster John Knox, 2009) have also shaped me and this work. Her emancipatory-radical democratic paradigm includes transformational and activism-based responses to the biblical text and its role in the communities that value them and recognize religious authority in them. This work is also activist work intended to transform congregations and classrooms and the persons who study, worship, and teach in them.

Other influences include Kahlil Gibran's *Jesus, the Son of Man* (A. A. Knopf, 1928), which, along with Ellen Frankel's *The Five Books of Miriam* (Putnam, 1995), modeled first-person *midrashim* that have stayed with me through the years and serve as a template for my own work. Sermons, *drashes*, conversations beyond numbering or naming, and a lifetime of hearing, thinking, questioning, and later reading, studying, and translating all shape this project.

At one level this work originates in the text; the Hebrew text and translation is the genesis of this project. Everett Fox is the translator who has influenced me most. His *Five Books of Moses*, *Give Us a King* and recently released *Early Prophets* are for me the finest translations of the Hebrew Bible available in English (Schocken, 1995, 1999, and 2014). At the same time Hugh Page's translations in *Israel's Poetry of Resistance: Africana Perspectives on Early Hebrew Verse* (Fortress, 2013) plumb the dialects of the Africana diaspora, offering a companion discourse to womanist translation and midrash.

While my womanish, womanist feminism has its individual characteristics, I am not the first black woman to do this work. I stand, write, and wrestle in the company of sister-scholar inheritrixes of an ancestral tradition of black women scrutinizing and questioning the text and the god of the text, including Julia A. J. Foote, Zilpha Elaw, Jarena Lee, Florence Spearing Randolph, Anna Julia Cooper, Maria W. Stewart, and Pauli Murray. Some of the black feminist and womanist Hebrew biblical scholars who have been my conversation partners in the maturation of this project are Valerie Bridgeman, Cheryl Anderson, Kimberly Russaw, Cheryl Kirk-Duggan, Mitzi Smith, Madipoane

Masenya, Vanessa Lovelace, and Musa Dube, along with feminist male voices Hugh Page and Randall Bailey.

I would like to thank the members of the Dorshei Derekh Minyan of the Germantown Jewish Center in Philadelphia, for the opportunity to share in a community of Torah study, teaching, and living; the RevGalBlogPals, for their reception of and feedback on the earliest version of this book; the Womanist Consultation of the American Academy of Religion and the Womanist Biblical Scholar Group of the Society of Biblical Literature, for creating a space for the flourishing of black feminist and womanist scholars, activists, preachers, poets, painters, and practitioners of womanist ethics; Sharon Watson Fluker and the Fund for Theological Education, for nurturing my vocation; my colleague Mark Brummitt, for naming this work and methodology as *womanist midrash*; my students at the Lutheran Theological Seminary at Philadelphia and the Reconstructionist Rabbinical College, for their questions and observations throughout the years; the sisters at the Episcopal Carmel monastery in Rising Sun, MD, for facilitating my sabbatical retreat; Susan Cole, my spiritual director, for accompanying me in prayer during this project; the All Saints Episcopal Church of Kapaa on the island of Kauai and the Diocese of Hawaii, for their gracious hospitality in calling me as a scholar-in-residence and providing a retreat house in which to craft this project; the Tantur Ecumenical Institute and St. George's Anglican Cathedral of Jerusalem, for granting me space and place in which to read, write, and reflect; the faculty and board of trustees of the Lutheran Theological Seminary at Philadelphia, for granting me a year's sabbatical; the Diocese of Pennsylvania, for supporting me during my sabbatical; Ron Townsend and Rachel Zimmerman, for running down obscure references; and Marianne Blickenstaff and Bridgett Green of Westminster John Knox, for your kind and gracious support.

This work was made possible in part by a 2010 Lilly research grant through the Association of Theological Schools in the United States and Canada.

Abbreviations

AYBD	*Anchor Yale Bible Dictionary*
BDB	Brown-Driver-Briggs Hebrew and English Lexicon
BigS	*Bibel in gerechter Sprache*
DCH	*Dictionary of Classical Hebrew*
Fox	*The Five Books of Moses*, trans. Everett Fox
GSJPS	A Gender-Sensitive Adaptation of the JPS Translation
HALOT	*Hebrew and Aramaic Lexicon of the Old Testament*
IB	The Inclusive Bible
JPS	Jewish Publication Society *TANAKH*
LXX	Septuagint
MT	Masoretic Text
NRSV	New Revised Standard Version
SP	Samaritan Pentateuch

Introduction

Women of the Torah and the Throne

PROLOGUE: YOU'RE INVITED TO SUPPER
(OR, IS THIS BOOK FOR YOU?)

I'd like to invite you to supper. My family is from the South, and I mean supper and not dinner. Supper is the larger (and earlier) of the two meals. You are most welcome to this table. Don't worry, it's no trouble, there's plenty to eat, and there are extra places at the table. Help yourself.

The supper table for many black women (women of African descent, primarily but not exclusively in the Americas, Caribbean, Europe, and on the continent of Africa) is often mother's or grandmother's table; it may have now become our table. The table (and everything on it) is womanist biblical interpretation, the content of this book, to which you are invited. That your host is a black woman who cooks and serves the way she does in no way makes you less welcome or even unwelcome because you may not be a black woman and/or set and serve your table differently. This book is an invitation, and its contents are meal (and recipes) and table talk.

In my house the dishes are not limited to those my mother and grandmother knew and loved. The dishes I love come from all over the world: India, Turkey, Jordan, and Morocco in addition to my ancestral North Carolina and Texas. All are welcome at this table, and as a sign of that welcome I offer not only dishes I like; I try to meet the dietary needs of my guests—which is not the same as cooking exactly what they want exactly the way they want. I am no short-order cook, yet some of the dishes on my table are kosher vegetarian; others are vegan. When there is meat, it may be halal. And, as the daughter of a southern woman who brought macaroni salad to family reunions, I can't pass myself off as a southern-style soul food cook, not even in this opening parable. So there is an explicit invitation for you to bring your own dish to share.

All are welcome to this table. The tables of our mothers and grandmothers (and sometimes fathers and grandfathers) in the African diaspora include multicultural marriages (Korean on my mother's side, Mexican on my father's side) and bi- and multiracial children in addition to our own multiple heritages (Native American, Irish, and African American on my mother's side; German and African American on my father's side). To be black in America is no singular thing; accordingly there is no singular black biblical interpretation. To be a black woman in the Americas is to navigate and negotiate multiple identities and perspectives, as so many womanist thinkers, writers, scholars, readers, preachers, teachers, and interpreters illustrate.

The supper invitation is the guiding metaphor for this book. Schoolmates, family friends, and some folk who we never figured out just how they arrived at our tables were all welcome. And so you are welcome, whether womanism and feminism[1] are familiar, beloved, or altogether new and strange dishes. You are most welcome.

If you are trying to figure out whether a womanist and feminist book about the Bible is for you, pull up a seat; dig in. Accepting this invitation to this table doesn't mean you can't go home and cook (or order in) the way you used to. It just may mean you won't want to. This text is an invitation for readers, hearers, and interpreters of the Scriptures to read and interpret with me. This text is written for those who read the Bible as a religious text, who look to it for teaching and preaching, inspiration and illumination; to offer religious readers an exegetical and hermeneutical resource that delves deeply into the canon(s) and draws on marginal and marginalized women as scriptural exemplars.

WOMANIST MIDRASH

My exegetical approach in this project is *womanist midrash* inspired by rabbinic midrashic approaches to the literal texts of the Scriptures, their translations, and interpretations for religious readers. My approach combines

1. Womanism is often simply defined as black feminism. It is that, and it is much more. It is a richer, deeper, liberative paradigm; a social, cultural, and political space and theological matrix with the experiences and multiple identities of black women at the center. Womanism shares the radical egalitarianism that characterizes feminism at its basic level, but without its default referent, white women functioning as the exemplar for all women. Feminism here is both the justice work of women on behalf of women in public and private spaces that seeks to transcend boundaries, and feminism

translation-based exegesis with literary and contextual, ancient and contemporary readings of the biblical text as Scripture. I offer "A Note on Translating" as an appendix. As religious readings, rabbinic readings discern value in texts, words, and letters, as potential revelatory spaces; they reimagine dominant narratival readings while crafting new ones to stand alongside—not replace—former readings. Midrash also asks questions of the text; sometimes it provides answers, sometimes it leaves the reader to answer the questions.

My friend and Hebrew biblical studies colleague Mark Brummitt coined the term "womanist midrash" for my work, and I am indebted to him for it. The expression captures my articulation of a womanist hermeneutic influenced by classical rabbinic and continuing contemporary midrash. Specifically, womanist midrash is a set of interpretive practices, including translation, exegesis, and biblical interpretation, that attends to marginalized characters in biblical narratives, especially women and girls, intentionally including and centering on non-Israelite peoples and enslaved persons. Womanist midrash listens to and for their voices in and through the Hebrew Bible, while acknowledging that often the text does not speak, or even intend to speak, to or for them, let alone hear them. In the tradition of rabbinic midrash and contemporary feminist biblical scholarship, womanist midrash offers names for anonymized characters and crafts/listens for/gives voice to those characters. This particular hermeneutic, womanist midrash, is an outgrowth of my experience from pulpit and pew with the *sanctified imagination* in black preaching; I have come to recognize the sanctified imagination as a type of African American indigenous midrash.

The exercise of the sanctified imagination may be unfamiliar for some readers. The concept of the sanctified imagination is deeply rooted in a biblical piety that respects the Scriptures as the word of God and takes them seriously and authoritatively. This piety can be characterized by a belief in the inerrancy of Scripture and a profound concern never to misrepresent the biblical texts. In this context the preacher would be very careful to signify that what he or she is preaching is not in the text but is also divinely inspired. In this practice a preacher may introduce a part of the sermon with words like "In my *sanctified imagination* . . . ," in order to disclose that the preacher is going beyond the text in a manner not likely to be challenged, even in the most literal interpretive communities. The sanctified imagination is the fertile creative space where the preacher-interpreter enters the text, particularly the spaces in the text, and fills them out with missing details: names, back stories, detailed descriptions of the scene and characters, and so on.

---

as it is in the Western world with historical and contemporary racism, classism, and transphobia characterizing it to differing degrees.

Like classical and contemporary Jewish midrash, the sacred imagination tells the story behind the story, the story between the lines on the page. For example, the sanctified imagination reveals that Rachel was athletic and long-legged. The sanctified imagination declares that Samson's locks of hair were dreadlocks. The sanctified imagination explains that Bathsheba always walked with her head held high, never refused to make eye contact with anyone, but David could not meet her eyes and hung his head in her presence until the day he died. Exercise of the sanctified imagination is also a form of what biblical scholars call reader-response criticism.[2]

A preacher may also engage in the practice without a formal disclosure, signaling with extreme and/or asynchronous descriptions, for example, Joseph's chariot wheels as "dubs" or "22s."[3] The invocation of the sanctified imagination also gives the community permission to resist the exegetical license taken by the preacher without rejecting or critiquing the sermon as a whole.

As sanctified imagination in this womanist midrash is rooted in the Afro-diaspora, specifically in the black church (a dynamic, diverse collection of peoples and practices with elusive boundaries), a womanist engagement looks to the experiences and articulations of black women throughout the diaspora (but in this work focusing on the Americas) as an authoritative source and norm for biblical interpretation. My practice of womanist midrash draws heavily on my knowledge of and experience with classical Jewish midrash as a scholar and with classical and contemporary midrash in congregational teaching (including my own) in Jewish spaces. As neither Christianity nor Judaism (nor even religious identity) is constitutive for womanist work, I include perspectives from the *hadith*[4] for characters with a legacy in Islam. And I try to articulate ethical observations in ways that transcend religious identity.

In Jewish sacred literature, *midrash* is the primary rabbinic term for exegesis. In Biblical Hebrew the verb *d-r-sh* means, "to seek"; later it would become specifically "to exegete"; *midrash* is its derived noun. Rabbinic exegesis is characterized by close reading of the biblical text, particularly the Masoretic Text (MT) and occasionally a targumic (Aramaic) text. Traditional midrash is also mystical, imaginative, revelatory, and, above all, religious. Midrash interprets not only the text before the reader, but also the text behind and beyond the

---

2. Reader-response criticism recognizes that the meaning of a text is not solely located in the text, but that the reader brings an authoritative interpretive framework to the text with her.

3. Custom twenty- or twenty-two-inch automobile wheel rims.

4. *Hadith* is the Arabic word for traditional sayings of and traditions about the Prophet Muhammad attributed to his companions. These teachings are not found in the Qur'an. They are authoritative to differing degrees.

text and the text between the lines of the text. In rabbinic thinking, each letter and the spaces between the letters are available for interpretive work. Midrash is rarely comprehensive and occasionally contradictory, raising as many questions as it answers. Midrashic exegesis can and does intersect with Western historical critical and philological approaches to the text.

There are formal, carefully delineated rules for midrash that rabbis Akiva and Ishmael promulgated between 100 and 135 CE, which can be found dispersed throughout rabbinic literature.[5] Midrashic exegesis is not limited to rabbis or the authoritative classic literature of rabbinic Judaism.[6] It continues whenever and wherever people study and teach the Scriptures.

Christian biblical exegesis from the patristic fathers to contemporary lay and specialized biblical interpretation holds much in common with traditional rabbinic midrash. Indeed, the writings of Christian mystics from the desert mothers and fathers to contemporary poets and preachers are as creative, insightful, and revelatory as classic midrash. Christian and rabbinic fathers share allegorical and metaphorical readings of the text, in many cases coming to surprisingly similar conclusions—for example, the tendency to read the Song of Songs as an allegory about the relationship between God (or Christ) and people (Israel or church-as-new-Israel). In some cases, biblical interpreters from different traditions come to the same conclusion about a text; in others, interpreters from the same tradition come to wildly differing conclusions about the same text.

As a product of African American Christianity, I emerge from an ancient tradition of biblical piety and reverence for the Scriptures as the Word of God. As an Anglican (Episcopalian) priest and preacher, I have learned to look and listen for the Word of God in, between, over, under, behind, and beyond the words in the Word. As a (now former) member of a *minyan* and occasional Torah teacher in Jewish congregations, I experienced midrash as *God-wrestling*. The bruising/blessing, God-grappling encounter between the man who is Ya'aqov (Jacob), the Heel-Grabbing-Sneak who becomes Yisra'el (Israel), the God-Wrestler, and a mysterious divine combatant in Genesis 32:25–32 is one of many biblical images that can be read as a metaphor for *drashing* (interpreting) Scripture. In this womanist midrash I will struggle with God and the text and God-in-the-text explicitly as a religious reader.

---

5. There is a tradition ascribing some of that work to the first-century rabbi Hillel.
6. I.e., the Mishnah, the Babylonian and Jerusalem Talmuds, the Zohar, and the *Midrash Rabbah* (exegetical treatises on each book of the Torah and the Megilloth—five small scrolls read for festivals: Esther, Song of Songs, Ruth, Lamentations, and Ecclesiastes), the halakhic *midrashim* (*sifras, sifreis, mekiltas,* etc.).

WOMANIST FRAMEWORK

Womanism takes its name and draws its guiding and interpretive practices from Alice Walker's definition (here in full):

1. From "womanish." (Opp. of "girlish," i.e., frivolous, irresponsible, not serious.) A black feminist or feminist of color. From the black folk expression of mothers to female children, "You acting womanish," i.e., like a woman. Usually referring to outrageous, audacious, courageous, or willful behavior. Wanting to know more and in greater depth than is considered "good" for one. Interested in grown-up doings. Acting grown up. Being grown up. Interchangeable with another black folk expression: "You trying to be grown." Responsible. In charge. Serious.
2. Also: A woman who loves other women, sexually and/or nonsexually. Appreciates and prefers women's culture, women's emotional flexibility (values tears as a natural counter-balance of laughter) and women's strength. Sometimes loves individual men, sexually and/or nonsexually. Committed to survival and wholeness of entire people, male and female. Not a separatist, except periodically, for health. Traditionally universalist, as in: "Mamma, why are we brown, pink, and yellow, and our cousins are white, beige, and black?" Ans.: "Well, you know the colored race is just like a flower garden, with every color flower represented." Traditionally capable, as in: "Mamma, I'm walking to Canada and I'm taking you and a bunch of other slaves with me." Reply: "It wouldn't be the first time."
3. Loves music. Loves dance. Loves the moon. Loves the Spirit. Loves love and food and roundness. Loves struggle. Loves the Folk. Loves herself. Regardless.
4. Womanist is to feminist as purple is to lavender.[7]

Most simply, womanism is black women's feminism. It distinguishes itself from the dominant-culture feminism, which is all too often distorted by racism and classism and marginalizes womanism, womanists, and women of color. Womanism emerged as black women's intellectual and interpretive response to racism and classism in feminism and its articulation and in response to sexism in black liberationist thought. Womanism includes the radical egalitarianism of feminism, the emancipatory ethic and reverence for black physical and cultural aesthetics of the black liberation movement, and the transformational trajectories of both movements; it is operative in religious and nonreligious literary disciplines. Yet womanism is also more complex, now in its third (and perhaps fourth) wave, troubling its ancestral gender, ethnic, and religious categories.[8]

7. Alice Walker, *In Search of Our Mothers' Gardens: Womanist Prose* (San Diego: Harcourt Brace Jovanovich, 1984), xi.
8. Monica A. Coleman, ed., *Ain't I a Womanist, Too? Third Wave Womanist Religious Thought* (Minneapolis: Fortress Press, 2013).

Womanists and feminists ask different questions of a text than do other readers and different questions from each other. And we also ask some of the same questions, and we arrive at similar and dissonant conclusions. Privileging the crossroads between our Afro-diasporic identity (embodiment and experience) and our gender (performance and identity), we ask questions about power, authority, voice, agency, hierarchy, inclusion, and exclusion. The readings enrich all readers from any perspective. The questions we ask enrich our own understanding and the understandings of those with whom we are in conversation.

The overlapping[9] categories of womanism and black feminism create an inclusive interpretive framework that transcends the interests and questions of those who most easily identify with black- and woman-centered approaches to biblical interpretation. In womanist practice, the voice and perspective of the whole community is sought and valued. Womanist interpretation does not privilege the embodiment and experiences of black women at the expense of other members of the interpretive community. Rather, while affirming the interpretive practices of black women as normative and as holding didactic value for other readers, womanist interpretation makes room at the table of discourse for the perspectives of the least privileged among the community and the honored guest of any background: the child who is invited into "adult" conversation around the table with "Baby, what do you think?" and the extra place at the table for whoever may come by. In addition, as black women who reside in communities and families whose constituent members include black men and children and biracial and multicultural bodies and families, womanism courts the voices of those around the table without regard to race, ethnicity, gender, age, ability, orientation, or trans/cis embodiment. Womanism is committed to the wholeness and flourishing of the entire community.

Given that womanism is as much perspectival as ideological, and phenomenological as much as analytical, it resists methodology as the category is articulated and wielded in male-stream and other traditions of biblical interpretation, including feminist interpretations. I have great difficulty with the notion that methodology functions as a recipe that when followed will yield a womanist product, as much difficulty as I have reproducing my grandmother's sweet potato pudding. Perhaps the theological equivalent of reverse engineering a recipe is praxis. Praxis is the practice of an art or skill, best supplemented with reflection that leads to more praxis in an action-reflection cycle. Questions that emerge from womanist praxis are questions that anyone can ask, and commitments that womanists bring to the text that many share. Some of those questions and commitments are:

9. That womanism and black feminism are not entirely synonymous may be best demonstrated by the varied ways in which individuals self-identify.

1. Who is speaking and/or active?
2. Where are the women and girls, what are they doing, and what are their names?
3. When women or other marginalized characters speak and act, whose interests are they serving?
4. Who (and where) are the characters without which the story could not have unfolded as articulated?
5. What are the power dynamics in the narrative?
6. What are the ethical implications of the text when read from the perspective of the dominant character(s)?
7. What are the ethical implications of previous (especially traditional) readings of the text for black women?
8. How have black women historically related to the text?
9. In what ways do the contemporary circumstances of black women readers shape new and renewed interpretations?
10. How do the values articulated in the text and its interpretation affect the well-being of the communities that black women inhabit?
11. How does (can) this text function as Scripture for black women?
12. Who is (what is the construction of) God in the text? Is s/he/it invested in the flourishing of black women, our families, and our worlds?

The primary womanist principles that shape this text are (1) the *legitimacy of black women's biblical interpretation* as normative and authoritative, (2) the *inherent value of each member of a community* in the text and interpreting the text, (3) *talking back* to the text, and (4) *making it plain*, the work of exegesis from translation to interpretation.

In this work those principles mean that I wrestle with the biblical canon, its contents and contours, seeking to empower others to assert a claim on the Scriptures and to interpret them for themselves, pursuing the well-being of the whole community, land, nation, and earth. I do so as a classically trained biblical scholar, using tools that have traditionally figured in male-stream approaches to the biblical text: textual criticism, linguistic and literary analysis, even historical-critical approaches, employing them as a feminist, as a womanist.

Womanists at the intersection of biblical scholarship and religious faith and practice engage the Scriptures of our communities as members of those communities. No matter how misogynistic, how heavily redacted, how death-dealing, how troubled, troubling, or troublesome the text, womanists who teach and preach in the black church do not throw the whole androcentric text with its patriarchal and kyriarchal lowlights out of our stained-glass windows because of its Iron Age theology. We wrestle with it because it has been received as Scripture. Our wrestling should not be taken to mean that we affirm texts that do not affirm us.

Simply teaching women's narratives is important work. All too often the texts chosen for preaching and teaching in and out of organized lectionaries exclude or minimize women's biblical narratives. One of my aims in preparing this work is to introduce readers to biblical women and their stories, with which they may not be familiar, and to reintroduce them to familiar stories through new lenses. Some feminists are hostile to the notion that simply teaching women's biblical narratives is a feminist project. Such a posture takes the ability to know the contents of the Bible for granted. Because of legal prohibitions against African literacy in the Americas and normalization of androcentric interpretations intended to disempower nonmale and nonheterosexual readers, direct access to the text in the company of a learned sister is an empowering and transformational experience for many black Christian women and men.

Above all, this work is womanist because it is *womanish*. That is, I am talking back to the text, challenging it, questioning it, interrogating it, unafraid of the power and authority of the text, just as a girl-growing-into-a-woman talks back to her elders, questioning the world around her in order to learn how to understand and navigate it.

TEXT SELECTION

There are, depending on how one counts, 111 or so named female characters in the Hebrew Bible. There are hundreds more who are unnamed. Then there are the largely unacknowledged women who make up the peoples of Israel and the nations with whom they are in contact. The number of women and girls submerged under the story lines of the text are beyond counting. Those were the women who interested me: The daughters of the ancestral stories whose fathers were said to live hundreds of years. Were they nearly immortal as well? The women of Israel behind the scenes of each text and story. The women of Canaan targeted for extermination in Joshua's campaign. The royal women of Israel and Judah, many of whose names are preserved in the text. The women of the empires that dominated Israel at one point or another: Egypt, Assyria, Babylon, Persia. Who were these women? What were their names? What stories would they tell? What do they have to teach us, we who read Israel's Scriptures as our own?

I found myself with more material that I could publish in a single volume. I have decided to present the archetypal and ancestral women of the Torah and the women associated with the thrones archived in the annals of the two monarchies. The texts, narratives, and characters that I have selected for this work are necessarily idiosyncratic, but I hope they are of interest to the reader.

OVERVIEW AND FORMAT

In each of the two parts, which focus on Torah stories and throne stories, I address women and their stories and offer some contemporary contextual and exegetical (application) questions. Some of these discussions will be quite brief, no more than a paragraph; others will provoke more questions than discussion based on their limited presentation in the text. When appropriate, I will make connections to other texts (and testaments) in a sidebar.

This volume is a collection of shorter exegeses, from a few paragraphs to a few pages, written with teaching in both classroom and congregation in mind, prefaced by brief introductions, and accompanied by the occasional sidebar. Each proper unit begins with my translation of a primary text. The exegesis takes a variety of shapes, suggested by the text itself. My treatments are not uniform, nor should they be, given the diversity of the biblical texts themselves. In general I craft names for women and girls who command my attention, drawing them from the languages of the text and its context. I read the text in light of its ancient context and my own womanist one. Some tellings follow the contours of the canonical texts, some read against them, and some construct new paths from their paths. In some cases I give voice to characters known and unknown.

This womanist midrash seeks to reintroduce readers to the shared Jewish and Christian Scriptures through the stories of women in the text. These women may be obvious, named, active and speaking in the text, or they may be hidden in expressions like "all Israel" or "all flesh." They may even be obscured in the binary gender forms of Biblical Hebrew, including the form that has traditionally been treated as masculine plural. I will seek, *drash*, these women and their stories, telling them again and anew as a womanist, drawing on the wisdom of black women and our interpretive practices, starting with my own.

HEARING THE WORD: TOWARD PROCLAMATION

Finally, I have had two experiences as a hearer of the Scriptures, in Jewish and Christian congregations. In churches, I have listened to women and men read and preach a very few texts in which I could hear myself; but mostly I have heard women and men read and preach texts that assume a normative male subject. In synagogues, that pattern continued during Torah chanting and recitation of the *haftarah* (selection from the Prophets accompanying the Torah). However, on some occasions—many more than in Christian congregations—I found myself hearing Hebrew Scripture addressed to women and female characters in a way that I never have heard in English, in Christian communities. I am also writing this book so that readers and hearers of Scripture who do not have access to Biblical Hebrew will be able to experience the Scriptures in a different voice, with a different inflection.

PART I

Womanist Midrash on the Torah

1

Genesis

BEFORE BEGINNING: GOD-WHOSE-NAME-IS-TOO-HOLY-TO-BE-PRONOUNCED

Four Hebrew letters, *yud-he-vav-he*, corresponding to YHWH (or YHVH) represent the Divine Name in the Hebrew Scriptures. The Divine Name is God's Most Holy Name. It is holy and cannot be pronounced. Unlike other words in the Hebrew Bible, the Four Letters are not accompanied by vowels enabling pronunciation; rather, they are accompanied by vowels from a different word, usually *adonai* (Lord), indicating an acceptable substitution that can be pronounced. Sometimes *elohim* (God) is called for; see Ezekiel 2:4. The combination of the sacred four letters, called the Tetragrammaton, and these vowels produce a word that simply cannot be articulated (try combining the consonants *q-r-s-t* with the vowels *a, e, i*; there is no such word). This rabbinic practice led to the substitution of "Lord," "God," and other titles (e.g., "the Name") when reading the text and to the contemporary practice of writing "the Lord" in mixed large and small capital letters to represent the Most Holy Name. A tradition of sacredness evolved around the Name so that it was recited only in specific liturgical contexts.

Some biblical scholars have disregarded the religious conventions around the Divine Name and have offered a hypothetical pronunciation and spelling. That practice has deep ties to the anti-Semitic and anti-Judaistic roots of Enlightenment and post-Enlightenment Western biblical studies, and I do not use it.[1] Lastly, since there are feminine and masculine names, titles, and

---

1. Johanna W. H. Wijk-Bos has written on this brilliantly and succinctly in "Writing on the Water: The Ineffable Name of God," in *Jews, Christians, and the Theology of the Hebrew Scriptures* (Atlanta: Society of Biblical Literature, 2000), 45–59.

images for God in the Scriptures, I gender God variously in translation—
sometimes feminine, sometimes without an articulated gender. Knowing that
male constructions dominate in the biblical text, interpretive literature, and
worshiping contexts of many if not most readers, I rarely use masculine constructions. As a womanist translator, I am committed to uncovering God-
language that empowers black women and girls, locating their reflection of
the divine image in the biblical text. Though calling someone out of (or outside of) their name is a serious violation in many black cultural contexts, the
Divine Name is a name that cannot be named and can be substituted for only
with inadequate language, calling for manifold options.

TORAH: SHE IS A TREE OF LIFE

The Torah is a transformational text. God transforms space, time, land, and
peoples in the narrative that begins with a *beginning* (the first word of the
Torah) and moves to *Israel* (the last word of the Torah in Hebrew). In one
mystical tradition, the very letters of the Torah are agents of transformation.
The Torah is so much more than the Law to which it is often reduced (and
then thrust into a binary opposite "Gospel"), particularly in some Christian

---

She Is a Tree of Life . . .

Proverbs 3:18 speaks of wisdom and extols her virtues (see vv. 13–18)
and rewards. One common rabbinic interpretation is that the "wisdom" extolled by Proverbs is the Torah, as in the midrash on Genesis
in *Bereshit Rabbah* 17:5. A Torah scroll is an exquisitely sacred object.
As a repository of divine Wisdom, and in some perspectives for the
very Divine, a Torah scroll is treated reverentially: wrapped, dressed,
and sometimes crowned, laid down, and rolled out with care, only a
pointer (not human flesh) touching the sacred text, with dedicated
space for repose (storage) and a place of honor for its reading. Special
honors are given to those who approach and read and recite prayers
in proximity to it, and there are special criteria for who can approach
and when. There are also special criteria for who can write a Torah
scroll and how, how the letters must be shaped, what color ink to use,
what kind of ink to use, what kind of scroll to use, what prayers to pray
before, during, and after the process. Some of this reverence extends
to the Torah in book form: it is not appropriate in the Jewish contexts
with which I am familiar to put a Torah (book) on the floor. The fall
of a Torah scroll to the floor would be a communal calamity, requiring
all who witness it to fast for forty days, according to some traditions.

interpretations. The Torah is instruction, revelation, and sometimes law. Torah (with a capital *T*) is the first five books of the Scriptures and all that is in them: story, song, genealogy, geography, legal material, and lessons from the ancestors. *Torah* (with a little *t*) is instruction and jurisprudence. So, while there is *torah* in Torah, not all Torah is *torah*, and there is *torah* outside of the five books of the Torah! *Toroth* (plural of *torah*) can be found in any of the many genres of Torah. Torah then is the first five books, their teaching, in whole or part, other teaching in other parts of the Bible, and religious *teaching* from beyond the Bible, in classical or contemporary midrash, for example.

The Torah is a locus of divine revelation (and divine self-revelation). The word *torah* comes from the verb *y-r-h*, "to throw" (e.g., "to cast lots") or "to shoot" (arrows). With regard to *torah*, *y-r-h* also means "to throw" rain or instruction from the heavens; see Leviticus 10:11, "You are *to teach* the daughters and sons of Israel all the statutes that the HOLY ONE OF OLD has spoken to them through the authority of Moshe."[2]

In a mystical sense, Torah can be seen as an embodiment of divine Wisdom and for some as the Word of God (with a capital *W*). When the Torah is praised and celebrated in biblical and postbiblical prayers, psalms, and songs in Hebrew, the verbs and adjectives are feminine, because *torah* is grammatically feminine. This will be the case for other images, metaphors, concepts, and portrayals of God in the text. The feminine gender of *torah* stands in sharp distinction to the masculine Word or *logos* (from the Greek) with which many Christians are familiar. And it stands in concert with the wisdom traditions of both canons; *chokmah* (Hebrew) and *sophia* (Greek) are both feminine. In her all-encompassing embrace, Torah includes womanist wisdom. However grammatical gender may be understood, *torah*-language ensures that liturgical language preserves feminine and masculine sacred language and images.

As a text, the Torah emerges in layers from varied ancestral oral traditions to discrete revised written traditions brought together in a massive editorial project. In one sense it is useful to think of the Torah as being produced starting with Deuteronomy, which serves as its theological anchor—portions of which were written in the seventh century BCE—and concluding with Genesis, which was most certainly edited during (if not after) the Babylonian

---

2. Unless otherwise acknowledged all translations of Scripture in this volume are mine. I use the transliterated names of biblical characters to provide the reader with a sense of their phonetic equivalence in Hebrew in the translations and midrashes. In the commentary I use the more familiar forms of the names. "Israelites" includes daughters and sons; but I have found that unless the daughters are rendered visible in translation, they are often not seen. Here in Leviticus 10:11 I argue it would be ludicrous to translate *beney yisrael* as the "sons of Israel," as though Torah were not applicable to the whole community; at the same time I acknowledge the more restrictive reading is a possibility whose implications must be considered.

exile in the sixth century BCE, along with the rest of the Torah. This dating provides a sense of theological urgency; the collection and compilation of these sacred stories is a response to the trauma experienced by survivors of the Judean monarchy (including those remaindered from the remnants of the northern monarchy) in the face of the defeat of the nation, dismantling of the monarchy, burning of Jerusalem, and razing of the temple. These tragedies and their attendant horror provide the impulse for *scripting* theology. Yet there are ancient texts scattered throughout the Scriptures, including in the Torah, that are older than their surrounding texts, such as Miriam's Song[3] in Exodus 15, and the Song of Deborah in Judges 5 next to its much younger prose sibling in Judges 4. Perhaps one ought not think of the Torah or indeed the rest of Scripture in chronological terms; the books are not in chronological order in either Jewish or Christian configuration.

The story of the Torah is a story of relationships: relationships between God-Whose-Name-Is-Holy and creation, the Holy God and human beings, human beings and creation. The Bible privileges some of these relationships with text space; there are characters whose stories dominate the text: they speak and act, they speak to God, and God speaks to them. This volume explores the women and girls who are not prominent in the biblical text or interpretive traditions and seeks to reintroduce them. Arguably at one time some of these women were better known. There is presently, I believe, a significant body of female characters in the Hebrew Scriptures who are unknown even when they do speak and act in the text, even when they do speak to God, and even when God speaks to them.

The women in the Torah are distributed unevenly. Many are named or referred to in Genesis. Fewer individual women are named in the rest of the Torah; rather, there are collectives—frequently national groups, for example, Israelite women, Egyptian women, and Canaanite women. There are also hypothetical women in the jurisprudence sections, for example, a woman who makes a vow, a woman who is raped, a woman suspected of adultery. There are women whose names are called in the Torah with whom many, if not most, readers are unfamiliar. Meet them, listen to them, and learn from them. Among them are Adah, Zillah, Naamah, Reumah, Mahalat, Basemath, Oholibamah, Mehetabel, Matred, and Me-zahab. Then there are all of the women who are not named: the women in Canaan who are cursed by Noah, the women of Sodom and Gomorrah, over whom God and Abram haggle,

---

3. Miriam's Song, also known as the Song of the Sea, is placed first on the lips of Moses and the Israelites in Exod. 15, while Miriam appears to sing only one verse in Exod. 15:20. Rabbinic and contemporary scholars agree that Miriam and the women likely sang the whole song, in keeping with Israelite cultural practice; cf. Judg. 11:34 and 1 Sam. 18:6.

the women of Babel, and many, many more. And yes, there are women who may be more familiar: Eve, Hagar, Sarah, Keturah, Rebekah, Rachel, Leah, Bilhah, Zilpah, and Miriam.

IN BEGINNING, A BEGINNING

Genesis 1:1 In beginning, He, God created the heavens and the earth. ²The earth was formless and shapeless and darkness covered the face of the deep, while She, the Spirit of God pulsed over the face of the waters.

In Biblical Hebrew *b'reshiyt*, the first word of Genesis, is *a* beginning, not *the* beginning. It is most literally *in-beginning* or *in-a-beginning* or even *when-beginning*.[4] The translation "In-the-beginning" for this single word stems from the Greek version of the Israelite Scriptures, the Septuagint (LXX), and certainly represents one way the text has come to be understood. It is neither the literal meaning nor the only way of reading or hearing this word. *A beginning* gestures to spiraling creation and its stories and to multiple contextual ways of hearing, imagining, and retelling these stories, including womanist midrash.

The second word of the text, *bar'a*, is a simple (Qal), masculine, singular, active verb, *he-created*. One womanist or feminist translation might be *In beginning God created the heavens and the earth*. While *elohiym*, the singular Israelite "God" with a plural grammatical form (also "gods" in non-Israelite contexts), is gendered in Biblical Hebrew, it appears to be less so in English. Or at least that is a common claim. My experience in classrooms and congregations demonstrates that while some reader/hearers read and hear *God* as gender-neutral or gender-inclusive, many read and hear "God" as male, as the polar opposite of "goddess" (which in their construction does not merit the capital *G* of "God").

In the second verse, a second verb articulating divine action occurs, *merechepheth*, a Piel (not-so-simple, sometimes intensive form), feminine, singular active verb, *she-pulsed*. The verb, *r-ch-ph*, can mean "hover," "flutter," or "tremble." The verb occurs only twice in Hebrew Scripture, in Deuteronomy 32:11 to describe an eagle over its young and in Jeremiah 23:9 in which all the prophet's bones shake, rattle, and/or roll. Its subject in Genesis, *ruach*, "spirit" (and occasionally "wind"), is feminine.

---

4. I use hyphens to indicate when one Hebrew word is translated by more than one word in English.

Though the Divine is articulated with feminine and masculine gender in the Scriptures, in translation and tradition God became virtually exclusively male. The gendering of God's Spirit as feminine calls for the feminine pronoun, yet generations of sexist translations have gotten around this by religiously avoiding the pronoun altogether. So in each case the text will say, "The Spirit [verb]. . . ." No unacceptably feminine pronoun is needed. But she is still there.

She, the Spirit of God

Imagine hearing the Scriptures proclaimed with the gender of God's Spirit restored: the Spirit, She rested on them . . . (Num. 11:26); then the Spirit of God, She wore Gideon (like a garment) . . . (Judg. 6:34); the Spirit of God, She came upon David . . . (1 Sam. 16:13); the Spirit of God, She has made me . . . (Job 33:4). This occurs more than thirty times: Gen. 1:2; Num. 11:26; 24:2; Judg. 3:10; 6:34; 11:29; 13:25; 14:6, 19; 15:14; 1 Sam. 10:6, 10; 11:6; 16:13–14; 19:20, 23; Isa. 11:2; Ezek. 2:2; 3:12, 14, 24; 8:3; 11:1, 5, 24; 43:5; Hag. 2:5; Ps. 143:10; Job 33:4; 1 Chr. 12:18; 2 Chr. 15:1; 20:14.

She, the Spirit of God, She-who-is-also-God, at the dawn of creation fluttered over the nest of her creation at the same time as He, the more familiar expression of divinity, created all. They, Two-in-One, are the first articulations, self-articulations, of God in (and the God of) the Scriptures. God is female and male, and when God gets around to creating creatures in the divine image, they will be female and male, as God is. Feminine language occurs in the text repeatedly of God; this means that feminists and womanists advocating for inclusive and explicitly feminine God-language are not changing but restoring the text and could be considered biblical literalists.

THE FIRST WOMAN

Genesis 2:18 It is not good that the *adam* is alone; I will make a mighty-helper correlating to it.

The detailed account of the creation of a human woman is without parallel in the available ancient Near Eastern literature. It is curious; the animals are created with the ability to partner and mate; yet the *adam* is singular, pluripotent, but singular. I have translated the *adam* as "it" because the previous description, singular and plural, bearing male and female in a single body, transcends the masculine singular to which Biblical Hebrew is limited.

Genesis 2:18ff. offers a detailed account of the culmination of creation, the creation of woman from *ha'adam*, "the human" created from the *humus* or the "earthling" created from the *earth*. There is an intentional relationship between *adam* and the red-brown (*edom*) *adamah* missing from the traditional translations of "man" and "ground." With the definite article "the," the text is not using *adam* as a personal name; it will omit the article when the individual named Adam is meant. The *mem* at the end of the word is a common indicator of plurality; correspondingly *adam* often means all of humanity.

The "mighty-helper," the *ezer*, is difficult to translate into English without a modifier; in all other places in the Scriptures it refers to God and the divine help God renders. In English a helper is often of lower status than the one being helped; not so here. The physical source material for the creation of this mighty-helper is within the pluripotent earthling. God puts the creature to sleep and divides it in half. This idea stems from rabbinic exegesis; Rabbi Samuel ben Nachman taught that God split the earth-colored *adam* into two equal portions.[5] I think of the division as something like mitosis in cell division.

The *tzela'* that God removes is a "side" and not a "rib" as commonly mistranslated. Throughout Exodus the *tzela'* of the ark of the covenant on which its poles are alternately set are its sides.[6] There is no other place in Scripture in which *tzela'* is translated as a rib. The NRSV supports this translation by adjusting the text of Genesis 2:23 to "this is at last bone of my bones and flesh of my flesh; this one shall be called Woman for *out of* Man this one was taken" (emphasis added). The words "out of" suggest removing a rib or other discrete part from the *adam*'s body. But the text actually says, "from a Human this one was taken," as in the GSJPS and Fox.[7] I find that there is more room in "from" than in "out of" for the traditional rabbinic understanding of a bifurcated being. From this point forward in Genesis, *adam* will refer to humanity (5:1), the two earthlings (3:22), and occasionally to the singular male earthling (3:12).

After the division the human persons are called "man" and "woman" for the first time. They are as brown as the earth from which they were created, an essential point in womanist exegesis. This is the point in the narrative at which gender as many understand it—social construction in response to biological indicators—arguably first occurs in the Scripture. In Genesis

---

5. *Bereshit Rabbah* 8:1.

6. See Exod. 25:12, 14; other examples include the hillside in 2 Sam. 16:3 and the side of the temple in 1 Kgs. 6:5–34.

7. The IB provides a poetic gloss in the text, "because we are of one flesh," and a literal translation in a footnote: "God took one of its sides [or possible ribs]"), while the JPS has the masculinist "from Man. . . ."

2:24—"Therefore a man [*ish*, not *adam*] leaves his father and his mother and clings to his woman and they become one flesh"—the significance of this new term, "man," is overlooked if the *adam* has been mistranslated as "man" in the preceding passage. For the *adam*, there was no corresponding creation; for the *ish*, man, the corresponding creation is the *isshah*, woman. The corresponding or correlating nature of the creation points back to their origin, two halves of a whole. They are neither identical nor mirror images. Together and individually they reflect the divine image.

The man and his woman—in Genesis 3:6 it will be the woman and her man—are in a relationship that is not named in the text. The translators of the NRSV and JPS Bibles along with the GSJPS interpret this relationship by introducing the words "wife" and "husband," in spite of the fact that Biblical Hebrew does not have designated terms for "husband" or "wife." *Ish* means "man"; *ba'al* means "lord" and can refer to a feudal-type lord or a spouse.[8] *Isshah* means "woman." The mutuality of their belonging to each other is lost when the terms "husband" and "wife"—with all of their burdens and baggage—are applied to the text. In addition, throughout the text it will always be correct to translate *isshah* as "woman," but not all women are married in the biblical text (or beyond).

Their relationship gives rise to an etiological proverb in verse 24 that intends to explain the origin of a particular relational pattern, that men—and apparently not women—leave their parents (household? land?) and form a new enduring attachment with and to their women. While contemporary readers have tended to look to Genesis for guidance on the appropriate form for intimate, conjugal relationships, it is not the case that biblical readers, authors, and editors did so. The relationship described between the first two people is ultimately rejected in favor of patriarchal and polygamous relationships.

The long saga of the first woman includes her subsequent conversation with the serpent and its aftermath. In chapter 3 the reader is introduced to a new character, a God-made, crafty, talking snake. It is very difficult for modern readers, particularly Christian readers, to read or hear this text without imputing negative or even satanic attributes to the snake. However, snakes, serpents, and dragons[9] in ancient Near Eastern literature were revered as the forms of a variety of goddesses and gods and associated with a wide range of

---

8. "Husband" is introduced in Gen. 3:6; Fox and the IB retain the Hebrew "woman."

9. These terms share a common vocabulary. The relative paucity of words in the closed canon of Biblical Hebrew, slightly more than seven thousand, compared to more than one million words in the perpetually expanding English language, means that the same word in Hebrew conveys distinctions that another language would convey with different words.

benefactions: immortality, wisdom, renewed youth; medicine, royalty, power, and more. The snake is apparently unlike any of the other animals in its ability to speak; this may be related to how creatively intelligent—crafty—it is. I like to translate the serpent's acumen as "naked intelligence," because the words for the nakedness, *arumim*, of the humans in verse 25 and the snake's craftiness, *arum*, in the next verse share the same consonants.

The snake asks, "Did God really[10] say that you two were not to eat from any tree in the garden?" The use of the second-person plural for "you" is not apparent when reading the text in English; it harks back to the time when the woman and the man were literally one flesh as the *adam*. In their ensuing conversation the woman repeats the instruction that God gave the *adam*, though she omits the phrase "on the day you eat of it" when repeating the death sentence. She says further that God also said that they should not even touch the forbidden tree of the knowledge of good and evil in the center of the garden. For many interpreters, that there is no corresponding conversation recorded previously in the narrative means that the woman is embellishing. Without critiquing her for doing theology, interpreting her conversation with God, I hold open the possibility that the woman is faithfully repeating a conversation that the narrator did not record.

Rabbis and Torah scholars have long asked how humanity is to keep the commandments of God. One solution, the principle of building fences around the commandments or individual instructions, consists of developing a teaching that will enable the community to easily fulfill the specific *torah*. To wit, one will not eat fruit from a tree that one does not touch. In this reading of the story, the woman offers the first (proto-) rabbinic teaching in the newly created world.

The talking snake responds to the woman's *torah* with theology. It (he in the text) presents a novel perspective of God: God has not told the whole truth. The creation can transform themselves and become like God or like the gods who make up the divine council; both translations are equally possible.[11] The woman took a good look at the tree and its fruit and found it extremely desirable. The desirability, *ta'avah*, of the fruit is the same word

---

10. The "really" is missing from the MT but present in a Dead Sea manuscript, 4QGen^k.

11. "God" and "gods" are the same word differentiated by context. In the ancient world the realm of the gods, including that of Israel's singular God, was envisioned as a royal court in which there were other entities variously understood as gods, angels, or other kinds of divine beings. See Gen. 6:2; Jer. 23:8; Job 15:8; Pss. 82:1; 89:6–9. The council includes adversarial characters such as the lying spirit in 1 Kgs. 22:19–22 and the adversary of Job in 1:6 and 2:1; "the satan," *hasatan*, should not be identified as Satan there.

that is used for the Israelites' "craving" for meat in the wilderness in Numbers 11:4. While it seems to have a negative connotation in that text, in its other uses it communicates godly and wholesome desires, including for God (Isa. 26:8; Ps. 21:2; Prov. 19:22). When she saw that the tree would indeed increase her intellect[12] (*lehaskiyl* refers to intellectual acumen), she gave some of the fruit to her man who, it turns out, was with her while she and the snake engaged in conversation.

Then something happens between verses 6 and 7. Or rather something does not happen. The woman and her man did not die in the day that they ate from the proscribed tree in the middle of the garden. Their eyes were opened, as the snake had said, and they learned/discovered/knew that they were naked, the last thing revealed by the narrator before the snake spoke to the woman. Then they, the two of them, together sewed loincloths for themselves.

The newly expanded intellects of the woman and man led to their covering their genitalia; perhaps we are to understand that with their new knowledge, the shame that the narrator told us was previously missing has now been acquired. It is important to note that there is no mention of sin, of a fall from grace or innocence, or of loss in this text. Those are much later interpretations and interpolations of this story.

The couple works together in their project. Their labor is not gendered. Sewing is not "women's work." I imagine that there was some criteria for leaf selection: Were other plants considered and rejected? What did they use for needles? What did they use for thread? Were their coverings simply functional or were they ornamental? Were they hiding or accentuating their genitalia? And, since the *goroth*, "girdles or loincloths," cover only a portion of their lower bodies, the woman is bare-breasted. In comparison with our culture, in which breasts—even nursing breasts—are highly sexualized, I find the lack of shame imputed to her bare breasts refreshing and noteworthy.

Together, the woman and her man hear the sound of God walking in the garden (the use of the reflexive Hitpael stem here suggests that God is taking Godself for a walk). Together they hide themselves. In verse 9, God calls to the *adam* a single word, "Where?"[13] The *adam* is in two bodies, the woman and the man. The question is directed to both of them, the whole of humanity at that time. "He says . . ."; the speaker is not identified as "the man" or "the *adam*." He says, "I . . . , I . . . , I . . . , I . . ." Four times he says, "I." They are no longer together. God's questions invite accusation and confession. "You" is no longer plural. "Who told you . . . ?" And "Did you . . . ?" In verse 12 the

---

12. Gen. 3:6: "To make [one] wise" in many translations; however, the word for "wisdom," *chokmah*, is not used here.

13. "Are you" is lacking.

(male) earthling speaks; he blames the other earthling. God invites confession from the woman and receives accusation; she blames the serpent. But since God made the serpent, she is also accusing God.

God's response is to curse the snake that God made in the first place. And God curses the ground that God made, explaining that God does so because the male God-made earthling listened to (really obeyed here) the voice of his God-made woman. God also redesigns the snake; it will now crawl on its belly in the dirt; this is the first hint to the reader/hearer that the talking snake walked upright, opening the possibility that this story was at one time a performance piece, so that people would have seen the snake walking around.

God continues to reconfigure creation; however, this reconfiguration is not cursing. The offspring of women and snakes will no longer engage in conversation; they will be enemies. The text does not actually say that snakes will no longer be able to speak. Many and great will be the woman's work (not pain) and her conceptions (not full-term pregnancies or live births). Childbearing will be difficult, hard work. There will be pain, and there will be desire. And her man will rule *with* her. The preposition *b* means "in" and/or "with." If one uses one of the standard lexical tools, one will have to go quite a ways into the entry on the preposition *b* to find occasions when it is translated "over."[14] "In" and "with" are its primary meanings; the verse is intelligible with the simple, straightforward, primary meaning: *he shall rule with you*.

Some religious communities tout the Eve-Adam pairing as the normative biblical archetypal and prototypal conjugal partnership. In so doing, they add words and concepts to the narrative: "wife," "husband," "marriage." The Eve-Adam pairing represents one biblical model and is soon joined by a wholly human-conceived model (male conception in this case): polygynous polygamy. Religious readers who insist on a single scriptural paradigm for human intimacy and family composition ignore all of the social evolution that follows: the normative and pervasive portrayal of polygamy, regular practice of rape-marriage on and off the battlefield, and, most significantly, the divine silence on these biblical relational patterns.

MOTHER CHAVAH (EVE)

Genesis 3:20 Then the *adam* proclaimed the name of his woman, Chavah[15] (Life-woman, Eve), for she became the mother of all living.

14. Brown-Driver-Briggs (BDB) or the *Hebrew and Aramaic Lexicon of the Old Testament* (*HALOT*).
15. I use the traditional names for biblical characters in the translations and the forms with which English readers are more familiar in the discussion.

The English name "Eve" seems to come from discarding the first and last consonants in the Chavah. The adjective *chaiy*, "living," refers to all life and not just human life.[16] God is "the living God" in Jeremiah 10:10 and many other places. The title becomes ironic with the death of Abel; she remains the mother of the living in the text, but is now also the mother of the dead.

As the story unfolds, the biblical authors focus on Adam and subordinate Eve. God does not. God kills for Eve, sews for Eve, clothes Eve. God made tunics for Eve and her man from skins. It seems that God brings death to paradise. God had said that on the day that the humans ate from the forbidden tree, on that day they would surely die. Instead, unidentified animals die. Then God evicted Eve. It is not reasonable that only Adam was evicted or that God was concerned that Adam alone would stretch out his hand to eat from the tree of life. Eve and Adam are banished together. *Ha'adam* means the whole of humanity, even when there are only two of them.

> Genesis 3:22 Then the Sovereign God said, "Look! The human-creation[17] has become like one of us, knowing good and evil; and now, it might stretch out its hand and take also from the tree of life, and eat, and live forever." [23]So the Sovereign God sent it forth from the garden of Eden, to work the humus from which it was taken. [24]God cast out the human-creation; and God settled at the east of the garden of Eden the cherubim, and a flame sword turning itself about to guard the way to the tree of life.

In chapter 4 Eve conceives and gives birth to Qayin, Cain. She names him, saying, "I have fashioned (*qaniyti*) a man with the Holy One." Then Eve gives birth to Hevel (Abel).[18] Neither Eve nor Adam is described as naming him, and no etiology is given for his name. Nothing of Eve's life between these births is related. She is not even mentioned in the story of one of her sons killing the other and God's banishment of the killer. She is not mentioned in connection with the marriage of her sons. Genesis is unconcerned about the conflict in claiming that Eve and Adam are the first people and that there are people somewhere else for her sons to marry. Eve is not mentioned when her grandchildren are born. She is not mentioned by name again (until the book of Tobit).

In Genesis 4:25, Eve and Adam have sex "again"; surely we are not to believe that they had sex only two or three times! Eve names her son Seth,

---

16. See the "living creatures" of Gen. 1:20 and Lev. 11:46.
17. "The humanity" is awkward and "the man" misleading.
18. The text doesn't even say that "Adam knew Eve" this time. Eve is not "known" by name; she is simply Adam's woman.

"placed," whom God placed with her in place of her murdered son Hevel, Abel. Eve never speaks again in the Scriptures. In these last words she and the text acknowledge her sense of loss for her son. God has given *her* Seth; Adam is not mentioned. Eve appears once more indirectly in Genesis 5:3. The author reveals that Adam had other daughters and sons after Seth. Eve is not named as their mother, but Adam has not been associated with anyone else. And in spite of the mysterious origin of Qayin's (Cain's) wife and daughters-in-law, Eve is still functioning in the story as the first woman, the mother of all living. There is a subtle irony here: the mother of all living has given birth to the father of murder, who is inscribed in Scripture as the first to succumb to sin on earth, signaled by the first use of the word *chata't*, "sin," in Genesis 4:7.

The story of Eve and Adam in Genesis has enjoyed something of a resurgence in religious discourse since the first century of the Common Era. New Testament, rabbinic, patristic, and pseudepigraphal authors all weighed in on lessons learned from Eve and Adam. But prior to that, most notably during the composition and editing of the rest of the Hebrew and Greek First Testament Scriptures, there was silence on Eve and Adam. They are not reflected on by name in the rest of the Hebrew canon. (Isa. 47:27 mentions an unnamed "first father" [or ancestor].) The Exodus narrative by far outweighs any other biblical story in number of internal biblical citations and reflections.

The story of Chavah, Eve, west of Eden is left to the imagination of the reader. What womanist wisdom did she pass on to her daughters and daughters-in-law that has been lost to indifference? How much of the work necessary to survive in the new world did she do with her own hands? Did she build a home, plant a farm or garden, do herding, go hunting? What recipes did she hand down to her daughters that recalled the memory of the garden's delights?

ADAH, ZILLAH, AND NA'AMAH BAT ZILLAH

> Genesis 4:19 Then Lamekh (Lamech) took for himself two women. The name of the one-woman was Adah, and the name of the second-woman was Tzillah (Zillah).

Seven generations have passed from Eve and Adam through an otherwise unknown Eastern woman and Cain to the time of Adah and Zillah. These two women, Adah and Zillah, are the first named in the text since Eve, and they are the first to participate in a polygamous—polygynous—partnership. From this point forward in the Scriptures, Lamech-style partnership (polygamy),

---

Polygamy

What happens to polygamy between the Testaments? Nothing in the biblical texts outlaws polygamy, although Jesus of Nazareth proclaims the Eve/Adam model normative and original in divine intent (Matt. 19:5–6; Mark 10:8). Arguments about the permissibility of polygamy—after all, the patriarchs did it—appear in the writings of the rabbinic and church fathers. Ultimately the Romans, not the church, outlawed polygamy.

---

rather than Eve/Adam-style monogamy, becomes normative. Lamekh reinvents what many translators and interpreters call "marriage."

Lamech offers in 4:23–24 what may be intended to be a rationale for the invention of polygamy. Someone, we do not know who, has caused Lamech some injury. He killed the man (or boy), invoking the memory of Cain. In the process he also justifies Cain's murder of Abel as vengeance. In comparing himself to Cain, Lamech acknowledges the wide gulf in the degree of their respective vengeances: By murdering his brother, Cain got sevenfold vengeance (against whom—Abel or God—is not specified); by killing the man whom he also calls a boy, Lamech gets seventy-seven-fold vengeance. What has this to do with his taking two women as intimate partners? It seems to be part of the same pattern: Lamech does and takes more in the same circumstances than do other people.

I have avoided calling the relationship between intimate partners in the Scriptures "marriage" thus far—even though the cohabitating and normatively child-producing relationship seems to conform to Western notions of marriage—because the word is not used in the text. In fact, there is no specific term in Biblical Hebrew for "marriage"; nor are there specific terms for "wives" or "husbands." Sometimes *ish* means "man" or even generic "person," and sometimes *ish* indicates a conjugal relationship. *Ba'al* means "lord," "master," and sometimes "male conjugal partner." It is also used to describe Abraham's relationship to two other men whom the NRSV translates as his "allies" but not his "husbands" in Genesis 14:13.

There are three verbs that are used to express conjugal unions: (1) *l-q-ch*, "to take" generally and with "woman" as the object, describes normative conjugal unions and is the most frequently used (about seventy-five times). (2) *b-'-l* carries connotations of hierarchy and dominion. Sarah is called *be'ulat ba'al*, "mistress of a master," to explain her relationship to Abraham in Genesis 20:3. It is also used of the rule of other lords over Israel in Isaiah 26:13.

(3) *ch-t-n* means "to marry" in its sixteen occurrences, and in its one nominal use means "wedding," but it is not regularly used. There are obviously more than ninety-six conjugal couples in the Hebrew Bible. Their unions are simply not named. Should unions that encompass polygamy and permit sexual access to abducted women, slaves, sex-workers, non-Israelite women, and widows without sanction be called "marriage," as the term has come to be used? Should they be called something else?

How did Adah and Tzillah feel about this new social structure Lamech invents? Was their participation voluntary? What did God think about this new development? Why is God silent on this development in the text? Since neither God nor the text critiques the practice, is it permissible? Is it simply a matter of human volition? Does this text mean marriage, coupling, or partnering, by whatever name, is ultimately just a human, social construction?

Adah gave birth to Yaval and Yuval (Jabal and Jubal). Through Jabal, Adah became the mother of all tent-dwelling women and men and all shepherding women and men. Through Jubal, Adah became the mother of the women and men who take up the lyre and/or the flute. Zillah gave birth to Tubal-Cain, named for his infamous ancestor; through him Tzillah became the mother of all bronze-workers and iron-workers. Zillah also gave birth to a daughter, Na'amah.[19] Nothing further is said about Na'amah bat Tzillah; the preservation of her name in the text is never explained. Hers is a paradigm-shifting family, naming women in the androcentric chronicle of a patriarchal family.

According to Genesis, this family changed "biblical marriage"[20] and invented the shepherding life that would become synonymous with biblical peoples and metaphors. In addition they gave birth to creativity in musical and metallurgical arts. Religious readers looking to and beyond the text for relational and other paradigms might do well to consider this family's legacy. The creativity of Adah and Zillah and their children rivals God's and foreshadows that of womanists; they brought into the world culture, craft, art, and music that had never before existed.

---

19. Her name will resurface in the text as the name of a Canaanite town destined for Judah (Josh. 15:41) and the first Judean queen mother, mother of Rehoboam and wife of Solomon in 1 Kgs. 14:21/2 Chr. 12:13; 1 Kgs. 14:31.

20. The recent insistence that the Eve-Adam story prescribes normative marriage for religious readers of the Scriptures must neglect the immediate aftermath of their union and the totality of conjugal unions in the Bible to proclaim "one man, one woman" as normative.

SARAH (FORMERLY KNOWN AS SARAI)

Genesis 17:16 "I will bless her, and more than that, I will give from her, for you, a son. And I will bless her, and she will become nations; rulers of peoples shall come from her."

The names "Sarai" and "Sarah" occur more frequently than the name of any other woman in the Bible, fifty-five times in the First Testament and four in the New Testament. Compare that to twenty-eight citations of Rebekah's name in the Hebrew Scriptures and one in the NT. Sarah bat Terah, Sarah neé Sarai, is introduced along with her sister-in-law Milcah (who is also her niece) in verse 29. Nothing else of her life matters or is disclosed. The discerning reader can ferret out the details of the incestuous unions that characterize this family, though her parentage is not disclosed until Genesis 20:12; she and her husband Abram share their father, Terah. The text withholds the relationship between Sarai and Terah for a dramatic reveal later in the story. There is another glaring omission in the text; it says nothing about the mothers of Sarai and Abram. We do not even know if Nahor and Haran (Abram's brothers) have the same mother as either Sarai or Abram.

In the next verse the text reveals that Sarai is infertile—as the biblical authors understood it, "barren." Barrenness is an agricultural term, implying that the soil—Sarai's womb—is inhospitable to life. In this understanding, men (and only men) produce "seed"; the woman's contribution to conception was unknown until very recently in human history. However, I find it curious that nowhere in the Bible is a man accused of having "bad" seed. The farmers who provided the language for the metaphor certainly knew that poor

---

Sarah and Abraham, an Incestuous Family

Sarah and Abraham are sister and brother, and they are married. Incestuous, intrafamily unions run in their family. Iscah and Milcah are Abram's nieces, the daughters of his brother Haran. Milcah is also Abram's sister-in-law. Milcah is Abram's niece and sister-in-law because she married her uncle Nahor, Abram's brother. Abram, Nahor, and Haran are brothers, the sons of Terah (and grandsons of another Nahor.) Milcah and Iscah are also Lot's sisters. The normative or at least regular practice of incestuous marriage in Lot's family may have some bearing on his subsequent conduct with his daughters. It is not clear whether the women in these relationships had any say in the matter. Neither is it clear whether the practice represented local culture or was characteristic of this family. The Torah will eventually proscribe such unions.

ground conditions were not the only cause for a failed crop. Surely they had seen mildewed or otherwise blighted seed stock. At any rate, quite some time must have passed between verse 29 and verse 30 in order for Sarai's infertility to become known.

In Genesis 11:31, Terah functions as a patriarch and moves the clan under his control. Terah takes his unacknowledged daughter Sarai, her brother and husband, Abram, and their nephew Lot on a journey from Mesopotamia to Canaan. It is possible that Terah took one or more women with whom he had children; it is also possible that he left women and progeny behind. Did Terah take Lot's widowed mother, his father Haran having died in 11:28? If not, why take a widow's son? Or had she died by this point as well? Lot appears to be her only son; he has two sisters, Milcah and Iscah. Did Terah take his other son, Nahor, his woman, and their family with them?

More than five hundred miles later they stopped in Haran, which the biblical writers associated with Abram's brother Haran.[21] Sarai and her family stay in Haran long enough for her father to die at a supernaturally ripe old age. Sarai and Abram have spent decades together, more than half a century, and their life together does not rate any discussion in the text.

In Genesis 12:4, Abram has reached the age of seventy-five. We have to read forward to 17:17 to discover that Sarai is a decade younger than Abram. She is sixty-five. Thinking back on the inauguration of their union, a ten-year age difference between partners seems more significant the younger they are. How old were Sarai and Abram when they became conjugal partners? They are on a journey that they have undertaken because God has called Abram to go on a journey, the end of which Abram does not know. In calling Abram, God blesses Abram, but God does not bless Sarai in Genesis 12:1–3. God does promise Abram female and male descendants, since a "nation" cannot be composed of only one gender.

Sarai's age is significant, because in the following stories she will be at risk of kidnapping (and likely worse) because of her great beauty. It is a rare and unprecedented thing in the Scriptures, or in the times in which they have been translated and interpreted, for a sixty-five-year-old woman to be recognized as extraordinarily, maddeningly beautiful, drawing the covetous sexual attentions of monarchs. Yet the Scriptures would have us believe that Sarai is so coveted twice.

These two stories (and their triplicate starring Rebekah and Isaac) undoubtedly come from disparate sources and do not reflect a chronological narrative. Their canonization into a narrative structure that claims coherence is an invitation to read them as separate, repeating events. In the case of the Sarai/

21. Haran the person and Haran the place are spelled differently in Hebrew, Sumerian, Assyrian, and Babylonian.

Sarah iteration, the duplication serves to emphasize her beauty and desirability, along with Sarai's and Abram's vulnerability to powerful "foreigners." The idea of these rulers as "foreigners" in their own principalities is comprehensible only when reading the text through Israelite eyes.

Israel's Iraqi, Babylonian Origins

Sarah and Abraham will become the founding parents of the people who will come to be called Israel, but they are not Israelites. Sarah, Abraham, and their brothers Haran and Nahor are from the Sumerian city of Ur (Gen. 11:28, 31). Ur is described as a "Chaldean" city. Chaldea became interchangeable with Babylon and Mesopotamia (2 Kgs. 25:13–36; Ezra 5:12; Isa. 47:1, etc.). Contemporarily, Ur is in Iraq, so the ancestors of Israel are also the ancestors of Iraq, since the entire family did not migrate.

As a result of a famine in Mesopotamia, Sarai and Abram went to the prosperous Egyptian empire. The text does not tell us if Lot went with them. What the text does say is that Sarai was beautiful and her beauty was a liability to Abram. Abram feared death more than he feared giving Sarai to another man. If she is known as his sister, a more powerful man might take her from him but let him live; if he were known as her man, he might be killed for her (see Gen. 12:12). The deception is for his benefit, not hers. In Genesis 12:15 what Abram feared most happened; Sarai was seized because of her great beauty and taken to the pharaoh. The account in Genesis 12 makes clear that the pharaoh took Sarai as his woman. And the text is clear that they lived together as a conjugal couple long enough for Abram to receive and enjoy sheep, oxen, male donkeys, male servants and female servants, female donkeys, and camels, and for some sort of plague to break out in the palace.

The *midrashim* reveal that the rabbinic interpreters understood Sarai was available for the pharaoh's sexual use, even when they did not want to admit it. The midrash on Exodus teaches that The-God-of-Sinai personally came down to deliver Sarai from the pharaoh. God tells Moses, "By your life, I will go down and save the Israelites. One woman came into Egypt and on her account I went down, and I saved her." When was this? When Pharaoh took Sarah, as it says, "And the HOLY ONE plagued Pharaoh. . . ."[22]

Abram did not object to Sarai's seizure. He relinquished her to the pharaoh and accepted a rich settlement for his loss. Her brother-husband sold her to

---

22. *Shemoth Rabbah* 15:14

a man he knew would use her for sex. A hip-hop womanist reading of this text would say that he pimped her out. This behavior on the part of the great patriarch has proved quite vexing to generations of interpreters. Rav Huna minimizes it in *Bereshit Rabbah* 3:1 and 41:1, saying it was only one night and the pharaoh never got any closer to Sarai than her shoe. But I think there is value in honoring Sarah as a survivor of sexual violence and domestic abuse and acknowledging her partner's complicity in that abuse. That is the plain truth for which womanist truth-telling calls. In a later section of the midrash on Genesis, Rabbi Simeon ben Yohai said that to compensate her for her troubles, the pharaoh gave Sarai his daughter Hagar, as reparations.[23]

In Genesis 12:19, the pharaoh admits that he took Sarai for his woman because he did not know that she was Abram's woman. Apparently the pharaoh has scruples about abducting partnered women, but not unattached women. The pharaoh confronts Abram about the deception, but Abram does not respond; he leaves with his woman and all that the pharaoh has given him in exchange for her. In Genesis 13:1 Sarai and Abram have left Egypt; they are very wealthy—the herd animals that Abram received in exchange for Sarai's body have made him a wealthy man. In Genesis 13:18, Sarai and Abram move to Hebron (although the text does not name her.)

Sarai is absent from the narrative when Lot is carried off as a war captive and when he is rescued (Gen. 14:12–16). Sarai is absent from the narrative when Abram gives the mysterious Malki-Tzedek (Melchizedek) one tenth of "everything," including the goods he received in exchange for Sarai from the pharaoh in Genesis 14:18–20. Given that wealth was accrued at her expense, perhaps she should've had a say in what happened to it. Sarai is absent from the narrative when the Holy One promises Abram descendants and makes a covenant with him in Genesis 15.

Sarai returns to the narrative in chapter 16. She is reintroduced along with her barrenness in the first verse. In spite of God's previous reassurance to Abram, he is still "going about childless" as he lamented in 15:2, without daughter or son from which his great nation may spring forth. The text links Sarai's childlessness with her possession of the person and services of an Egyptian slave-girl, *shiphchah* here, called Hagar (see Excursus, "The Torah of Enslaved Women"). The pain of Sarai's infertility transcends time. Every year that Abram and Sarai lived together as husband and wife was a year that passed without a child, with or without miscarried pregnancies or even

---

23. Giving a sexually exploited woman another woman to exploit sexually is "biblical" justice. I am not reading this as a historical or ethical claim but am acknowledging its Iron Age morality.

the hope of a child. In her desperation, Sarah turned to surrogacy, forcible surrogacy.

The girl—she is young enough to be presumed fertile—is called Hagar, a masculine Hebrew name meaning "foreign thing," from the root *g-w-r* that means "foreigner" or "sojourner." I very much doubt that her Egyptian parents gave her such a name. It is more likely that Hagar is what she was called after she entered a Hebrew-speaking household. I find it noteworthy that her name is not feminine, "foreign woman," even though it is her female body that will be colonized to gestate the hopes of Sarai and Abram.

Sarai gives Hagar to Abram as a surrogate wife, not as a "concubine," as some translate.[24] Concubinage does not exist in biblical Israel, in spite of the deployment of the term "concubine" in the dominant NRSV and JPS translations in a number of narratives. Concubinage generally refers to sexual use of a subordinate woman; if children are produced, they are illegitimate. In the Israelite two-tier conjugal system, the children of primary and secondary (or low-status) women in Israelite households are legitimate. Primary women are *nashot* (the plural of *isshah*, "woman"), regularly translated "wives." Secondary women are *pilegishiym nashot*, "women of secondary status." The terms are used together, and *pilegesh* (*piylegesh*, "secondary woman") also occurs alone.[25] The type of union, not sequence, determines the status of the union; a man's only woman may be of secondary status, or he may have several of primary status.

In Genesis 16, when Sarai gives Hagar to Abram, she gives her, *l'isshah*, "as a woman/wife," using the same term, *isshah*, for Sarai's own relationship with Abram. Secondarily, Sarai intends to use Hagar to produce a child to fulfill the divine promise; the child will be a legitimate heir. The biblical text has compressed ten years into one verse. It has been ten years since Abram has settled in Canaan. This does not include the first leg of his journey or his stay in Egypt. They have waited for God to provide them with a child for more than ten years; they are desperate. Sarah's barrenness seems to be secondarily—and temporarily—ascribed to God.

Sarai and Hagar are cowives. Both are matriarchs; both will entertain the Divine. Both will mother dynasties. But there is hierarchy between them, internal and external.[26] Sarai employs that hierarchy against Hagar; first

24. In Gen. 16:3 Hagar is called an *isshah*, "woman," situationally translated "wife" as in the NRSV and Fox. IB, JPS, and GSJPS use "concubine," which has traditionally indicated low-status marriage signaled by the use of the word *pilegesh* (*piylegesh*), which is not present in this text.

25. See Judg. 19:1; 2 Sam. 15:16; 20:3, where *pilegesh* (*piylegesh*) modifies *isshah*.

26. Renita Weems's powerful articulation of this point in *Just a Sister Away: A Womanist Vision of Women's Relationships in the Bible* (San Diego: LuraMedia, 1988) remains influential; see 1–19.

she offers her man Hagar's body and presumed fertility. Then Sarai claims and ultimately rejects Hagar's child and blames her man for doing what she told him to do in the first place (Gen. 16:5). Sarai invokes divine judgment between herself and Abram for the violence, *chamas*, that she claims has been done to her, then takes matters into her own hands and violently abuses, *t'a'nneha*, Hagar herself. Many translations downplay Sarai's abuse of Hagar in verse 6: NRSV, "dealt harshly"; JPS/GSJPS, "treated harshly"; IB, "treated badly." Fox's "afflicted" is somewhat stronger. Yet Sarai's abuse is described with the same verb, *'-n-h*, that led to God's redemption of Israel from Egypt (cf. IB, NRSV, JPS, and GSJPS "oppress" in Exod. 1:11). When Shechem abuses Dinah using the same verb, he rapes her, as does Amnon, Tamar. Sarai orchestrates Hagar's sexual abuse by Abram and is a party to and beneficiary of it. The biblical text makes plain the unwelcome truth that women participate in the trafficking and sexual abuse of other women. Understandably, Hagar runs away.

Sarai's story continues in Genesis 17, when she is eighty-nine years old according to the narrative. In spite of Sarai's violent abuse of Hagar, in spite of her forcible surrogate impregnation of Hagar, God keeps God's promise and Sarai becomes miraculously pregnant. God's fidelity to Sarai exceeds Sarai's fidelity to Hagar. God expresses that fidelity to Abram through a covenant expressed in Genesis 17:1–22; God also changes Abram's name to Abraham. In that same conversation, God speaks to Abraham about his woman. But first Abraham must circumcise himself and the males of his household. The sign that God chooses for the covenant between Godself and Abraham, his household, and his descendants excludes Sarai, the women of their household, and all of the women among their descendants. So is God really the God of the uncircumcised Sarai and her daughter descendants?

God tells Abraham that Sarai's name is also changing. God does not speak to her. God does promise to bless her and bring forth a line of royal rulers from her. This differs from the promise made to Hagar in chapter 16: she will be the mother of nations, but there is no mention of royalty among her descendants.[27] Abraham's response is to fall down laughing, questioning whether Sarah can give birth at her age. He does not consider that God can bring this miracle to pass. Just as Sarah is absent from the conversation about the covenant between God and Abraham, she is absent from the ritual that inscribes it on the flesh of Abraham, Ishmael, and every free and enslaved male in Abraham's household (Gen. 17:23–27). Does the covenant then extend to Sarah and the other women in her household?

---

27. It is worth noting that Abraham initially resists the idea of another heir, asking God in Gen. 17:18 to bestow these blessings on the child he has, a child God seems to have disregarded: "If only Yishmael existed before your face."

In Genesis 18:9, mysterious visitors ask Abraham about Sarah. One promises that she will indeed conceive and give birth within the year. From within the tent Sarah laughs to herself, as Abraham had previously laughed in God's face. After telling us that the eighty-nine- or ninety-year-old woman is indeed menopausal, God demands that Abraham explain Sarah's laughter, although he is never called to account for his own. Sarah denies laughing, and someone—the lack of an explicit subject makes it impossible to know if God or Abraham is speaking—rebuts her denial.

In 18:12, Sarah asks a fascinating intimate, explicit question: "After I have been completely dried out, will there yet be for me, wetness?"[28] The text offers a surprising acknowledgment and affirmation of women's sexual pleasure even as it supposes that at some age—perhaps with menopause—women are past the age for intimate moisture and its pleasures.

Sarah disappears from the text for several chapters. She reappears in chapter 20, when Abraham (and his unmentioned household) moves to Gerar. Once again Sarah's beauty brings peril. Once again Abraham identifies Sarah as his sister and not as his woman. In 20:13, Abraham explains that he asks that Sarah only identify herself as his sister in every place they travel. On one hand, that level of fear seems completely paranoid; on the other, Sarah is taken from him to be the woman of a wealthy man on two occasions (if we read the narratives sequentially as they appear in a canonical reading). Their deception has apparently saved their lives, although it has not preserved Sarah from abduction and rape or forced marriage.

This time the Scriptures would have us believe King Avimelekh (Abimelech) of Philistia takes Sarah from Abraham for the second time. But the text assures us that she is not violated this time. Now, this sister-wife-surrender story is most likely an alternate version of the one in chapter 12. But combined with that narrative as a second canonical story, it serves to emphasize Sarah's great beauty at her great age, the number and nature of threats to the promises God has made to Abraham, and God's continual intervention to protect Sarah, Abraham, and their progeny—including Hagar and her progeny. In 20:18, the text reveals the lengths to which God is willing to go to protect Sarah: God inflicts infertility on all the women in Abimelech's household—his woman and female slaves, whose duties appear to be sexual and reproductive—until Sarah is released.[29]

---

28. In his Jewish Publication Society *Commentary on Genesis*, Nahum Sarna offers the translation "abundant moisture" in lieu of the traditional "pleasure."

29. Obviously it would take some time for this infertility to manifest, but the text has specified that there was no sexual contact between Sarah and Abimelech, so the reader must imagine that he was somehow too busy to make use of the woman he had seized.

In chapter 21 Sarah conceives at long last; no further mention is made of her intimate pleasure and concomitant wetness. Instead, she celebrates the "laughter" that God has brought into her life through her son (a pun on Isaac's name in Hebrew). She rejoices particularly in the thought of nursing, *y-n-q*, her son. In her barrenness Sarah responded to Hagar's fertility with violence, driving her out in chapter 16. The text does not address Sarah's reception of the returned Hagar. In her fertility Sarah once again turns hostile eyes to Hagar. This time Sarah does not lay a hand on Hagar; instead, she sends her out into the wilderness to die with her now unwanted and superfluous son, Ishmael. In Genesis 21:12 God gives Abraham a command that has vexed and inspired biblical commentators through the ages: "Whatever Sarah says to you, obey her." In the rabbinic exegetical tradition expressed in the *Midrash Rabbah, Shemoth* 1:1, Sarah was a prophet whose prophetic abilities surpassed those of Abraham.[30]

Sarah disappears from the text at one of its most crucial junctures, Abraham's decision to sacrifice their son. The reader can only imagine that Abraham did not tell Sarah of his plan, or speculate what might have happened had Sarah been included in the conversation with the Divine, or had she been apprised of Abraham's intent. One can only wonder what she said when the day's events became known, retold, ultimately to be canonized.

Sarah's death at the age of one hundred and twenty-seven is memorialized in Genesis 23:1. The deaths of women in the Scriptures are rarely detailed; accounts of their burials are even more rare. On Sarah's behalf, Abraham negotiates for a burial ground with a Hittite clan that has taken up residence in Canaan. In the moment of her death and in the days and weeks and months following, Sarah is beloved, bewailed, and bemoaned, and Abraham is bereaved and bereft. When the number and complexities of Sarah's lives are measured (23:1 uses the plural), she is woman and wife, mother and matriarch, female patriarch and flawed person, blessed and beloved.

Daughterless, Sarah was the mother of Yitzchaq (Isaac), the mother-in-law of Rivqah (Rebekah), and the grandmother of Israel. Sarah's stature as an ancestor grew with the canonization of each volume of Scripture. Isaiah invokes her name in 51:2; one of the heroines of Tobit is named for her; and she is named in Romans 9:9; Hebrews 11:11; and 1 Peter 3:6—although the author of the Petrine epistle has not based his assertions on the extant First Testament. Sarah also appears in the pseudepigraphal books of *Levi, Abraham, Asenath* (in which we learn that Sarah was quite tall), *Lives of the Patriarchs*, and the *Prayer of Levi*.

30. Abraham was called a prophet by Abimelech in Gen. 20:7. Most commentators regard this an indication of regard for Abraham, given he does not actually function as a prophet.

The biblical Sarah is a complex character who exercises privilege and experiences peril. In her complexity she can be iconic for contemporary religious readers who may not find themselves on a single side of a contrived privilege-peril binary scale. Women of color who are imperiled in the United States and the wider Western world because of race and ethnicity can also exercise privilege if they are Christian and/or cisgender[31] and/or heterosexual. Women who exercise white privilege can be imperiled through Muslim identity or sexual minority status. Male privilege—even white male privilege—can be eclipsed in part by sexual orientation or broader gender nonconformity.

Sarah's economic and social privilege and national origin separate her from Hagar, even though they share gender peril. Their biological privilege-peril spectrum is inverted: Hagar's fertility offers little privilege, while Sarah's barrenness poses significant peril. Sarah chooses the role of female patriarch and enforces the patriarchal hierarchy on Hagar, even when Abraham does not require her to do so. She has another option, as Renita Weems demonstrates in *Just a Sister Away:*[32] solidarity and sisterhood. In this reading Sarah serves as a cautionary tale bearing witness to the temptation to exercise whatever privilege we may have over someone else, rather than stand with them in shared peril, thereby extending and transforming privilege.

HAGAR

> Genesis 21:17 God heard the voice of the boy, and the messenger of God called to Hagar from the heavens, and said to her, "What is with you, Hagar? Fear not, for God has heard the voice of the boy there where he is."

The biblical portrayal of Hagar has served as the launching point for contemporary womanist discourse and premodern protowomanist analyses, and continues to fire the exegetical imaginations of readers/hearers of African descent in multiple religious traditions. The biblical account of Hagar intersects with and diverges from the traditional Islamic accounts of the Hajar narrative; it should be noted that Hajar's story is not told in the Qur'an.[33] Muslim readers

---

31. "Cisgender" refers to having one's gender identity perceived as corresponding with one's biological sex.

32. Renita J. Weems, *Just a Sister Away: A Womanist Vision of Women's Relationships in the Bible* (San Diego, CA: LuraMedia, 1988), 9–10, 14, 16.

33. Hadiths are reports of the words and deeds of the Prophet Muhammad. I have used the collection of classical Islamic scholar Sahih Bukhari (810–870 CE) in the public domain and the *tafsir* (commentary) of Al Tabari, widely considered to be authoritative (Muḥammed Ibn-Garīr al-Ṭabarī and William M. Brinner, *The History*

Messenger/Angels

English speaking hearers and readers are used to encountering "angels" in the biblical text, but the images that are invoked by the term were virtually unknown to those who crafted and those who first encountered the Hebrew Scriptures. The word *mal'ak* (*mal'akiym*, plural) means "messenger," not necessarily a supernatural being. The human messengers of Genesis 32:3; Numbers 20:14; Deuteronomy 2:26, and so on are *mal'akiym*, as are the supernatural messengers that Jacob saw on the ladder in Genesis 28:16, the messenger in the burning bush in Exodus 3:2, and the messenger Balaam and his donkey encounter in the road in Numbers 22:31. (The messengers in Gen. 19:1 cannot be clearly identified as supernatural or human, in spite of the translation "angels" in NRSV and JPS; Fox, the GSJPS, and IB use "messenger" exclusively.) These messengers do not have wings—hence Jacob's ladder—and they do not play musical instruments. There are supernatural beings with wings: the cherubs (Hebrew *cheruviym*) have two; the fiery seraphim have six. Neither the cheruviym nor seraphiym are ever called "messengers" (*mal'akiym*) in the text. The practice of calling the messengers "angels" stems from the translation of the Hebrew Scriptures into Greek. The Greek word *angelos*, "angel," was used to translate *mal'ak* for human and divine messengers. However, the primary meaning of *angelos*, a human messenger, has been lost in contemporary popular usage.

---

and hearers of the tradition that identifies Hajar as the mother of Ibrahim's promised heir affirm Hajar's status as a matriarch and that Hajar was a servant in Sarah's household. Christian womanist readers/hearers have reevaluated the biblical Hagar narrative for its affirmation of her place in the divine narrative and that of her descendants, in spite of her enslavement and use as a surrogate. Among these, the reading of Delores Williams has had the most significant impact on my scholarship.[34]

Perhaps more than any other scriptural (in the broadest sense) narrative, the Hajar/Hagar story emphasizes the import of naming and of names. Muslim feminist scholar Amina Wadud taught me that the name we use for Hajar/Hagar immediately privileges one tradition over the other. This volume is

---

of al-Ṭabarī. *The Children of Israel*, vol. 3 [Albany: State Univ. of New York Press, 1991]).

34. Delores S. Williams was the first scholar to highlight for me (and many of my peers in seminary and graduate school) the significance of Hagar as the only person in the canon to name God (*Sisters in the Wilderness: The Challenge of Womanist God-Talk* [Maryknoll, NY: Orbis Books, 1993]).

exegesis of and commentary on the shared Scriptures of Judaism and Christianity, yet the expansive nature of womanism that is deeply entrenched in the lived reality of black women and all whom they (we) love in the world includes women and men from a broad range of religious traditions and those from none. In this discussion the biblical Hagar will share space on the page with Hajar from our sister tradition Islam and its sister-texts, the hadiths, given the silence on Hajar in the Holy Qur'an. The account that follows is a conversation between the stories of the matriarch who has come to be called Hagar in the Jewish and Christian Scriptures and Hajar in Islamic sacred texts.

In all of the stories, Hajar's/Hagar's story begins not with transcendence but with subjugation. In the hadith, Hajar is given to Sarah by a tyrant.[35] Genesis 16 does not reveal under what circumstances Hagar initially entered servitude; Hagar's previous life is of no interest to the authors and editors of Genesis—or, they may have supposed, to their readers and hearers. To be fair, they may not have imagined a generation of readers/hearers who would call themselves "Hagar's children," even as they identify with the God of Abraham.[36] There is a rabbinic midrash that Hagar's subordination was compensation for Sarah's subordination to the pharaoh who bought her from Abraham; in this reading Hagar was the pharaoh's daughter. This midrash answers questions I have as well: Who and where were her parents? How did she come to be enslaved? Was she born into servitude? These questions have particular resonance in the Americas for readers and hearers of African descent, whose ancestors were enslaved and whose foremothers were regularly subjected to the theft of their bodies, inside and out.

Hagar's *otherness* is at the heart of her portrayal in the Torah, Tanakh[37] and New Testament. Her name, I have contended, is not *her* name: *HaGar* means "the foreigner," "alien," or "sojourner" in Biblical Hebrew. The alien is one who resides in a land that is not their own, as in Abraham's family residing in Canaan as aliens, and the familiar protections in the Torah for the aliens in the midst or gates of the Israelites.[38] It strains credulity to imagine an Egyptian mother naming her child "alien" in the language of the people to whom she will be subjected in servitude, and not just because *HaGar* is masculine in Hebrew.

---

35. *Sahih Bukhari*, narrated by Abu Huraira, vol. 7, book 62, number 21.

36. I grew up hearing African Americans refer to themselves as "Hagar's children" in black churches, because Hagar is African, and unlike the broader culture as demonstrated through media portrayals, we knew Egypt was in Africa.

37. Tanakh, sometimes rendered as TaNaKh, is a vocalized acronym for the tripartite Hebrew Scriptures in Jewish tradition; the three parts are the Torah, Nevi'im (Prophets), and Ketuvim (Writings).

38. See Exod. 6:4; Lev. 16:29; Num. 9:14; etc.

There is another way of understanding Hagar's name. In the Islamic tradition, Hajar does not derive from "alienation." Rather, the range of potential meanings for Hajar's name includes "splendid" and "nourishing" in the wider cognate Semitic language system.[39] There is an established history of the name Hajar being given to women on the Arabian Peninsula and elsewhere in ancient Semitic languages, for example, Ethiopic and Nabatene, some two millennia before the Common Era. It is, I think, a supreme irony that the names Hajar and Hagar evoke such different semantic ranges and that they overlap and intersect in the body of a woman who transcends scriptural canons and traditions.

The Hebrew text beginning with Genesis 16 makes it clear that Hagar has no say over her body being given to Abram or her child being given to Sarai. Hagar is on the underside of all of the power curves in operation at that time, as noted by Renita Weems,[40] Delores Williams,[41] and many, many others: she is female, foreign, enslaved. She has one source of power: she is fertile; but she lacks autonomy over her own fertility. Sarai is infertile, and the text suggests that, as a result, Hagar held Sarai "in low esteem." Hagar's disposition towards Sarai is framed with the word *q-l-l*, "to curse" or to "hold worthless," that is, "light," "little," or "nothing." It may not be that Hagar views Sarai as nothing because Sarai is infertile and Hagar is fertile. Rather, it may be that Hagar regards Sarai as nothing and/or curses her because Sarai uses Hagar's body for her own reproductive purposes. Why should a sex-slave, forced into gestating someone else's child, think highly of or bless her enslaver? Perhaps the text singles out Hagar's feelings toward Sarai because Sarai is primarily responsible for Hagar's sexual subjugation. Abram's complicity is secondary. Sarai is free; she has some societal privilege as Abram's woman and Hagar's mistress. But she is still an infertile woman in a male-dominated world, both of which imperil her status; she seeks to attain/restore her status on and in Hagar's body.

Sarai inscribes the hierarchy between herself and Hagar on Hagar's body. In the hadith, Sarah is jealous of Hajar.[42] First Sarah perpetuates patriarchal values deliberately and intimately, seizing Hagar's sexuality and fertility. Then she continues her domination of Hagar in anger. Sarai initially takes her anger out on Abram, within limits; no actions accompany her words to him. She calls on God-of-the-Holy-Name to do justice on her behalf in 16:5. God

---

39. See Ernst Knauf's entry on Hagar in the *Anchor Yale Bible Dictionary* (*AYBD*), 3:19. The ancient Egyptian language is a sibling Afro-Asiatic language along with Semitic languages.

40. Weems, *Just a Sister Away*, 12–15.

41. Williams, *Sisters in the Wilderness*, 3–6.

42. Narrated by Ibn Abbas, *Sahih Bukhari*, vol. 4, book 55, number 584.

remains silent. The silence of God offers a fecund space for midrash, which frequently addresses silence in the text. As a contemporary womanist midrash, I offer the reading that God's silence is a response to Sarai's charge that God judge between her and Abram. Abram has not wronged Sarai. Abram and Sarai both wrong Hagar, and God does not permit them to compound that wrongdoing by destroying her and her child.

When Abram removes himself from the fray, Sarai takes her anger out on Hagar. Sarai brutalizes Hagar. The standard translations do not capture the physical violence that is represented by this verb, '-n-h.[43] In fact, Sarai's oppression of Hagar in Genesis 16:6 is the same as Egypt's oppression of Israel in Exodus 1:11, ultimately leading to God's liberating intervention. This is one of a series of inverted parallels between the stories of Hagar's sojourn with Sarai and Abram and Israel's sojourn in Egypt.

But Hagar liberates herself; she runs away.[44] A messenger of God-of-the-Holy-Name finds Hagar in the wilderness. This messenger of God is a supernatural being. But there is more to this messenger; in 16:7, the messenger of God-of-the-Holy-Name functions as God in disguise, or perhaps better, God in (human) drag.[45] The holy messenger uses the first person in 16:10, speaking as God, and in 16:13 Hagar realizes that she has seen God. This is extraordinary, for Exodus 33:20 will insist that no one can see God and live; perhaps those verses ought to be translated as "no *man*."

God's message to Hagar is disturbing. She must return to Sarai and submit to her violent and vicious abuse. It does not appear that she will be subject to Abram's sexual use again, but that is entirely up to him—or perhaps Sarai in that family. The biblical text reifies her enslavement. God's words are unwelcome, but there is hope. Sarai will not destroy her; Hagar will survive. In 16:10 Hagar receives the first divine annunciation to a woman in the canon of a promised child and promise of a dynasty. Hagar will become the Mother of Many Peoples.[46] Beyond the biblical narrative, *Hagar* functioned as an ethnic signifier for peoples on the Arabian Peninsula from 2000 BCE to the Middle Ages, including Darius I in hieroglyphics (*AYBD*, 3:19).

43. Cf. "dealt harshly" (NRSV), "treated harshly" (JPS and GSJPS), and "treated badly" (IB). "Afflicted," Fox's translation, is somewhat closer.

44. She will run again in chapter 21; there is a parallel text for that episode in the hadith, but not for the journey in chapter 16.

45. "Drag" initially referred to women's clothes worn by men in live theater. It now functions more generally as wearable markers of identity that transform one person— or, in the case of God, being—into another.

46. Early readers of the Scriptures may well have connected Hagar to the "Hagrites" mentioned in Ps. 83:7, who also appear several times in 2 Chronicles, although some modern scholarship discounts a link between them; Baruch 3:23 mentions "the descendants of Hagar."

This portion of Hagar's story contains an episode without peer in all of Scripture. In Genesis 16:13, Hagar names God: *El Ro'i*, "God of seeing," meaning, "Have I seen the One who sees me and lived to tell of it?" She is the only person in the canon to give God a name. There is no parallel for this part of Hagar's story in Hajar's story in the hadith. Hagar's story continues in Genesis 21. But where was she during the stories that took place between chapters 16 and 21? Where was Hagar when God changed Sarai's and Abram's names to Sarah and Abraham? Where was Hagar when Ishmael was circumcised? Where was Hagar when the mysterious visitors predicted a miraculous pregnancy for Sarah? Where was Hagar when Sarah was taken into Abimelech's household?

Without answering these questions, Hagar reappears in Genesis 21. Sarah has given birth to Isaac. One day she sees Ishmael playing and demands that Abraham put him and his mother out. She does not want Ishmael to inherit anything along with Isaac, even though God had made promises to Hagar for her son and to Abraham for all of his descendants. Genesis 21:11 says that Abraham was greatly troubled by Sarah's demand on account of his son; he expresses no feelings for Hagar. God comforts Abraham on account of Hagar *and* Ishmael, although the text does not name Hagar and refers to her repeatedly as Abraham's (not Sarah's) woman-servant in verse 12. The text also confirms Isaac's status as the primary heir. God also affirms (v. 13) the promise that God has made to Hagar and Abraham, that Ishmael will be a great nation of his own.

Abraham provides some provisions, bread, and water for his family and sends them on their way, into the wilderness. In the hadith, Ibrahim goes with Hajar and their child.[47] In both the Bible and the hadith, Hajar/Hagar weeps, and heaven hears her cry. In the hadith,[48] the angel Jibril (Gabriel) hears Hajar and responds to her cry. In the Bible God hears her cry and the boy's, and an unnamed messenger responds to Hagar. This is her second supernatural encounter. As in Genesis 16, the messenger is more than a messenger; the messenger is God, who speaks in the first person in verse 18, repeating the promise to make Ishmael a great nation.

In both accounts Hajar/Hagar receives life-sustaining water. The hadith specifies that the water replenishes Hajar's breast milk. In the Bible Hagar discovers a well. The stories diverge at this point, and the characters go in separate journeys. In the hadith Ishmael grows into a hunter, marries, and divorces. Ibrahim and Ishmael go to Mecca to build the Kaaba.

---

47. Ibn Abbas, *Sahih Bukhari*, vol. 4, book 55, number 584.
48. Ibid.

In the Bible, Hagar and Ishmael live first in the wilderness of Paran, where he develops as a martial artist, specializing in the bow. Eventually Hagar and Ishmael go home to Egypt. Hagar finds a wife for Ishmael. Were they reunited with Hagar's family? To what city did they go? Into what family or community did Ishmael marry? Hagar's journey to Egypt, where she procures a wife for Ishmael (as does Hajar in the hadith), creates a final inverse parallel with the Israelite sojourn in Egypt: Hagar the Egyptian is abused by Sarah the proto-Israelite; Israel is abused by Egypt. Hagar escapes into the wilderness; Israel escapes into the wilderness. Hagar heads toward Egypt; Israel heads away from Egypt. Hagar's name is never called again in the Hebrew Scriptures, though she is named in Baruch 3:23. Her name may live on in the Hagrites of the First Testament;[49] she is reinterpreted in the Second Testament (see Gal. 4:22–25), and midrashed and exegeted in the sacred literatures of Judaism, Christianity, and Islam.

I read Hagar's story through the prism of the wholesale enslavement of black peoples in the Americas and elsewhere; Hagar is the mother of Harriet Tubman and the women and men who freed themselves from slavery. I see Hagar as an abused woman. I see God's return of Hagar to her servitude and abuse as the tendency of some religious communities to side with the abuser at the expense of abused women and their children. Frequently that advice is couched as "God's will." Ultimately Hagar escapes her slaveholders and abusers and receives her inheritance from God, and God fulfills all of God's promises to her. Sarah's complicated relationships with Abraham can be read as exemplars of the complicated relationships between women and men across lines of privilege and hierarchy. Abraham's sexual use of Hagar has resonances in the sexual and reproductive uses of women's bodies in the American slavocracy and in countless other global contexts across time, including the present day and every context in which this volume will be read. Sarah's actions evoke both complicity with dominant male abuse of subordinated women and the independent abusive actions of dominant-culture women against subordinated women. The legacies of the relationship tropes among Hagar, Sarah, and Abraham survive them and transcend their cultures of origin.

The deaths and burials of Sarah and Abraham are preserved in the text. Hagar's are not. I will borrow from Ishmael's depiction at his father's funeral (Gen. 25:7–18) and the death of Sarah (Gen. 23:1–2, 19–20) to construct a midrash for Ishmael's burial of his mother and fill in the blanks with my sanctified womanist imagination.

49. Their linkage of the Hagrites with Ishmael and Edom (see Ps. 83:6) suggests ancient readers indeed recognized them as or associated them with Hagar's descendants. See 1 Chr. 5:10, 19–20; 27:30.

And Hagar lived one hundred seventy-seven years; this was the length of Hagar's life. Hagar breathed her last and died in a good old age, an old woman and full of years, and was gathered to her people. Hagar died at Heliopolis[50] in the land of Egypt; and Yishmael her son went in to mourn for Hagar and to weep for her. And Hagar's daughters and sons from the man she chose for herself mourned with Yishmael and his daughter Mahalat.[51] After this, Yishmael had his mother embalmed and mummified and placed Hagar his mother in a sarcophagus in a tomb in Heliopolis in the land of the Nile. The tomb and the land that is around it passed through the generations of the Hagrites as a burying place. There Hagar was buried, with her man.

These are the descendants of Yishmael, the son of Hagar who God promised would become the Mother of Many Nations. These are the names of the grandchildren of Hagar, the children of Yishmael, his daughter Mahalat and these, named in the order of their birth: Nebaioth, the firstborn of Yishmael; and Qedar, Adbeel, Mibsam, Mishma, Dumah, Massa, Hadad, Tema, Jetur, Naphish, and Qedemah. These are of the grandchildren of Hagar, the children of Yishmael, and these are their names, by their villages and by their encampments, twelve princes according to their tribes.

This is the length of the life of Yishmael the son of Hagar, one hundred thirty-seven years; he breathed his last and died, and was gathered to his people. He was buried with his mother Hagar in her tomb.

RIVQAH (REBEKAH)

Genesis 24:60 Our sister, may you become a thousand, ten-thousand-fold.

Rivqah (Rebekah) is one of the most dominant matriarchs in the Israelite story; she has agency and she uses her voice. A close reading of her story indicates that she is portrayed as one of the most active women in the canon. The sixty-seven verses that comprise Genesis 24 are full of her comings and goings, words and deeds; there are at least twenty verbs devoted to her actions in chapters 24–27. Rebekah's voice and agency are located in a matrilineal household, identified as her mother's household in Genesis 24:28. Her father identifies himself with a matronymic (maternal name) in Genesis 24:15 and 24

---

50. Inspired by Joseph's marriage to Asenath of Heliopolis, then called On, by Isaiah's reimagining of the relationship between Israel, Egypt, and Assyria in 19:19–25, and by the construction of a Jewish temple there about 160 BCE.

51. See Gen. 28:9 for Mahalat(h), Ishmael's daughter.

Matronyms

Jacob identifies himself as the son of Rebekah (*ben Rivqah*) but does not mention Isaac or even Abraham in Genesis 29:12. Other persons in the Scriptures identified by their mother's names include David's chief warriors—and nephews—Joab, Abner, and Abishai, the sons of Zeruiah, who is David's sister, more than two dozen times in Samuel, Kings, and Chronicles, for example, 2 Samuel 19:21–22; 1 Chronicles 2:16. In the case of Rebekah, the use of the matronym is associated with matrilineality; her home is a *beyt 'em*, "a mother's household" (Gen. 24:28), not the more common *beyt 'av*, "a father's household." Other matrilineal households in the Scriptures include the families of origin of Ruth and Orpah in Ruth 1:8 and the bride in the Song of Solomon 3:4 and 8:2.

---

as Bethuel ben Milcah, Bethuel the son of Milcah, his mother, the niece and sister-in-law of Sarah and Abraham.

Rebekah is introduced in Genesis 24 as the key to the fulfillment of God's promise to Abraham. Even though Abraham has Ishmael and Isaac, and Ishmael has likely become a father by this time, Abraham does not want to go to his death without seeing Isaac's children, the next step in the fulfillment of God's promise. Abraham seeks a marriage for his son in accordance with his family practice of incestuous unions. Rebekah's grandmother Milcah is also Isaac's first cousin as the daughter of his uncle Haran, and she is also his aunt, since Milcah is married to another of his uncles, Nahor. This makes Rebekah and Isaac second and third cousins.

Abraham sends a servant to acquire a bride for Isaac from his family. It is not clear if he consults with Sarah. The servant works out a plan whereby he will know that the girl he encounters will be divinely chosen. Rebekah appears in the text with a disclosure of her ancestry, emphasizing that this will be an intrafamily union in Genesis 24:15. Yet Rebekah, more specifically her brother Lavan (Laban), will come to be called Aramean (Gen. 25:20). Indeed, Israel will be said to have been descended from "a wandering Aramean" in Deuteronomy 25:9. In Genesis 24:16 there is a description of her qualifications, physical attractiveness, and sexual inexperience. Each description is compounded; she is "extremely good [or pleasing] to look at" (*tovat mar'eh m*ᵉ*'od*) and "unpenetrated, no man had known her" (*bᵉtulah ve'ish lo yᵉda'ah*). Yet the rest of her story will make it clear that she is not reduced to the sum of her parts. There is no way of determining her age; we can only conclude that she is marriageable and of childbearing age.

When Rebekah provides the emissary with potentially life-saving water, he knows that she is the one "designated" by God (although the verb *y-k-ch* has this sense only here in 24:14). When the servant drapes her with gold, Rebekah appears to take it in stride or as her due. She does not in any way object to his largesse. The servant asks who she is and if he might go with her to her *father's* house (24:23); he does not know that she lives in her *mother's* house (24:28). Rebekah identifies her father as the son of her grandmother in verse 24 and extends the offer of hospitality herself (24:25); she does not need to check with anyone. Rebekah's brother Laban does the necessary housework to prepare their mother's house for their guest (see 24:31).

In verse 50, patriarchy appears and attempts to raise its head. Bethuel, Rebekah's father, and Laban, her brother, tell the servant to take her and go. However, Bethuel and Laban do not have the final word and may not have the authority to issue the command. At the end of the chapter, during the family conversations Rebekah agrees to marry Isaac. When Rebekah's mother is consulted, she and Laban in verse 55 first ask the servant to delay his return for ten days. Then in verse 58 Milcah makes sure that Rebekah's wishes are consulted and honored.[52]

When asked whether she will return with the servant and marry Isaac, Rebekah answers, "I will." Rebekah rides off into the sunset in a narrative in which she will continue to be active. She is not alone when she journeys to meet her new husband; she takes with her women-servants from her mother's household, including her nurse from her infancy, Devorah (Deborah).[53] As she departs, her household blesses her, marking a canonical first[54] in the preservation of the words of blessing in verse 60: "Our sister, may you become a thousand, ten-thousand-fold; may your seed inherit the gates of those-who-hate-him."

52. Laban is with her, and the text frames the dialogue as a joint undertaking. However, Laban is also listed as speaking with his father, telling the servant to take his sister. It seems that he agrees with whatever parent is speaking.

53. Deborah's name is given in Gen. 35:8.

54. There are very few blessings spoken to women and preserved in the Scriptures. In Gen. 17:16 God speaks to Abraham of blessing Sarah, but the text does not record divine words of blessing spoken to Sarah. Deborah blesses Jael in Judg. 5:24. Boaz blesses Ruth, and the women of their community bless Naomi in Ruth 3:10 and 4:14. In Tob. 11:17, Tobit blesses his new daughter-in-law Sarah. Judith is thrice blessed: First in Jdt. 13:18–20 she is blessed by her town elder, Uzziah. Then in 15:9–10 the high priest and Israelite elders in Jerusalem bless her. Last, the women of Israel bless Judith in the next verse, but their words of blessing are not preserved in the text. Elizabeth reprises Deborah's blessing of Jael and Uzziah's blessing of Judith when she blesses her pregnant virgin cousin, Mary, in Luke 1:42.

On her journey with her promised husband's servant, Rebekah notices a man and asks who he is (24:64–65). It turns out that he is her intended, but she did not know that when she made her inquiry. Rebekah's status as a promised woman does not keep her from looking at men or inquiring about them. She is a bold matriarch in every sense of the word. In verse 64 Rebekah's veil may indicate her status as a bride; in general, women in ancient Israel are not described as wearing veils in the Bible. There is no description of a ceremony to mark their union; the Scriptures do not indicate that there were any formalities beyond gift-giving, consent, and the occasional celebratory meal.

With her union to Isaac, Rebekah moves from a matrilineal family—where her father is known only by the name of his mother—to a patrilocal one, in which she as a new bride moves into her husband's mother's home (24:67). In verse 67, for the first time in the canon, the relationship between a woman and her man is characterized by love. Abraham has "played" with Sarah and been fearful of losing her to another man, but the only love ascribed to him is for Isaac (Gen. 22:2). Indeed, Isaac's love for Rebekah introduces the verb '-h-v, "love" (including romantic love) into the text. No previous character in the Scriptures is described as loving or being loved.[55] Love and the quest for love will be a hallmark of the next portion of Rebekah's story and that of her daughters-in-law, Leah and Rachel.

Rebekah's story continues in Genesis 25:19 after a break in the text. Purporting to list the descendants of Isaac, verse 19 instead provides Isaac's parentage; his age at his union with Rebekah follows—her age is never disclosed—and then the text announces her infertility. However, since the text has already promised offspring, the reader/hearer knows Rebekah's barrenness will be short lived. Rebekah seems to be reduced to object status for a while. The narrator speaks about her, Isaac prays for her, God acts on her, and her children move within her. She is not the subject of any of these verbs.

In verse 22 Rebekah's agency returns; her unborn children pitch so violently in her womb that it feels like one is "crushing [the life out of]" the other.[56] Rebekah gives voice to her feelings in a difficult-to-translate expression.[57] A generous translation might be "If this is to be so, then why am I here?" Rebekah seems to be questioning why she is pregnant with twins, only to lose one in an internal struggle. She takes her question directly to God, using the verb d-r-sh, "seek." When the object of the verb d-r-sh is God, the one from whom knowledge is being sought, the inquiry is prophetic.

---

55. God's steadfast, faithful love, is expressed with another root, ch-s-d.

56. *Vayitrotzatzu*, (r-tz-tz, "crush," "suppress," or "oppress") is used reflexively in the Hitpael here.

57. Most literally she says, "If so for-what this I?"

God speaks directly to Rebekah, without an intermediary, prophet, or messenger. God promises that both children will become great nations, but they will be divided in an inverted hierarchy, based on their age. God does not promise Rebekah that she will survive their birth or live to see them fulfill their destinies. Rebekah gives birth to the first set of twins mentioned in the Scriptures.[58] Genesis 25:26 states that Isaac is sixty when the twins are born; he was forty when he married Rebekah. That means that Rebekah lived with her infertility for twenty years. The text credits Isaac with one successful prayer on Rebekah's behalf. Did he really pray only once? Did God wait twenty years to answer his prayer, or did he wait twenty years to pray? It defies credulity to believe that the most active matriarch in the canon never offers a prayer on her own behalf during each of the twenty years in which the reader must imagine that she and Isaac looked and hoped for a child. Yet the text never mentions Isaac taking another woman or fathering children with anyone else. That is exceptional among the patriarchs of Israel.

Rebekah's story hurtles forward to the adulthood of her children. The only reference to their childhood is that somewhere along the way Esau becomes a hunter, to the pleasure of his father, who loves him. Rebekah loves her younger son, Ya'aqov (Jacob), the one God said would dominate his older brother, Esav (Esau). Rebekah is absent from the story in which Esau sells his birthright though she is implicated in it. Even if she was absent from the scene, what did she have to say when she found out?

Genesis 26 is a triplicate version of the matriarch-desired-by-a-foreign-monarch theme, previously deployed in Genesis 12:10–20 and 20:1–18 featuring Sarai/Sarah. A canonical reading treats them as separate stories, in spite of the textual evidence arguing that they are merely duplicates. Indeed, the pat villain in Genesis 20 and 26 is King Abimelech of the Philistines; the reader is to imagine that he has failed twice, in two successive generations, to commandeer a woman. Perhaps an additional intent of this story is to ridicule the Philistines. In any case, the cumulative effects of these stories is to reinforce the desirability of the matriarchs, the threat of the surrounding peoples, and the fidelity of God in perpetually delivering the members of this family from danger throughout the generations. Rebekah fades from the text again, but in truth she is just under the surface, between the lines, in the most fertile space for midrash, which frequently begins with questions.

Rebekah appears to move with Isaac several times as he feuds with the Philistines over wells producing life-giving water in the valley of Gerar.[59] When

---

58. She will be followed shortly by Tamar in Gen. 38:27; the only other canonical mention of twins is Thomas, the disciple of Jesus known as "the Twin," John 11:16.

59. The text does not mention anyone other than Isaac relocating.

Isaac "pitches his tent" (Gen. 26:25) in Beer-sheba, it seems that he has settled in with his family, in spite of their absence from the text. When Isaac builds an altar to the God of his ancestors, does Rebekah participate? When Isaac sacrifices to the God-of-ancestors, does Rebekah participate? When God/the text/God-in-the-text self-identifies as "the God of Abraham" (Gen. 26:24), does God/the text mean that God is not the God of Sarah, Hagar, and/or Keturah? When the Philistines and Isaac feast together in reconciliation (Gen. 26:30), is Rebekah there? Does she eat with them, or even cook for them? Even this most active of matriarchs is a literary character to be shelved in the imagination of the biblical writers and editors when she is of no use or interest to them.

Rebekah reappears from the shadows when her son Esau marries not one, but two Hittite women, Yehudit bat (Judith, the daughter of) Beeri and Basemath bat Elon. Rebekah and Isaac are made bitter by their Hittite daughters-in-law. Here Rebekah and Isaac provide a united front against these marriages. Why are they opposed to the marriages? Textually speaking, anti-Hittite bias as a form of general Israelite xenophobia is a later development than the setting of the narrative. The only contact between the Hittites and the kinfolk of Sarah has been the purchase of a burial plot from a Hittite landowner. At the time of Sarah's death Abraham purchased it from Ephron ben Zoar in Genesis 23:20, and Abraham is buried there in turn by Ishmael and Isaac. It will become the family burying place.

The Hittites are a dominant force in the ancient Near East. Their wealth and power made it possible for them to move into Canaan and buy up desirable land before there was a people called Israel. They will be added to the list of inhabitants with whom Israel will struggle for dominance in the land. While the memory (or imagination) of interethnic hostilities affects the authors and editors of the text, the characters have yet to experience any hostility at the hands of the Hittites. So why do Esau's unions make his parents so unhappy? Are they disappointed that he has broken the generations-old tradition of marrying within his family? Do Rebekah and Isaac just dislike these women as individuals? Is the author simply attributing a later ethnic bias in the belief that such bias was timeless and required no further explanation? Rebekah will come to fear that Jacob will also marry a Hittite woman (Gen. 27:26).

Perhaps it is because of the Hittite women that Rebekah decides to defraud him of his rightful blessing as Isaac's firstborn. It is not clear if her decision is based on opportunity—the overheard conversation in Genesis 27:5—or if it is premeditated. Is she spying on Esau and/or Isaac, looking for an opportunity to discredit or disinherit Esau? The text has previously revealed that Rebekah loves Jacob, saying nothing of her feelings for Esau. Now it appears that she has none for him at all, not that she just loves Jacob more. I say that Rebekah and not Jacob defrauds Esau because it is her plan, and she works her plan, including working her son. Rebekah overcomes Jacob's fear of receiving a curse instead of a blessing by taking ownership of the consequences; she will take the curse if Jacob will take the risk. Her plan works, and Jacob receives the blessing of the firstborn. Rebekah is silent during and after the blessing; she is not even present in the narrative. How did she respond to the fruit of her handiwork? Did she celebrate or gloat? Did she congratulate Jacob? Did she say anything to Esau? Did they have any kind of relationship left?

The blessing itself may provide a glimpse into an aspect of Rebekah's life that is not further detailed in the text; it seems that she has given birth to more than two children. Genesis 27:29 says in part, "Be mighty over your kinfolk and may your mother's children[60] bow down to you." *Acheyka* can mean "kinfolk," "siblings," or "brothers." The second phrase, *baniym emeka*, "children of your mother," makes it clear that Isaac is referring to Rebekah's children and not more distant relatives. The plural suggests that there is at least one other child:[61] whether the blessing is directed toward Esau or Isaac, his siblings are to bow to him. Isaac confirms that he has indeed given Esau the service of his siblings, using the plural again in verse 37. Yet the text discusses only these two brothers. Who were Rebekah's other children? How many were there? Are the unmentioned children daughters?

Esau's disappointment becomes hatred directed solely toward Jacob (Gen. 27:41). I wonder if that means he did not know his mother's role in the loss of his inheritance or if he simply could not bring himself to hate her. Later Esau will marry more women from outside the family, because he knows it will displease his father, but the text does not mention any feelings for his mother as part of his motivation. Esau plans on killing Jacob as soon as the mourning period for his father has passed; however, Isaac is not yet in his grave. Someone tells Rebekah of his plans—but not Isaac. How widely were Esau's plans known? How often did people in the household go to Rebekah and not Isaac with news or problems? Did Isaac know the extent of Rebekah's actions? Jacob is unaware until their mother tells him. Did anyone else know? Rebekah arranges for Jacob to leave town for his own safety. But Rebekah does not want Jacob to marry a Hittite woman like his brother when he is out of her immediate control. She arranges for Isaac to direct Jacob to return to the practice of intrafamily marriage and marry one of his mother's nieces, his first cousins. In so doing, she limits his ability to choose a partner for himself.

60. *Baniym* are "children," "sons," "daughters-and-sons," and occasionally "descendants."

61. The expression could refer to her grandchildren, but grammatically it supports a reading referring to her own children.

This is the last time that Rebekah appears alive in the text. Jacob will tell his prospective in-laws that he is her son—and never name his father—in Genesis 29:12, but the reader/hearer has no way of knowing if Rebekah is alive or dead. We will discover in Genesis 49:31 that she has been buried with Isaac and Sarah and Abraham when Joseph asks to be interred with them. The death of Rebekah is not recorded, yet the death of her childhood servant Deborah is. It is surprising that the most prominent matriarch is not laid to rest in the text. To correct this omission, I offer the following epitaph:

> *Rivqah bat Bethuel ben Milcah*
> *was the mother of Esav from whom she withdrew her mother love*
> *and Rivqah the daughter-in-law-of Sarah*
> *was the mother of Ya'aqov the Heel-Grabbing-Sneak who became Israel*
> *the God-Wrestler.*

QETURAH (KETURAH)

Genesis 25:1 Avraham (Abraham) did it again; he took a woman, her name was Qeturah (Keturah).

Genesis 25 describes Abraham's third intimate union, with a woman named Keturah (Qeturah). It is not clear whether the announcement is concurrent with the union or if the text is reporting a previous union. The latter is more likely; the names of their six children follow immediately and likely represent at least a decade, if not more. In Genesis, Keturah is described as a primary woman, an *isshah*; in 1 Chronicles 1:32 she is described as a secondary woman, a *piylegesh* (*piylegseh*).

The timing of her presentation leads me to ask when and where did Abraham meet Keturah? Under what circumstances did they become a couple? That she is not mentioned until after Isaac reaches sexual maturity could suggest a late-in-life union. But Abraham is one hundred (Gen. 17:17) when Isaac is born, and Isaac is forty when he marries (Gen. 25:19). The text will grant him 175 years; perhaps we are to understand that he was still potent past the century mark, at 140 years of age.[62]

Whatever one thinks about the years ascribed to Abraham, Keturah and the peoples she mothered with him are an enduring part of the Israelite story. Keturah and Abraham are the ancestors of nations with whom Israel will have complicated relationships: Zimran, Yoqshan (Jokshan), Medan, Midian, Yishbaq (Ishbak), and Shuah. Their storied offspring will include Dedan and Sheba. Keturah, who is Qantura bint Yaqtan in Islamic tradition, does not

---

62. His great age reflects the power and fidelity of God, not a biological reality.

appear in the Qur'an and hadiths; she is in the influential al-Ṭabarī commentary, where she is also recorded as giving birth to six children.[63]

Because the biblical text discloses this union after the death of Sarah, and Isaac is described as being comforted after the death of his mother through his new relationship with Rebekah, the rabbis understand Abraham's union with Keturah to be his source of comfort in his bereavement (*b. Bava Qamma* 92b).

In my midrashic imagination, I see Keturah as the one woman Abraham chose for himself. His family practiced incestuous unions; he may not have had a choice in marrying his sister Sarah, or he may have been prevented from marrying outside of his family. Sarah insisted that he marry Hagar; he may not have felt that he had a choice, in that he was desperate for the heir God promised. But Keturah he chose for himself. He had done all that God had required of him, moved halfway around the world (as he knew it), and ensured that his primary heir was well on his way to becoming a patriarch in his own right. And he chose something, someone, for himself, Keturah. Perhaps he wanted more children; perhaps he was not satisfied with Isaac and Ishmael, a mere two sons. He and Keturah had six children; it is not possible to gender these children based on their presentation as a list of names, with the exception of Yoqshan (Jokshan), who appears in Genesis 25:3 with a masculine singular verb. In 1 Chronicles 1:32 they are listed as the children, *beney*, of Keturah. The common plural is used for all-male groups, mixed-gender groups, and occasionally all-female groups.[64]

The number of children that Keturah and Abraham shared invokes potential relational paradigms. Was their relationship more than childbearing? Did they share a home, meals, and laughter, in addition to a bed? Was there love between them? And how did Keturah feel about Abraham's other women and children? Abraham's polygyny transcends text and culture. The phenomenon of male access to multiple sexual partners, while limiting women to a single partner, is among the most common historical social-sexual configurations and endures to a lesser degree to the present age. What does it mean that this paradigm is enshrined in Scripture, tolerated or even sanctioned by God?

ABRAHAM'S LESSER WIVES

Genesis 25:5–6 Avraham (Abraham) gave all that was his to Yitzchaq (Isaac). And to the children of his lesser women Avraham (Abraham) gave gifts, while he was still living, and he sent them away.

63. Al-Ṭabarī in al-Ṭabarī and Brinner; *History*, 129.
64. Naomi uses other common plural forms to address Ruth and Orpah (Ruth 1:8–11).

Who are Abraham's lesser or low-status wives? Are there women in addition to Hagar and Keturah? If so, then neither they nor their children are identified. I read them as other wives because Hagar and Keturah are never called lesser wives in the Torah. While Keturah is called a lesser wife in Chronicles, Hagar is never called a lesser wife anywhere in the Scriptures. So even if Keturah is included in the lesser wives of Genesis 25:6, there is at least one and possibly more to account for the plural.

What is clear from the text is that the children from these unions do not receive a sizable inheritance; this is standard for children born of such unions. It is not clear what sorts of gifts he gives them; the inference of the text is that these gifts pale beside the inheritance of Isaac. As a modern reader/hearer, I am troubled that Abraham continued to produce children who would not be provided for after his death. The text does not suggest that the women who gave birth to these children received even gifts. It is sad to contemplate Keturah, and possibly other nameless women, in their later years with nothing but their children, on whom they have to depend for everything. The traditions around primary and secondary unions in ancient Israel neither required nor prevented Abraham from providing an inheritance for all of his children. He could have been more generous than customary. After all, God had both enriched him and extended his life, virility, and potency. The favoring of one child over others seems inherently unfair. Yet if I am honest, I do not always have control over whom I like more than another person. Why then would I expect parents—biblical, literary, or contemporary—to control their affections?

RACHEL

> Genesis 29:9 While Ya'aqov (Jacob) was still speaking with them, Rachel came with the sheep of her father, for she was a shepherd.

Rachel, the future daughter-in-law of Rebekah, was as active a matriarch as her mother-in-law, who was also her aunt. Rachel is busy shepherding her father's sheep when Jacob encounters her. This introduction is striking for many reasons. Shepherding in the Bible is a powerful and dominant metaphor for leading the people of Israel as a civil (monarch) and religious (prophet) leader and for God's own care of God's people.[65] Civil and religious shepherding are combined in descriptions of messianic leaders in the biblical text. The term has come to be virtually synonymous with clergy vocation, particularly

---

65. See Num. 27:16–17; 2 Sam. 5:2; Ps 80:1.

in Christianity. Yet most readers/hearers whom I have asked cannot identify any women shepherds in the Scriptures.[66]

The presence of female shepherds in the Scriptures seems not to have contributed to the dominant image of the clergyperson/shepherd as a male person. I note with curiosity that the NRSV translation of *ro'ah hiw'* in Genesis 29:9 reduces Rachel to merely "keeping" sheep, without naming her as a shepherd, as do the JPS, GSJPS, and Everett Fox (Jewish) translations.[67] This means that readers/hearers in many Christian contexts will not encounter Rachel as she is presented in the text, as a shepherd. What did Rachel shepherd? Rachel's flocks may well have included sheep and goats together (see Gen. 30:25); the word *tz'on*, "flock," in Biblical Hebrew does not distinguish between sheep and goats.[68]

The second aspect of Rachel's presentation that invites notice is that she is near or with men who are not introduced. It is not clear if they are relatives, servants, or neighboring shepherds. There is no apparent concern about Rachel working in close proximity with these men as a woman in general or because she is both marriageable and not yet married. Rachel is not described as being in the company of other women (shepherds, servants, or sisters). The stereotype of biblical women being confined to the home, to women's company, avoiding the public sphere and the company of (unrelated) men, falls on its face with the introduction of Rachel in the Bible. Jacob kisses Rachel before telling her (or the men with her) that he is related to her, and no one is disturbed by this intimate contact. There is no other narrative in the Hebrew Bible in which a man kisses a woman who is not related to him.[69]

The third noteworthy aspect in Rachel's story is the absence of her mother. That she is never named or mentioned makes it impossible to know if she is

66. There are others: Zipporah and her seven sisters in Exod. 2:26 and the poet-woman in Song 1:8; there is no reason to believe all of the shepherds in plural constructions are male.

67. Literally, *ro'ah hiw'* is "she was/is a shepherd," or "she-who-shepherds, she," (the feminine singular Qal participle followed by the feminine singular-subject pronoun). Cf. "which she tended" in the IB.

68. The bias against goats, with which many Christian readers/hearers are familiar, seems to be a New Testament issue and ought not be imported into the First Testament. Hebrew "flocks," *tz'on*, which can be either sheep or goats, become *probaton*, sheep, in the Greek Scriptures of both Testaments, even though there is no way of determining the composition of the herd. In the Septuagint, Rachel is not described as a shepherd.

69. Primarily men kiss men, usually in their family (e.g., Gen. 27:26–27; Exod. 4:27). There are theoretical kisses of unacceptable women (Prov. 7:17), and Orpah kisses Ruth (Ruth 1:14). Laban does kiss his daughters good-bye (Gen. 31:55). Though not a narrative account, the Song of Solomon is significant for the full range of sensual and sexual intimacy between the woman and her man.

living or dead. I am inclined to read her as dead because of the number of characters who do appear in Rachel's story. It is also possible that she is alive and no longer a part of the family. Divorce is not unknown in the canon, although it is rarely described in narrative texts.

There is a gap in Rachel's story. What sort of relationship do she and Jacob have during his first-month stay? Does she know that his mother, her aunt Rebekah, has commanded him to choose her or her sister as his wife? How much time do they spend together? What do they talk about? Do they talk about making a life together? Are they in love? Do they share the work of shepherding her father's flocks? Does she know that he plans to talk to her father about marrying her? Did Jacob tell her that the reason he has journeyed to meet her family is to find a woman who will be acceptable to his mother? In Genesis 29:20, the text reveals that Jacob loves Rachel so much that seven years of service to her father pass in the twinkling of an eye for him. What sort of relationship do they have during the seven years of their betrothal? What sort of relationship does Jacob have with Leah? What sort of relationship does Rachel have with Leah? What is known about Rachel is that she is "beautiful in body and face," according to Genesis 29:17.

How does the deception go forward? Is Rachel in on it? Is she waiting to be brought to her new mate? Does she not get suspicious as time passes? Does she not notice her sister is nowhere to be found? Do none of the servants tell her what is going on? It seems incredible that Rachel does not know what was going on around her. Even when the deception becomes known, Rachel says nothing in the text. The spaces in this story are fertile ground for midrash. I offer the following from Rachel's perspective:

> *Rachel and Leah were ordinary sisters. They had largely separate lives. Leah preferred indoor life, and Rachel preferred outdoor life. Neither was much interested in marriage. Following the rules of the household established by Milcah, their great-grandmother, whose name their grandfather Bethuel ben Milcah bore, they were asked if they would marry each time a suitor came forward, as their aunt Rivqah had been asked. And each time they said no. They said no to their brothers and cousins. They said no to intrafamily unions. They said no to the neighbors and to strangers. They said no to unions outside of their family.*
>
> *Then one day their cousin Ya'aqov came to town looking for a woman from their family, his family. Their father said one of them would have to marry him. Auntie Rivqah would not take no for an answer. Ya'aqov asked for Rachel and offered seven years of his labor in exchange for her. She spent the seven years getting to know him, but she never came to love him. He turned to Leah to help him win her over. The more he pursued her, the less*

interested she became. The more time he spent with Leah, the more she came to love him.

When the time for the wedding feast and consummation came, Leah and Rachel agreed to switch places and told their father what they had decided. They waited until deepest night and put out all the lamps in the wedding tent. Leah hoped that Ya'aqov would realize that is was she whom he truly loved. Ya'aqov was angry and disappointed. He demanded Rachel. Lavan tried to dissuade him. Rachel hoped he would give up, but he stayed another seven years. Ya'aqov's pursuit of Rachel broke Leah's heart. The love she held for him and for her sister soured. When Rachel finally consented to marry Ya'aqov, she was at the end of her childbearing years. He did not care. He wanted her, and finally he had her. That Rachel still did not want him and that he never wanted Leah wounded Leah deeply. Leah carried that hurt to her grave. She held on to and acted out of her deep hurt. She was never reconciled to her sister.

This midrash gives Rachel an agency with regard to her marriage that the text does not. As the story progresses in the canon, it will appear that Laban used his daughters to secure Jacob's labor.

Genesis 29:30 suggests that Jacob loves Leah; he just loves Rachel more. Rachel's story continues with a common literary device in the literature of the ancient Near East: the barren woman. Like their neighbors, biblical authors used this theme to illustrate both the power of God and the prominence of the one conceived against all odds. In desperation, Rachel in Genesis 30:1 demands that Jacob provide her with children, or she will die. In my midrashic reading she succumbs to the societal pressure to bear children. And Leah taunts her. Rachel feels shame that her elder sister is so fertile while she is not. Jacob "becomes furious" in Genesis 30:2 (the expression denotes a snorting bull). Jacob correctly blames God for Rachel's infertility. Like her mother-in-law before her, and many women of means in her culture, she chooses the option of surrogacy. Like the women before her, she does not consider her slave a person with the right to grant or deny access to her body. Rachel gives Jacob her slave Bilhah (formerly her father's slave, see Gen. 29:29) as a surrogate and tells him to "come in(to) her." Bilhah is first Laban's slave and then Rachel's; the only service she performs in the text is reproductive. The traditional translation "enter her" unnecessarily softens the explicit nature of the expression; the double entendre works in Hebrew as it does in English. The biblical authors were not as prudish as some of their translators and interpreters.

Jacob obeys Rachel as he obeyed his mother. He takes Bilhah as an *isshah* (a primary woman, the same category as Rachel and Leah and Leah's slave

---

Slave or Servant?

I choose the translation "slave" rather than "servant" for *shiphchah* and *amah* (both feminine) and *'eved* (masculine singular; plural *'avadiym*, inclusive) to emphasize that these persons were bought and sold, used for sex, impregnated, and completely subjugated to the power of those called their mistresses and masters. "Servitude" suggests employment, which is not the case for slaves in the biblical corpus. See the essay "The Torah of Enslaved Women," at the end of this chapter, for a detailed discussion.

Zilpah) and fathers two sons whom Rachel names with reference to her sister, Dan (Judge) and Naphtali (Struggle) in Genesis 30:6–8. At one point (Gen. 30:14ff.) Rachel attempts to heal her own infertility using "love-fruit," *duda'ei*, generally identified with mandrakes, a tuber relative of the potato. Rachel's root-work is not censured by the text; it may well have been regarded as within the bounds of legitimate healthcare, given how widely mandrakes were used in the Mediterranean to treat infertility. Leah's son Reuben finds the mandrakes, and Leah will let Rachel have some only if she, Leah, gets to have sex with Jacob. (Jacob goes where he is told and does what he is told, to whom he is told.) The text does not say that Rachel gets to complete the mandrake ritual by having sex with Jacob.

Unlike Rebekah, Rachel does not seek the God who promised offspring to Hagar, Sarah, and Rebekah—either personally or through a professional intermediator, a prophet. Even in her desperation, Rachel does not turn to the God of Jacob. In Genesis 30:1 she demands that Jacob give her children, much to his consternation. He asserts that conception is a divine prerogative, that he is not God, and that God has closed her womb. Neither of them prays for her fertility. When naming her surrogate son Dan, born for her by her womb-slave Bilhah, Rachel says, "God has judged me [*danani elohiym*]." The sense is that God has found in her favor over her sister by granting her a surrogate son, but the text does not indicate that Rachel sought out this verdict. This is one of three times Rachel speaks any name for the God with whom her family would come to be so closely identified.

Finally, in Genesis 30:22–24 God remembers Rachel. Has God forgotten her because she does not worship or seek God? Jacob returns to her bed—which is not mentioned in the text—and God opens her womb, and she has a son whom she names Joseph (Yosef, "Addition") in hopes that she will have another child. She says that God has taken away her reproach and immediately invokes the Most Holy Name of God to express her hope that she will conceive again. Her exclamation, "May the HOLY ONE add to me another son" (Gen. 30:24), is spoken about, not to, God. I do not think that we can say Rachel ever prayed to (or praised) the God of the text. Further, crediting Jacob's god with providing her children would not necessarily mean rejecting her own gods (Gen. 31:19).

This is a touching story with many familiar overtones. While most Western Christians do not practice polygamy, there are many blended families as a result of widowhood and divorce, and many people enter into marriage with children from previous relationships. The elements of sibling rivalry, jealousy, infertility, and desperation transcend time and location. Yet God loves this family and has promised fidelity to them throughout all their generations. Does this fidelity extend to all of the branches of this twisted family tree? Is Rachel the recipient of divine favor? In the world of the text, yes; she has a child, and she has the love of the father of her child, and very few men in the biblical text are described as loving their partners. Is the divine favor that Rachel receives for *her*, or is she the instrumental beneficiary of patriarchal divine favor? What about the enslaved women whose bodies they use as livestock? Are they blessed?

Eventually, Jacob desires to head his own household and seeks the permission of his father-in-law to take his women and children and leave. Laban divines—divination was a rarely sanctioned magical practice in the Scriptures—that God has blessed him through Jacob and desires to reward his son-in-law before sending him off. Jacob practices a form of magic that is not sanctioned in the Scriptures and takes the bulk of Laban's herds as his wages. Jacob's use of magic is comparable to Sarah's sibling marriage; both will be proscribed later in the Torah, but the ancestors are not held accountable to those standards. Jacob's magic strikes me as retributive; I believe he is punishing Laban for saddling him with Leah. He has negotiated all of the striped and speckled goats (and possibly sheep). But rather than take them and leave, he uses magic wands to affect their breeding and produces a larger, stronger flock for himself and a weaker, smaller flock for his father-in-law. When Laban and his other children become hostile, Jacob shows his handiwork to his women and tries to convince them that he is justified because he has been cheated.

Jacob credits God for his wealth but does not quite credit God with the magical mechanics, just the result. In Genesis 31:15 Rachel answers that their father has sold them and is running through the wealth he received for them; they want to leave with Jacob. (The verb is singular ta'an, "she answered," indicating that the first person in the double subject, Rachel, is the most active.) Rachel's words mark the complete breakdown of the family bonds across the generations; Laban has lost the love and respect of his daughters and son-in-law. This development allows the reader/hearer to reinterpret the bride deception. Apparently Laban deceived Jacob in order to keep Jacob and his free labor as long as possible. In Genesis 31:16 Rachel stakes a claim to the property that Jacob has taken from her father; it is not just for her children. In other texts, women will inherit when they have no male siblings, but this is apparently not the case for Rachel and Leah (see Gen. 31:1).

Rachel decides that they have not taken enough from her father and takes their household deities. I say "their" and not "his," as does the text, because there is no reason to believe that Rachel does not share her father's religion. Rachel has told Jacob to do what God tells him; I believe she means *his* god, and she will take care of *her* gods. While the text (Gen. 31:20) credits only Jacob with deceiving Laban by running away, Rachel and Leah support him, keep the secret, and escape with him, their children, and their flocks, camels, and donkeys.

I think that the lengths Rachel goes to in order to keep the gods—her gods—indicate that Rachel did not worship Jacob's god, or at least not exclusively. Jacob has pronounced death on whoever stole the gods; in spite of his earlier magic prowess, these words have no power over Rachel. Laban searches each tent, and we learn that Rachel and Leah each have their own tent (Gen. 31:32). Rachel keeps her gods. I believe the text continues to avoid calling them Rachel's in order to avoid acknowledging her non-Yahwistic religious commitment. In Genesis 35:4, when members of Jacob's household surrender "foreign" deities, it is not clear if Rachel is in their number.

Only in his leave-taking does Laban show any paternal tenderness to Rachel or Leah or their children. He lays claim to them and their wealth (Gen. 31:43) and in verse 50 adjures Jacob not to take any other women or have any children with any other women, presumably to protect their inheritance. This is a rare demand in an androcentric society. In the same verse Laban enjoins Jacob not to mistreat his daughters, for God will watch him and hold him accountable to this covenant. The text does not explain Laban's newfound relationship with Jacob's god. It may be that he enjoins Jacob in the name of his god because of the power the Name held for Jacob. It should be remembered that these characters reflect the ancient world in which multiple, even conflicting, religious claims were easily tolerated in polytheism and henotheism (elevating one god above others).

The covenant of Mizpah, which many know as "May the LORD watch between me and thee while we are absent one from the other," is actually a covenant about the treatment of women as the neglected portion indicates: "If you abuse my daughters or if you take women above my daughters, though no person is with us, look—God is a witness between you and me" (Gen. 31:49–50). The "May the LORD watch . . ." is really "May the LORD watch to see if you mistreat my daughters." It is unfortunate that the context of the Mizpah covenant has been all but forgotten, particularly in the industry that has sprung up around selling it engraved on jewelry and other memorabilia. Using my sanctified imagination, I can hear this covenant as part of a wedding ceremony and wonder that it is not part of the regular wedding liturgies of religious communities—notwithstanding how it may be used by individuals.

Neither Rachel nor Leah is present when Jacob has two encounters with supernatural beings, the first in Genesis 32:1, with messengers of God in what Jacob names Mahanayim, "God's Camp," and the second in Genesis 32:24, the bruising, blessing wrestling match between Jacob and his unnamed assailant. Their absence may be because the text has established that God of the Holy Name is Jacob's god and not Rachel's or Leah's. In addition, while Jacob is wrestling by the Jabbok, Rachel, Leah, and their children have been sent ahead.

The next morning, Jacob will fear for their safety from Esau and the four hundred men he is bringing with him. Jacob exposes them to the risk of armed conflict based on his love for them: he exposes Bilhah and Zilpah and their children to the most danger by placing them at the front of the column; next come Leah and her children, and finally Rachel and Joseph in Genesis 32:1–2. He takes the most risk by riding to meet Esau, who has previously pledged to kill him. The text does not reveal what conversation passes between Rachel, Leah, and Jacob about Esau. When they meet him, they bow down before him, perhaps a polite greeting, perhaps a conciliatory one. Esau and Jacob are reconciled, and Esau's people escort Rachel, Leah, Bilhah, Zilpah, Jacob, and their children on their way.

Rachel becomes an unnecessary character in Jacob's story. Rachel is absent from the story in Genesis 34 of the rape of Dinah, Jacob's daughter with Leah. She is not mentioned by name in chapter 35, when the household relocates to Bethel, but may be referenced in Jacob's instruction for everyone to surrender their deities. He seems to have forgotten his previous promise to kill whoever has Laban's gods. Rachel is absent or silent when God changes Jacob's name to Yisrael (Israel) in Genesis 35:10. God does not change Rachel's name, as God changed Sarai's name.

In Genesis 35:16 Rachel dies in childbirth. The name Rachel chooses for her second son, Ben-oni, "son of my sorrow," is not honored by Jacob-turned-Israel. He renames the boy Ben-yamin, Benjamin, "right-hand son." Rachel is buried, and her grave marked in the text, unlike that of Rebekah. In Genesis 48:7 Israel recounts Rachel's death to Joseph. Jeremiah invokes Rachel in the Scriptures with a lament in 31:15 (quoted in Matt. 2:18), and the people of Bethlehem invoke her along with Leah in a blessing (Ruth 4:11). Lament and blessing characterize the portrayal of Rachel in the Scriptures: a pawn of her father, in conflict with her sister, loved by a man she does not say she loves, ashamed of her infertility, and finally a mother granted fertility by God, dead before seeing her children grown and married, her deathbed wishes disregarded.

Rachel's story (like that of her aunt and mother-in-law Rebekah) claims a great volume of text in comparison with the stories of other individual women in the canon. She is canonized as the beloved of Israel. Her love is not considered. Rachel has difficult relationships with her father, sister, and husband. Rachel's mother is mysteriously missing from her story, raising unanswered questions. Where was her mother? Did her absence contribute to these difficult relationships? There is someone else with whom Rachel is in some sort of relationship. God is involved in Rachel's life in the most intimate way, granting her the desire of her heart, even though she does not turn to God for help and may not have subscribed to the worship of this God as she worshiped the gods of her ancestors.

Rachel offers many tropes for womanist midrash. She is for all intents and purposes, in the words of the Negro spiritual, a motherless child, a long way from home. She is a root-worker in a Bible that many would use in order to burn women for their knowledge of herbal remedies under the label "witchcraft." Many in the African diaspora have been taught that their ancestral medicinal practices are incompatible with the Scriptures and the God of the Scriptures, but Rachel teaches us that this is not so. Neither God nor the text proscribe her root-work (or her husband's use of magic wands). Rachel's life is full of drama. Her family of origin is complicated and dysfunctional, and even when the word "love" is spoken, it has virtually no meaning. Willingly or unwillingly, Rachel gives up her life for her child, begetting another generation of motherless children.

LEAH

> Genesis 29:31 When the Giver of Life saw that Leah was unloved, God opened her womb.

There was something about Leah, the way she looked (or perhaps the way she *saw*) that defies description: "Leah had peculiar eyes." In Genesis 29:17 the word that describes Leah's eyes, *rakkoth*, is inscrutable. She was literally "tender-eyed," whatever that means. In any case Leah was overlooked. From the beginning of her story it is clear that the story is not her story but her sister's story—itself a subplot in Israel's (person and people) story. Leah is older than Rachel, and whatever we are to understand about her eyes, how she is seen is clear: she is not "beautiful of form and face." That description is reserved for her younger sister, Rachel.

But how did Leah and Rachel come to be? Who was their mother? And what happened to her? Was she alive and well, erased and silenced by the text, its authors and editors? Was she dead and gone? Did she die in childbirth? Who mothered Leah and Rachel? Did they have an "other mother" to nurture them into womanhood, as is frequently the case in the African and other diasporas?

By design neither Leah nor Rachel married in the womanish midrash I composed for the entry on Rachel; Leah and Rachel rejected their would-be suitors. There was another possibility. Perhaps their father, Laban, rejected their suitors, not wanting to pay a dowry, let alone two. Laban's attachment to his material wealth lies beneath all of these stories. Leah is not described as ugly, deformed, or blind, which may have impacted her ability to marry. As the daughter of a relatively wealthy man, Leah was a desirable bride. Nothing in the canon to this point suggests that women were chosen as potential mates based on their looks alone—however much female beauty might occasionally be celebrated in the text. And Leah was from a family that practices internal marriage: Her aunt Rebekah married her cousin Isaac. Her great-grandmother Milcah married her own uncle, Nahor. Her great-grandaunt Sarah married her own brother, Abraham. And her great-granduncle Lot fathered children with his own daughters. I submit that in the tangled branches of this family tree there were certainly viable candidates, but for some reason they were all rejected. In this reading, I choose to place that responsibility squarely on Laban.

It is clear that Laban is the primary actor in the wedding deception. He takes Leah to Jacob. And in an odd note in Genesis 29:24, he gives her his slave-woman Zilpah, seemingly as a consolation prize, on the way to the marriage bed. The text does not offer a conversation between Laban and Leah. It does seem to suggest that Leah does not have a choice to marry. This is very much at odds with her aunt Rebekah's choice whether or not to go with Isaac. Surely she had heard the story. Laban's excuse that tradition required the deception in Genesis 29:26 does not hold water. The so-called tradition was not previously voiced in the text or in the canon, and if it were so, then why not tell Jacob when he asks for Rachel?

Leah is in a horrible position. She has heard her whole life how beautiful her sister is. But she has never been called beautiful. Perhaps she's been told by well-meaning folk that her eyes aren't *that* noticeable. She is unmothered. Her father has used her for his own devices. She is married to a man who does not love her as much as he loves her sister, if he loves her at all. For whatever reason, she enters into competition with her sister for Jacob's love. There is no competition. She is eclipsed the moment Jacob sees Rachel. But she tries and finds that he has a weakness; he cannot stay away from her bed, even when he has a male heir and a spare (and another, and another); Jacob returns over and over again to her bed. What is that about?

The All-Seeing One takes note of Leah in Genesis 29:31, that she was hated (*s'nu'ah*) and grants her children. God knows that Leah is not (merely) loved less by Jacob than Rachel, as in Genesis 29:30, or that she is not only "unloved," as the IB, NRSV, JPS, and GSJPS translate verse 31; in truth, she is *hated* (so Fox). The text does not say that she is hated by Jacob, leaving open the possibility that she is hated by her husband, sister, and/or father, and perhaps others. What is compelling here is that God-of-the-Holy-Name cares about Leah when no one else does, and gives her the one thing that will grant her status and standing in her androcentric society and now-patriarchal household.[70] Moreover, God withholds children from Rachel for Leah's sake. This begs the question, was God punishing Rachel for being loved, or was she guilty of something else? And what does it say that God afflicts one woman with infertility in that culture to assuage the betrayed broken heart of her sister? The text does not say God made Rachel infertile or did so because of the hatred for Leah. However, in the text the link between Rachel's love, Leah's hatred, and their wombs is not incidental. Another possibility is that Leah was simply God's favorite, as God would prefer David over Saul.

Leah's childbearing, and, more, child naming reveal her desperation for Jacob's love:

> When the GOD OF LOVE saw that Leah was hated, God opened her womb; yet Rachel was barren. [32]Leah conceived and gave birth to a son, and she proclaimed his name "Re'uven" (Reuben, meaning "Look! A son!"); for she said, "Because the GOD WHO SEES ALL has looked on my affliction; now my man will love me." [33]She conceived again and gave birth to a son, and said, "Because the GOD WHO HEARD MY CRY has heard how hated am I, God has given me this one also," and she proclaimed his name "Shim'on" (Simeon, meaning "Hearing"). [34]She conceived again and gave birth to a son, and said, "Now, this time my man will be joined to me, because I have given birth to three sons for him"; therefore his name was proclaimed "Levi" (Joining). [35]She conceived again and gave birth to a son, and said, "This time I will give-thanks-and-praise GOD WHOSE NAME IS HOLY"; therefore she proclaimed his name "Yehudah" (Judah, meaning "giving-thanks-and praise"); then she stood-and-stopped giving birth. (Gen. 29:31–35)

---

70. Laban is from a matrilineal family; he is the grandson of the matriarch Milcah, whose name was preserved when her male partner's was forgotten. The absence of Leah's and Rachel's mother enabled Laban to shift the power paradigm in his matrilineal home. Now and only now is it patriarchal.

Perhaps by the time she gives birth to Yehudah (Judah), Leah has ceased to hope that Jacob will love her and is resting in God's love for her. But then, in Genesis 30:9–13, the now infertile and most likely menopausal Leah competes again with Rachel for Jacob's love by ordering him to take her woman-servant turned womb-slave Zilpah as her surrogate—which he does. He has just fathered two children with Rachel's slave, Bilhah. Zilpah gives birth to sons whom Leah names Gad (Fortune) saying "*B*'*Gad*" (the origin of "By Gad," meaning "What fortune") and Asher (Blessed). This time Leah is hoping to be vindicated by her peers, other women; when naming Asher she says, "In this I am blessed! Women-born-of-women[71] will call me blessed!" These verses account for years, anywhere from a year to conceive and birth each baby to six or more, allowing for five years in which the previous child was being nursed before the next child was conceived.

In Genesis 30:14–18, Leah reveals her deep pain—Rachel has taken from her everything that matters and seeks to take even more: Reuben, Leah's son, found "love-fruit" (*duda'ei*),[72] a plant used medicinally, believed to treat infertility. In exchange for some of the love-fruit Rachel barters a night with Jacob to Leah. Leah says in verse 15, "Was it not a small thing for you to take my man? Must you now take my son's love-fruit?" Rachel is desperate for children of her own; she is not satisfied with her surrogate children. Rachel's promise to permit Jacob to sleep with Leah this one night must have sounded condescending to Leah. The conversation raises the question, how often did Jacob sleep with Leah? It seems that he was with her on a regular basis in order to father four children with her; they will also produce a daughter later. It also seems that Rachel is his gatekeeper.

Without comment or complaint Jacob complies with the arrangements his women have made for his sexual favors. Leah's infertility is reversed, and she gives birth to Issachar (Payment). In verses 19–20, in spite of his professed preference for Rachel and in spite of having several male heirs, Jacob continues to have sex with Leah, who does not have to buy his time or services. Jacob fathers another son, whom Leah names Zebulun (Cohabitation). They continue in conjugal intimacy. Finally, in verse 21 Leah gives birth to a daughter whom she names Dinah (Judgment), without explaining her name, as was done for each of Jacob's sons. However, Jacob returns to Rachel's bed and finally impregnates Rachel.

71. Literally "daughters."
72. Traditionally identified with *atropa mandragora* or *mandragora officinarum*, mandrakes, *Dictionary of Classical Hebrew* (*DCH*).

Leah and Rachel are absent from the narrative when Jacob performs what might be called root-work or juju[73] on the flocks to increase his wealth at their father's expense. They reappear and agree with him that they should leave because they no longer have any inheritance with their father. What they do not say is that Jacob has taken it. They assert a claim on their own behalf and on behalf of their children; they share the wealth with Jacob. After their flight Laban pursues them but is more interested in his missing gods. When he enters Leah's tent in 31:33, he does not speak to her. Yet Laban initiates the lovely covenant at Mitzpah to hold Jacob accountable for his treatment of his daughters and grandchildren. Laban pauses to kiss his daughters and grandchildren before he leaves.

Leah endures one final insult from Jacob before she exits the narrative; when Jacob fears retribution from Esau, he separates his women and children and positions them according to their value to him (Gen. 33:2). Leah and her children are more important to him than Bilhah or Zilpah and their children, but not as important as Rachel and Joseph.

In Genesis 34, Leah's daughter Dinah is raped, and Leah is conspicuously absent from the narrative. Leah is also absent from Rachel's death scene and its aftermath. In Genesis 49:31, Leah's death is reported. She, not Rachel, is buried with Sarah, Abraham, Rebekah, and Isaac. In death, if not in life, Leah is finally accorded the dignity of a matriarch. Her name will be linked with Rachel's in the townswomen's blessing in Ruth 4:11; then Leah fades from the Scriptures. She is not invoked in the Prophets, Writings, or New Testament. It is Jacob's deathbed request to be buried with Leah and not Rachel (Gen. 49:29–33).

Leah the loveless matriarch is a heartbreaking character. The sage in Proverbs 30:21–23 writes that the earth cannot bear the weight of an unloved woman when she finally gets a husband; perhaps the sage had Leah in mind. Leah's story is a reminder that marriage and love do not go together any more than do love and sex. Leah's relationship with Jacob indicates that loveless marriages, man sharing, jealousy, and competition are not just contemporary issues. There is no happy ending for Leah; she is not fulfilled as a person or as a woman in motherhood. She is not the last woman to go to her grave longing for the love of a man who does not love her but is willing to sleep with her. Pious women readers/hearers may not choose to be Leah, but I suspect that

73. "Juju" covers a broad swath of traditional religious practices dispersed by the trans-Atlantic slave trade, pejoratively called witchcraft or magic on both sides of the Atlantic. "Root-work" is a related category of traditional practice involving plant matter, often (if not most often) performed by women in the African diaspora, similar to Jacob's use of "rods" to affect the fertility of flocks and enrich himself at his father-in-law's expense in Gen. 30:37–41.

Leah's story canonized her lovelessness as well as her fruitfulness because it rang true to human experience. Leah offers a cautionary tale to women looking for fulfillment in someone else's love: you cannot make someone love you.

BILHAH

> Genesis 30:3 Rachel said, "Look! My womb-slave Bilhah—come in her, and she will give birth on my knees that I may also build babies, through her."

Bilhah is one of two slave-women whose bodies were used to produce a full third of the twelve tribes of Israel. Bilhah and Zilpah are often overlooked—in prayers naming the matriarchs in Judaism and Christianity—and sometimes combined, and in my experience as a congregant and student they are conjoined as a footnote to Israel's story. For that reason, I treat them separately. Bilhah is first enslaved to Laban, the father of Leah and Rachel, before being passed on to his daughter Rachel. While she is enslaved to Laban, Bilhah is initially referred to as a *shiphchah*, a type of female slave; later, she is called an *amah*, another type of female slave. Both terms connote sexual servitude by means of their literary contexts in the Bible.[74] Bilhah figures more prominently in the Scriptures than does her sister in slavery, Zilpah.[75] There are eleven references to Bilhah; there are only seven for Zilpah.

The text is not interested in how a girl (or woman young enough to be presumed fertile) came into Laban's household. Was Bilhah the bond-woman of Laban's mysteriously missing wife? Was Bilhah born in captivity or captured as a spoil of war? How long was she in Laban's service before he gave her to Rachel? What sorts of services did she provide Laban? Given the absence of Laban's wife from the narrative, it is entirely possible that Laban used Bilhah sexually.

Bilhah's sexual subordination to Rachel (with or without the possibility that Laban used her sexually) evokes the sexual abuse of enslaved Africans in the United States, the Caribbean, and other places. Religious readings that valorize Rachel place the descendants of those held as chattel in the American slavocracy in the position of identifying with slave-holding values and against the interests and experiences of their foremothers. Rachel, like her foremother Sarah, does not hesitate to use the body, womb, and sexuality

---

74. The two terms are used nearly interchangeably in the Hebrew Scriptures, although there was likely once a distinction between them.

75. Bilhah and Zilpah are not necessarily biological sisters or even relatives. The text is uninterested in their identity or heritage.

of another woman for her own purposes. There is no pretense that Rachel does not know about her husband's sexual use of her slaves; there is nothing differentiating her from the white women who benefited from slavery in and around their homes, often meting out punishment to pregnant slaves and their children who looked like their children. When Rachel gives Bilhah to Jacob, she gives her as a primary wife, an *isshah*. Yet Bilhah remains Rachel's slave; she is regularly referred to as a slave, a *shiphchah* (but preferentially translated as a "maid" or "servant").[76] Rachel initiates Bilhah's sexual subordination. Bilhah proves fertile and gives birth to Dan and Naphtali.

In each slave-surrogate story, the text portrays a singular accounting of the sexual contact between Abraham and Hagar, Jacob and Bilhah, and Jacob and Zilpah. The reader must imagine how many times the slave-women were forced/required to have sex with these men in order to provide their mistresses with the children they craved. Rachel, like other women who use their slaves as child-bearing surrogates, claims the children; this is not comparable to the vast experience of enslaved women of African descent forced to bear children at the whim of their enslavers, whose children were sold off or abused to punish them for a sin that was not theirs.

A modern, and admittedly imperfect, parallel to Rachel's use of Bilhah's body might be the women of privilege who travel to the two-thirds world, India in particular, to pay a surrogate to bear their children at a tenth of the cost of an American surrogate. While the women do consent to the practice, the financial disparities and cultural consequences of carrying someone else's child in traditional societies complicate that consent. It becomes more complicated when racial disparity parallels the economic disparity.

Bilhah's body is used again in Genesis 35:22. Reuben ben Leah, Jacob's firstborn son, rapes Bilhah. That Bilhah does not consent is indicated by the Hebrew, *vayishcav et-bilhah*, "he lay Bilhah." There is no "with" indicating consent, in spite of the misleading NRSV, JPS, GSJPS, and Everett Fox translations. Bilhah is the grammatical and sexual object of Reuben's actions. Reuben is young enough to be her son. He may have been like a son or nephew to her. But he uses her nevertheless, whether for his own sexual pleasure or as a pawn in a battle with his father. The pain, anguish, rage, and shame that Bilhah must have felt are difficult to imagine. In the text no punishment is meted out to Reuben. No comfort is offered to Bilhah in the text. Was she supported by other slave women, by Zilpah, who shared her lot in life? It seems unlikely that Rachel or Leah came to her aid. Bilhah's body has belonged to Laban,

---

76. NRSV, IB, JPS, GSJPS, and Fox use "maid" and "maidservant" preferentially in Gen. 30:3 and other texts. See Gen. 29:29; 30:3, 4, 7; 35:25; and 46:25, where she is simply "given."

Rachel, Jacob, and now Reuben. In this narrative Bilhah is described as a secondary wife, a *pilegesh* (*piylegesh*). She has been degraded in body and status.

Yet something of Bilhah endures and transcends the abuse heaped on her body. In 1 Chronicles 4:29 there is a town named Bilhah, settled by the descendants of Simeon. Textually speaking, the town is likely the same town called Ba'alah in Joshua 15:29. Since Ba'alah and Bilhah are more than one letter apart, scribal error does not seem to be responsible for the discrepancy. There are very likely two different traditions or sources about the ancient city list. The space between the two traditions provides a midrashic space. Perhaps Bilhah is the Ba'alah ("lady" or "mistress") for whom the town is named, regaining the dignity that had been stripped from her. Finally, in Genesis 46:23–25, Bilhah takes her place in the genealogy of Israel as a matriarch, credited with seven children and grandchildren; this is largely repeated in 1 Chronicles 7:13.

Bilhah represents the woman who has had more than one abusive relationship, the woman who has been raped by more than one perpetrator, the woman who has been betrayed by women and men, the woman who has never known anyone to value her for more than what they think about her body, in part or the whole. And Bilhah represents the woman who survives her abuse.

In Eucharistic Prayer C in the Holy Eucharist, Rite Two, in the *Book of Common Prayer* of the Episcopal Church, the celebrant invokes "Lord God of our Fathers; God of Abraham, Isaac, and Jacob." I always add Bilhah (and Zilpah) to this prayer when I celebrate, not because the text indicates that the God of Israel and these dysfunctional family dynamics claimed or even accepted Bilhah, but because she is one of the mothers of Israel. After all that she has been through, after all that was done to her, to erase her name from the chronicle of her descendants and their people is to do further violence to her. Likewise, when I pray the *Amidah* in a Jewish congregation, when the *siddur* (prayerbook) blesses "the God of our fathers, the God of Abraham, the God of Isaac, and the God of Jacob" in many liturgies and "the God of our mothers and fathers" in Reconstructionist settings, naming Sarah, Rivqah, Rachel, and Leah, I add Bilhah and Zilpah for the same reason.[77]

Lastly, calling the names of familial and spiritual ancestors is a womanist practice with roots in a number of African societies.[78] In ritual practice, the

77. After sharing an early version of this material with the Dorshei Derekh Minyan (prayer congregation) of the Germantown Jewish Centre in Philadelphia, Pennsylvania, where I was a member at the time, the congregation decided to do a study of the use of the names of Bilhah and Zilpah in the liturgy and ultimately made space for individuals to add them if they so chose.

78. James Evans traces out some of these practices in the American context in his discussion "History and Hope in the African American Experience" (James H. Evans,

affirmation "Ashé!" from the Yoruba tradition concludes the name-calling of the ancestors. *Mother Bilhah, womb-slave of Israel, we call your name. Ashé!*

ZILPAH

> Genesis 30:9 When Leah saw that she had ceased giving birth, she took her womb-slave Zilpah and gave her to Ya'aqov as a wife-woman.

Zilpah is the second womb-slave whom Jacob impregnates. Her story parallels Bilhah's in many respects, yet there was one significant difference. Her predecessor, Bilhah, was given to Jacob because Bilhah's mistress, Rachel, was infertile. Zilpah was given to Jacob because her mistress, Leah, was not satisfied with four children (Gen. 30:9). As Bilhah gave birth to new children for Rachel and Jacob, Leah, desperate for his love, ordered Jacob to use Zilpah, who had been given to her by her father Laban, to make more children for her. And as with Bilhah on Rachel's command, Jacob complied with Leah's demand.

The text tells us nothing about Zilpah before Laban gives her to Leah on the occasion of her wedding. How did she come to be enslaved in their household? Where was her family? Did Laban use her sexually before giving her to Leah (given his wife's complete absence from the narrative)? Zilpah was passed from Laban to Leah to Jacob. Zilpah gave birth to Gad and Asher for Leah and Jacob. The text does not record any further abuse of Zilpah. She is mentioned only seven times. In the genealogy in Genesis 46:16–17, Zilpah is the mother and grandmother of fourteen. She even has a granddaughter who will figure prominently in classical rabbinic midrash, Serach.

Zilpah is presented as another pawn in the war for Jacob's attention and affection. The battlefield for that war was the bodies of Bilhah and Zilpah. Through the sexual and reproductive occupation of their bodies, people who would be known as Israel came into being. Through the wombs of Rachel, Leah, Bilhah, and Zilpah, Israel's people were birthed by choice and by force. The text says nothing to suggest that the God of Abraham, Isaac, and Jacob is the God of Bilhah and Zilpah. They are casualties of nation building. But their children, their grandchildren, and their descendants will claim and be claimed by the God of their patriarchs, and some of us who claim the God of Israel, including through the life and teachings of Yeshua ben Miryam, Mary's child, Jesus, also claim Zilpah, Bilhah, Hagar, and all of the unnamed

We Have Been Believers: An African American Systematic Theology [Minneapolis: Fortress Press, 1992], 143–44).

womb-slaves in what has become our spiritual ancestry. *Mother Zilpah, womb-slave of Israel, we call your name. Ashé!*

ASENATH

> Genesis 41:45 Pharaoh gave Yosef (Joseph) the name Zaphenath-paneah; and he gave him Asenath daughter of Potiphera, priest of On, as his woman. Then Yosef went out over the land of Egypt.

The story of Asenath the African matriarch of Israel is a treasure in the shared canon, a treasure that has scarcely been mined in feminist and womanist scholarship, teaching, and preaching—even, and particularly, in African diasporic and African American Christian contexts. Asenath is a woman of status in her native culture and in the Israelite narrative; she is among the treasures of Egypt with which Joseph is rewarded for his service and his loyalty. Her city On, also known as Heliopolis, was the primary site of the worship of Ra, the sun god. Her father was a priest in the god's service, likely a high-ranking priest, since marriage to Asenath is an indication of how high Joseph has risen in the pharaoh's estimation. In Genesis 41 Joseph has integrated so well into Egyptian society that he has been given an Egyptian name, clothing, and jewelry, including the pharaoh's own ring, in addition to a new family.

The people of Israel, from Sarai and Abram of Ur to Ephraim and Manasseh *beney*[79] Asenath are a product of a multicultural, multiethnic, multilingual mélange. Asenath is the only African matriarch credited with producing tribes in Israel. Since Joseph was never counted as a tribe, and the tribe Levi didn't get an inheritance in the promised land, Asenath's two sons with Joseph, Manasseh and Ephraim, were counted to round the number of tribes back up to twelve. Asenath becomes an Israelite matriarch without ever setting foot in Israel or Canaan. She and Joseph die in Egypt. Joseph's body is preserved, and his bones are eventually carried into Canaan (Gen. 50:25; Exod. 13:19; Josh. 24:32), but no mention is made of Asenath's remains. Were her bones (or her mummy) carried out of Egypt with Joseph's? Was she given a traditional Egyptian burial?

The Hebrew Bible regularly shows strong connections between mothers and their children, which gives rise to questions in Asenath's story. When Zaphenath-paneah/Yosef reunites with his family of origin in Genesis 48:3–6, his father Jacob-turned-Israel asserts a claim to her children, perhaps because they are more Egyptian than Israelite. How does Asenath feel about Joseph's

---

79. "Sons of."

family? Is she present when they reunite? How does she feel about Jacob's claim on her children? Does she see it as an attempt to erase her identity in her children?

Asenath is one of a number of non-Israelite women to partner with significant patriarchs in the Israelite ancestry. The rabbinic practice of reckoning identity through the mother does not apply in this biblical text. Asenath's children count as Israelites in the text because their father is an Israelite. At the end of Genesis, Joseph makes choices that will affect Asenath's descendants in Israel; he rations food to everyone in need, from Egyptians to hungry refugees from every known tribe and tongue. When he arranges for the Egyptians to sell everything they own to buy food, including their own bodies, he sets up the slave-making system that will enslave his own descendants born of his union with Asenath, meaning that there will be Egyptian blood on both sides of the slave divide.

SPECIAL SECTION:
THE TORAH OF ENSLAVED WOMEN

> Exodus 21:7 When a man sells his daughter as a slave, she shall not go out as the male slaves go out.

For me as a black feminist and womanist descended from enslaved Africans in the Americas, biblical slavery is a particularly pernicious and personal issue. Slavery in the Bible represents more than the ubiquity of slavery in the ancient world; it represents the theological bulwark on which the Atlantic slave trade rested. There were financial and social imperatives and rationales upon which the American slavocracy rested, to be sure; but the Bible of the church that baptized me and communes me and ordained me and called me to teach in a seminary of the church—*that* Bible, which is also *my* Bible—calls for the enslavement of human beings. One of the pillars of that biblical slavery is the sexual use of female slaves for the personal, individual gratification of slave-holding males and perpetual production of subsequent generations of slaves through forced pregnancy.[80] While unaddressed in the text, with the possible exception of the Joseph saga, there is no reason to imagine male slaves in ancient Israel were free from sexual use. Sexual assault is not limited by culture or gender of assailant or target. Whether or not one understands the stories of Exodus to have any historicity, slavery and sexual subjugation were

---

80. I am defining any impregnation of an enslaved girl or woman by or for her enslavers as forced, even while acknowledging the complexity of intimate associations, some of which certainly had some elements of choice.

part of the world in, before, and behind the text. It is extraordinary that the Hebrew Scriptures, which do not shy away from sexually explicit and violent stories, do not acknowledge the systemic nature of sexual abuse of enslaved persons in its accounts of Egyptian slavery.

Is the God of Abraham, Isaac, and Jacob truly the God of Hagar, Sarah, Keturah, Rebekah, Leah, Rachel, Bilhah, and Zilpah? For me, no issue forces this question more than the biblical sanction of the sexual subordination of women in and through chattel slavery. How might Bilhah answer the question "Is this god whose people were bred in her unwilling womb her god?" A broader question is "How was it possible to treat any human being this way?" There were ready justifications for enslaving foreigners: they were different; their worship was different and wrong. What about enslaving members of one's own community with whom one shared the worship of the one God? Under what circumstances might one enslave one's own daughter? The Torah and subsequent texts provide occasion and rationale for slaveholding. The legacy of these codes includes Israelites enslaving Israelites; Christians enslaving Christians; and American slave owners raping their enslaved daughters, sisters, nieces, and cousins to make more slaves. That one of these texts is enshrined in the heart of the exodus is grotesque and obscene.

There are for me two iconic expressions that capture the liberation of the exodus: *shalach et 'ami*, "Let my people go"; *hotziy'anu adonai mimitzrayim mibet 'avadiym*, "The HOLY ONE brought us out of Egypt out of the house of slavery." The verb in the second expression, *y-tz-'*, is the primary verb of the exodus, used nearly a hundred times in the book of Exodus alone—virtually always in Hiphil, the causative stem, signifying that God made it happen. It is the verb that God uses in the first conversation with Moses on Horeb in Exodus 3:10, and it is the primary verb through which successive generations recall and remember the exodus.[81] So I was stunned when I read in Exodus 21:7, *lo tetze'*, "She shall not go out," that is, she shall not be liberated. Under what circumstances could a woman's liberation be abrogated, her exodus be annulled, and she be returned to bondage—on the way to the promised land, which she will enter as enslaved as she was in Egypt?

The geographic and literary location of this text is crucial; it is written as though the Israelites are between slavery and freedom. While their feet have not yet reached the promised land, the Israelites and their God are ensuring that some men can disenfranchise their own daughters and return them to slavery while making a profit off the sale. Therefore, if and when the father of an Israelite woman or girl decides to sell her into slavery, which is thinly disguised sex-slavery, the liberating acts of God, Miriam, and Moses are of no avail to her.

---

81. See Josh. 2:10; Judg. 6:8; 1 Sam. 12:8; Jer. 7:22, 25; Dan. 9:15.

For the purpose of this womanist (most definitely womanish) midrash I will emulate[82] the system of rabbinic commentary in which a piece of Torah is commented on by the rabbis in the Mishnah and further discussed in the Talmuds and/or elaborated upon in the midrash:

When a man sells his daughter as a slave, *lo tetze'*, she shall not go out as the male slaves go out.

> Rabbah Amunah asked, What does it mean, *lo tetze'*, "She shall not go out"? Rabbat Dinat answered, "When a father sells his own daughter into slavery, knowing full well that she will be used as a sex-slave, there is no liberation for her. For *y-tz-'*, is liberation, the 'ex' in 'exodus.' There will be no exodus for such a daughter. She will arrive in the Land of Promise a slave, a breeder of slaves."

Non-Israelites were the preferred slave-stock (Lev. 25:44–46), although in a pinch impoverished Israelites could serve as "hired-workers," *sakhir*, until the jubilee year. The broader passage in Leviticus 25:39–46 is convoluted, using *'-v-d*, "slave," as verb and noun in *lo ta'vod avodat eved*, "you shall not enslave [them] in the slavery of a slave," in verse 39 and describing their labor as "hired-workers" in verse 40, *ya'vod imak*, "they shall serve/slave with you." The justification is that they, the Israelites, are God's slaves (v. 42). Foreigners may be enslaved and held in slavery and passed down in slavery (vv. 44–46), practices gleefully embraced as biblical in the trans-Atlantic slave trade.

Biblical slavery depended in part on "otherness," the characterization of some people as wholly "other," particularly along ethnic and gender lines. That otherness extended to excluding slaves from the categories of neighbor and stranger, for whom the Israelites had some ethical obligations, for example, "Do not covet your neighbor's slaves."[83] Your neighbor is your fellow and fellow slaveholder—not his, or even her, slaves. Likewise, the Sabbath is for Israelites, their families, slaves, livestock, and resident aliens; these are separate categories. Therefore the commandment not to oppress resident aliens (Exod. 22:21) was not interpreted as do not hold or abuse slaves, even with the caveat, "for you were resident aliens in Egypt," because slaves, resident aliens, and Israelites were distinct categories. This has implications for the erasure of Israelite identity for Israelites who are held in slavery by other Israelites, particularly girls and women. Women represent a particular kind of otherness in the canon, distinct from the generally male speaking voice of the Scriptures and

---

82. These *rabbatoth*, female rabbis, live only in my sanctified imagination. Their titles Rabbah and Rabbat are among the options that some women rabbis use contemporarily.

83. The Decalogue uses the second-person masculine singular, addressing itself to a singular, male, married and slave-holding subject. See "Women in the Commandments" in chapter 2, on page 104.

their predominantly male addressee. The compounded otherness of foreign women produces a near-hysteria in biblical tradents while Israelite identity is not sufficient to counter that otherness in women in the community. Not surprisingly, there is no corresponding text for Exodus 21:7 in which a man may sell his son into slavery.

There are three primary lexical terms for the enslaved in Biblical Hebrew: *'eved, amah,* and *shiphchah.* The first term, *'eved,* is the generic term for slave, commonly and misleadingly translated "servant." In the singular it nearly always refers to a male slave; the plural (*'avadiym*) represents men and both genders; for example, the whole people of Israel were slaves, *'avadiym,* in Egypt. While *'-v-d* is the dominant lexical expression denoting slavery, it has a broader semantic range than does its primary English translation. "Slavery," "service," and "worship" are all appropriate contextual translations, and in some passages the root is used with more than one meaning.[84] Whereas the term "servant" may be intended to focus on the nature of their duties, the translation "slave" addresses their estate—bought, sold, and captured, many held in perpetuity, with their children born into their estate; limited opportunities for manumission; bereft of autonomy, particularly with regard to their persons, sexuality, and reproduction.

The next two terms, *amah* and *shiphchah* (*amahoth* and *shiphchoth,* plural), are used together and so interchangeably that it is no longer possible to distinguish between them.[85] Both are sometimes translated "maid." Genesis 30:3–4 is illustrative of the broader translation pattern: The NRSV, JPS, GSJPS, and IB translate *amah* as "maid," while Fox uses "slave-girl" in verse 3.[86] Both *amahoth* and *shiphchoth* are enslaved women or girls regularly associated with sexual and reproductive duties. Translating either as "maid" intentionally obscures the sexual nature of their servitude. Both terms seem to refer primarily to foreign women; Leviticus 25:44 stipulates that they should be bought from foreigners. However, a survey of the passages in which these terms occur does not indicate that these women are entirely or even preferentially non-Israelite. The two terms for enslaved women, *amah* and *shiphchah,* occur about 120 times in the canon.[87]

84. See the following for some of the variety of its use: Gen. 2:5, "work" or "till" the ground; Exod. 1:13, Israelite slavery in Egypt; Josh. 1:1, Moses as God's slave/servant; 1 Chr. 6:49, Aaron's work in the tabernacle.
85. See Gen. 30:3–4, in which Bilhah is called both an *amah* (v. 3) and a *shiphchah* (v. 4).
86. All translate *shiphchah* as "maid" in v. 4 (except IB, which does not translate it at all).
87. As a side note, I find it interesting and not entirely insignificant that *amah* is a homophone of *ammah,* which is used to indicate body parts such as "arm" and "penis," a measure of length drawn from the arm, "cubit," and a "channel" that corresponds in

Exodus 21:7 allows for an Israelite man to sell his daughter as an *amah*-slave for sexual use and does not require him to be destitute to do so. In fact, the text places no limitations on him as it pertains to selling his daughter into sexual subjugation; he can do so for any or no reason. The restrictions in the following verses are for the man who buys her, to keep him from using her and passing her on to his son, using her and selling her to foreigners, replacing her and then starving her to death, or depriving her of clothing or the opportunity to conceive children who would theoretically help support her if they were not held in bondage themselves. (This very specific list of potential fates suggests real-world awareness of the vulnerability of enslaved women beyond the literary constructions of the passage.) If the buyer's use of the woman or girl violates these terms, then he must release her (to what fate, after being so used?) with no specified compensation.

In its broader literary context, the Exodus passage distinguished female slaves from male slaves who were to be freed (*yetze'*—"He shall go out") in the seventh year of their bondage unless they chose to remain. Even then, any slave woman provided to male slaves and her children remained enslaved. However, Deuteronomy 15:12ff. corrects this text by calling for the freedom of female and male slaves in the seventh year and for them to be compensated "liberally" with foodstuffs and livestock they helped produce. How long is the rhetorical, literary, midrashic, and imaginary space between Exodus and Deuteronomy? How long did it take God and Moses to correct themselves or get corrected? All these texts are specific to Israelites; non-Israelites were held in perpetuity, making these texts available to provide a scriptural foundation for the enslavement of Africans, read as others by Europeans, who saw themselves as the legitimate heirs of the Israelites, even as they often demonized Jews. Bearing this in mind, imagine the horror evoked by Deuteronomy 28:68, in which one of the penalties for failing to observe the covenant was that God would ship Israel back to Egypt (in actual seagoing ships) and they would offer themselves for sale as *'avadiym*-slaves and *shiphchah*-slaves, but no one would buy them. There is no horror expressed in the text for Israel's reenslaved daughters.

In some of the narratives I address, I translate *amah* and/or *shiphchah* as "womb-slave." In these cases, the girls are given by other women to men for sex for the express purpose of impregnating them. This is forcible surrogacy.

---

some way to the measure of length. The two words have different philological origins and are not related, although they have similar spellings and sound alike. I hear echoes of sexual reductionism in the juxtaposition of the two words, e.g., that an *amah*-slave is as much a receptacle as an *ammah*-channel.

In addition, I believe that it is more appropriate to describe the womb-slaves as girls, because they would have been young enough to have been presumed fertile and possibly virginal in order that the paternity of their children not be disputed; however, it may be that in some cases, they were already proven fertile.

The term "sex-slave" may conjure up abducted girls imprisoned in dungeons, whose stories litter contemporary news reports. In modernity, sex slaves are kidnapped and trafficked women and girls (and sometimes boys and men) who are forced to have sex with one or more men (overwhelmingly) for the duration of their captivity, and are sometimes forced to bear their captor's children. If their captors force them to perform other services—such as dealing drugs, soliciting other victims, domestic chores—that does not mitigate against their sexual enslavement. Therefore I am calling these women in the Bible sex-slaves to make their sexual servitude visible and to center it for the religious reader/hearer of these texts, not to suggest that they do not perform any other duties. Here are some of the texts that make their sexual servitude most explicit:

> Genesis 16:1 Now Sarai, Avram's (Abram's) wife-woman, did not give birth for him. She had an Egyptian *shiphchah*, a slave-girl whose name was Hagar, [2]and Sarai said to Avram (Abram), "Look at this! The GOD OF ALL FLESH has prevented me from giving birth to children; please go in to my *shiphchah*-slave-girl; perhaps I shall construct-children[88] from her." And Avram (Abram) obeyed Sarai. [3]And Sarai, Avram's (Abram's) wife-woman, took Hagar the Egyptian-girl, her *shiphchah*-slave-girl, after Avram (Abram) had lived ten years in the land of Canaan, and gave her to her husband-man Avram (Abram) as a wife-woman.[89]

> Genesis 21:10 And Sarah said to Avraham (Abraham), "Drive out this womb-slave with her son; for the son of this *amah*-womb-slave will not inherit along with my son, with Yitzchaq (Isaac)." . . . [12]And God said to Avraham (Abraham), "Let it not be evil in your sight on account of the boy and on account of your *amah*-womb-slave; whatever Sarah says to you, obey her, for it is through Yitzchaq (Isaac) that seed shall be named for you. [13]And also, for the son of the *amah*-womb-slave, I will make a nation of him, because he is your seed."

88. The verb *b-n-h*, "build," "construct," is a homophone of *ben*, "child," and is a double entendre.

89. Hebrew uses "*isshah*," making Hagar the same category "woman" or "wife" as Sarah, counter to the JPS translation, "concubine." Since *isshah* describes all women, including those not in conjugal relationship with men, the translation "wife" is secondary and largely an artifact of the translation language. The same issue applies to *ish*, "man," "husband."

Genesis 30:3 Rachel said, "Here is my *amah*-womb-slave Bilhah; go in to
her, that she may give birth on my knees and that I too may construct-
children[90] from her." . . . [9]When Leah saw that she had ceased giving birth,
she took her *shiphchah*-womb-slave Zilpah and gave her to Ya'aqov (Jacob)
as a wife-woman.[91]

Exodus 21:7 When a man sells his daughter as an *amah*-sex-slave, she shall
not go-out-in-freedom as the male slaves do.

Leviticus 19:20 When a man lies-down emitting-seed with a woman
who is a *shiphchah*-slave-woman, designated for another man and neither
ransomed nor released or freedom given to her, there will be an inquiry-
of-compensation. They shall not be put to death, since she has not been
freed.

Leviticus 25:44 And your male slave and *amah*-woman-slave who are
yours, from the nations that surround you, from them you may buy a male
slave and an *amah*-woman-slave.

Seeing and hearing sexual servitude and forced surrogacy in the Scriptures
whenever female slaves or "handmaids" are mentioned gives new meaning to
texts like Exodus 20:10 and 20:17. In the former, the command to observe
Shabbat in the Decalogue extends to the women and girls in sexual servitude;
perhaps this means that the Sabbath is the one day when they will not have
to have sex with the man who enslaves them. In the second text, men are
commanded not to covet the slave-women of other men. While the Torah in
general and Decalogue in particular are directed to the whole of Israel, this
individual *torah* has a heterosexual and heteronormative framework that does
not invalidate it for women of any orientation or gay men, but rather one that
articulates the sexual desire of one (presumptively but not necessarily male)
Israelite for the enslaved girl or woman in his (or her) neighbor's household
destined for sexual servitude, forcible surrogacy, and/or breeding other slaves.
So "Do not covet your neighbor's *amah*-womb-slave" means "Do not covet
sex with your neighbor's sex-slave." Indeed it is hard to imagine one man coveting another's slave-girl *without* coveting her sexual exploitation. Likewise
the command not to covet your (male) neighbor's male slave should be heard
with regard to the likelihood of sexual abuse of male slaves.

I do not believe that it is an overstatement to read sexual subordination
on the surface of each text in which enslaved women and girls are specified
as *amahoth* and *shiphchoth*. Similarly it beggars belief that male slaves would

90. See note 82 on *b-n-h*, "build," "construct."
91. The text stipulates that Bilhah and Zilpah are in the same marital category as
Rachel and Leah, counter to the JPS translation, "concubine."

be coveted but not for sexual use. There are a few passages (e.g., Isa. 24:2; Ps. 123:3) where an *amah*-slave or *shiphchah*-slave is linked only with her mistress, but the Torah makes clear that female slave owners used the bodies of their female slaves for their own benefit, including through forced surrogacy as illustrated in the stories of Hagar, Bilhah, and Zilpah.

In a number of other texts, *amahoth* and *shiphchoth* are used as something akin to class signifiers. In the story of Abimelech (Gideon's son), the first monarch in Israel, who ruled Israel for three years (Judg. 9:22), his mother is derided as an *amah* by those who reject his rule (Judg. 9:18), although the text identifies her as a legitimate but secondary wife, a *pilegesh* (*piylegesh*) (Judg. 8:31). In Samuel, women abase themselves, referring to themselves as the *amah*-slave or *shiphchah*-slave of males with power and authority, human and divine: In 1 Samuel 1:11, Hannah identifies herself as God's *amah*-slave repeatedly while petitioning for a child. Later, in verses 16 and 18, she calls herself first the *amah*-slave, then the *shiphchah*-slave of Eli, as she offers her apologia for her heretofore unorthodox practice of praying without speaking aloud. While Hannah may not have been making herself sexually available to God or Eli, her self-identification could be read something like, "I am an unworthy sex-slave." Further, part of Job's self-defense in Job 31:13 against the injustices rained down upon him is that he treats his *amah*-slaves (and male slaves) justly, hearing their complaints against him; surely extending justice to sex-slaves illustrates his righteousness. In some cases, men identify themselves as sons of *amah*-slaves, abasing themselves in their prayers (see Pss. 86:16 and 116:16).

In some cases it appears that a woman's self-identification as an *amah*-slave or *shiphchah*-slave was also intended to convey sexual submission. In 1 Samuel 25:24ff., Abigail throws herself at David's feet, proclaiming that she is his *amah*-slave, although she has a husband. When her husband dies, she becomes one of David's many women. In 2 Samuel 6:22 David's wife Michal critiques him not for "dancing before the Lord," as is often reported, but for uncovering his body in the sight of the *amah*-slaves of his slaves—*amhoth 'avadayv*, "the sex-slaves of his slaves," the lowest of the low. In response, in verse 22 David says that he was dancing before the one God *and* that he will further debase himself, *unqaloti*, in the eyes of those very sex-slaves. In 1 Kings 3:20ff., the sex-worker who petitions Solomon to award her custody of her stolen child refers to herself as his *amah*-slave. And Ruth famously makes herself sexually available to Boaz as first a *shiphchah*-slave and then as *amah*-slave (in Ruth 2:13 and 3:9 respectively).

In other texts, women with their own power and authority use the self-abasing formula in their dealings with men, seemingly to disarm them. The resident woman of Tekoa repeatedly identifies herself as David's *shiphchah*-slave while critiquing his treatment of his sons in her conspiracy with Joab in 2 Samuel 14. The resident woman of Abel-Beth-Maacah says she is Joab's *amah*-slave when negotiating with him to break the siege of her city in 2 Samuel 20:17. When Bathsheba abases herself as David's *amah*-slave in 1 Kings 1:13ff., she is likely invoking David's previous treatment of her as she seeks to hold him to his word (of which there is no sign in the text that he ever gave) that her son Solomon would reign after him. The subtext may well be transactional. Bathsheba has paid for Solomon's throne, on her back, and she will not be cheated out of it.

In a few instances, the prophets proclaim liberty for *shiphchah*-slaves.[92] The prophet Jeremiah calls for the liberation of Hebrew slaves, male *'avadiym* and female *shiphchah*-slaves, in Jeremiah 34:13ff. The people comply but then think better of their slaveholding and take them back into bondage, much to his consternation. Joel famously announces the bestowal of God's spirit on *shiphchah*-slaves and *'avadiym*, "male-slaves." In 2 Chronicles 28:8ff. the prophet Oded demands that the Judeans free the Israelite women and men that they have taken captive as spoils of war as *shiphchah*-slaves and *'avadiym*, "male-slaves." The people do so, and the text notes that they clothe those among the slaves who were naked (v. 15) as they heed the prophet. The public nudity of the slaves in that context calls up images of slave markets and the public stripping of slaves intended for sex-work, so that their potential buyers may more easily assess their value.

The sexual subjugation of women, including Israelite (Judean) women, continues into the return from Babylonian exile. Ezra 2:65 and Nehemiah 7:67 note that the exiles returned with 7,337 male and female slaves, now using *amah* exclusively for female slaves. It is a morbid commentary that the new community could not function without enslaved humans, including enslaved women and girls available for sexual and reproductive use. In a particularly telling episode, some Judean women and men complain to Nehemiah (5:5) that "we are forcing our daughters and sons to be slaves (*'avadiym*), and some of our daughters have been raped." In 5:1–5 they confess selling their children and taking liens on their fields to pay the Persian imperial taxes and feed themselves. One of Nehemiah's responses is to pledge to buy them

92. That they do not do so for *amah*-slaves may indicate that the terms had preferential regional or other use. Given the lack of literary distinction between *amah*- and *shiphchah*-slaves and the somewhat randomized deployment of the terms (one appears fifty-six times in the canon, the other sixty-three), *shiphchah* may come to represent all enslaved women and girls. Indeed, the term *amah* drops out of some prophetic books (and is lacking from 2 Kings to Zechariah), suggesting that *shiphchah* becomes the dominant vernacular term, for a while, contextually.

back (v. 8); however, the text seems to suggest that the women were raped as soon as they were bought. The term *amah* appears in the archaeological record; a number of seals and seal impressions from the sixth century BCE indicate that *amah* evolved to designate a woman with administrative authority, as did *na'ar*, "boy."

In the LXX, *amah* and *shiphchah* are both translated by *paidiskē* (seemingly more servant than slave and more girl than woman) preferentially, some eighty-eight times. However, in the Former Prophets (Judges–Kings) and stray single citations in Ruth and Esther, *doulē* (female slave) is the translation of choice, some fifty times. In the New Testament, *paidiskē* is the term of choice, used thirteen times to the three uses of *doulē* restricted to Luke-Acts. Luke has *doulē* for Mary's self-articulation as the "slave-woman of the Lord" in Luke 1:38 and 1:48—perhaps based on Hannah's self-articulation as God's *amah*-slave, given the intertextuality between Hannah's and Mary's psalms. Correspondingly, Acts 2:18 has *doulē* for the slave-women on whom the Spirit falls on Pentecost, citing and conforming to Joel in the LXX. Luke also uses *paidiskē* twice, once along with the corresponding masculine form for slaves in a parable (Luke 2:45) and once for the slave-girl at the temple during the arrest of Jesus (Luke 22:56). Galatians 4:22 calls Hagar a *paidiskē* in order to contrast her with the free Sarah. There is no clear distinction between the two terms, nor is one more easily identifiable as sexualized than the other.

The Mishnah prefers *shiphchah* to *amah* (fifty-nine citations to five); in addition, none of the references to *amah*-slaves mentions progeny with their enslavers, but many references to *shiphchah*-slaves do. The *mishnayoth* that deal primarily with issues of marriage and progeny, *Yevamoth* and *Kethuvoth*, use *shiphchah* exclusively.[93]

There is one significant attribute of sexual subjugation in the Scriptures that differs in no small amount from the experiences of enslaved African women and girls in the Americas. The sexual subjugation of women in the Scriptures is not racialized; the category "race" does not properly apply to the Scriptures, even when ethnic identity is at stake. While foreign women are constructed as particularly sexually tempting, and the Israelites do bring them into their community as sexual and reproductive slaves, notwithstanding whatever other domestic chores they may have also had, the Israelites also buy, sell, and use women and girls from among their own people as sex-slaves and breeding stock.

The pervasiveness of Israelite sexual servitude of women from their own people in addition to other peoples stands in sharp contrast to the sexual subjugation of African and native women by European colonizers. Virtually any

93. See *mishnayoth Qiddushin* 1:2; *Baba Qamma* 4:5; 5:6; *Yadaim* 4:7 for *amahoth*; and *Yevamot* 2:5, 8; 7:5, etc., and *Kethuvoth* 1:2, 4; 2:9; 3:1, etc., for *shiphchoth*.

Israelite (or Judean) girl or woman could be sold as or treated as an *amah*- or *shiphchah*-slave. Even with the maintenance of rigid gender hierarchies in Europe and Colonial America and with the commodification of some classes of white women as sex-workers and sexually available through class distinctions—including sexual abuse of servant populations—white women were (and to some degree still are) positioned as sexually pure and chaste, over and against women of color, with black women representing promiscuity and sexual perversion in the extreme. One characteristic of imperial and enslaving, colonizing social hierarchy was to protect an elite class of white women as the embodiment of pure womanhood, inaccessible to any defiling touch. There seems to be no biblical, Israelite equivalent of the construct of white ladyhood, particularly as it was reified and constructed in the American South.

This also means that there is no exact biblical corollary to the wholesale depiction of black and brown women's bodies as publicly sexually available, promiscuous, and uniquely suited for sexual depravity that undergirds and frames American history and contemporary culture. Ironically, the abuse of the bodies of black and brown women and girls by black and brown men and boys in our own communities does correspond to the Israelite experience of sexual subordination of their own women and girls by their own men, drawing a rebuke from the prophet 2Pac:

> Since we all came from a woman
> got our name from a woman
> and our game from a woman
> I wonder why we take from our women
> why we rape our women,
> do we hate our women?[94]

The widely chronicled experience of female slaves in ancient Israel used sexually by their enslavers presages the experience of enslaved African girls and women in the Americas and subjugated women and girls around the world; it lives on in religiously sanctioned gender hierarchies that appeal to the biblical text. The sexual use of enslaved women and girls that pervades the canon also begs the following questions: How are these texts Scripture? How are they true? How are they illuminating? How are they authoritative? What enduring Word is there in these words?[95]

---

94. Written and performed by Tupac Shakur, *Keep Ya Head Up*, from his 1993 album *Strictly 4 My N.I.G.G.A.Z.* on Interscope Records.

95. These questions, like this project, begin with the claims of the religious reader/ hearer that the Bible—in any configuration—is *Scripture* and as such is authoritative, illuminating, revelatory, etc.

To those questions I can answer only that the truth of these passages of Scripture is the truth of the world in which they originated. The biblical world was one in which women's autonomy over their own bodies, sexuality, and reproduction was nearly inconceivable.[96] The truth of the text is that the framers of the text were so convinced of the rightness and ubiquity of slavery that they could not imagine—or hear—a divine word of dissent. As a rule the biblical text is not concerned about the conversion of the women whose enslaved wombs produce significant figures in Israelite history, though the rabbinic discourse will go out of its way to construct conversion narratives for the many non-Israelite women in Israel's lineage.

The biblical text is fundamentally androcentric and regularly (though not exclusively) patriarchal. Yet there are texts in which God or the narrator addresses women directly, texts in which women and their children and other vulnerable people are the primary concern of God and the text (not to mention texts in which feminine language and imagery is used for God). Women in the Scriptures function in various capacities: monarch, prophet, judge, shepherd, entrepreneur, musician, slave, and slaveholder.

The complexity of the biblical texts is part of what draws me to them and commends them to me. I wrestle with the texts, more bruised than blessed while God-wrestling the Torah as a surrogate for the One who revealed her and the ones who claim(ed) clear and certain apprehension of that revelation in the name of the One. These passages illuminate the gulf between the god of the text and God beyond the texts. The authority of these texts is the authority that is given to these texts by the communities that canonized them and those that receive them. One aim of the American slavocracy was to make the god of the slaveholders, whom they identified as the God of Israel, the god of the enslaved. The success of that project is very much in doubt; the god of the slaveholder has in fact not become the god of the enslaved, leading to no small amount of consternation for some. Some of us outright reject the god of slavery in or out of the Scriptures.

As a God- and Torah-wrestling woman, I say:

> *A father does not have divine sanction to sell his daughter into sexual slavery, knowing as I write these words that there are girls being pimped out and sold by their own fathers who do not need or seek the permission of a text or its god before selling their daughters as sex-slaves. A man does not have the right to capture a girl—whether from the sanctuary of her own home or neighborhood or even if she runs away from home—and rape her and*

96. The Song of Solomon occupies the space between "nearly" and "totally."

impregnate her. Women do not have the right to give or sell their daughters or to provide their men with the bodies of other girls.

As I write these words, another truth emerges from the Scriptures: the reprehensible gender and sexual mores of the Stone and Iron Ages are still in effect for some of the women, men, boys, and girls living in the Digital Age. Our sacred texts do not proclaim or even envision a world without slavery and the subordination of women, but they lay a foundation for us to transcend them and their limitations—the limitations of those who claimed to hear God enshrining human bondage of all sorts: "Remember that you were slaves in Egypt." "Do to others what you would have them do to you." "What is hateful to you, do not do to another." "In the Messiah there is no longer slave or free, male or female."

In the same text in which God delivers some of the Israelites from Egyptian bondage and orders others into sexual bondage, I hear words of liberation and release from an unlikely voice, *Laban ben Milcah av Leah v'Rachel*, Laban the son of Milcah and father of Leah and Rachel. Many know it as the Mitzpah covenant in Genesis 31:49–50 but cite it only in part; in whole it proclaims God's interest in the welfare of Laban's daughters and prohibits Jacob from taking any more women. That he violates this at the bequest of his own women suggests that he invites divine judgment on himself and his descendants. Perhaps this verse extends beyond these two women; perhaps God's concern for womankind is more inclusive:

> *May the* HOLY ONE OF OLD *watch between you and me, when we are absent one from the other. If you ill-treat my daughters, or if you take women in addition to my daughters, though no one else is with us, remember that God is witness between you and me.*

RESOURCES ON BIBLICAL SLAVERY

Anderson, Cheryl B. *Ancient Laws and Contemporary Controversies: The Need for Inclusive Biblical Interpretation.* Oxford: Oxford University Press, 2009.

Brooten, Bernadette J., and Jacqueline L. Hazelton. *Beyond Slavery: Overcoming Its Religious and Sexual Legacies.* New York: Palgrave Macmillan, 2010.

Haynes, Stephen R. *Noah's Curse: The Biblical Justification of American Slavery.* Oxford: Oxford University Press, 2007.

Hopkins, Dwight N. *Down, Up, and Over: Slave Religion and Black Theology.* Minneapolis: Fortress Press, 2000.

Patterson, Orlando. *Slavery and Social Death: A Comparative Study.* Cambridge, MA: Harvard University Press, 1982.

Pinn, Anthony B. *Terror and Triumph: The Nature of Black Religion*. Minneapolis: Fortress Press, 2004.

Reddie, Anthony. *Black Theology, Slavery, and Contemporary Christianity*. Farnham, Surrey, England: Ashgate, 2010.

Smith, Mitzi J. "Slavery in the Early Church." In *True to our Native Land: An African American New Testament Commentary*, Brian K. Blount, general editor. Minneapolis: Fortress Press, 2007.

Wimbush, Vincent L. *The Bible and African Americans: A Brief History*. Minneapolis: Fortress Press, 2003.

2

Exodus: These Are Not All the Names

Exodus 1:1 These are the names of the sons of Israel, the ones who went to Egypt, each man and his household.

The Hebrew name for the book of Exodus, *Shemoth* ("Names"), comes from the opening words of the first verse. The text does not in fact provide the names of all of Israel's sons; it names only the twelve who were accounted as patriarchs in the later tradition. Genesis 46:15 and 46:26 number Israel's children at thirty-three and sixty-six respectively. However one understands the two numbers, they mean that Israel has more than twelve sons. These are not all of the names.

Israel also has an unknown number of daughters. There are daughters among the thirty-three or sixty-six, perhaps a dozen or more. Only one of their names is ever called: Dinah. But there are more. In Genesis 35:37, after Joseph is sold into slavery, "all of [Jacob's] daughters," along with his sons, seek to comfort him. Dinah's name is called in Genesis, but in Exodus her name is not called among the roster of Israel's children who went with him to Egypt. These are not all of the names. The names of Dinah's sisters are never called, nor are their numbers verified, but they are acknowledged in Genesis 37:35; 46:7; and 46:15. These are not all of the names.

The number of female characters in Exodus drops almost tenfold when compared to those in Genesis. In Exodus, stories of individual women, let alone women whose names are preserved and/or spoken, will be few and far between. Many will be hidden in the expression *beney Yisrael*. *Beney Yisrael* means "sons of Israel" in Exodus 1:1. It can also mean "children of Israel"—Israel the person and Israel the people—and will come to mean "Israelites." I will translate *beney Yisrael* inclusively, with gender specificity, that is, "daughters and sons of Israel" and "Israelite women, men, and children," when it is clear that it is functioning as an inclusive plural. Gender-neutral inclusive plurals like "children" and "descendants" obscure the women who are surely present in these expressions and in this verse. Women are not the only hidden class of people in these passages; children are rarely mentioned. I make the presence of children among the Israelites explicit when they are implied in the narrative. This is not always clear; for example, were minor children required to drink the ashes of the golden calf? I will begin with a discussion of women buried in the *beney Yisrael* and continue with specific verses identifying and/or invoking women.

Exodus is a story of becoming. The women, children, and men born to and through the descendants of Sarah, Rebekah, Rachel, Leah, Zilpah, Bilhah, Bat-Shua, Tamar, Asenath, and countless unnamed mothers and matriarchs become the people of Israel through the exodus story recorded in Exodus and Numbers, after a lengthy pause in Leviticus. The exodus story includes wonderful, rich stories of the Israelites' formative encounter with their God while wilderness wandering from promise to fulfillment. The individual narratives use fire and cloud, blood and water, ritual and worship to deal with calling and ordination, community and individual response to divine providence, stewardship and personal piety. Exodus calls for the extermination of indigenous women, men, and children and the seizure of their land, by God in the name of God.

Exodus looms large in biblical and postbiblical interpretation. Jewish and Christian writers—liberationist, womanist, feminist, postcolonial, queer, and more—have crafted a secondary canon interpreting Exodus that is itself the subject of interpretation. The story of exodus provided a template for American expansion into the West and subjugation (and extermination) of America's native peoples, and for the self-liberation of enslaved African peoples in the Americas. Its liberating paradigm supplies rhetoric and imagery for LGBTQI folk coming out of spaces in which human dignity has been eclipsed. Themes from the exodus even appear in a wealth of science fiction, providing paradigms for (interspecies) intercultural contact.

Exodus calls only a handful of women by name: Shifrah (Shiphrah), Puah, Yocheved (Jochebed), Zipporah, and Elisheva (Elisheba). But there are other women: Israelite, Egyptian, Amorite, Hittite, Hivite, Perizzite, Jebusite, and Canaanite women without whom the story of Exodus cannot be told.

SHIPHRAH AND PUAH

Exodus 1:15 Now the king of Egypt said to the Hebrew birthing-women, whom the name of one was Shiphrah and the name of the second, Puah, [16]he said, "When you birth the Hebrew women, and see them on the birth-stools, if it is a son, you will put him to death; and if a daughter, she shall live." [17]But the birthing-women feared God; they did not do as the king of Egypt commanded them, but they let the boys live.

Shiphrah and Puah are described in Exodus 1:15ff. as Hebrew birthing-women, *m'yaldoth ha'vriyoth*. It appears that they are Hebrew women themselves, rather than Egyptian women or women from some other community who provide midwifery services for the Israelites. Shiphrah's name is based on a Semitic-language root, *sh-p(h)-r*, "to be beautiful" in Hebrew and "to be pleasing" in Aramaic; the word *sapphire* may be related. Puah's name is also attested as a Semitic name.[1]

Given their presentation, we can read Shiphrah and Puah as the "mothers" or "heads" of the Israelite midwifery guild. It seems incredible that just two women are responsible for (attending) all the births of the Hebrew people, a people who are described in Exodus 1:7 as "filling the land." In a surreal tableau Shiphrah and Puah find themselves in the presence of the unnamed pharaoh of the exodus, who in Exodus 1:16 commands them to kill every male baby they deliver on the birthing stools, that is, before presenting him to his mother. One can only imagine what that encounter was like. Using my sanctified imagination, I see them both maintaining their calm, showing proper respect in every way as though they were seasoned diplomats and courtiers. And after the meeting with the pharaoh,

Shiphrah and Puah call all the birthing-women to assemble, telling their overseers that they are passing on Pharaoh's instructions. One Egyptian lingers longer than the others; Puah shoos him out with the ancient womanist refrain: "This is women's business." He leaves. Hundreds of women come to the place of Shiphrah's tent. Many bring daughters, granddaughters, and nieces whom they are apprenticing in the profession. Some are pregnant; others are nursing. It takes more than a day for everyone to gather, eat, and rest from their journeys. And there is talk. Shop talk, women's words, shared

1. It may be possibly Ugaritic "girl-child"; cf. Spanish Nina and Arabic Walidah.

experiences, and new techniques: herbs to stop bleeding, herbs to bring on labor, teas to increase milk production, ways to limit pregnancies.

Finally Shiphrah speaks. She tells them Pharaoh's words. The women gasp. Some mutter. Some shout. Some of the children are frightened. Shiphrah and Puah shush them and call for calm. Shiphrah begins to prophesy: "God has brought our people a mighty long way. And I don't believe God has brought us this far to leave us. Do not fear this pharaoh or his warriors, not his warhorses nor his chariots. God will blow them away like smoke in the wind. In our days, before our eyes God will break the back of Egypt and wash away its might. God will raise up one of our sons to lead us and all our children out of this house of slavery. Our hands and our wombs do God's work. We will deliver the deliverer. We will keep him safe until the day that God calls him to lead us to freedom. We shall receive our freedom, dancing to woman-song if we trust in the mighty power of Shaddai, who drew us from her holy womb, whose spirit covers the earth."

Shiphrah takes her seat. Puah speaks: "Trust in God-Whose-Name-Is-Holy. This is what we shall do: deliver the babies; hide as many of the boys as you can. Raise others as girls. Do not worry about the Egyptians; they will not come house to house to check on women! They cannot imagine that we would defy the pharaoh whom they revere as a living God."

The women leave the convocation of birthing-women. Days, weeks, then months go by. Pharaoh is too busy to think about the Hebrew birthing-women. Someone mentions that the Hebrew people are still growing, in spite of the pharaoh's commandment. He summons them back to explain themselves.

In the text, only a single verse passes between the pharaoh's genocidal command and his realization that the birthing-women have failed to curb the population of Israel. This is another fertile space for midrash. How long did it take Pharaoh to figure out that the birthing-women have not stemmed the tide of Hebrew births? A month? A year? How did he find out? Was he keeping track? Was there a bureaucrat in charge of "the Hebrew problem"?

The reader may be astounded that Shiphrah and Puah are not thrown in jail or in a dungeon, or taken out and summarily executed. But the narrative has told us that the women are God-fearing women. God and/or their fear of God protects them. And while the pharaoh is capable of brutality, he seems unwilling to get his own hands dirty or even to have violence done in his presence. Instead he calls the women back. Shiphrah and Puah lie.

They use the pharaoh's cultural bias against him. In Exodus 1:19 they say, "The Hebrew women are brutish, animalistic, *chayoth*—not refined, like

Egyptian women. Their babies just plop out of them." The word *chayoth* occurs only in this place. However, it is a homophone for and likely related to the noun *chayah*, "wild animal." The pharaoh seems to be at a loss for words. In fact, he never speaks to them again. The birthing-women leave the royal audience unscathed, in spite of their disobedience. More than that, they leave with divine favor. At some point in their future the birthing-women become matriarchs, heads of their own households (Exod. 1:21). The divine largesse is noteworthy for at least two additional reasons: (1) there is no mention of men in their lives, even if they are married; they, not husbands or other men, will be the heads of their households; (2) the promise of a house—or better, a dynasty—is the same one God gives to David in 2 Samuel 7:11. However, Shiphrah's and Puah's resistance appears to be in vain; the pharaoh orders the deaths of all Hebrew baby boys. This time, the pharaoh does not trust the women to do his dirty work; he commands his own people to become his genocidal agents.

The liberation of the Israelite people in Egypt begins with Shiphrah and Puah. They are the mothers of a revolution waged by women. They likely enlisted untold numbers of birthing-women and expectant mothers in their resistance movement. It is not clear whether they deliver Moshe (Moses), Aharon (Aaron), and/or Miryam (Miriam). In any case their act of resistance sets the stage for those to follow. Shiphrah and Puah become the first deliverers in the book of deliverance.

YOCHEVED (JOCHEBED)

> Exodus 6:20 Amram married Yocheved (Jochebed) his father's sister and she gave birth to Aharon (Aaron) and Moshe (Moses), and the length of Amram's life was one hundred thirty-seven years.

> Numbers 26:59 The name of Amram's woman was Yocheved (Jochebed) bat Levi, who was born to Levi in Egypt; and she gave birth to Aharon (Aaron), Moshe (Moses), and their sister Miriam for Amram.

Yocheved (Jochebed), the mother of Moshe (Moses) is not named when her story is first told; neither is Amram, Moses' father. She is first named in Exodus 6:20 but has a more complete introduction in Numbers 26:59. Her name bears a trace of the Divine Name. The "Yo" is derived from the "Y" in YHWH. Her name means something like the honor (or weightiness) of YHWH. Her naming further deepens the mystery of why Moses did not know the Divine Name. Jochebed is *bat Levi*, a daughter of the tribe of Levi. In Exodus 6:20, she is the paternal aunt of her spouse, Amram. The term *dodah*, aunt, is used for wife of the father's brother in Leviticus 18:14 and 20:20 and here is taken to mean father's sister.[2]

According to the MT, SP, and dominant Targumim, Jochebed is the daughter of Levi the patriarch himself, literally *bat Levi*, and not just a woman among his descendants. Amram's father is Kohath (Exod. 6:18), so Jochebed is the sister of Kohath and of Gershon and Merari, their brothers. Numbers 26:59 affirms this reading, stipulating that she was born to Levi in Egypt. Given that Jochebed was born in Egypt, she may well have been significantly younger than her brothers, and she and Amram may have been age mates. In any case, Sarah's descendants have returned to their incestuous roots. The narrative says nothing about Jochebed's mother, Moses' grandmother, and whether she or Jochebed consented to this union.

Being born in Egypt, Jochebed did not experience the famine in Canaan and immigration to Egypt or witness the dramatic family reunion with Joseph. She may have lived through the death of the pharaoh her elders knew and the ascension of the pharaoh whom they did not know. She would have watched the material circumstances of her people change from abundance, to sufficiency, to lack. She would have lived through the edicts restricting and oppressing her people until the pharaoh happened upon his final solution. I see Jochebed prefiguring European Holocaust victims, watching the governments and people they knew turn into monsters whom they no longer knew or even recognized. In response, Jochebed became an agent of resistance: the very decision to give birth was an act of defiance. At some point Jochebed gave birth to a daughter, Miryam (Miriam), who would become her partner in resistance. It is not clear whether Miriam was born under the genocidal edict of the pharaoh. It is clear that by the time of her next pregnancy, Jochebed was aware of the imperial prohibition of keeping and raising male Hebrew children.

2. These are the only occurrences of the word in the Hebrew Scriptures. The primary manuscript from which the Hebrew Scriptures are translated, the Masoretic Text (MT), dates from only 1008 CE, so it is common to compare it to other ancient manuscript traditions. Parallel versions of the Scriptures in Aramaic, Targumim *Onqelos* and *Pseudo-Jonathan*, and the Torah of Samaritan Judaism, the Samaritan Pentateuch (SP), preserve the identification of Jochebed as her husband's aunt. In the *Pseudo-Jonathan* Targum she is the aunt of Amram using a different word, *chevyah*. In the LXX and another Aramaic text, *Targum Neofiti*, she is the daughter of her husband's brother, making her the cousin and not the aunt of her spouse.

The text does not specify the age differences between Jochebed's children, but the narrative presents the as-yet-unnamed Miriam as old enough to negotiate on her mother's behalf in Moses' infancy, in Exodus 2:8 calling her an 'almah—a girl of marriageable age, suggesting an age difference of at least a decade, if not more. Aaron is not mentioned in the initial narrative; however, Exodus 7:7 will make him three years older than Moses. Aaron was likely born before the genocidal edict. The text presents the decision to keep and hide the baby Moses as Jochebed's alone (Exod. 2:1–3). Amram is neither named nor consulted. Jochebed imitates God: God sees that each stage of creation is "good," *tov*; and Jochebed sees that the child she brings forth is also good, invoking the same word, *tov*, preserved in the IB translation.[3] Jochebed certainly hides Moses from the Egyptians, but does she also have to hide him from her own people? Are there informants among her people? Perhaps there are women who have lost or even killed their baby boys, who cannot bear to see anyone else keep hers. Does Jochebed hide Moses from Amran? That seems unlikely, yet the passage presents only women in relationship to the baby Moses: first Jochebed and Miriam, then *bat pharaoh*, the princess, and her women servants.

When the baby is three months old, and perhaps beginning to roll over, Jochebed knows she cannot hide him once he starts crawling, so she conceives an ingenious and desperate plan. Perhaps, just perhaps she has heard the midrash of another mother long ago who trusted her son, Sargon, twenty-third century BCE, to the waters of her river in a pitched reed basket.[4] Jochebed's last act in the Scripture is to secure a place as her son's wet nurse. How long did she nurse him? Did she tell him that she was his mother? If so, when? What lullabies did she sing him? What stories did she tell him? Did she ever tell his foster mother who she was? Foreshadowing the story of Hannah and Samuel centuries later, Jochebed nurses her son and then sends him away to be raised by someone else.

At some point, Moses learns who he is; by Exodus 2:11 he is an adult and knows that he is a Hebrew. I will suggest that Jochebed is responsible for his self-knowledge. Using my sanctified imagination, I see Jochebed talking

3. Other translations disrupt this symmetry; Moses is "fine" in the NRSV, "beautiful" in the JPS and GSJPS, and "goodly" in Fox.

4. Sargon was the legendary king and empire builder after whom subsequent kings of Assyria named themselves, including the Sargon who occurs in the Hebrew Bible (Isa. 20:1). The legend of the ancient Sargon's birth was preserved in cuneiform and is widely available, e.g., in Don C. Benjamin and Victor H. Matthews, *Old Testament Parallels: Laws and Stories from the Ancient Near East*, 4th ed. (Mahwah, NJ: Paulist Press, 2016), 89.

to her son, singing to her son with the full knowledge of the princess, her partner in the deception they perpetrated against the pharaoh and his edict. I imagine that she nurses him for as long as she can, five or six years. I imagine that Moses maintains his relationship with his birth mother with the full knowledge of the princess, his foster mother and his other-mother. As a result of his contact with his mother and sister, Moses is also able to maintain relationships with his father and brother.

Jochebed's experience, trying to maintain family unity as a slave woman— albeit one with a beneficent mistress—is comparable to the experiences of enslaved African women in the American South, regularly separated from spouses and children, even if they labored on the same plantation. Indeed, the experience of Moses having more than one mother has ongoing corollaries in many African diasporic contexts, where mothering is not limited to women who give birth. Many black churches in the Americas celebrate birth mothers, adoptive mothers, foster mothers, heart-mothers, other-mothers, and single fathers on Mother's Day.

Exodus 6:20 states that Moses' father lives for one hundred thirty-seven years. Yet he disappears from the narrative, while Jochebed decides to keep and hide their son and to stay in his life while continuing to nurse him. The reader/hearer can only wonder if Amram had any further contact with his son. There is no family reunion scene in the Scriptures. While the exodus narrative in Exodus and Numbers mentions both Miriam and Aaron, neither of Moses' parents is ever mentioned again. It is unimaginable that they were left behind in Egypt. It is likely that the reader/hearer is to understand that in spite of the great length of Amram's life, he and Jochebed have died by the time Miriam and Moses lead their people to freedom.

I see Jochebed in Moses, specifically in his character as he is subsequently portrayed in the biblical text: I see Jochebed in Moses' love for his people in Exodus 2:11ff., in his inability to watch as his people are injured (even by one another [Exod. 2:13]), in his pursuit of justice—even if he has to take matters into his own hands. That Moses does not identify himself with the empire and claim imperial privilege for himself—intentionally passing as an Egyptian—is for me fruit of Jochebed's life and nurture of her son. I see Jochebed in her son in his initial dealings with the woman who would become his and with her sisters, when he risks his life and freedom to help them in Exodus 2:15ff. Moses is a wanted man, yet when he sees some men taking advantage of women, he goes to their defense. He does not know them and has no expectation of a reward. He endangers himself by involving himself in their affair. They could turn him in. He risks discovery because helping those who are unjustly oppressed is the right thing to do. I believe Moses learned that from his mother, Jochebed.

MIRYAM (MIRIAM)

Exodus 15:20 And the prophet Miryam (Miriam), Aharon's (Aaron's) sister, took a hand-drum[5] in her hand; and all the women went out after her with hand-drums and with dances. [21]And Miryam (Miriam) sang to them all:
"Sing to the HOLY ONE, for he has triumphed gloriously; horse and rider he has thrown into the sea."

Micah 6:3 I brought you up from the land of Egypt, and from the house of slavery I redeemed you; and I sent before you Moshe (Moses), Aharon (Aaron), and Miryam (Miriam).

I start with verses from Exodus and Micah to demonstrate Miriam's prominence among her people some five hundred years after the time in which the story of her life is set.[6] The prophet Miriam has spawned much exegetical and interpretive scholarship, from rabbinic literature to contemporary biblical scholarship.[7] Miriam is one of two girl children who has an active narrative during her childhood in the Scriptures: The other, an unnamed slave girl in 2 Kings 5:2–4, appears and disappears within three verses and lacks the pedigree of Miriam bat Yocheved[8] bat Levi.

Miriam is the mother of the women prophets in the Hebrew Scriptures. She is the first woman in the canon identified as a prophet. She is named in more biblical books than any other woman, including Eve, Sarah, and Rebekah. Miriam appears in Exodus, Numbers, Deuteronomy, Chronicles,

---

Exodus's Two Prophets

Exodus knows only of two prophets: Aaron, whom God calls Moses' prophet in Exodus 7:1, and Miriam. Aaron does not hear from or speak on behalf of God. Moses hears from and speaks on behalf of God, but he is not described as a prophet until Numbers 12:6–8, nor given the title until Deuteronomy 18:15. As a result, Miriam is in many regards the only prophet acknowledged in Exodus.

---

5. Though regularly mistranslated as a "timbrel" or "tambourine," a *toph* is hand-held drum; see the note in GSJPS.

6. Though there is no historical evidence to corroborate it, a late date for Exodus is 1250 BCE; Micah dates to the mid-seventh century.

7. See Wilda C. Gafney, *Daughters of Miriam: Women Prophets in Ancient Israel* (Minneapolis: Fortress Press, 2008).

8. I am intentionally naming her matrilineally, calling her by her mother's name in the traditional formula.

and Micah. Her name became the most common woman's name in the world that produced the Christian New Testament: all of the Marys in the NT—six or seven, depending on how one counts—are Miriams. Likewise there are any number of Miriams in the rabbinic literature. In the Midrash there is Miriam bat Boethus, Miriam bat Nakdimon, and Miriam bat Tanhum (all in *Eicha Rabbah* 1:47–50); and in the Talmud there is Miriam bat Bilgah (*b. Sukkah* 56b) and Imma (Mother) Miriam, whose son Abba (Father) Saul made a number of rabbinic rulings in *b. Ketubbot* 87a–88b (he is identified only by her name; his father is never identified, suggesting that she is his most prominent ancestor). There is also a Maryam in the Qur'an; an entire *sura* (chapter) is devoted to her.[9]

Miriam's name has two meanings. In Hebrew it means "bitter-water-woman"; in Egyptian it means "beloved" (see *HALOT*). Miriam was undoubtedly the beloved of her family, her people, and her God, and she tasted the bitter waters of slavery. In addition, she is known in rabbinic tradition for providing water for her people (*b. Ta'anit* 9a), based on the narrative of her death, in which there ceases to be water for the people as soon as she dies (see Num. 21:1–2).

Miriam and Aaron are Moses' older siblings. Aaron is three years older than Moses according to Exodus 7:7, making him too young to have negotiated his brother's placement in the royal household. I read Miriam as the oldest because she was the one who negotiated with the Egyptian princess on her mother's behalf. Miriam (like her mother Jochebed) is not named when she first appears in the Scriptures, perhaps because she and her family are so well known and their names are all supplied elsewhere. There are very few biblical families in which the names of both parents and all of the children are preserved.

It is likely that Miriam went with her mother into royal service (see previous entry on Yocheved/Jochebed). Also, she may have helped to care for her younger brothers, splitting her time between her parents. I find it unlikely that Amram accompanied Jochebed into the pharaoh's household; female childcare providers are not typically accompanied by a male spouse. My sanctified imagination finds Miriam exposed to Egyptian culture, as the child of a slave in service to the princess and a slave herself, behind the scenes. Perhaps

9. Sura 19, titled "Mary," has ninety-eight *ayat* (verses) devoted to Maryam (Mary) the mother of Issa (Jesus); however, in 19:28, Maryam is described as "the sister of Haron (Aaron)" just as Miriam is in Exod. 15:20. It appears the two Miriams/Marys/Maryams have been confused. However, normative religious readings of the Qur'an do not allow for that possibility. Standard Quranic exegesis holds that "sister of" here means "descended of." See Seyyed Hossein Nasr et al., *The Study Quran: A New Translation with Notes and Commentary* (SanFrancisco: HarperOne, 2015), 771.

her place in or association with the pharaoh's household protected her from the predation that so commonly befalls girls and women in service to others, particularly among the enslaved. Miriam would have been fully aware of the harsh realities of the slavery she and her people endured, in spite of her perspective—through the bars of a gilded cage.

Miriam's maturation into womanhood is missing from the Scriptures. She is a child, and then she is an elder woman. In Exodus 7:7, Moses is eighty and Aaron is eighty-three when they first enter divine service to demand the release of their people. By any calculation Miriam is at least eighty-five and more likely closer to ninety when she leads her people across the Reed (Red) Sea to freedom from slavery. As a girl and later as a woman, Miriam had few real choices in her life, circumscribed as it was by the enslavement of her people. One choice that she seems to have exercised was not to marry, not to give birth, not to offer to the Egyptian empire any children of her body, her womb.

Given the near ubiquity of conjugal partnering in the text, I read the lack of a partner for Miriam as an intentional choice on her part.[10] Miriam's lack of a partner has proved quite vexing for some of her rabbinic interpreters. The rabbis devote no small amount of ink to marrying Miriam off to any number of biblical worthies, most notably Caleb and his brother, in order to trace David to and through her (see *Shemoth Rabbah* 48:4).

The text confines Miriam's prophetic gift to the Nile River crossing in Exodus 15. Moses does not come into his gifts until just before he approaches the pharaoh; there is no indication when Miriam begins her prophethood, nor any reason to limit it to her senior years. The rabbinic literature, for example, *b. Sotah* 11b–12a, suggests Miriam's prophesying began as a child, In my own midrashic reading, while Moses was in hiding, building a new life with no intent of his own of returning to his people and no inkling that God would call him and send him back, Miriam was the people's prophet, their only prophet. Whether Moses was twenty or even thirty when he fled, decades passed before his return to the pharaoh's court. In my sanctified imagination, I see Miriam as the pastor for her people in Egyptian slavery. Her preaching and teaching reminded them that God was real and did hear their prayers; no matter how many generations it would take, God would deliver them.

---

10. Prophets as a class form a significant exception. (Deborah's title, *eshet lappidoth*, means "woman of flames" or "fiery woman" and not "woman/wife" of Lappidoth.) Marriage is rare among prophets. Only Huldah among women prophets is married. Of those to whom books are attributed, only Hosea is married—if the Gomer story is not an elaborate metaphor; Ezekiel is widowed. It may be not just that their spouses are not mentioned in the canon. Progeny and descendants are important markers of success and God's faithfulness, yet with the exception of Moses and Samuel there are no descendants of prophets in the Bible's many genealogies.

Freedom came just as she prophesied. Exodus 14 tells the narrative of the exodus event in prose, describing Moses holding open and then closing the waters of the Reed Sea by extending and retracting his arms. Exodus 15 tells the story of the moment of liberation through song, one of the oldest in the canon, placed in Moses' mouth at the beginning of the chapter in its current form and in Miriam's at the end. Within that chapter is what may be an even older version of the story, Exodus 15:20–21. It is widely understood by scholars that the Song of the Sea (as it is called) is actually Miriam's. In this reading, Miriam sings the whole song, referenced by its initial verse, and she leads the people through the waters while Moses stands holding the waters open, with the Mosaic ascription a later interpolation.[11]

Additionally, the song represents the first liturgy of liberation. Miriam, followed by the women, directs the whole assembly in verse 21: "And she answered them." Miriam sings a call-and-response song, which would later become a staple of the Psalter and African-derived worship. In answering "them" (lahem, common plural), Miriam commands the community to "sing to God-Whose-Name-Is-Too-Holy-to-Be-Uttered." Miriam's command, "Sing!" is common plural, shiyru; Miriam's ministry is to all the redeemed, not just the women, as some have claimed. However since the common plural can function as a masculine plural, Miriam's instructions could have been for the men. The women were already following her dancing and drumming and required no instruction to join the song of liberation.

Miriam is unnamed and unmentioned in the wilderness wandering that concludes the book of Exodus, pauses in the book of Leviticus, and continues in the book of Numbers until chapter 12. Yet she was present. Miriam was present for the struggle to feed and water the people. In rabbinic tradition Miriam provided water for the people through the supernatural well provided to her by God; when she died, they lost the well along with her. Miriam was present for the gifts and challenges of quail and manna. She was there when the people complained and grumbled and when they fell prey to hostilities.[12]

Miriam was there when Moses' father-in-law brought his woman, Zipporah, and their children to him in Exodus 18:1–3, after he had sent her away, apparently divorcing her in 18:2. When Yitro (Jethro) advised Moses on setting up a legal system, she was there. How did Miriam's prophethood figure into their plans? Miriam was there when God descended to God's people

---

11. Verse 21 begins with "and," not "then" as in the NRSV; it may well have been moved around in the narrative.

12. Exod. 16:2 says that the people grumbled against Moses and Aaron but does not mention them grumbling against Miriam.

veiled in smoke and fire. Was she on the mountain when God wrote the Ten Commandments? Did she remain with the people when Moses went up on the mountain of God? Did the men who made the golden calf break Miriam's earrings off when they ripped them from the other women in Exodus 32:2? Miriam was with her people when they constructed a fabric canopy under the heavenly canopy for their God to inhabit. Miriam returns to the story in Numbers. To be continued . . .

A PHARAONIC PRINCESS

Exodus 2:10 When the child grew up, Miryam (Miriam) brought him to the pharaoh's daughter, and he became her son. She named him Moshe (Moses), saying, "For from the water *meshitihu*, I-drew-him."

One curiosity of the biblical narrative is the intentional anonymity of the Egyptian princess who rescued, named, and raised Moses and that of her father, the pharaoh of the exodus. It is as though the authors do not want to identify the specific regime. This may have something to do with the lack of extratextual support for the exodus narrative. In some traditions she is conflated with another Egyptian princess, named Bithia in 1 Chronicles 4:17, who becomes the mother of the first recoded namesake of the prophet Miriam in the canon. I treat them separately.

In this volume I call the princess who nurtures Moses Sheshan (the Egyptian word for lotus); she appears only in Exodus 2:5–10. The story does not tell us how old she is, if she is married or single, if she has other children or is infertile, if she has siblings, or if she was the firstborn of the pharaoh struck down in the plague. Her entrance and immediate exit from the text leave many questions: What was her relationship with her father like? Did he know that she was fostering a Hebrew child? Did she publicly differ with her father on his treatment of the Hebrew women, men, and their children? Was she a beloved and indulged daughter? Or was she one of so many children by so many women that he could not keep them straight?

I read Sheshan as an ally of the Hebrew people. In contemporary antioppression work and discourse, an ally is a person who uses his or her privilege to work for justice on behalf of oppressed people. There are white allies who use their white privilege to combat racism. There are male allies of feminists and womanists who use their male privilege to combat sexism. There are heterosexual allies who work with and on behalf of non-gender-complying people and sexual minorities to combat bias against those minoritized for their orientation, gender identity, or expression. The drash I offer constructs her as an ally who works to bring Moses into the world of her privilege. Note that she doesn't work to dismantle that privilege. Allyship has its limits.

> *Sheshan was the flower of Egypt. Her father thought her too sentimental and overly attached to their slaves. He thought she would grow out of it. He turned a blind eye to the way she ran the small household that he permitted her. What did a few dignities afforded to a few slaves matter in the long run? He had more slaves than he needed, and it was time to thin the herd.*
>
> *Sheshan was appalled at her father's policies. She thought that if he could see the Hebrew people as people he could never sanction the wholesale slaughter of their babies. Sheshan sought to prove to her father that a Hebrew was just as good as an Egyptian. She would show him by giving the right education, clothes, cultural training and values to a Hebrew child, taking him as her son and her father's grandson. Sheshan's plan was doomed to fail. No matter how well integrated and assimilated Moshe was, he and his people would always be "other" in her father's eyes. Nonetheless, Sheshan and Yocheved conspired to give Moshe a rich bicultural formation in both heritages, believing that his access to privilege could one day be used in service to his people. Who knew, perhaps Moshe might one day ascend the double throne of Upper and Lower Egypt and free his people.*

CONSECRATED FIRSTBORN DAUGHTERS

Exodus 13:1 The HOLY ONE OF OLD said to Moshe (Moses), [2]Sanctify to me every firstborn child; all that are the first to open the womb among the Israelites, female or male, of human beings and animals, are mine.

The firstborn daughters and sons of Israel are equally sacred to God in this text. In Exodus 13, *every* human and *every* animal that is firstborn within Israel is sacred to the God of Israel. The passage does not allow for distinctions along gender lines; *kol* means "all," "each," and/or "every," denoting every firstborn human and each firstborn animal, all the firstborn of any sort. The text does not discuss the mechanism or ritual of sanctification or its significance beyond birth order. However, the commandment to "sanctify," "consecrate," or "make-holy" (*qadesh*) does occur repeatedly in the canon, and its use, particularly in Exodus, offers some understanding of what is meant here.

In Exodus 19 God commands the women and men of Israel to sanctify themselves two days in a row, before God appears in their midst on the third day. Because the divine instructions also include washing their clothes in the same verse (Exod. 19:10), many interpreters understand that washing one's self is the first act of sanctification. In the same account in verse 15 Moses adds that the Israelite men should segregate themselves from their women, either completely or just to refrain from sexual activity. However, this is an addition to the command of God in the narrative and not a part of the requisite sanctification.

In other places in Exodus, sanctification occurs through other, ritual means: Aaron's vestments sanctify him (Exod. 28:3, 41; 40:14); anointing with oil sanctifies a bull for sacrifice (Exod. 29:36); God sanctifies Aaron and his sons and the desert sanctuary by manifesting the divine glory in their presence (Exod. 29:44); and Aaron and his sons are sanctified through anointing with oil (Exod. 30:30; 40:13). Following the logic of these texts, the sanctification of the newborn firstborn daughters and sons of Israel would have included at a minimum washing and anointing with oil. It is not clear whether any words were spoken as part of the anointing ritual. On one level, sanctification is hygienic; on another, it is dedicatory. The two are intertwined and inseparable.

In my reading, the midwives who delivered the babies would have performed the ritual of sanctification, in part or whole. Washing of the newborn is a long-attested practice of midwifery, as is anointing with oil. Other possibilities are that the mother or a religious functionary performed the anointing. It does not appear that men attended Israelite births in any form; so it is less likely that the father or a priest or Levite performed the anointing.

There were women in Levitical and priestly families—the daughters and wives of male Levites—who were obligated to preserve their cultic and social status by avoiding specific taboos and who were entitled to eat sacred meals along with their menfolk.[13] I have often wondered if there was a specific ritual function fulfilled by these women. Among the ritual tasks I find most likely are facilitating ritual baths for women; consulting on other women's issues, like those associated with birth and bleeding; examining women's bodies for evidence of skin disease; and, in this text, anointing the firstborn. If the anointing was part of the ritual of birthing, the women of priestly and/or Levitical families may have performed it.

The initial presentation of the sanctification of the firstborn in Exodus 13:1–2 clearly includes daughters, through the repeated use of *kol*, "all." Later in the chapter the consecration of the firstborn is elaborated upon, first acknowledging the sanctity of them all, but eventually seeming to narrow the focus to firstborn males:

---

13. See Lev. 22:12–13; I will discuss them more fully in the chapter on Leviticus.

Exodus 13:11 "And it will be that the FIRE OF SINAI will bring you into the land of the Canaanite women and men and their children, as God swore to you and to your ancestors, and will give it to you. [12]You shall pass over to the HOLY ONE OF OLD whatever is the first to open the womb, female or male. All the firstborn of your animal holdings that are males shall be the Holy One's. [13]But every firstborn donkey you shall ransom with a sheep-or-goat; if you do not ransom it, you must break its neck. Every firstborn person among your children you shall ransom. [14]And it shall be that when one morrow your child asks you, 'What is this?' you shall say, 'By strength of hand the GOD OF OUR SALVATION brought us out of Egypt, from the house of slavery. [15]When Pharaoh was hardened refusing to let us go, the GOD OF ALL FLESH killed all the firstborn in the land of Egypt, from human firstborn to the firstborn of animals. Therefore I sacrifice to the GOD OF ALL every male that first opens the womb, but every firstborn of my children I ransom.'"

This attempted clarification in the passage leaves more questions than it answers. One question is whether this passage really includes girl-children as I insist. There is a long-standing practice in Judaism of *pidyon ha-ben*, "redemption of the firstborn son," based in part on this verse and its subsequent interpretive history. In order to read Exodus 13:13 as pertaining only to males as do NRSV, JPS, GSJPS, and Fox, one has to disregard the use of *kol* ("all," "each," and/or "every") in verses 1 and 12, and one has to translate *kol bekor adam* as "every firstborn male" rather than as "every firstborn human-person." This is a long-standing traditional Jewish interpretation, based in part on seeing parallelism between *hazakariym*, "the males," applied to animals in verses 12 and 15 and *adam*, "human," in the latter portion of verse 15. However, *adam* without the definite article ("the") means "human," "humankind," "person," generic and collective. In the Torah and in the bulk of the Scriptures, *adam* is simply not used for "male" or "man."[14] The use of *ben* as "child" of either gender in verse 14 is in keeping with its customary usage (whether singular *ben* or plural *baniym*): "child" or "children," of either or both genders. For example, see Jeremiah 15:20, in which *ben* is modified by *gibor* to specify "man-child." I and the translators of the IB prefer the gender-inclusive "children" in Exodus 13:15.

A second question is what it means that the firstborn, animal and human, belong to God. It appears that God claims the firstborn animals through death. Verse 13 makes it clear that nonransomed donkeys must be killed (sanctified) by having their necks broken. Ransomed donkeys are sanctified through the sacrifice of their ransom, a sheep or goat sacrificed in their place.

14. The sole exception is Eccl. 7:28, which is a much later text than Exodus, significantly postdating the production of the Torah and formation of the bulk of the canon.

Seh, used in this passage, like *tzo'n* used elsewhere, means either sheep or goat. The verb *p-d-h* is rendered "redemption" in the NRSV, JPS, GSJPS, IB, and Fox translations; however, "ransom" is the primary meaning of *p-d-h*. Both BDB and *HALOT* reserve "redeem" to translate *go'el*.

The occasion of being firstborn is worthy of and bestows the obligation to sacrifice, even if the animal itself is not sacrificed. The text does not say, but implies, that firstborn sheep and goats are sacrificed as part of their own ritual of sanctification; hence the need to make arrangements for donkeys, which could not be legitimately sacrificed, but which were still required to be sanctified when firstborn. When the firstborn donkeys are killed, they are not killed like sacrificial animals, having their throats slit and having their blood drained; instead, their necks are broken. In the text, the killing of the firstborn donkeys is linked to the sacrifice of the herd animals as a ransom for a firstborn donkey. Sanctification of the firstborn calls for a death, at least as it pertains to animals.

The killing of firstborn animals, whether through ransom or on their own accord in a ritual of sanctification demonstrating divine ownership of all of the firstborn, raises the question of human sacrifice. While this passage does not call for human sacrifice, it seems to point to an ancient understanding that required sacrifice of the firstborn and developed the ransom system as an alternative. The Exodus 13 passage does not say with what firstborn children are to be ransomed; the narrative is repeated and condensed in Exodus 34:19–20, reiterating that all the firstborn, animal and human—and therefore girls and boys—are God's, that donkeys must be redeemed with a herd animal, and that Israelite children must be redeemed through unarticulated means. Between these two passages, Exodus 22:29–30 says in part, ". . . the firstborn of your children you shall give to Me. You shall do the same with your oxen and with your sheep." Males are not specified for humans or animals, long-standing traditional translation practices notwithstanding.

Numbers 18:15 will eventually specify five shekels as the means for human redemption. Exodus as a literary unit remains mysteriously silent on the matter. It may be that the ransom ritual and requirements were so well known that there was no need to record them in the text. The text is also silent on whether firstborn status brings with it any religious or cultural status, apart from the general practice of birth-order hierarchy and decided preference for and bias toward males.

These texts recover a brief moment of equanimity between girls and boys at the moment of their birth. This rare instance of equal standing in the sight of God in a religious context between girls and boys may (or may not) extend to women and men. While contemporary readers/hearers may not want to revisit a practice that conveys even a modest amount of privilege on one child in a family above all who follow, the washing and anointing rituals have been incorporated in whole or in part in a number of welcome rituals for children, from baptism to adoption, in some forms of Christianity and Judaism.

WOMEN IN THE COMMANDMENTS

> Exodus 20:12 Honor your mother and your father, so that your days may be long in the land that the HOLY ONE your God is giving you. . . . [17]You shall not covet your neighbor's house; you shall not covet your neighbor's woman, or female slave or male slave, or ox, or donkey, or anything that belongs to your neighbor.

As part of the Israelite community, women are included in the commandments given. Sometimes they are explicitly mentioned, as in the commandments above; other times women are implicitly mentioned, as in Exodus 20:14, "You shall not commit adultery." The divine address in the communal material is second-person masculine singular. While "you" has neither gender nor number in English, it is clear in Hebrew that the commandments are addressed to a singular male subject. Contextually, that subject is an individual, adult, free male, presumed to hold slaves.

Regardless of whether a specific commandment uses inclusive language, the command was applicable to women. For example, "You, *sir*, shall not steal" (my use of "sir" here makes visible the gender and number specificity of the pronominal grammar) does not mean that *you, madam, may steal*. Religious communities have decided for themselves which of these commandments addressed to an individual male subject apply to all persons, for example, not bearing false witness, and which, if any, pertain only to male citizens.

Women are woven in and out of the Ten Commandments in Exodus 20. They are hidden in the reminder that God delivered the Israelites from slavery in verse 2. The commands to have no other gods and not to misuse the Divine Name in verses 3–7 are addressed to the singular male subject, but surely apply to women, whether free or enslaved, as they do to men in bondage. Free women, enslaved women and men, livestock, and foreign residents are included in the Sabbath commandment in verse 10. Mother and father are to be honored in verse 12. The single male subject (and by implication women as well) shall not steal (v. 13), commit adultery (v. 14), kill (v. 15), or bear false witness (v. 16). The woman who commits adultery is not addressed specifically until Leviticus 20:10; they both, she and he, are to be stoned for their transgression.

In Exodus 20:18, all the people of Israel, woman and man, child and adult, enslaved and free, citizen and alien, behold the living God veiled in smoke, attended by lightning and thunder; no amount of androcentric, gender-exclusive language can change that. The mass theophany is unparalleled in the Scriptures. Moses will proceed even further, granted intimate audience in verse 21.[15] That the women and their community saw God shrouded does not invalidate their witness any more than it does the many men credited with seeing the Divine.

In Exodus 18:12, Jethro officiates a sacred meal in which Moses, Aaron, and all the elders of the people eat in the divine Presence. Later, in Exodus 24:9–11, Moses, Aaron, his sons Nadav (Nadab) and Avihu (Abihu), and seventy elders share another sacred meal during which they see God. It is not clear whether the seventy elders are women and men together. It is clear that "elders" is a broadly inclusive term, as is every other collective throughout the Scriptures, and could include women. The theophanies of women are few and far between. Hagar sees God in Genesis 16, but none of the first mothers of Israel do so. Miriam sees God in the conversation about Moses' prophetic status and hers in Numbers 12. On the day that the Torah was given on Sinai, all the people saw God for themselves.

The theophanies of men from Elijah to Ezekiel portray the Divine in their experience—no matter how fantastical—as gendered (whether biologically or linguistically) and as corresponding to their own culturally dominant male gender. Using my womanist sanctified imagination, I can imagine some of what the women saw when they saw God. Perhaps women saw the God in whose image they were created in their shared, feminine image. I imagine that they did not all see the same thing. The Scriptures contain such rich feminine imagery for God, some of which perhaps stems from this great epiphany.

As the daughters of Israel gazed upon God on the mountain, they saw smoke and fire. Within the flames and of the flames some saw great wings fluttering over the people, spreading over them her shelter of peace. Others saw an everlasting rock, She-Who-Gave-Birth and to whom her children cling as a sure defense in the time of trouble. Yet others saw a Tree of Life stretching out her branches over all the earth, feeding her children from the sacred fruit of her body. Some heard thunder and some heard birdsong. Some saw lightning and some saw rainbows. Some saw a robe of many colors, others blinding white, yet others deepest midnight spangled with the stars of heaven. Some felt the earth move and others felt the winds blow. And all of them saw God. Yet none of their descriptions alone, nor all of them together, were sufficient to convey the majesty of the FIRE OF SINAI.

15. Chapter and verse numbers often differ in Hebrew and English because they were inserted separately. In this unit the MT numbers the section from vv. 15–18.

DAUGHTER FOR SALE

Exodus 21:7 When a man sells his daughter as a slave, she shall not go out as the male slaves go out. [8]If she is unacceptable in the sight of her lord, who designated her for himself, then he shall let her be ransomed; he shall not sell her to a foreign people—he does not have the authority to do so because of his treachery against her. [9]If he designates her for his son, he shall treat her justly as a daughter. [10]If he takes another woman for himself, he shall not diminish the food, clothing, or intercourse of the first woman. [11]And if he does not do these three things to her, she shall go out for nothing—no money.

In the Bible slavery is an all-encompassing construct that includes Israelite slaves and Egyptian slave owners, Canaanite slaves and Israelite slave owners, and Israelite slaves and Israelite slave owners, in addition to non-Israelites enslaved by other non-Israelites. The import and impact of biblical slavery on womanist thought cannot be overstated (see "Special Section: The Torah of Enslaved Women" in chapter 1, page 72).

God-talk: What We Call God Matters

The divine title "Lord," *adonai*, is the plural possessive (literally "my lords") of *adon*, lord. And since "lord" is a substitute for the four sacred letters of the Divine Name that cannot be pronounced, it is not actually God's name. "Lord" is also a male honorific and is applied to human men in the Hebrew Bible several hundred times. In Exodus 21:8 the slave owner who decides the fate of female slaves based on whether or not they please him sexually is called "her lord." As a woman and as a feminist woman, I have great difficulty extending the title of the male slaveholder to the deity, particularly when the slaveholder's authority extends to sexual use of enslaved girls and women. I follow longstanding rabbinic practice and substitute language drawn from the wider biblical tradition for the Tetragrammaton.

3

Leviticus: The Heart of the Torah

Leviticus is the heart of the Torah. It is the center book in the collection, occasioned by a pause in the exodus journey begun in Exodus and concluded in Numbers. It is a text that strikes fear in the hearts of many of my seminarians and experienced preachers and teachers; yet it is simply (and not so simply) a text about how to live in relationship: how to live in relationship to God and how to live in relationship to others in the community. It is in the communities of Israel and their neighbors that people occur in Leviticus.

There are very few individual characters named in Leviticus; more than half of the proper nouns refer to God, and Israel makes up a significant portion of the names in Leviticus. There is a handful of individual names: Abihu, Abraham, Aaron, Ithamar, Eleazar, Elzaphan, Dibri, Jacob, Isaac, and Nadad. There is one woman named in the whole of Leviticus: Shelomith bat Dibri in chapter 24. There are some two dozen verses in Leviticus that specifically mention women, many more in which women are included as part of the people of Israel, and a number that deal exclusively with the all-male priesthood.

As a communal, relational text, Leviticus is primarily about boundaries and categories: boundaries between God and humanity, boundaries between human persons, and proper categories for people, animals, food, and behavior. The ritual acts of Leviticus help to maintain proper boundaries and categories and, in so doing, maintain the health of the community and its individuals. Leviticus can also be viewed as a public-health text; many of its provisions are designed to prevent transmission of diseases and other vectors of ill health, including those with cultural, religious, and spiritual significance. Leviticus concerns itself with everything your body squeezes or squirts out, extrudes, expels, leaks, or flakes, with the exception of snot, spittle, urine, feces, and vomit. With this focus Leviticus extends from the health and well-being of a single individual to the health and well-being of the whole people.

Leviticus suggests that good health—physical, spiritual, and societal—starts with the individual and spreads to the community; likewise, the ill health of an individual can affect—literally infect—the community. Here are some public-health policies that can be read from Leviticus: (1) *Hygiene*. Hand washing is one of the simplest defenses people have against infection and disease. The expression "cleanliness is next to godliness" is not found in the Bible, but the authors of Leviticus might well approve. Ritual bathing was as much about physical cleanliness as it was symbolic of other transforma-tions, for example, from diseased to restored, and/or preparatory for a change in status. (2) *Nutrition*. While it is not clear to what degree the Israelite dietary codes are to be understood in terms of contemporary nutrition standards, they function as an individual and community guide to contextually appropri-ate dietary practices, which when properly observed maintain the health of the community. One subtext of the dietary codes is that the food called for was actually accessible to the community. Access to affordable, healthy food within walking distance, along public transportation, is an issue that affects contemporary individual and community health. (3) *Quarantine*. The periods of separation called for by Leviticus to evaluate and diagnose disease, and to monitor its spread or remission, are the most obvious examples the function of Leviticus as a public-health text. (4) *Ethical standards*. The attention Leviti-cus devotes to who is and who is not an appropriate intimate partner adds an ethical dimension to the public-health provisions of Leviticus. Maintenance of societal standards regarding sexual activity, marriage, procreation, and transgressive sexual behaviors is one aspect of the text that includes physical, spiritual, and communal health concerns.

Drawing from the individual and community concerns in Leviticus as a womanist reader, I argue that taking one's health and the health of one's com-munity seriously as a religious obligation also means taking seriously one's own sexual health and the health of one's sexual partners. In this light, these texts can be read as a calling for sexually active persons to determine and monitor their HIV or other sexually transmitted-infection status, share that information with their partners, use condoms as appropriate, and maintain sexual fidelity. Maintaining one's health with regard to other infections such as colds, flu, tuberculosis, staph, and so on may also be read from this text. The importance of health-care providers, treatment, and prescription medi-cation can be read from Leviticus as a public-health text.

The world that Leviticus envisions and creates is a gendered one with a gender-based hierarchy. Specific texts assign space and place to human beings based on gender. It is also a world that sees some human experiences as egalitarian. The issues of bodiliness presented in Leviticus when read as Scripture transcend religious, cultural, and ethnic identity, even though they are expressed in religious, cultural, and ethnic idiom. Leviticus, like the whole of the Torah, addresses itself to an adult, free, Israelite man as representative of the whole community. Israelite women are rarely addressed; the address of non-Israelite resident aliens and enslaved women and men from various backgrounds is rarer still. Part of being human is having a physical body, and this text discusses the implications and consequences of human physicality, female and male, literally from conception to death, possibly passing through various states of disease. In this perspective Leviticus is—in its own (and in spite of its own) religious, cultural, and ethnic idiom—egalitarian. Healthy and natural processes, like lovemaking, affect women and men and their children. Unhealthy, but still natural, processes like disease and death affect women and men and children.

The world that Leviticus envisions, like the Scriptures themselves, is heteronormative. The authors and editors of the biblical corpus produce these texts to support their nation-building and expansion agenda. They require bodies for labor, for (re)settlement and (re)building, for food production, for defense, and for nurturing the hopes of their own imperial dreams. Leviticus, and the broader canon, therefore valorize and prioritize heterosexual unions and reproduction.

With its focus on boundaries and categories and relationships, Leviticus seeks to bring order to a chaotic world. That the world tilts toward chaos was most poignantly expressed in the exile that gave birth to the codification of much of this material; this means that, even for its authors, the prescriptions of Leviticus may have represented an idealized world and not the inhabited world.

WOMEN WHO GIVE BIRTH

Leviticus 12:2 Speak to the women and men of Israel, saying: If a woman is-sown-with-seed and gives birth to a male, she shall be quarantined seven days; as the days of her menstrual separation, she shall be quarantined. . . . ⁵If a female she births, she shall be quarantined two weeks, as the days of her menstrual separation and quarantine; her time of blood restoration shall be sixty-six days.

The issue of blood taboo surrounding menstruation and childbirth, combined with the differing treatment of women who give birth to daughters and women who give birth to sons, is one of the attributes that mark Leviticus in particular and ancient Israel in general as androcentric to some readers and hearers of the text as Scripture, and as patriarchal and misogynistic to others. The traditional language that has been employed in translating this text— "unclean," "purification," and so on—conveys a particular image of women as impure and dirty, if not sinful.

The standard English translations "clean" and "unclean" suggest thesis and antithesis. However, these are two different Hebrew words, from completely different verbal stems: *t-h-r* and *t-m-'*. As English-speaking readers and hearers, we are saddled with "clean" and "unclean," largely because of the history of translation of the Scriptures. The practice of treating these words as polar opposites began with the LXX. From the translation of John Wycliffe in 1382 to the NRSV in 1989, including the first two versions of the JPS translation (1917 and 1962), "clean" and "unclean"—with a variety of spellings—were the standard translations in English-speaking Judaism/s and Christianity/ies. "Defile" is the translation of choice for *t-m-'* in Genesis 34:5 and 13 in the rape of Dinah.

English-language translations of the Bible in the past ten to fifteen years have begun to wrestle with these terms. In his critically acclaimed 1995 translation *Five Books of Moses*, Everett Fox used "ritually-pure" to translate *tahor*, and left *tamei* untranslated.[1] While not a translation, Ilona Rashkow's *Taboo or Not Taboo: Sexuality and Family in the Hebrew Bible* translates these terms similarly to Fox, as "ritually-pure" and "taboo."[2] *The Contemporary Torah: A Gender-Sensitive Adaptation of the Original JPS Translation* uses "pure" and "impure."[3] All these readings stigmatize affected persons and their property; given that some of these people were marginalized before they were stigmatized, this is profoundly negative othering. All of these translations are difficult because of the great number of differing circumstances that are lumped together under the same term: childbirth, potentially contagious disease, and sex with animals are all classified with some form of the root *t-m-'*; yet not all are intentional actions or choices and appropriately guilt- or sin-bearing.

While *tahor* can include cleanliness in the hygienic sense, it is in the broadest sense to be "ritually fit," "prepared-for-participation" in the community and its sacred observances, and after a period of quarantine, "restoration." The lack of fitness or preparation can be remedied by ritual or other means,

1. Everett Fox, *The Five Books of Moses: Genesis, Exodus, Leviticus, Numbers, Deuteronomy; A New Translation with Introductions, Commentary, and Notes* (New York: Schocken Books, 1995).

2. Ilona N. Rashkow, *Taboo or Not Taboo: Sexuality and Family in the Hebrew Bible* (Minneapolis: Fortress Press, 2000).

3. David E. S. Stein, Carol L. Meyers, Adele Berlin, and Ellen Frankel, eds., *The Contemporary Torah: A Gender-Sensitive Adaptation of the Original JPS Translation*, (Philadelphia: Jewish Publication Society, 2006).

including the passage of time, bathing, anointing, fasting, sacrifices, and offerings. Being unready for liturgy is not sinful and often is akin to having not bathed before one goes to worship. *Tamei* can be "taboo," "contagious," and/or "quarantined." The person who is *tamei* is a person who needs to perform a ritual that is relatively simple in most cases, even when the periods of time associated with them are not clearly explained. Only in the most severe cases—an incurable contagious disease—is a person perpetually unable to participate in the life of the community. In most cases, there is a set duration for a person's time apart from the community in the *tamei* category—frequently only until sunset, which marks the beginning of a new day (see Lev. 11:24ff.).

With specific reference to menstruation at the end of Leviticus 12:2, where a form of *tamei*, occurs, John Wycliffe also uses "corrupt"; Tyndale uses "disease"; the 1917 edition of the JPS uses "sickness"; the 1985 edition JPS uses "infirmity"; Fox combines "infirmity" with "remaining-*tamei*"; and the GSJPS refers to menstruation as a "condition." The persons who are subject to this labeling are menstruating girls and women; women who give birth; those with diseases—particularly highly visible, potentially communicable diseases; those with suspect, perhaps defective or deficient possessions and homes; and those who live at the margins of the community. These folk are by turns *tahor* and *tamei*.

The unfortunate association of guilt (the verb *asham*) with *tamei* adds the appearance of an element of wrongdoing to the notion of *tamei*. For example, Leviticus 5:1ff. makes clear that anyone who accidentally touches a dead animal is both *tamei* and *asham; asham* here should be understood as "responsible" because of the accidental nature of the contact. The person is affected by her or his unintentional contact (and becomes *tamei*), for which they become responsible (*asham*) when they realize what has happened. Failure to address their lack of ritual fitness then becomes an issue of sin, which is distinct from "responsibility."

I want to suggest, following the teaching of Rabbi Phyllis Berman, with whom I have studied, that *tahor* and *tamei* represent different kinds of holiness.[4] Rav Berman's teaching resonates with the biblical notion that the holiness of God is so powerful that it is destructive, like radioactivity. If one is too close or improperly clothed or prepared—that is, lacking obscuring layers of smoke and incense—or does not maintain appropriate distance or perform the necessary preparation rituals to come in contact with divine holiness, then one will not survive the encounter. I generally choose variations of the terms "restoration" and "restriction" to translate *tahor* and *tamei* and preserve the

---

4. Rebbe Berman's commentary on *Tazri'a*, this portion of Leviticus, is available in the Torah Commentary section of the Shalom Center's website, theshalomcenter.org.

alliteration; however, in this text I use "quarantine" because of the medical context. A third term, *niddah*, refers to menstruation and is traditionally translated "impurity." In some contexts I use "ritually appropriate." Following the practice of the editors of the GSJPS, briefly annotated in its glossary, I translate *niddah* with "menstrual separation and quarantine" in Leviticus 12:5.

However one understands and translates these terms, there remains in Leviticus 12 a difference between the number of days of a woman's separation from the community after the birth of a boy (seven days for the period of restriction and thirty-three days for the period of restoration) and the number of days after the birth of a girl (fourteen and sixty-six days). This practice may simply reflect cultural biases, although it is not clear how mother, baby, or community benefits from more or less time apart. It is also not clear to what degree the mother and baby are isolated: Are they in the home with the father? Does the midwife monitor the woman for postpartum bleeding? Can other women visit? The practice does function to socially construct gender at birth. A child, along with its mother, is categorized and placed in gender-cued circumstances immediately at birth.

The biblical texts do not allow for the possibility of intersex persons and do not conform to human experience. The rabbis were aware of the varieties of human genital configuration and discuss androgynous persons (*'ndrwgynws*) and persons whose gender is indeterminate (*twmtwm*). The rabbinic approach to ambiguous and indeterminate gender was simply to make a determination in order fit the person into the appropriate gender construct with its requisite behavior.[5]

As a womanist reader/hearer, I see deep, ancient sexist beliefs and practices in and behind this text. The belief that women are "less than" men—less competent, less capable, less intelligent, less capable of contributing meaningfully to society, a lesser reflection of the image of God—finds good support in some parts of the Scriptures. This is one such place. I name it and preserve it as Scripture, teaching that all of our human institutions and productions, including and especially religious ones, are flawed. Sexism is one of those ancient, enduring flaws.

WOMEN WITH A SKIN DISEASE

Leviticus 13:29 When there is a woman or man in whom there is a diseased-spot on the head or in the beard, [30]the priest shall examine

5. See the discussions in Mishnah *Bikkurim* 4 and *b. Yebamoth* 81a, 82b–84a; *Bekoroth* 41a–42b and 57b; and *Shabbat* 134b—137a, as representative of the broader discourse.

the diseased-spot. If it appears deeper than the skin and the hair in it is yellow and thin, the priest shall pronounce her or him restricted; it is scale-disease, a skin-disease of the head or the beard.

As an Afro-diasporic reader in a Euro-centric world that frequently embodies white-supremacist norms, I was delighted as a young reader to discover a text that demonstrated blond was not a normative hair color for the people of Israel. Blond hair can be only a potential indicator for disease in a community in which blondness is uncommon or perhaps unnatural. This was long before I understood the implications of geography; Sinai, Canaan, and subsequently Israel form the land bridge between Africa and Asia; neither continent is known for indigenous blonds.[6] In modernity, blonds signify a particular construction of whiteness as a category that excludes so-called people of color and leads to the intentional exclusion of black and brown girls from dominant-culture beauty standards, even though blond hair naturally occurs in persons of African descent. However, yellow hair bears a different significance in the text. According to Leviticus, the presence of yellow hair is a call for closer inspection to determine whether quarantine and other subsequent procedures are in order to protect the community.

The skin disease of Leviticus 13–14, called *tzara'at*, has generally been translated "leprosy," even though it does not conform to the symptomatology of leprosy, Hansen's disease, as it is currently understood. The biblical disease manifested quickly enough for a seven-day quarantine period to be a useful diagnostic tool (Lev. 13:4, 5, 21, 26, 31, 33); leprosy develops over a much longer period of up to several years. The biblical condition occasionally went into spontaneous remission (Lev. 14:3); however, leprosy cannot be cured without pharmacological treatment. The biblical disease is described as occurring with scaling or flaking of the skin, translated "itching" in the NRSV (Lev. 13:30–37); but it is never described as coincident with the loss of extremities, perhaps the most common and obvious sign of leprosy. Lastly, Leviticus uses the term *tzara'at* to describe some sort of fungal or mold infestation in buildings and garments;[7] the human disease does not infect inanimate objects.

Leviticus 13:38 begins a unit that explicitly includes female subjects, unlike the bulk of the Torah:[8] "When a man or a woman has shiny-spots on the skin of the body." Verses 13:2 and 13:9 use "human person," *adam*, to indicate that this larger discourse applies to women and men, even though the grammatical

---

6. The Modern Hebrew word for blond, *blondindi(t)*, is derived from contemporary English; there was apparently not a need for the word until relatively recently.

7. See Lev. 13:47–59 and 14:34–54.

8. Lev. 13:29 does the same in a discussion of women and men with burned skin.

forms are masculine. In a number of verses from 13:29ff., women and men are specified in conjunction with a masculine singular verb, pronouns, and so on. Whatever this disease (or collection of diseases and other conditions), *tzara'at* affected women and men equally and called forth the same communal response: the spot is examined, and a judgment is made. If the questionable spot is deemed benign, no further action is called for. If the spot is deemed suspicious the afflicted persons are quarantined for a week and then reexamined. There is a second week of quarantine, which may be accompanied by shaving the head and face and perhaps other body parts. A *kohen*, a priest, performs the diagnostic examination. The text is clear that women and men experience the same disease, diagnostic rituals, and treatment program. However, it strikes me as unreasonable that, given Israel's modesty codes, men would examine women's bodies for any reason, including disease or contagion. It is possible to read *kohen* as "person from the priest-clan," which would include women:

> Leviticus 13:2 When a human has on the skin of their flesh a swelling or a scab or a shiny-spot, and it becomes a plague-mark of skin-disease on the skin of their flesh, that one shall be brought to Aharon the priest or one from his descendants, the priest-clan.

Leviticus 13:2 uses *mibanayv hakohaniym* to designate authorized diagnosticians other than Aaron. One possible translation is certainly "from Aaron and his sons, the priests." Only Aaron and his sons are priests. Israel does not have a female priesthood, even though women do serve in other capacities, including at the wilderness sanctuary and temple. However, *banayv* (plural possessive) means more than "his sons"; it can mean "his children," "his descendants," or even "his disciples/apprentices." I believe it likely that the daughter of a priest, a *bat kohen*, examined the suspicious areas on women's bodies and consulted with her father, brother, or husband, perhaps concealed behind a curtain, who made the final determination.

As a daughter of the clan, a *bat kohen* is a Levite and part of the Kohenic community; a Levite's wife might be a *bat kohen*, but that was not a requirement. This is the rabbinic understanding indicated by the word *kohenet*, literally a female *kohen*, meaning here family or clan member, not priestess— though some contemporary Jewish feminists claim the term with a priestly resonance. Subsequent texts (Lev. 21:9; 22:12–13) give behavioral guidelines for a woman who is *bat kohen* to maintain her familial ritual status and privileges, such as eating holy food from the people's sacrifices. Grammatically speaking, the daughters of priests would be included in *mibanayv hakohaniym*, at the end of Leviticus 13:2, therefore the translation "from one of Aaron's descendants" reflects all of the lexical possibilities.

In Leviticus 13:45, in a passage that uses only masculine grammar, the person with a current outbreak of the skin disease must live outside the community until they are restored. The ritual priestly inspection and certification are explained in detail in chapter 14, which uses masculine language exclusively. My womanist midrash provides the ritual of restoration according to Leviticus 14 for a woman previously diagnosed with skin disease, with the understanding that the *kohen* who inspects women is a *bat kohen*. It invites the reader to think about how the ritual may have affected women differently than men, for example, to envision women with shaved heads and eyebrows and to see women explicitly as ritual participants.

> *The HOLY ONE OF OLD spoke to Moshe, saying: ²This shall be the ritual for the woman with skin-disease at the time of her restoration:*
>
> *She shall be brought to the priest-clan; ³the priest-folk shall go out of the camp, and the priest-daughter representative shall make an examination. If the disease is healed in the woman with skin-disease, ⁴the priest-folk shall command that two living clean birds and cedarwood and crimson yarn and hyssop be brought for the woman who is to be restored. ⁵The priest-folk shall command that one of the birds be slaughtered over fresh water in an earthen vessel. ⁶The priest shall take the living bird with the cedarwood and the crimson yarn and the hyssop, and dip them and the living bird in the blood of the bird that was slaughtered over the fresh water. ⁷The priest shall sprinkle it seven times upon the woman who is to be restored of the skin-disease; then he shall pronounce her restored, and he shall let the living bird go into the open field. ⁸The woman who is to be restored shall wash her clothes, and shave off all her hair, and bathe herself in water, and she shall be restored. After that she shall come into the camp, but shall live outside her tent seven days. ⁹On the seventh day she shall shave all her hair: of head, and eyebrows; she shall shave all her hair. Then she shall wash her clothes, and bathe her body in water, and she shall be restored.*

SEXUALLY ACTIVE WOMEN

Leviticus 15:18 A woman with whom a man lies-down—yielding a flow of seed—shall both bathe in water and be restricted until sunset.

This is a difficult verse to render into English standard grammar. Most literally it is "And-a-woman whom he-lies-down a-man with-her flow-of-seed and-they-shall-wash in-water and-they-will-be-restricted until-sunset."[9] There

---

9. Words connected by hyphens represent a single word in Biblical Hebrew.

is no verb accounting for the production of semen, "flow of seed"; I have supplied "yielding." Other translations supply similar verbs. Grammatically speaking, there is no reason for the text to be this awkward. Listening for midrash, I can hear the speaker stumbling over these words: "And a woman who, *um, you know [gestures with hands], when* a man lies down *with [more gesturing] and anyhow you get* ejaculation, both should wash and be apart from the community until the next day. *Whew. [Wipes face.] What's next on the list?*"

Leviticus generally regulates sexual activity with an eye to communal boundaries, relationships, health, and well-being. Here the primary issues seem to be basic hygiene and space for intimacy. The verb *r-h-tz*, "wash" or "bathe," is used for ritual and nonritual bathing.[10] The period of restriction, *tamei*, is shared by the sexual partners. They are quarantined from the rest of the community, but not from each other. They share their restriction, and possibly their space, until sunset, which marks the beginning of a new day. Declaring them "unclean," as do other translations, obscures the particular holiness of their intimacy.

A curious omission from the perspective of some religious readers/hearers is that the text does not limit sexual activity to conjugal or "married" couples. While terms like "wife" and "husband" do not exist in Biblical Hebrew, and "marriage" is seldom used, the expressions "her man" and "his woman" designate community-recognized unions translated as "marriage" by most interpreters, who then use "wife" and "husband" contextually. None of that language is present in this text, perhaps because the subject of the passage, an adult, male, free Israelite, is not limited to "his woman" for sexual intercourse. Israelite men had legitimate sexual access to sex-workers, who were generally foreign (and probably not expected to comply with this *torah*), and to female slaves, to whom they had some limited ethical obligations, along with their own women or wives.

This passage is constructed as *torah* for the Israelites, so both the woman and man here are adult Israelites; since the *torah* is binding on both of them, it is not likely that slave women are the intended recipients—however common washing after sexual intercourse might be. When the enslaved are included in a *torah* provision, they are specified, which suggests that the rest of the Torah does not apply to them. For example, Shabbat rest is extended to slaves and resident aliens (Exod. 23:12; Deut. 5:14). I believe there is an economic, productivity rationale for excluding enslaved women from this *torah*. If they were required to be restricted from the community until the next day each time they were used sexually, their enslavers would be deprived of their labor on a regular basis. I do not believe that the Israelite householder was secluded with

10. See Gen. 18:4; Exod. 2:5; Lev. 1:9; Num. 19:19; Deut. 23:11.

his slave after he had used her, or that there was space for her seclusion after every sexual encounter. The intimacy called for by the text, with the couple remaining restricted until evening, has class implications.

The partners in the text experience some measures of equality. They are from the same community (Israelite), share the same broad economic class (free), and have consented to their sexual encounter. The verb *sh-k-v* ("lie-down") when combined with "with her/him" indicates consent.[11] The partners are required to bathe and share the *tamei*-state for the same length of time. The text is heteronormative, as is the whole of the biblical text. The primary concern of the Israelites with biological reproduction as a means of nation building through food production and military capabilities, combined with the lack of articulation of sexual variety, explains the focus on heterosexual coupledom.

As a womanist, I observe that sexual intimacy is nearly ubiquitous in Afro-diasporic communities, as it is everywhere else, while conversations about sexual activity in black America are not ubiquitous, especially in religious black America, most especially in black Christian communities. While it is difficult to imagine starting (or advertising) a conversation about sexual ethics from Leviticus, this *torah* offers a number of key discussion points: (1) equality between partners, (2) consent to sexual intimacy, (3) hygienic (read: healthy, "safe") sexual practices, and (4) intimacy as a constituent element of sexual activity. One principle of rabbinic exegesis is that texts have multiple meanings, including literal (*peshat*) meanings and interpretive (*drash*) meanings, and they are not limited to either or the combination.

A midrashic reading therefore permits an articulation of a radical equality between partners that transcends what occurs in the larger corpus of the Scriptures. For while the sexually active couple in this passage are subject to the same *torah*, in the bulk of Leviticus, Torah, and Scripture there is pervasive androcentrism, frequent impositions of gender-based hierarchy, and virulent misogyny. Given the plural, multicultural nature of the people(s) assembled under the name Israel, it would be a mistake to read the social equality of partners in ethnic, national, or racial terms. That both are "free" does not even mean that both are in the same socioeconomic stratum, but it does suggest that one is not financially or otherwise vulnerable to the other.

The issue of consent is partially located in the majority standing of the partners. The Bible does not address itself to minor children. When commands to "children" are issued, they are issued to adult children. This means that both partners are statutorily capable of granting consent, even though the age of

11. Rape is signaled by other verbs indicating force and the lack of "with"—e.g., "he lay her"— though the latter is not always clear when reading in English.

sexual maturity was largely reckoned at puberty in ancient Israel, and sexual activity and the production of children were markers of adulthood. While there were most certainly abduction and rape of prepubescent girls as war captives, this text does not seem to be set in those circumstances.

Likewise the hygienic underpinning of the text can be read with a focus on spiritual, emotional, physical, sexual, and societal health. Ethical sexual behavior then is not limited to what one does after sex as it is in the text, but can and must include what one does before and during sex, even though those are not the specific categories of the text. This also speaks to the decision to have sex and with whom, which the text leaves open for discussion.

The fact that both partners are *tamei*-restricted together, in the same space, speaks to me of a sexual ethic that does not divorce sexual activity from intimacy. The activities of the couple during the time they are apart from their community are not prescribed. Subsequent sexual activity is not proscribed. They have until evening. If they are sexually active at night, they have the whole day until the next evening draws near. While I have been discussing the *tamei* state in terms of "restriction," "space," and "intimacy," it does not mean that persons who were *tamei* for sexual reasons were fully secluded or quarantined, like those suspected of contagion or women bonding with their newborns. There were clearly degrees of seclusion. *Tamei*-restriction after sex is a set ritual of practices or avoidances, such as not handling foodstuffs or coming into physical contact with other persons, rather than remaining in a physical space. This is why holding enslaved women to the requirements of this *torah* would have been untenable in my view.

WOMEN WHO DO SEX-WORK

Leviticus 19:29 Do not profane your daughter by making her a prostitute, and the land will not become prostituted and full of premeditated-wickedness. . . .

Leviticus 21:7 The sons of Aaron shall not take a woman who is a prostitute or has been penetrated; neither shall they take a woman driven-away from her man. For they are holy to their God. . . . [13]The priest shall take only a woman who is a virgin. [14]A widow-woman, or a driven-away-woman, or a penetrated-woman, a prostitute-woman, these he shall not take, for only a virgin-woman of his own people shall he take,

Sex-work, although scorned, is tolerated in biblical Israel—up to a point. Leviticus is the first text in the canon to attempt to deal statutorily with sex-

Sex-work, Prostitution, Harlotry, and Whoredom

Actual sex-work, metaphorical sex-work, and accusations of sex-work and name-calling based on the low regard for sex-work and sex-workers run together as tangled, nearly inseparable threads in the biblical text and in its history of translation and interpretation. In the biblical canon, the language of prostitution, harlotry, and whoredom is used nearly indiscriminately for (a) women who do sex-work, (b) anyone who works in the service of a deity other than the Israelite one, (c) anyone who worships another deity, and (d) the land as a result of foreign worship (and occasionally immoral acts including sexual ones). The translation of z-n-h terms reflects the cultural biases of each generation of translators, myself included.

work. In Genesis 38, Judah has sex with a woman he doesn't realize is his daughter-in-law Tamar, because he thinks the woman is a sex-worker. The story is about her right (affirmed in the text) to have a child from his line, apparently through any means necessary (also affirmed in the text). But the framework of the story portrays his use of sex-workers as normative: He is widowed and has sexual needs. He knows where to find sex-workers and what they look like. He may be out of practice, because he doesn't bring appropriate currency with him—or the encounter was unexpected. He is desperate for sexual services and gives her all of his personal identification as surety against his bill. He seeks to pay off his balance and asks his friend to help him find the woman. There is no shame or stigmatization in his conversation or in the narration of his actions.

When Tamar's pregnancy is revealed, someone accuses her of sex-work. This is both the equivalent of calling a woman a "whore" for having sex outside of culturally accepted boundaries and an ironic pun—she has performed sex-work with him. Based on the accusation, Judah decides to have her burned alive. This illustrates the disdain Israel has for sex-workers among its own women, while permitting its men to seek sex-workers of other national and ethnic identities. Ultimately the truth comes out, and Judah proclaims that Tamar is more just (or "righteous," KJV) than he.

In Exodus, the sole reference to sex-work is bombastic, describing the worship of other peoples of their own gods. The inference in Exodus 34:15–16 is not that there are sexual rites associated with the worship of the peoples of the land, but rather that any worship of any other deity is an infidelity to the God of Israel who is perceived as the God of all and often as a male spouse. However, some interpreters will invent all manner of sexual worship for non-Israelites, including "cultic prostitution," which in spite of its presence in modern Bibles, simply did not exist.[12]

In Leviticus the root z-n-h is used both for nonsanctioned worship (see 17:7; 20:5–6) and for commercialized transactional sex, (19:29; 21:9). Leviticus 19:29 addresses a singular male subject[13] forbidding him from turning his daughter into a sex-worker, using the Hiphil (causative stem) of z-n-h. The act of prostituting one's daughter is "profanation," ch-l-l, a homophone of the stem from which "pierced/penetrated" arises, but an entirely separate word. I read this text as I do the one in Exodus 21 in which fathers sell their daughters into slavery: These pieces of legislation are necessary because these practices exist in the community. There were men selling their daughters as sex-slaves—designated for the use of one partner, which was permitted with some minor regulation—and there were men who sold their daughters as sex-workers to an unknown number of men. This last practice was disallowed by this torah. However, the practice likely endured in Israel, which explains the prohibition for priests taking sex-workers as their women or wives.

This text presumes an absolute patriarchal control of a woman's body and sexuality by her father. It is possible that this text is addressed to the whole of the community; surely women were not permitted to prostitute their daughters either. But the language places authority on (and recognizes the power of) the singular male subject. The setting of Leviticus—an extended pause on Sinai during which torah continues to be revealed—highlights the inequities among the peoples newly liberated from Egyptian slavery and sets the stage for the grumbling of the people in the book of Numbers to come.

Focusing one's attention on the problem of the text rather than on a solution many contemporary readers find inadequate, one gets an image of ancient Israel, whether in the wilderness, Canaan, or their own land(s), in which the commercialization of women's bodies was such a widespread problem that God and/or the editors of the Torah endeavored to address it. The verses that forbid men in the priestly clans from marrying sex-workers illustrate another reality, particularly if one understands these regulations to arise in response to concrete situations in the community. These women were not shunned by their people. They were seen as acceptable marriage partners, just not in the priest clan; they married into and perpetuated the lineages of the families in

12. See the extensive discussion in endnote 5 in chapter 1 in my *Daughters of Miriam: Women Prophets in Ancient Israel* (Minneapolis: Fortress Press, 2008), 174.

13. As with the Decalogue and larger Torah, the putative addressee is an adult, male, presumptively heterosexual, free Israelite citizen.

ancient Israel. And before this *torah* was pronounced, they apparently married into priestly families too.

WOMEN WHO COMMIT ADULTERY

Leviticus 20:10 When a man commits adultery with the woman of his neighbor, both the male-adulterer and the female-adulterer shall surely be put to death.

The adultery statute is largely egalitarian on its face. Women and men are subject to the same penalty for sexual contact with someone other than their spouse. This text is heteronormative, as is the whole of the biblical text. The primary concern of the Israelites with biological reproduction as a means of nation building through food production and military capabilities, combined with the lack of articulation of sexual variety, explains the focus on heterosexual coupledom. However, behind the text a married man has legitimate options for multiple sexual partners, options that do not extend to married women.

Israelite men have sexual access to the women they enslave (Exod. 21:7–11) and can perpetually acquire more, including through abduction of women in war (Deut. 20:1–14). There is also some degree of tolerance for professional sex-work (Gen. 38:21–23; Josh. 2:1; Judg. 11:1); Israelite women are prohibited from being sex-workers, but Israelite men are not prohibited from patronizing them (Lev. 19:29). Neither using a sex-worker nor having sex with a slave constitutes adultery for men. Even if a man has sex with a slave intended for another man, he is merely assessed a fine and not subject to execution (nor is she). There were separate penalties for having sex with a virgin-girl intended for someone else in marriage. A woman who had sex with any man other than her husband would be subject to execution. A man would be subject to execution under the statute only if he had sex with the woman/wife of another man. There is no allowance for Israelite women to have sex with male slaves (the text seems not to know of same-gender sexual contact between women) or to capture men in battle for the purposes of breeding. And there is no mention of female sexual abuse of subordinate males.

The means of death for an adulterer of any gender is not specified in the text. None of the adultery statutes specifies the means of execution: Exodus 20:10 and Deuteronomy 5:18 say, "You shall not. . . ." This passage, Leviticus 20:10, simply calls for the execution of both parties. In Leviticus, stoning is reserved for offering one's children through fire to Molech (20:2), consulting ghosts or other sources of secret knowledge (20:27), and blaspheming (24:14–

16, 23). Rabbinic texts do call for stoning (and strangulation) in cases of adultery, repeatedly in the Talmud Babylonian volume on women, *Nashim*.[14] The association of adultery with stoning postdates the Hebrew Scriptures and for many readers is indebted to the Gospel story in John 8.[15]

The adultery statutes make an interesting case for the *toroth* in the Torah *not* being the law of the land in subsequent books in the canon. There are no texts in which women or men are executed for having sex with someone's spouse or with someone other than their spouse. Laying aside the cases in the book of Genesis, on the principle that they predate the revelation at Sinai— at least in the narrative—there are a number of texts where the penalty of execution ought to apply but is simply never brought up. In 2 Samuel 12:9ff. Nathan does not invoke execution as the penalty for David's sin against Bathsheba (against Uriah in the logic of the text); this is not simply an issue of the monarch being above the law, because the whole point of Nathan's rebuke is to hold David accountable, pronounce judgment, and reveal the penalty for his actions. In 2 Samuel 16:22 Absalom rapes his father's secondary wives in public; no one calls for his execution. Applying a statutory penalty to Absalom would have legitimately ended his contestation for the throne and benefited David. Monarchal privilege does not apply to Absalom; while he is trying to establish himself as monarch, there is a price on his head as a rebel—not as an adulterer. Proverbs makes seven references to a stereotypical adulteress; she is expected to live to continue her wayward way of life with no threat of execution. There is no talk of execution in the rhetoric of Hosea about Gomer, who is described repeatedly as a sex-worker and an adulteress. The rhetoric of adultery is commonplace in the biblical text, as are violations of this ethical standard. If indeed these *toroth* were widely known and available, the lack of application of this penalty may suggest that the Israelites heard and understood their own Scriptures with nuance rather than literalism.

SHELOMITH BAT DIVRI (DIBRI)

> Leviticus 24:10 The son of an Israelite woman came out (now he was the son of an Egyptian man among the women and men of Israel);

14. See *Talmud Bavli, Ketubbot* 11b; 45a for exemplars. *Nashim* contains the tractates on sisters-in-law (*Yevamot*), marriage contracts (*Ketubbot*), and the suspected adulteress (*Sotah*), among others.

15. The suggested methodology in the John text, individuals picking up stones and participating in a mob action, evokes the stoning of Stephen in Acts 7:54–8:1. However, that approach is in conflict with the stoning ritual described in the Mishnah, in which a person is pushed off a cliff, a crushing stone placed on the chest if necessary, and mob stoning is a last resort (*Mishnah Sanhedrin* 6:2–4).

and the son of the Israelite woman and an Israelite man fought in the camp. [11]The son of the Israelite woman violated the Name and cursed. And they brought him to Moshe (Moses); the name of his mother was Shelomith bat Divri (Dibri), of the tribe of Dan.

Shelomith bat Dibri, a woman from the tribe of Dan, is the only woman named in the book of Leviticus. She was impregnated in an unspeakable way by a man who is not named. She gave birth to a son who would be known for the scandal of his origin—which is also her scandal—and for the crime for which he would be executed, but for not his own name. She and her story have become infamous[16] in biblical and rabbinic discourse. At first glance, the story is not about her; it is about her son, whose name is strangely absent from the text and the tradition. But then there is the matter of his parentage; his father is an Egyptian. His parentage is his story, and it is his mother's story, Shelomith's story.

The Scriptures do not say how Shelomith came to be impregnated by an Egyptian. Their silence invites speculation. The rabbinic speculation blames Shelomith and circuitously calls her an adulteress.[17] The two options for She-lomith's conception, consensual and nonconsensual, are both problematic for the authors and editors of the canon, particularly those in the priestly com-munity responsible for Leviticus.[18]

A consensual sexual relationship between an Israelite woman and non-Isra-elite man is so problematic in and for the text that it is nearly unimaginable. Even consensual relationships between Israelite men and foreign women are fraught in the canon. While such intermarriages are quite common in the Torah, especially among leading figures, Deuteronomy 7:1–3 will attempt to outlaw the practice. Judah, Simeon, Joseph, and Moses all have such unions and children from these unions. In Numbers 25, a Midianite woman is exe-cuted by Moses' brother Aaron on her wedding day, even though Moses him-self is married to a Midianite woman. With the exception of Miriam's rebuke of Moses in Numbers 11, these unions are not critiqued in the canon. Abra-ham's relationship with Keturah could fall into the same category; although Israelite identity is not at stake—it does not yet exist—she is an outsider, not part of his extended family within which it was their practice to form unions. Some may cite Ruth as a singular example of acceptable interethnic unions.

---

16. She is called a shame to her father, family, and tribe (*Shemoth Rabbah* 48:2 and *Vayiqra Rabbah* 32:5–6, where she is blamed for her son's death).

17. See *Shemoth Rabbah* 1:28.

18. Her interpreters in the Zohar (the major mystical rabbinic text) don't care whether she was raped or not, and neither does her husband in that midrash. In Zohar C 105b–106a "an Egyptian comes to her in the middle of the night," leading to her husband divorcing her.

However, Ruth 1:4 says that Ruth and Orpah were "lifted" or "abducted" into marriage, *yis'u*, using the verb *n-s-'*, which indicates abduction, forced marriage, and rapine in other passages (see Judg. 21:10ff.), rather than the traditional verb for a consensual union, *l-q-ch*. Abduction or rape-marriages were relatively normative in ancient Israel as they were in the wider ancient world and were not subject to the same critique as consensual interethnic unions in the Hebrew Bible.

The possibility that Shelomith chose an Egyptian partner would have been scandalous and salacious at best, especially given the enslavement of the Israelites to the Egyptians. Among subjugated peoples, women who chose to cohabitate with, marry, or give birth to the children of the men whose people oppress their own are regularly viewed as traitors and sometimes whores. The second possibility is that Shelomith did not consent to sex with the Egyptian man who impregnated her. Rape by their oppressors of subjugated women (and men and children of both genders) is horrifyingly common in subjugated and enslaved communities, yet there are almost no accounts of Israelite women and girls being sexually abused by their oppressors.[19]

Lamentations 5:11 seems to be the sole account of rape of Israelite women by their oppressors. Yet there are multiple accounts of the systematic rape of Israelite/Judean women by their fellow Israelites. Judges 21 records the abduction and rape of virgin girls from Jabesh-Gilead and the house of God at Shiloh, to provide women for the tribe of Benjamin. During the return from Babylonian exile, impoverished Judean girls sold to pay off family debts were raped as soon as they were exchanged by their own kin (Neh. 5:5). Also relevant is the public nudity of Israelite women held in captivity by their own people in 2 Chronicles 28:10–15. The lack in the canon of stories of sexual violence against Israelite women at the hands of the Egyptians or later the Assyrians, Persians, Greeks, or Romans is stunning and does not reflect the reality of war and occupation. It is all the more striking because the Israelites model the practice of slave-rape in using the bodies of enslaved women and girls for reproduction and in capturing women in war as "spoils of war," "booty" in some texts (see Num. 21 and Deut. 20).

Whether viewed as consensual or nonconsensual, Shelomith's conception and gestation of an Egyptian child were cast in shameful terms. I say that her unnamed offspring is Egyptian because the Scriptures reckon identity paternally, allowing for the impregnation of slaves and abducted women as a benefit (and net population increase) to the people of the assailant. Her

19. The Joseph story in Gen. 37:7–18 is framed as a failed seduction and false accusation of rape, rather than as attempted rape, but the moment the Egyptian woman grabs his garment some sort of assault is underway.

son's copugilist is an Israelite in the text; Shelomith's son is not. Her son's name is not preserved, even though this is a narrative that is ostensively about his conduct. Clearly, at one level this narrative is about his identity and the unwelcome fact of his existence, making it about her—hence the inclusion of her name in the text. The man's missing name stands in sharp contrast to his mother's threefold identification: she is Shelomith, she is a/the daughter of Dibri, and she is from the tribe of Dan.[20]

The text juxtaposes the origin of Shelomith's son an undetermined number of years prior with the present conflict. Shelomith's son and a man who counts as an Israelite fight over an undisclosed provocation. It is easy to imagine that Shelomith's son was in many fights because of the circumstances of his birth, but there is no way to determine the cause of the current conflict. What is known is that Shelomith's son—I'll call him Ben[21]—"violates" the Divine Name while fighting. The verb n-q-v, vayyiqqov here, means "to pierce," that is, "to violate," and also "to designate," that is, "to name." As it pertains to "piercing," the semantic range includes ornamental or functional piercing of objects (2 Kgs. 12:9) and piercing with weapons (2 Kgs. 18:21; Hab. 3:14; Job 40:24) and provides the basis for "female" in Genesis 1:28, that is, "able to be pierced or penetrated." The second semantic range of the verb has to do with designating someone or something, that is, "naming" them.[22] One can hypothesize a naming system that involves both elements, for example, engraving, but that would be purely speculative.

I invoke both ends of the semantic range in my translation, because the "naming" in the text—uttering the Divine Name—is a "violation." The naming/violation occurs in the context of cursing, vay'qallel (q-l-l), in verse 11. In the canon it is possible that, unlike current traditional practice, simply pronouncing the Divine Name is not a transgression; a few texts seem to indicate that in addition to the high priest, some few individuals also used the name ritually.[23] The biblical practice of saying the Name presupposes actually knowing the correct pronunciation and/or spelling, not the case with the common contemporary scholarly speculation found in many publications.

The form of the curse that would qualify as a violation, ultimately termed "blasphemy" in the tradition, most likely would have differed from

20. Dibri is more likely a parent than a place at this stage in the narrative, although nothing conclusive, not even gender, can be drawn from the name.

21. "Ben" means "son" as well as "child" and "descendant" and is also used to relay geographical or characterizing information. The choice is influenced by the comparable practice of Mieke Bal in *Death and Dissymmetry* (Chicago: University of Chicago Press, 1988).

22. See Gen. 30:28; Num. 1:17; Ezra 8:20; 2 Chr. 28:15.

23. See Ps. 68:4 in particular and Gen. 26:25; 2 Sam. 6:18; 1 Kgs. 18:24.

contemporary curses. "God curse you" or even "God damn you" would not have necessarily drawn rebuke; people blessed and cursed each other in the name of their gods, including in Israel, with some frequency.[24] The type of curse that would have elicited the death sentence would involve cursing God specified in verse 15, for example, "I curse you and your god ____."[25]

Ben Shelomith is seized on Moses' orders and put under guard (*bamishmar* in v. 12), making him the first incarcerated man in ancient Israel and the OG[26] of Israelite penal system. His crime is apparently novel and requires a divine consultation. In verses 13–16 his capital sentence is decreed and codified as a legal precedent for anyone else who violates the sanctity of the Divine Name, whether Israelite or not—and, by implication, whether woman or man.

My womanist reflection on Shelomith bat Dibri begins with the last thing revealed about her in the text, her name. Her very name highlights a gender-identity issue in the canon. Shelomith's name is perpetuated[27] in the canon by women and men and by one person whose gender is indeterminate: Shelomith bat Dibri would have lived alongside Shelomith ben Izhar, a cousin of Miriam, Moses, and Aaron (1 Chr. 23:18); Izhar was their father's brother. In the line of David, Shelomith was the sister of Zerubbabel, who oversaw the restoration of the temple in the return (1 Chr. 3:19). Also among the returnees was a man named Shelomith ben Josiphiah (Ezra 8:10). In 2 Chronicles 11:20, Maacah, daughter of Absalom and granddaughter of David, gave birth to a number of children, including one named Shelomith, whose gender cannot be determined by the text. In spite of being constructed by the text as the "mother of blasphemers," the reoccurrence of her name throughout Israel's chronicles indicates that neither Shelomith's name nor her memory is perpetually tarnished by the story. While Leviticus reduces her to what may be the two most awful events in her life, the Scriptures preserve her name as one to be perpetuated throughout the generations. The name also appears on the seal of a woman from a prominent family who serves the governor of the Yehud province (formerly Judah) in an official capacity.[28]

---

24. See Num. 5:21; Josh. 6:26 and 2 Kgs. 2:24 for some acceptable biblical curses invoking God.

25. See 1 Kgs. 21:10–13 and Job 1:5; the principle extends into the New Testament in 1 Cor. 12:3.

26. "Original Gangster," a/the founding member of a crime family, gang, or other criminal enterprise or surviving, retired, gang member of a previous generation.

27. It is unlikely that they were all named for her, but perhaps some were.

28. The seal reads, "Shelomith the woman-slave of Elnathan the Governor." She has been identified as the daughter of Zerubbabel, who figures prominently in Haggai, Zechariah, Ezra, and Nehemiah. See Eric Meyers, "The Shelomith Seal and Aspects of the Judean Restoration: Some Additional Reconsiderations," *Eretz Israel* 17 (1985): 33–38.

Shelomith's history is revealed before her name and is exposed in the text in a way that suggests that she did not have a happy loving partnership or that, if she did, it was accepted by her people or the text. The phenomenon of having one's history, especially one's sexual history (or fantasies about one's sexual history) proceed one into a conversation is familiar but not unique to womanists. Women of color can identify with the experience of being engaged solely in terms of one's sexuality, relationships, and/or progeny. Shelomith is the mother of a child who was accused—rightly or wrongly—of a crime, imprisoned, and executed. And Shelomith is the mother of a child whose ethnic identity has significant social implications. Nothing else of her parenting is disclosed in the text. Many mothers of color find themselves helping their children navigate (or watching as they learn on their own to make the crossing) the dangerous waters of race and ethnicity, whether or not their biological parents have differing constructions of race. Categories like "black" and "Latina" are far from monolithic and are subject to interpretation by the bodies that inhabit them and the bodies that construct them from a distance. The reader is left to wonder what Shelomith told her son about who he was and how he came into the world, what his name was (Egyptian or Hebrew or a hybrid), who his father was, and whether his father was still in his life, even at that moment—but erased from the canon, because of what his parents' relationship represented.[29]

Lastly, Shelomith is the mother of a child caught up in the criminal justice system. Like many in its clutches, Ben is guilty of the crime of which he is accused, and he is still her son. The overrepresentation of black and brown women and men in the criminal justice system of the United States rests on the incarceration of the innocent and the guilty alike. Shelomith is known in the canon as "that woman" whose son did "that thing." She is guilty by association, as a result of the press her son's story has generated, digging into her own past. The text talks about her; it does not invite or engage her in the conversation. The text does not give Shelomith a voice with which to express her feelings for her son: whether she welcomed his birth or not, whether she loved him fiercely whatever his origins, whether she struggled to provide for him or raise him, whether her family supported her and welcomed him, whether she was surprised at his fighting or used to it, whether she feared the impending judgment on his crime or welcomed it, whether she loved him more than God, loving him enough to forgive the unforgivable sin. For each possibility, there are women with children in the criminal justice system for whom those feelings in sum, or in part, are their lived reality.

29. The book of Numbers will laud the execution of those in consensual interethnic unions and reward the killers with divine blessing.

Shelomith is the most visible woman in Leviticus: a woman with a son conceived and born in some kind of scandal, who was convicted and executed for blasphemy. But the Scriptures reduce her to a skeleton; without the flesh of her story, Shelomith is one-dimensional. Nevertheless, the shadow she casts has familiar contours. As a Christian womanist I see echoes of Shelomith's story in the story of Miryam, Mary of Nazareth, and the scandalous conception, birth, and execution of her son, Yeshua ben Miryam, Jesus, Mary's child.

4

Numbers: Exodus, Part 2

The book of Numbers may well be regarded as Exodus, Part 2. Many of the narratives that many biblical readers associate with the exodus narrative occur in Numbers rather than Exodus. The supply of quail and manna, wandering and whining in the wilderness, the sending of spies into Canaan, divine guidance in a pillar of cloud and fire, and the episode with the golden calf are just a few of the exodus stories in Numbers. The book of Numbers includes wonderful, rich, multidimensional texts of the Israelites' formative encounter with their God while wilderness wandering from promise to fulfillment. The individual narratives invoke the senses with apparitions of fire and cloud, detailed descriptions of ritual and worship, calling and ordination—all to facilitate community and individual response to divine providence, stewardship, and the personal piety of Israelite women and men.

Numbers continues the social organization of the newly liberated community, shaping itself as an androcentric hierarchy. Women are put in a subordinate place frequently, from the prophet Miriam, to Israelite women who wish to make their own vows to God, to foreign women whose brutalization the text authorizes. The androcentric hierarchy articulated in Numbers and throughout the canon is not true patriarchy with all males, or even all male heads of households, holding power and authority over all women and children. Rather, certain males, and occasionally certain females, held sway over all others. For example, Moses was subordinate to Aaron in priestly matters, while Aaron was subordinate to Moses in prophetic matters. Ruling women will hold sway over all others, including men, while nonruling royal women will hold sway over all except for the ruling monarch.

Biblical Israel's androcentric hierarchy should not be misidentified as misogynistic (though there are certainly misogynistic texts in the corpus). Women were valuable contributors to society and preservers of the cultural heritage. The many tellings of the saga of Mahlah, Noah, Hoglah, Milcah, and Tirzah[1] are preserved in the biblical text because of their role in preserving the land as an inheritance. The importance of God changing the *torah* of inheritance to benefit these women cannot be overestimated.

In spite of the essential role of women in establishing and preserving the nation-state, biblical Israel could not be constructed as egalitarian. The abundance of narratives sanctioning violence against women belies that claim. In Numbers 31:1–20, the abduction, forced marriage, and rape of prepubescent girls directed by Moses raises male sexual violence to the level of divine commandment. The book of Numbers offers canonical space in which the religious reader/hearer can—and I argue *should*—wrestle with these issues.

DISEASED WOMEN

Numbers 5:1 The HOLY ONE OF OLD spoke to Moshe, saying: [2]"Command the women-and-men-of-Israel to send out of the camp every-woman-or-man who is diseased-in-skin, or has an-irregular-discharge, and everyone who is restricted through contact with a dead-soul. [3]Both male and female you shall send out, sending them outside the camp so they shall not render-restricted their camp. I dwell among them."

This passage includes and obscures women in *beney Yisrael*, traditionally rendered "Israelites," and in "every/all," *kol*, while specifically including women in "male and female." Specific diagnostic and quarantine procedures and restoration rituals associated with women and men with skin diseases and those who have penile and vaginal discharges are discussed at some length in Leviticus (see "Women with a Skin Disease" in the chapter on Leviticus). Anita Diamant's *The Red Tent* represents one populist midrashic approach to imagining the lives of some Israelite women sequestered during their menstrual, postpartum, and irregular periods of bleeding in and around one particular space. This passage in Numbers 5 evokes a separate camp, a group of tents: some for women, some for men, some for those with visible disease on their skin, some for those with irregular vaginal bleeding, and some for those with irregular penile discharges. Each condition had its own rituals and quarantine requirements. It is a question worthy of rabbinic pondering whether a person under one sort of restriction can be rendered further restricted by

1. See Num. 26:28–33; 27:1–11; 36:1–12; Josh. 17:3–6; 1 Chr. 7:15.

coming into contact with a person under another type of restriction. I imagine that the occupants of the "tents of restriction and restoration" would keep to themselves, so as not to multiply the nature of their own restriction.

But for those who showed no signs of restoration, those whose quarantines were permanently extended because their diseases had not gone into remission, there was no foreseeable path back to the larger community. Quarantines could be indefinitely or permanently extended because of unrelenting hypermenorrhea, recurrent or incurable gonorrhea, perpetually ulcerated skin continuing to crack and ooze and bleed. Surely some held out hope for medical remission, spontaneous cures, a miracle. But using my sanctified imagination, I see others getting on with their lives, making a life for themselves in the camp on the margins of the camp.

These are some of their stories: Avira did not bleed like other women. She bled for weeks at a time with scarcely a week's respite. Each time her bleeding stopped, she would go to the edge of the Camp of the Tents of Restriction and Restoration to have a kohenet—*a priest-woman, the daughter of a priest— confirm the beginning of her restoration so she could complete the rite, but her bleeding always returned.*

Matok lived at the edge of the camp beyond the camp. He had a yellowish discharge from his penis that no one would have noticed if his wife Einat had not gone to the kohenet. *She was already back in the main camp, restored from her last touch from him. He was here to stay.*

Dovevah lived in a small tent with other m'tzoraroth, *women with skin diseases. Some called them* q'rechahoth, *bald-headed women. Every time a new spot, patch, ulcer, blister, or boil broke out on their skin, they shaved all their hair and eyebrows, hoping to complete their rite of restoration. For each healed spot, though, Dovevah swore she saw two new ones erupt. She wanted to return to the camp where God lived in a holy tent among the people, but one of the elder-women, Ammah Husn, who came with the people from Egypt, said that her type of disease would never relent. Ammah Husn encouraged Dovevah to marry Ra'anan, a man from the neighboring tent with the same kind of skin-disease. Other couples had married and borne children in the camp beyond the camp.*

Orpaz was born and raised in the camp beyond the camp. She knew no other life. Her mother was one of the bleeding-women. She came to the camp to stay for her birth and the normal time of restriction. Instead she bled and bled and ultimately died. Orpaz was nursed by one of the women with skin disease. When she was weaned four years later, her foster mother took her to the kohenet *so that Orpaz could go through the rights of restoration and be returned to her family in the camp. But her father had taken another woman who had given birth to two sons. Neither of them wanted her. Orpaz*

was the first but not the last of a generation who lived and died on the mar-
gins of the Israelite community.

The camp beyond the camp moved with the main camp, seeking the same
promise of land and freedom as their kinfolk in the main camp. They saw
the same pillar of fire and smoke, their veiled God, leading them all to a new
place. They too heard the voice of God thunder across the wilderness when
God spoke to their prophets Miryam and Moshe. They too were God's people.

As a womanist reader/hearer, I reflect on the various communities that live
on the margins of the dominant culture. Some of those communities are gendered in particular ways; they are spaces which people who do not conform to
dominant-culture gender norms seek out, form, and are sometimes abandoned
to. Because they are lesbian and gay and bisexual and trans- women and men
and sex-workers, they find and create safe home spaces when they can. Some
of these communities are marked by physical otherness, for example, communities shaped by deaf culture or by architectural structures that accommodate
mobility and activity patterns associated with people in wheelchairs, or people
who use walkers or aging populations. There are also communities of people
who share living (and dying) space outdoors who have no other homes, who
may have untreated mental illnesses and/or addictions, and who may share a
life built around the substances to which they are addicted. Women of color
and their children are present in each of these communities, some occupying
space in more than one such community or subculture at a time.

There are literal equivalents to the afflictions in the Numbers 5 text that
affect black, brown, and beige women: skin diseases and discolorations like
vitiligo, eczema, and even albinism; bleeding disorders associated with uter-
ine fibroid tumors that affect women of African descent disproportionately;
sexually transmitted diseases and infections from HIV/AIDS to HPV, herpes,
gonorrhea, syphilis, chlamydia; and other life-imperiling social, moral, ethical, and religious issues for women of color and our communities. As womanists serve our communities in the disparate camps, some seek the well-being
of persons in their respective camps while others seek to dismantle the boundaries between the camps.

MIRYAM (MIRIAM) RETURNS

Numbers 12:13 Hear, HOLY ONE, hear and heal her. . . . [15]Miryam
(Miriam) was shut out of the camp for seven days; and the people—
the women, the children, and the men—did not move forward until
the gathering of Miryam (Miriam).

Miriam returns to the story in Numbers 12. There she leads Aaron in criticizing Moses' most recent marriage in verse 1. More specifically, I believe that Miriam is criticizing Moses' divorce of Zipporah in Exodus 18:2. Many commentators have racialized this narrative, claiming that Miriam objected to the African origins of this new wife, and as a result was turned white with disease, in spite of the fact that the word "white" is not in the Hebrew text (nor is it in the SP, LXX, or Peshitta). While there is xenophobia in the biblical canon, it is not constructed racially, as the category of race did not exist; the Israelites did not distinguish peoples based on skin color.[2] Rather, I find that the issue here is the abandonment of Zipporah and her children: Her father takes them all back home, as reported after the fact in Exodus 18:3, and brings them back to Moses in an attempted reconciliation in verse 6. Moses greets Jethro and does not acknowledge his family. There is no further mention of them. Then in Numbers 12 Moses shows up with another woman as his wife. That is arguably the substance of Miriam's objection.

Although Miriam and Aaron were every bit as much prophets as Moses, the form of her objection of Moses' marriage in Numbers 12 draws sharp rebuke from God, who overhears the conversation (v. 2) and summons them all for a talking-to (v. 4). In between verses 2 and 4, Moses' publicist inserts a verse trumpeting his great humility (v. 3), vexing those who claim that Moses wrote the Torah. How could he be humble and say that he is humble? God rebukes Miriam and Aaron, proclaiming the superiority of Moses' prophethood. Then God leaves in verse 9. While leaving, God's cloud "turns," and Miriam becomes disfigured with diseased skin. Her affliction will be invoked in Deuteronomy 24:8 as a reminder to take seriously the necessity for quarantine in such situations. Most interpreters read that God punished Miriam (the rabbis and I find Aaron subsequently afflicted) for speaking against Moses. But the passage does not say how Miriam becomes diseased. It is something of a surprise in the narrative, marked with the exclamation, *hinneh*![3] Miriam is stricken with a skin disease that Moses has been empowered to inflict and heal (Exod. 4:6–7). Then Aaron asks Moses for forgiveness for both of them and for Miriam's restoration.

Moses' prayer for Miriam in verse 13 is one of the most beautiful in the Hebrew Scriptures: *El na, rapha na lah*. Most translators abandon the breathy

---

2. See Rodney Sadler, *Can a Cushite Change His Skin? An Examination of Race, Ethnicity, and Othering in the Hebrew Bible* (New York: T. & T. Clark, 2005); and Peter T. Nash, *Reading Race, Reading the Bible* (Minneapolis: Fortress Press, 2003).

3. Often translated as "Look!" or "Behold!" The Rev. Dr. Beth LaRocca-Pitts taught me that *hinneh* is more akin to what one says when one discovers one's car has been stolen. She proffered "Shit!"

assonance, the repetition of the "ah" sound. I offer, "Hear, Holy One, hear and heal her," to preserve something of the poetry of the original. Miriam's healing is neither described nor attributed to God or Moses, mirroring her affliction. Drawing upon a cultural shaming analogy, God calls for a seven-day exile in verse 14; Miriam is banished from the people whom she served as prophet for decades and led in their dance of deliverance.

The daughters and sons of Israel vote with their feet on the banishment of Miriam: they refuse to move them. Or they vote with their behinds: they sit on them. In verse 15 the Israelites refuse to continue on their journey without their prophet. They wait for Miriam, and God apparently waits for them. Or perhaps it is God who waits, refusing to venture forward without God's prophet, Miriam.

One measure of the strength of the Miryamic prophetic tradition is illustrated in the refusal to leave Miryam behind after her affliction. The people sit with her, as Job's friends would sit with him. But they do not blame her for her affliction. She is their prophet, and they are her people. My womanist sanctified imagination populates the camp-beyond-the-camp where Miriam and her people who could not rejoin the assembly temporarily or permanently were sequestered:

> *Miryam's visit to the camp beyond the camp made of the Tents of Restriction and Restoration was her first visit. She had not come to the camp as had every woman for her monthly time of restriction and restoration, because she was in her nineties when Israel left Egypt. The other prophets and most of the priests came, most only until the next evening after making love. Some came to stay so often they might as well have had their own tents; others visited with less frequency. Some of their leaders, priests and prophets and elders, came to stay after a death in the family; but their child-bearing women came to the camp monthly and after the birth of their children, in addition to the times of their lovemaking. The elder-women came after their times of lovemaking. But Miryam never took a man; she had never had need of the Tents of Restriction and Restoration before.*
>
> *Miryam had been cast out as punishment for speaking out to God and Moshe over the scandal of his divorce. He had abandoned his first wife, Zipporah, and their children—after all she had done for him! She had saved his life from the hands of his own God. Her father had taught her about the God of Sinai, and she had taught Moshe, although he hadn't listened and grazed the sheep on the holy mountain. He's lucky God didn't kill him for sure. Moshe traded her in for a new woman—it wasn't Zipporah's fault she was abandoned like yesterday's garbage—and then Moshe had the nerve to try to keep up his relationship with Zipporah's own father; well, that wouldn't last. Someone needed to tell him about himself before the other men started*

getting ideas. And Miryam, our prophet, got in his face and told him about himself.

And then God struck her—God has always favored Moshe, just like Galit in the next tent over favors her nasty little Zvi over her sweet Nechamah, no rhyme or reason. But God immediately regretted it and took it back. But God had to save face with Moshe, who was acting all outraged, even though Miryam was telling the truth and everyone knew it. And Aharon, hiding behind her skirts the whole time, agreed with her but was afraid to say a mumbling word. Just like he's hiding in that tent over yonder. Never mind that, I wasn't supposed to say anything. You didn't hear it from me. No diseased priests in Israel's ranks. Hmph.

Now our Miryam, she's a real prophet. She goes to God on our behalf, and God speaks to her for us. God comes when she pounds her drum. And when she dances, God dances with and in her. That's my kind of prophet. And she's not just hiding in her tent either. She's not afraid of picking up another kind of restriction from one of us who can never go back to the main camp. Although some of the worst ones keep their distance out of respect.

Some say we ought to have moved on by now. The main camp before and those of us here after. God-in-Fire started to move, but a funny thing happened. Some of the women in the main camp refused to move without the prophet being gathered back in to the main camp. All of the women in the tribe of Levi, Miryam's kinswomen—including all of the priest-women— refused to move. The menfolk thought that they could pack up the God-Tent without them and move ahead. Well, now they know.

We'll be sorry to see her go. She is our prophet, and we are her people.

It is perhaps not insignificant that her final appearance in the text prior to her death is one in which her authority is contested. Miriam is submerged in the narrative from this point on. She is rendered invisible in the quarrels and rebellions that follow in the book of Numbers. One way of interpreting Miriam's absence from subsequent wilderness narratives is to suggest that neither Miriam's conduct nor her authority was contested, when those of Moses and Aaron were challenged repeatedly. Miriam emerges from her exile (chaps. 13–19) in chapter 20.

In Numbers 20:1, Miriam dies and is buried. Some commentators date this passage to the fortieth year of wilderness wandering, shortly before Aaron's death in Numbers 33:8; others find the perambulations of the Israelites impossible to sort out.[4] Her age at her death is not disclosed. She may

4. See the Adele Berlin, Marc Zvi Brettler, and Michael A. Fishbane, eds., *Jewish Study Bible* (Oxford: Oxford University Press, 2004) and the JPS Torah Commentary on Num. 20:1.

well have been a centenarian. Miriam is buried in Kadesh, in contemporary Syria.[5] The preservation of her death and burial in the Torah marks Miriam as an extraordinarily significant woman in the biblical tradition. Miriam is so esteemed in the Talmud that she is reckoned as the only woman included among the patriarchs—Abraham, Isaac, Jacob, Moses, Aaron, and Benjamin—over whom neither the angel of death nor the worms of earth had dominion (*b. Bava Batra* 17a). In the biblical text her death is juxtaposed with the lack of water, which dried up when she died, nurturing the tradition that one of Miriam's prophetic gifts was the ability to provide water for her people.

In the Targumim, Aramaic translations of the Bible, Miriam's well is explicitly mentioned several times in the accounts of her death and its aftermath.[6] The evolution of the Aramaic Scriptures can be compared to the evolution of the New Testament, in which different Gospels include different accounts of the same event with varied amounts of details, some expanding the texts—or oral account—of previous versions, for example, the multiple ending of Mark and the multiple accounts of the resurrection of Jesus. *Targum Pseudo-Jonathan* records Miriam's death thusly:

> Numbers 20:1 The women-men-and-children-of-Israel, the whole congregation, came to the wilderness of Zin on the tenth day of the month of Nisan. And Miriam died and was buried there. [2] Now, on account of the merit of Miriam a well was given. When she lay-down-in-death, the well was hidden. So there was no water for the congregation, and the congregation gathered against Moshe and against Aharon.

Targum Neofiti relates the hostilities the children of Israel face after Miriam's death to opportunism while they are grieving her loss and that of Aaron:

> Numbers 21:1 When the Canaanite, the king of Arad who was dwelling in the south, heard that Aaron, the pious man by whose merit the clouds of glory brought out Israel [from bondage], had been taken up and that Miriam the prophet by whose merit the well had gone up, had been taken up—for Israel had reached the road that the spies had gone up—then they waged war with Israel and took some of them captive.

---

5. The rabbis will see her interred on Mt. Nebo with her brother prophets; see *b. Sotah* 13b as a measure of equality.

6. See Neh. 8:8 for the inaugural account of translating the Torah into Aramaic. For the use and sanctity of the Targumim, see *b. Berakhot* 8a–b; *b. Shabbat* 115b; *b. Megillah* 3a; 17a; *b. Mo'ed Qatan* 28b.

Targum Pseudo-Jonathan, Numbers 20:1, provides a date for Miryam's death, the tenth of Nisan; according to tradition, it was on the first anniversary of Miriam's death that Joshua led the surviving generation of Israelite women and men and their children across the Jordan River. Miriam's last two appearances in the Scriptures bear witness to the strength of her legacy. In a complicated genealogy in 1 Chronicles 4:17, Miriam's name lives on through one of Caleb's daughter-descendants, indicating that the tradition of naming girls for the prophet Miriam began long before the first century and all of the Marys of the Gospels. And when God sues God's people in Micah for failing to "do justice, love kindness, and walk humbly with their God," God's opening argument is that God has not only redeemed God's people but sent before them Moses, Aaron, and Miriam.

WOMEN OF MOAB

> Numbers 25:1 While Israel was dwelling in Shittim, the people began to have unsanctioned-intimate-relationships with the women of Moav. [2]And the women invited the people to the sacrifices of the God of the women, and the people ate and bowed down to the God of the women.

Numbers 25 extends the portrayal of foreign women as dangerously seductive to a new realm. The people—*ha'am*, an inclusive term that includes women and men—began to "whore" with Moabite women, (the Fox and GSJPS translations of *liznoth*). The use of "people" suggests a large group between "some" and "all."[7] Adults categorized by the ability to be sexually active are indicated here.

In the Scriptures the Israelites are regularly accused of prostituting themselves with other gods or their intermediaries (e.g., Lev. 17:7; 20:6; Deut. 31:6; Ezek. 16 and 23). Worship of other deities is regularly characterized as adultery and prostitution (e.g., Jer. 5:7; Hos. 4:14; 1 Chr. 5:25). The charge of prostitution, *z-n-h*, can mean sex-for-money, worship of other deities, or intermarriage with non-Israelite peoples. This last is accompanied by the presumption that intermarriage will lead the Israelite spouse to non-Israelite worship; interestingly, the canon does not presume that authorized Israelite worship will draw outsiders into its fold. Yet not all intermarriages are so characterized. Joseph, Moses, and David are among the most prominent

---

7. Num. 25:9 offers a possible tally of at least 24,000.

Israelites who escape being labeled whoremongers for their unions with non-Israelite women. The notion is further complicated by the passages that call for Israelite men to abduct the women and girls of non-Israelite peoples as breeding stock after armed conflict in the name of God, without critique for the men in these unions.[8]

The Numbers 25 passage is unique in its assertion that the "people" of Israel are perversely intimate with the women of Moab, leaving open the possibility that both Israelite women and men are intimately involved with Moabite women (but not Moabite men) through its specific grammar. There is no comparable text in the Hebrew Scriptures even suggesting women's same-gender erotic activity.[9] Other passages accuse the people as a whole of sexual perfidy, by describing Israel collectively as God's female spouse and the foreigners in plural terms that indicate collective maleness (e.g., the Egyptian and Assyrian "lovers" and "warriors" in Ezek. 23). Some passages declaim the intercultural heterosexual unions as "prostitution" to other gods (e.g., Exod. 34:16: "And you will take women from among their daughters for your sons, and their daughters who prostitute themselves to their gods will make your sons also prostitute themselves to their gods").

Conversely, Numbers 25:1 can be understood as excluding women from the category "people" if the text is read as heteronormative and therefore referring only to male Israelites in relationship with Moabite women. However, this would read against the use of the term in the remainder of the biblical corpus, where it is clearly an inclusive term.[10] In any interpretive framework, this is a queer—in every sense of the word—text. The passage continues with the Moabite women inviting the people to participate in their religious rituals; again "people" is *ha'am* and gender inclusive. At these sacrificial feasts the Israelite women and men willingly yield themselves to the Moabite god and the worship of Ba'al of Peor. Peor was the mountain from which Balaam repeatedly blessed the people of Israel in the preceding chapters. He paid for those blessings with his life in Joshua 13:22.

The compression of time in this text makes it difficult to know how these events and relationships developed over time. Did the Israelites settle in or

8. See Num. 31:18ff.; Deut. 20:14; 21:11ff.; Judg. 21:10ff.

9. I address this notion more fully in Wil Gafney, "A Queer Womanist Midrashic Reading of Numbers 25:1–18," in Athalya Brenner and Archie Chi Chung Lee, *Leviticus and Numbers* (Minneapolis: Fortress Press, 2013).

10. Athalya Brenner argues against this in "The Decalogue: Am I an Addressee?" in Athalya Brenner and Gale A. Yee, *Exodus and Deuteronomy* (Minneapolis: Fortress Press, 2012). She deduces from the gendered language in the Decalogue that men are "the people." I cannot easily dismiss her observation; it is clearly the case for some biblical tradents that women are objects and not subjects. However, even when reduced to secondary status, women are still part of the people Israel.

just near a Moabite community? Did the two peoples share grazing land, water sources, and markets? Was there regular daily contact between the two peoples? Did the Moabites welcome the Israelites to their community? Were there other residents? Did the Moabite women extend invitations to their sacred meals as an expression of their culture, to welcome their new neighbors? Why did the Israelites find Moabite worship so compelling? Did any Moabites find Israelite worship compelling? What was the nature of the relationships between the Moabite women and Israelite women and men? Were they sexual, marital, and/or religiously but not physically intimate? For the authors and editors of the text, the relationships between the peoples are deeply problematic, as signaled by the verb *z-n-h*, meaning sex-for-money in a literal sense and infidelity to the Israelite God in the broader sense, though there is no suggestion that sex-work for hire is performed in the passage.

God through Moses pronounces judgment on the Israelite people. God calls for the "heads" of the people to be executed. The heads, or leaders, of the people are never defined in the text; they are usually presented as a group. There is no clear articulation of how many persons occupied this leadership role in the wilderness, or their gender.[11] While they are traditionally read as an all-male group, there is no grammatical reason to do so. The text does not say if the leaders were themselves involved with Moabite women and participated in the sacrificial meals. It does not seem likely that all of the heads of the people did so. Yet Numbers 25:4 says that all the heads are to be executed by being hung or impaled, *y-q-ʿ*.[12] Targeting only the leaders suggests that they are to be executed for failing to keep the people from yielding to the temptation of the Moabite women and their religion. If that is indeed the case, it might explain why, apart from the leaders, neither Israelite women nor men were to suffer any negative consequences in God's decree.

A number of surprises follow. In spite of their usual xenophobic rhetoric, the Israelites do not mistreat the maligned foreign women; they execute only their own people. Secondly, in verse 5, Moses commands the judges, perhaps synonymous with the heads of the people, to kill the Israelite women and men who have joined the Moabite community. In so doing, he simply changes the divine command without consultation or consequence. The judges never execute their fellow Israelites in the narrative. Moses' command has fared no better than God's. In the next unit, a Midianite woman and her Israelite husband are executed, impaled (different verb, *d-q-r*), but not by a judge. In Numbers

11. Ezra and Nehemiah will provide lists of these persons—without attestations of gender—in their respective writings.
12. Death by hanging for the crime of miscegenation cannot escape comparison to lynching.

31 the Midianites will be savaged by the Israelites (possibly as surrogates for the Moabites), but the Moabites and their tempting women and inviting God and religious festivals largely pass from the narrative as it is written.

One of the hermeneutical keys to this text is the identity of the Moabite God. In verse 2, *eloheyhen* appears twice. It can either mean "their (the women's) *God*" or "their (the women's) *gods*." The traditional translation choice has been the plural "gods," which offers the greatest contrast with the singular Israelite God—traditionally affirmed by use of the capital letter in translation—although Hebrew lacks capital letters. However, verse 2 mentions only one deity, Ba'al of Peor. Though *elohiym* normally means the God of Israel when read in the singular, it does occur as an individual non-Israelite deity in 1 Kings 19:37. By choosing the singular to reflect the specificity of Ba'al of Peor, I choose to capitalize "God," to reflect the view of the Moabite women who are the subject of this text, not the judgment of those who produced the text. I suggest that the worshipers of the Israelite and Moabite gods did not view them as polemically opposed, as did the many framers and interpreters of this text.

Many contemporary religious readers and hearers of this text see and hear in the name Ba'al of Peor something that is irreconcilable with the God of the Scriptures, with whom they identify. It may help to remember that "Ba'al" is a title that means "lord" and/or "master," and that the God of Israel is called by that title, leading to no small amount of confusion with the Canaanite god of the same name (see Hos. 2:16). The Canaanite deity Ba'al Haddu, or Lord Haddu, was often called just Ba'al, and the title became synonymous with his name. The Hebrew expression "Ba'al Peor" is simply Lord/Master of Peor.

In addition, *ba'al* occurs frequently in the text as an adjective without reference to any deity and does not necessarily evoke heterodox religion. Examples include the Genesis 37:19–20 text, a version of which is engraved on the tomb of the Rev. Dr. Martin Luther King Jr.: "Here comes this master dreamer. Come now, let us kill him . . . and we shall see what will become of his dreams." Most translators regularly omit *ba'al* here. Other references include as "husband" in Exodus 21:3ff. and elsewhere as "horse-master" in 2 Samuel 1:6.[13] Along with Ba'al, the God of Israel also shared the names El and Elohiym with Canaanite gods—along with some psalms, hymns, imagery, and sacred stories—so there was a good deal of overlap between religious traditions.[14] All of this is to say that Ba'al of Peor may not have been perceived as

---

13. Ba'al is also an element of many place names, e.g., Josh. 11:9; Judg. 3:3; 2 Kgs. 4:42.

14. Frank Moore Cross, *Canaanite Myth and Hebrew Epic: Essays in the History of the Religion of Israel* (Cambridge, MA: Harvard University Press, 1997).

significantly different from the Israelite God, whom the people knew by many names and associated with a number of specific places.

Reading from the perspective of those for whom Ba'al of Peor is the God they have chosen to worship—perhaps not differentiating *Ba'al Peor* from the God of Israel as *Ba'al Sinai*—provides the contours of this midrash. My sanctified imagination suggests to me that the Moabite women and the Israelite women and men who are intimately involved with them represent a type of womanist community. Alice Walker's classic definition of a womanist as "a woman who loves other women, sexually and/or nonsexually. Appreciates and prefers women's culture. Committed to survival and wholeness of entire people, male and female" offers a framework for understanding these relationships.[15]

In this reading, the Moabite women are the protowomanists. They are "other" in the Israelite Scriptures, as women of African descent are frequently "other" in Western discourse. The relationships between Israelite and Moabite women suggested by the bombastic text include sexual and nonsexual: The stem *z-n-h* can indicate erotic intimacy or any other relationship, worship, or act that is perceived as disloyal to the Israelite God. I suggest that the Israelite and Moabite peoples rediscovered their common ancestry; perhaps some Israelites thought that they had reached the land of promise when they experienced the hospitality of their distant cousins. Perhaps a significant number of Israelite households defected from the caravan and settled in Moab; that would explain why others were punished in their stead. In any event, the women and men of the Israelite people entered into a number of differing relationships with the Moabite women, including intimate unions, more formal interactions, conjugal child-producing unions, and nonsexual relationships. Perhaps the women of Israel and Moab loved each other sexually and nonsexually, as intimated or at least allowed for in the words of the text "*the people began to have unsanctioned-intimate-relationships with the women of Moav.*"

Next, the Moabite women offer sacred hospitality. For this reading I am suggesting that their hospitality be read as "women's culture," in part because it is restricted to the women of Moab in this text. There is also a suggestion in the book of Ruth that Moabite culture can be read as women's culture: in Ruth 1:8, when Naomi tells the Moabite women Ruth and Orpah to go back home to Moab, she tells them to return to their "mothers' households," describing Moabite culture in matrilineal terms. (Israel had both mothers' and fathers' households.) There is something compelling about these invitations;

---

15. Alice Walker, *In Search of Our Mothers' Gardens: Womanist Prose* (San Diego: Harcourt Brace Jovanovich, 1983), xi–xii.

enough Israelites accept them to provoke the censure in the text. The rituals themselves may well have been nearly indistinguishable from the Israelites' own slaughter-sacrifice rituals, or the distinctions may not have been as significant to the people participating in the liturgies as they were to the framers of the canon and its articulation of orthodoxy.

Womanists are committed to the well-being of the whole people of their community and indeed the larger world. This is indicated by the presence of Israelite men, boys, and girls—all included in "people"—forming relationships within their host community. This is, I think, what makes this a queer text—not the possibility of same-gender sexual contact between women, or the specter of an Israelite-Moabite orgy masquerading as worship of a god-who-is-not-God, but the choice of an untold number of the Israelite people to leave their pilgrimage and prophets for a different promise, a new home among a people who welcomed them to their tables, sacred spaces, homes, and communities. And because so many accepted that hospitality, someone had to die. Those to be executed did not join the protowomanist transcultural, transgressive community. They were presumably executed for permitting or not preventing the flowering of an alternative expression of Israelite religion and culture.

The manner of execution for the surrogate victims reflects the charge of *z-n-h*, as unauthorized intimacy, specifically, penetration. The verb *y-q-'* in Hiphil means to execute ritually and publicly, in other words, a public hanging or lynching. The mechanisms include hanging, dismemberment, and impaling. Death by impaling is particularly resonant here; impaling is violent penetration, a *lex talionis* retribution for forbidden intimacy. There may not have been penetration, or even sexual intimacy, in all of the relationships between the Israelite people and Moabite women, but their surrogates will be violently and lethally penetrated on their behalf. The heads of the Israelite people will not be the last surrogates penetrated on behalf of the Israelite people who chose to live and worship with Moabite women; women, girls, boys, and men from Midian will be penetrated sexually and nonsexually, lethally and nonlethally.

The ongoing narrative is interrupted by a new narrative. The following two entries, "Cozbi bat Tzur" and "Women of Midian," are part of one large narrative told in serial episodes. Suddenly, unexpectedly, an Israelite man brings his Midianite—not Moabite—woman, Cozbi the daughter of Tzur, home to his people and their sacred space, the tent of meeting. Instead of being offered a place at the welcome table, they are violently penetrated at the hands of Phinehas, Aaron's grandson. The silence of God in the story so far is deafening: Moses speaks for God but does not speak to God, and God does not speak to Moses.

COZBI BAT TZUR

Numbers 25:6 Suddenly, a man from the women and men of Israel came and brought a Midianite woman to his kinfolk, in the sight of Moshe (Moses) and in the sight of the whole congregation of the women and men of Israel, and they were weeping at the entrance of the tent of meeting! [7]Then Pinchas (Phinehas) ben El'azar (Eleazar) ben Aharon (Aaron) the priest saw; he rose from the midst of the congregation and took a spear in his hand. [8]He went after the Israelite man into the tent-chamber, and he stabbed the two of them, the Israelite man and the woman, through her inner-chamber, and the plague was stopped among the people of Israel. . . . [14]The name of the slain Israelite man who was killed with the Midianite woman was Zimri ben Salu, leader of an ancestral house belonging to the Simeonites. [15]The name of the Midianite woman who was killed was Cozbi bat Tzur; Tzur was the head of peoples, of an ancestral house in Midian.

Numbers 25 reads something like a serial drama. The last episode ended in verse 5 with a cliff-hanger; the judges of Israel are commanded to kill all of the women and men of Israel who have joined the community offered by the local Moabite women (see preceding section, "Women of Moab"). What happens next? Do the judges kill them all? Do the judges kill any of them? How many are guilty? The audience never finds out, because the next episode opens with a new outrage, which leads to killing and more killing, with last week's intended victims obscured in the bloody haze of this week's vengeful violence.

This week's episode opens with a wedding. However, instead of an Israelite wedding canopy, a *chuppah*, there is a foreign wedding tent, a *qubbah*. The wedding is held in the center of the Israelite camp, in front of the Israelite sanctuary. Everyone is there, but not just for the wedding. In a nod to the previous episode, those assembled are weeping, perhaps at the news that so many of their friends and families have been targeted for execution, or perhaps at the news that those who are judges have been charged with the executions of so many of their friends and family members.

Suddenly Pinchas (Phinehas) the priest runs to grab a spear and stabs the newlyweds to death in front of their friends and family and the assembly and the tent of the conspicuously silent God of Israel. The text names the dead as it makes a crude pun about just where Phinehas inserted his spear in the woman's body. The Moabite women, their God, and the Israelite women and men who joined their community sharing kinship ties and worship have been forgotten. This Midianite woman and her people become the focus of the saga. The Moabites and Midianites are interchangeable; they are all foreigners—never mind that Israel is migrating through inhabited lands to a settled one, uninvited.

Cozbi bat Tzur is a woman of some standing among her peoples. Her father is a leader of peoples, head of a Midianite clan. Numbers 31:8 calls Tzur, Cozbi's father, a king. Her people and the Israelites were already intermarried. Cozbi's Midianite people took Moses in when he fled Egypt after taking the life of an Egyptian. Cozbi's Midianite sister Zipporah took Moses for her man, gave birth to his children, and saved his life.[16] Cozbi's fellow Midianite Jethro (also known as Reuel and Hobab) was the priest of Midian who served the God of Israel's ancestors and the exodus on the sacred mountain, Horeb (also known as Sinai), when Moses did not know enough not to graze sheep on God's mountain. He was the same Midianite priest who offered the appropriate and acceptable sacrifice to God when Moses and his Midianite family were last together in Exodus 18:12. Jethro had even helped design the judicial system in Israel, because Moses did not know how to delegate or that he should (see Exod. 18:13ff.). However, the larger story in Exodus 18 also reveals that there was a serious division in Moses' own Israelite-Midianite hybrid family.

Even in dissolution, Moses' own Midianite intermarriage casts a shadow over this narrative. His grandnephew, Phinehas, executes a man and a woman for doing what Moses did repeatedly. Moses' first marriage to the Midianite *bat kohen* Zipporah and the close relationship between the Midianites and Israelites may explain why Zimri ben Salu, Cozbi's intended, planned a big family wedding in front of the Israelite sanctuary. Surely Zimri could not have imagined that he would be executed for following in the footsteps of Moses the lawgiver. Indeed, after sending Zipporah and their children back to her father, Moses' second marriage recorded in Numbers 12 was also to a non-Israelite, a Nubian woman.

Cozbi's death follows the death sentence pronounced on Israelites who had accepted the Moabite women's offer of sacred hospitality, but what did that have to do with Zimri and Cozbi? Cozbi is Midianite, like Moses' in-laws, not Moabite; yet the two peoples are conflated in malignant xenophobia. On his own, with no command from God or Moses, Phinehas takes up a spear and follows Cozbi into her *qubbah*, wedding tent-chamber; the foreign word occurs only this once in the Scriptures. With an uncertain meaning, *HALOT* relates it to Midianite tent-shrines.[17] In that case, it would have been a domed tent or structure, as a *qubah* in Arabic is most literally a dome, as is the Aramaic *qubbeta* (per *HALOT*).[18]

16. See Exod. 2:21–22; 4:24–26.
17. The editors of the *Jewish Study Bible* relate the term to its Arabic homophone, as Midian was partially located on the Arabian Peninsula.
18. The JPS Torah Commentary similarly relates it to a Bedouin sanctuary also used for weddings, associated with women of high status (like Cozbi) and with female

The *qubbah*, tent-chamber (my trans.), makes a pun with *qevah*, the place where Cozbi's body was penetrated. Neither word occurs again in the Scriptures. Cozbi's *qevah* is her body's "private chamber."[19] Fox preserves the nuance with his "private-parts." NRSV and JPS both use "belly," which, when combined with their respective "tent" and "chamber," completely miss the symmetry of the text. The IB does not translate the term. Zimri's fatal injury is not elaborated upon. Cozbi's deathblow is rendered a punch line: the Midianite woman is killed through the violent penetration of her womb and/or vagina—terminating and parodying the conjugal union that Cozbi, Zimri, and his family (perhaps accompanied by her family) were gathered in the presence of God to celebrate.

Verse 9 indicates that other killing has been occurring simultaneously. Twenty-four thousand Israelites are killed in a mysterious plague that stops as soon as Phinehas kills Cozbi and Zimri. It is not clear whether all of these Israelites have begun new lives with Moabite women or if, as Numbers 26:64–65 suggests, God just uses that occasion to kill off the remainder of those who left Egypt but are condemned to die before reaching the promised land.

Perhaps the only thing more disturbing than Phinehas's actions is the divine pronouncement that follows. While God did not speak in the previous subunit, leaving the responsibility for the execution orders against the Israelite people on Moses' hands and lips, God does speak in this portion of the saga, albeit after the fact. God vindicates and rewards Phinehas, with of all things a "covenant of *shalom*," superficially a covenant of peace, more broadly one of well-being, wholeness, and restoration (vv. 11–12). For the authors, editors, and God in the text, Phinehas has restored the community after its infestation by and infatuation with foreign women; for this, his zealous rage is commended. He is further rewarded in verse 13 with a perpetual priesthood.

While in traditional commentaries the slaying of Cozbi is linked with the defection of Israelites to Moabite families and worship, under the rubric of "apostasy," that is not what is happening in this passage. Unlike the people condemned to death in the beginning of the chapter, Cozbi and Zimri are not accused of worshiping other gods. The fact that they are having the wedding ceremony at the Israelite shrine may well indicate Cozbi's acceptance of the God of Israel as her own. Even if that were not her intent, Zimri's choice of a non-Israelite woman puts him in the company of the patriarchs Judah, Joseph, and Simeon, in addition to Moses himself. None of these unions was

---

religious leaders. The IB translates it as a "nuptial tent," the NRSV simply as a "tent," JPS as a "chamber," and Everett Fox as a "private chamber."

19. NB: The same letter makes the "b" and "v" sounds here; both words are spelled *qof-beyt-heh*.

punctuated by the imposition of capital punishment or plagues. What is it about this union in particular that sends Phinehas (and God) into a killing rage?

Cozbi and Zimri have violated a taboo. Specifically, Zimri and Cozbi have transgressed in a *consensual* intermarriage. This taboo does not necessarily reflect the wilderness wandering period in which this story is set; rather, it reflects the fears and concerns of the decimated survivors of a shrinking post-monarchal province under foreign domination when the written text would have been finalized, edited, and canonized. In that and subsequent interpretive contexts, intermarriage becomes a harbinger of extinction, but with some important caveats. David's intermarriages (and those in his lineage) are largely overlooked because of his role in crafting a monarchy with imperial ambitions.

I say that their crime was their *consensual* relationship because Numbers will go on to prescribe *torah* for abduction and rape-marriage of enemy women and prepubescent girls into sanctioned unions from Cozbi's own Midianite people. Deuteronomy will refine this *torah*, and the practice of abducting women and girls endures throughout the canon. As a foreign woman, if Cozbi bat Tzur had been captured in battle as a child or prepubescent girl, she would have been good enough to abduct and rape into marriage. But she was not good enough for Zimri ben Salu to choose of his own free will. She and he had to die. Indeed, some rabbinic commentaries interpret the deaths of Cozbi and Zimri as fulfilling the divine command that "all the heads of the people" be impaled in Numbers 25:4.[20] This interpretation is an attempt to address the fact that God's command goes unfulfilled in the previous story. Indeed, Moses gives an entirely different command in verse 5: that the judges should kill everyone among the people who transgressed, annulling God's command to kill the judges. Neither command is fulfilled, adding to the inscrutability of this chapter.

What is clear is that intermarriage is suddenly a grave problem. But what about the aforementioned patriarchs, Judah, Joseph, Simeon, and Moses, and their consensual unions with non-Israelite women? Perhaps Cozbi and Zimri are surrogates for them, and the viciousness of their executions reflects a suppressed rage against their untouchable leaders. What is a religious reader/hearer to make of this story, particularly of God's affirmation of Phinehas's actions? It is clear that the biblical text and the god in and of this text affirm lethal violence to enforce social, cultural, and religious norms. Turning to the context of canon shaping, a reader/hearer might take into account the fierce xenophobia and self-protectionism of the Israelites who survived the demise

20. See the excursus on what is called "The Apostasy of Baal-Peor" in the JPS Torah Commentary on Numbers.

of their own nation at the hands of the Assyrians and Babylonians and hear this episode as bombastic bravado. A religious reader-hearer might look to God-beyond-the-text and reject this text as an imperfect reflection of their God, who transcends social, cultural, and religious norms.

One terrible irony is that the foreign Midianites are no "pagan" Canaanites; they worshiped God of the Holy Name, YHWH, on the mountain before Israel did, and their priest Jethro instructed Moses in the ways of serving their shared God. How embarrassing! Better to eradicate any indication that there were predecessors to the chosen people. The pretense that the two peoples and their worship are completely different and their segregation must be enforced with lethal violence does beg comparison with race-based violence and the construction of racial categories that have characterized genocide in the twentieth and twenty-first centuries.

There is a familiarity in the profound otherness constructed for the Midianite people, so completely other that they are not worthy of human dignity in the eyes of the Israelite authors and editors. This ontological otherness evokes the otherness of blacks in the Americas from slavery through the civil rights era; the otherness of black folk was the antithesis to white supremacist ideologies, legislation, and social policies built and defended with lethal means. It is not that the Israelites are racially distinct from the Midianites, as the category of race doesn't exist in antiquity; it is that their ethnic distinctiveness functions like racial otherness. The ethnic differences between Midian and Israel are complicated by their shared religion, like the shared Christian identity claimed by the enslaved and slaveholders and the shared Christianity of the Hutu and Tutsi peoples of the Rwandan genocide. In this reading, Cozbi's killing is a lynching, and Zimri is killed as a race traitor, identifying with marginalized community over and against his or her own people.

The execution of Cozbi and Zimri has the depraved reasoning of a lynching, a lethal act of terror to put or keep a subjugated people in their place. The sexualization of Cozbi's execution evokes the rapine and sexualized torture of lynched women: Laura Nelson in Okluskee, OK, on May 23, 1911; Cordella Stevenson in Columbus, MS, on December 8, 1915; and Mary Turner in Lowndes County, GA, on May 17, 1918, in particular. Cozbi's killing evokes most the butchering of Mrs. Turner, who was stabbed in the belly, as was Cozbi; she was cut open to excise the full-term child she was carrying, who was then stomped to death as she was hung by her feet, set on fire, and shot.[21]

---

21. The National Association for the Advancement of Colored People (NAACP) holds extensive archives on lynching in America, and James Allen has assembled a comprehensive collection of photographs of lynched women and men in his 2000 volume *Without Sanctuary: Lynching Photography in America* (Santa Fe, NM: Twin Palms Publishers. 2000).

As lynching victims, Cozbi and Zimri become scapegoats who incarnate the sin conferred on them by those who sacrifice them to expiate their own perceived sin. The term "scapegoat" comes from Leviticus 16, in which a goat is sent to the wilderness after having had the premeditated and therefore unabsolvable sin in Israel transferred to it. Literally, the goat is sent *l'Aza'zel*, "to Aza'zel." Some rabbinic and Christian translators broke *l'Aza'zel* into two parts that they then translated "goat that escapes," yielding the "scapegoat" of the Tyndale, Bishops', Geneva, and King James Bibles. However, like *Mika'el* (Michael), *Gavri'el* (Gabriel), and *Rapha'el* (Raphael), *Aza'zel* is the name of a legendary supernatural being. While the beneficent Michael, Gabriel, and Raphael have been received as "angels," the demonic Aza'zel has all but disappeared. Aza'zel is the one who controls the realm beyond the realm where the God of Israel is sovereign. In sending the sin-goat to Aza'zel, the Israelite God was putting the sin of God's people out of the world that mattered.[22] Acknowledging another supernatural entity was not seen as a problem, because the Torah is henotheistic (hierarchy among gods) rather than monotheistic (denying the existence of all but one god)—hence the divine jealousy over worship of other gods. After the deaths of Cozbi and her intended Zimri, her father Tzur, who is killed in Numbers 31:8, and the other Midianite monarchs fall in battle, and tens of thousands Midianite women, men, and children are killed as scapegoats for the forbidden, largely sexual, desires of the Israelite people.

Cozbi's killing epitomizes the type of violence with which the Old Testament—when the Hebrew Scriptures are held in distinction from a "New" Testament—has become synonymous for many who express discomfort with the (sub)canon. This divinely sanctioned killing demonstrates the most profound othering of human beings in the name of religion and in the name of God. The unit even includes the quintessential expression of violence in the Hebrew Scriptures, "smiting" ("strike," *n-k-h*, in v. 17). Readers and hearers of the biblical text as Scriptures through which they (we) seek/hear/experience God must articulate how this passage and others like it function religiously in the contemporary world, in which there remains lethal religious violence, including some that appeals to the Bible for its justification.

This subunit ends with some victim blaming and by drawing a link from the Peor matter to Cozbi bat Tzur to all her people, but most particularly the women. In the section below, "Women of Midian," God sounds suspiciously like an Iron Age theologian justifying his people's actions in the name of their God and religion. The subsequent violence against the Midianite people is

22. "[B]eyond civilization" in Baruch J. Schwartz's commentary on Lev. 16:8 in the *Jewish Study Bible*; Jacob Milgrom identifies the wilderness to which the goat is sent as "the habitation of demons," *Leviticus 1–16*, *Anchor Yale Bible* (New Haven, CT: Yale University Press, 1974), 1020.

God's will. They bring it on themselves according to the God-in-the-text. However, the text is not clear. What is the initiating attack? Inviting the Israelites to their sacred meals and receiving them into their communities? Nor is the text clear how the union of Cozbi and Zimri in the light of day, at the center of the Israelite camp, is an act of deception. By placing these claims on divine lips, the authors and editors of the narrative may have sought to forestall questions, critique, and repudiation of the violence. But they have failed.

WOMEN OF MIDIAN

Numbers 25:16 The FIRE OF SINAI said to Moshe, [17]"Attack the Midianite women, men, and children, and strike them; [18]for they have attacked you all by the trickery with which they deceived you all in the Peor matter, and in the Cozbi matter, the daughter of a leader of Midian, their sister; she was killed on the day of the plague that resulted from Peor."

This call for the war with Midian, ("smiting" in v. 17), is supposed to be read as the logical conclusion of the wedding-day massacre of Cozbi bat Tzur and her Israelite groom Zimri ben Salu earlier in Numbers 25 (see the previous section, "Cozbi bat Tzur"). The accounts of hostilities against the Midianites carried out in Numbers 31 are linked with the Israelite defection at the invitation of Moabite women at the beginning of this chapter. And all of these subunits are linked to the (in)famous foreign prophet Balaam.

The expressions "the Peor matter" and "the Cozbi matter" in verse 18 are irrational incitements to violence: Peor was the place where Balaam blessed and refused to curse Israel (Num. 23:28–24:9), not the site of an attack or other violence, and the place where some Israelite women and men formed intimate relationships with some Moabite women and accepted their invitations to share in sacred meals (Num. 25:1–2). Cozbi was a prominent Midianite (*not* Moabite) woman, the daughter of a clan chief or king, who along with her groom was assassinated on the day of her wedding to an Israelite, with a spear thrust through her reproductive organs. Their wedding was open and public, as were their killings, in the sight of the people and in front of the Israelite sanctuary, presumably in the presence of God (Num. 25:6–15). None of this makes any sense, especially the shift from the Moabites, with whom some Israelites did enter consensual unions at the beginning of the chapter, to the Midianites, with whom Moses himself had intermarried some time ago. Neither Moses' marriage nor his in-laws are mentioned as their people are slaughtered and women taken captive for reproductive use. Where are his sisters-in-law and the rest of the members of Jethro's household?

The justification for the slaughter fails to meet the excuses given in the text. In none of these episodes were the Israelites "attacked" or even "tricked," as claimed in Numbers 25:18. The claim of trickery also makes Zimri ben Salu and other Israelite men look like hapless fools while emphasizing the danger of foreign women. The vitriolic language in the call to arms equates some voluntary intercultural worship and intimate unions with violent assaults, thereby justifying violence in retaliation for nonviolent intercultural contact that was interpreted as apostasy. It is more than ironic that the only Israelite to die violently in this episode was killed by another Israelite full of (divinely sanctioned) righteous indignation. The illogic of this episode contributes to the senseless rage holding these narratives together.

The anti-Midianite narrative breaks after the call to arms for a census. As a consequence of the census, there is a dispute about the allocation of land based on the census (see the next section, "Mahlah, Noah, Hoglah, Milcah, and Tirzah, Daughters of Zelophehad"). Following the census there are several chapters of religious instructions; then, without any transition, at Numbers 31:1 the story returns to the Midianites: "The Ancient One spoke to Moshe (Moses), saying, [2]'Avenge the Israelites on the Midianites; afterward you shall be gathered to your people.'"

In the ensuing verses God and Moses repeatedly call for vengeance against the Midianites. God does not tell Moses how to get this revenge, leaving the specifics entirely up to Moses. The intervening verses describe the muster of twelve thousand Israelite soldiers and the Israelite military victory over the five monarchs of Midian, whom they kill, including Tzur, the father of Cozbi. Cozbi's wedding-day assassination spirals into this war on the claim that her Midianite people have provoked it through trickery, exemplified by her union with an Israelite and the previous unions of some other Israelites with Moabite women. The text shows little interest in sorting out the various "-ites." After killing the monarchs of Midian, the first thing the fighting forces do in Numbers 31:9 is take Midianite women and girls captive to use sexually.

Three terms are used repeatedly and interchangeably in this narrative and others like it: *shalal* ("spoils of war"), *malqoach* ("booty"), and *baz* ("plunder"). All three terms are used to describe women and girls. For many readers there may be an apparent disconnect between the idea of booty as plunder and the understanding of booty as a colloquial term for a person's buttocks. Narratives such as this and others, from the slave trade to pirate lore—not the Disneyfied pirates but the slave-trading purveyors of forced prostitution—demonstrate the link between captive people, particularly but not exclusively women and girls, as sexual merchandise and other items of value captured during armed conflict. The concept of a person's physiological booty as spoils of war booty has passed almost unnoticed into the lexicon of American English and African American cultural rhetoric, in which booty has been reduced from a whole person to a person's anal and genital orifices, often accessed from the back. In addition, there is the most recent expansion of the lexicon to include "booty-licious" from the song of the same title by Destiny's Child.[23] Given the ongoing colonization and exploitation of African diasporic and African American sexuality, especially female sexuality, the veneration of young women who proclaim the deliciousness of their own booty is utterly fascinating.

As a consequence of the Midianite war, the Midianite women and children are taken as booty. The value among the women and girls is in their availability for rape-marriages. In the biblical text these unions are legitimate conjugal unions that produce children who are recognized as legitimate members of the Israelite community. These unions are rape-based because of the lack of consent to these unions and concomitant sexual intercourse, not just in the contemporary sense. The normative practices associated with conjugal unions in the Hebrew Scriptures—negotiations between families, consent of the parents or the woman herself—are not present in these narratives.

After securing their female booty the warriors secure livestock and other valuables. Then Moses becomes furious with them. The reasons for Moses' escalating rage are unclear. This war began in the aftermath of intermarriage between a Midianite woman and an Israelite man; there were earlier unions between Israelite women and men and Moabite women in Numbers 25:1. Is Moses angry that there will be *more* intercultural unions? Apparently not; the Israelites can keep Midianite women, or rather girls, as long as they are not sexually experienced. Moses also calls for the slaughter of all Midianite boys, including infants and toddlers, recreating the pharaoh's genocide at his birth. The text is nearly incoherent; I imagine Moses sputtering and shaking with rage:

> Numbers 31:15 Moshe (Moses) said to them, "You all have let-live all the females! [16]They, these females here, they were for the women and men of Israel through the word of Bi'lam (Balaam) the cause of turning away against the HOLY ONE in the Peor matter, so that the plague came among the congregation of the HOLY ONE. [17]Now then, kill every male among the little ones, and every woman who has known a man by lying with a male you all shall kill. [18]And all the little ones among the women who have not known a man by lying with a male, keep alive for yourselves. . . ." [32]The booty remaining from the plunder that the troops had taken totaled six hundred seventy-five thousand sheep, [33]seventy-two thousand oxen, [34]sixty-one thousand

---

23. Beyoncé Knowles et al., "Bootylicious," *Survivor*, Columbia Records, 2000.

donkeys, [35] and thirty-two thousand human souls in all, from women who had not known a man by sleeping with him.

Moses' instructions offer some rationale for his anger; he would have preferred to see all of the Midianite women dead. Does this include his wife and sisters-in-law? As with the internal logic of the chapter, there are conflicts with the events as they have been recorded. There is no account of the Midianite women entering unions with Israelite men other than Cozbi and Moses himself. As it is written, Moses seems to be angry that women who have been sexually intimate with their own men, including every wife and mother, were not summarily executed; they might give birth to other Midianites, and he is intent on genocide. That explains his anger that the Israelites have spared the baby boys. Moses' "corrective" is to order the deaths of the Midianite women who are sexually active and all of the baby boys. Moses' genocide is more effective and efficient than that of the pharaoh. He has learned well.

Moses, or the one who crafts this speech for him, blames the women among his Midianite in-laws for Israel's relationships with Moabite women, and he personally oversees the designation of thirty-two thousand sexually inexperienced girls as booty. The number is so astronomical as to be incredible. However one understands the number, its role in the passage is clear: the Israelites annihilate a significant portion of the Midianite people and will use the remaining virginal girls to breed them out of existence, paternity being reckoned patrilineally. Moses' Midianite family is unmentioned; with six sisters-in-law, surely he has nieces. What is their fate?

Moses then introduces a new element to the story: the Midianite women made the Israelite women and men join the Moabite women and are therefore responsible for Israelite faithlessness. The notion that forcing Midianite girls into conjugal and childbearing relationships with Israelite men is vengeance for consensual Israelite-Moabite unions, and one (more) Israelite-Midianite union is stupefying. Moses has in a fell swoop just added thirty-two thousand potential mixed marriages into the community. This illogic is entirely consistent with a dominant strain in the Hebrew Scriptures: Israelite men are helpless in the face of foreign women's seductive sexuality. They will give up anything, including their own God. The only way to protect them from themselves is to exterminate the foreign threat; rape and forced pregnancy were acceptable genocidal alternatives.

The issue of Moses' own Midianite family looms large over this narrative, even though (and because) the text says nothing of his own family. Moses is calling for the execution of sexually active Midianite women like his own wife, Zipporah. His father-in-law Jethro could have been among the dead. While his two sons "counted" as Israelites, what about their cousins, aunts, uncles, neighbors, and other kin? The text also neglects to mention the Abrahamic pedigree of the Midianites; they are the descendants of Keturah and Abraham. Did Moses *really* call for genocide for his own in-laws, kinfolk, and skin-folk?

Biblical scholars generally read the unit as the work of the priestly school of editors.[24] When the canon took its final shape, the priestly community was particularly concerned with intercultural relationships in the light of Israel's subjugation to Assyria, Babylon, and Persia. In this light I read the calls for vengeance against the Midianites, Midianite/Moabite conflation, and valorization of Phinehas placed on the lips of God and Moses as attempts to rehabilitate Aaron's grandson Phinehas and shore up the image of the priesthood. Underneath the disparate traditions there may be a narrative in which Phinehas starts the Midianite war by assassinating Cozbi, the royal daughter of the house Tzur, believing he is carrying out the will of God.

Even though the linkages and rationales are tenuous at best, the war chronicle functions as the conclusion to the trilogy comprised of the blessing of Balaam, the hospitality of the Moabite women, and the marriage of Cozbi and Zimri. Also connecting these stories is xenophobia, fear of foreigners—in particular foreign women, as seductresses who will entice the women and men of Israel away from their own God. Again it is clear that Israelite worship is not imagined to be equally compelling. When Cozbi appears to voluntarily choose the people of Israel and their God, she is violently repudiated. The Israelites don't appear to believe in evangelism or conversion.

The use of force, subjugation, and rape to restore order to the Israelite universe is telling. In this saga the agency, dignity, and humanity of non-Israelite women are so threatening that they must be destroyed through sexual subordination on an industrial scale. Rather than be permitted to enter into unions with Israelite men and women on their own terms or bear children who will construct their own cultural and religious identities—even if that means choosing to identify with Israel, as did Cozbi—these women and their future children are condemned to a life of subjugation, in which their identity and newly abased status are conferred on them through systematic, religiously sanctioned rape and forced impregnation.

The Torah will enact statutes (in Deut. 20–21) regulating the practice of abducting women and girls for procreative use and offering some limited protections to the abducted women and their children. This practice endured—and continues to endure in the world beyond the text—because it is effective. It demoralizes the conquered, and when the children of these unions are counted as the children of the victors through forced impregnation, they

---

24. See Baruch Levine's commentary, *Numbers 21–36, Anchor Yale Bible* (New Haven, CT: Yale University Press, 1974), 285–92.

simultaneously build up the community of the victor while eradicating the community of the conquered. Forced impregnation is a tool of genocide, particularly when combined with the extermination of all of the males in a conquered society. The modern world has seen it in Bosnia, Serbia, Rwanda, Darfur, and the Congo, and most recently in territories controlled by *Daesh*.[25] The othering of the Abrahamic Midianite people as a whole brings to mind the intractable conflict between Israelis and Palestinians. The shared ancestry is essentially erased by those who portray their sister and brother Semites as wholly other (albeit without the sexual subordination called for in this text). On a smaller scale, individual men abduct women and girls, imprisoning and impregnating them and making news in Europe and in the United States; some of these men and their female accomplices articulate religious rationales for their crimes.

My sanctified imagination reads against the text and against the portrayal of God in the text:

> *God! God didn't do this! A man did this. Pinchas ought to be ashamed of himself! His mother, Putiel, is beside herself with grief. The way he did that beautiful girl. He raped her with a spear in front of God and everybody. Talking about "It's God's will." God speaks to him. He may be hearing voices, but my God had nothing to do with that mess.*
>
> *What? What am I talking about? Child, where are you from? You can't be from anywhere around here if you don't know what happened yesterday at the Israelite camp—a cold-blooded murder on sacred ground. This war they're conscripting boys for today is because of that murder.*
>
> *You see the Midianites and Israelites are kinfolk from way back; they share the same old-father, Avraham, but have different great-mothers. The Midianites were born from Qeturah of the deserts; they say she was the love of his life at the end of his life. The Israelites were born from Sarah his own sister—I know, I know, we don't hold to them sorts of ways around here now, but that's what they did then. Anyway, they say she got his wealth and Qeturah got his heart. There was a 'nother woman, Hagar, mixed up with them . . . but where was I?*
>
> *The wedding . . . it was a big to-do. Her Ladyship, Princess Cozbi, only child of King Tzur, took an Israelite for her royal consort. His name was*

---

25. An acronym for *al-Dawla al-Islamiya fi al-Iraq wa al-Sham*, the Arabic name of the terror group initially called the "Islamic State" in Iraq, Syria, and other parts of the Levant. (Its most common appellation, ISIS, is an acronym for the Islamic State in Syria.) *Daesh* is the preferable nomenclature to many who reject the religious characterization of the group, as the word *daesh* in Arabic has derogatory implications.

Zimri; he was from good people; his father Salu was head of his local clan, but he was definitely marrying up. Everyone was looking forward to the celebration and, to tell the truth, some were looking for trouble. But no one expected this.

You see, a while back the Israelite head-man, Moshe, divorced the senior priest-woman of Midian, left her with their children, and went off and married another woman, even though her family took him in when he was nothing and had nothing. Her father, the great high priest of all Midian, took him as an apprentice in the priesthood, but Moshe didn't have the aptitude. His brother Aharon took his place. Abba Yitro even continued to mentor him, teach him something after he left his daughter, and he tried to get them back together too. That's the kind of man he is.

Well, people wanted to see if Zipporah was going to be at the royal wedding and what Moshe would say to her and her father. Soon enough, everyone forgot about that. . . . You should have seen the wedding; Cozbi was draped with so much gold and silver that she couldn't move. The royal Midianite wedding tent was set right in front of the Israelite sacred tent, symbolizing the union of the two peoples. Everyone was there. The feast was already set up: honey bread, date wine, roast quail, slow-grilled goat kid, and minced lamb. . . . And just as Zimri formally presented his beloved to his family, one of the Israelite priests—a priest!—stabbed him with a spear and killed him.

People started running, screaming; it was pandemonium. Then Pinchas turned on Cozbi. He chased her into her own wedding tent. A group of other priests grabbed her honor guard, wrestling them and delaying them just long enough—they had planned it all out. Pinchas was shrieking how he will cleanse the foreign influence from out of Israel by blood and fire if need be. He called her horrible names as he stabbed her in the belly and down below over and over again: "She-devil! Foreign whore! You'll never use your whore-parts to ensnare another Israelite man! With your blood I atone for the sin of Israel! God grant me and all who follow me peace from your kind forevermore!"

Pinchas and his folk started killing everyone they could find in the wedding party. Moshe ran into the tent of God and prayed for the plague of violence to pass him and his family by and to come to an end. When he finished praying, as they were gathering the dead and tending the wounded, Pinchas said that the Midianites would come looking for vengeance, and the only way to protect Israel was to strike them first. He'd planned it all along. Moshe was beside himself with grief. He stayed in the sacred tent while Pinchas spoke in his name, as his grandfather Aharon used to do. To get the people to go along with him, he promised them all the wealth of Midian. There were just enough greedy, craven souls to back him up. And then appealing to the lowest of the low, Pinchas promised every Israelite warrior a Midianite virgin and slaves for every family.

And now look at them. Gearing up for war. Trampling Cozbi's memory into the dust. They've already forgot how they done her. Hmpf. They've forgotten that they were slaves. You'd best get your family out of here. It's not safe for decent folk.

MAHLAH, NOAH, HOGLAH, MILCAH, AND TIRZAH, THE DAUGHTERS OF ZELOPHEHAD

Numbers 27:1 The women came-forward, the daughters of Zelophehad ben Hepher ben Gilead ben Machir ben Manasseh ben Yosef, a member of the Manassite clans. These are the names of his daughters: Mahlah, Noah, Hoglah, Milcah, and Tirzah. [2]They stood before Moshe, and before El'azar the priest, and before the leaders, and all the congregation, at the entrance of the tent of meeting, saying, [3]"Our father died in the wilderness; he was not among the congregation of those who appointed themselves against the Holy One of Sinai in the congregation of Korach, but he died for his own sin; and he had no sons. [4]Why should the name of our father be taken away from his clan because he had no son? Give to us a possession among our father's male-kin." [5]Moshe brought their case before the Holy One of Old. [6]And the Holy One said to Moshe; [7]"The daughters of Zelophehad are right in their speaking; you shall surely give to them a possession, an inheritance among their father's brothers and you shall pass the inheritance of their father on to them. [8]And to the women and men of Israel you shall also say, 'When a man dies and has no son, then you shall pass his inheritance on to his daughter.'"

Mahlah, Noah, Hoglah, Milcah, and Tirzah are some of the most important women in the canon. Many Jewish and Christian feminists and womanists know them as the daughters of Zelophehad. Their story is so important that they are mentioned in five different places: Numbers 26:33; 27:1–11; 36:1–12; Joshua 17:3–6; and 1 Chronicles 7:15. Only the prophets Miriam and Moses are mentioned in more books in the Hebrew Bible, and the iterations of their story outnumber the four canonical Christian Gospels.

Numbers 26:28–33 introduces Mahlah, Noah, Hoglah, Milcah, and Tirzah in the genealogy of their clan. It begins with an accounting of the descendants of Asenath the African matriarch and Joseph, who became the parents of the two half-Egyptian, half tribes of Israel, Ephraim and Manasseh. One of their tenth-generation sons, Zelophehad, fathered five daughters with a woman whose name has not been preserved. The mother of the daughters

---

"I Call Your Names"

I make a point to call Mahlah, Noah, Hoglah, Milcah, and Tirzah by their names as often as possible. When the names of so many women and girls in the Scriptures have been erased, those who remain are particularly precious. I have noticed that many women in congregations and classrooms know their story and the name of their father, Zelophehad, but not theirs. The practice of calling the names of African ancestors with the liturgical formula "I/we call your name" derives from West African religious practices, including but not limited to the Yoruba religion. The Yoruba-language affirmation "Ashé!," which concludes the ritual sentence, functions like the Judeo-Christian "Amen," with a slightly different semantic range, including "power" and "cosmic harmony." Mahlah, Noah, Hoglah, Milcah, and Tirzah, I call your names. *Ashé!*

---

of Zelophehad is not mentioned in any of their narratives. There is no way to determine if she is missing from their lives or just missing from the story. The rabbis in *b. Bava Batra* 119b suggest that Zelophehad was a widower. The recitation of the women's names in four of the five texts in which their story is told is extraordinary, given the paucity of women's names in Scripture. According to Carol Meyers, of the 1,426 personal names that appear in the Hebrew text, 1,315 are or are presumed to be male.[26] That means that there are only about 111 female personal names in the Scriptures of Israel, representing a mere 9 percent of the characters in the First Testament.

The second mention of Mahlah, Noah, Hoglah, Milcah, and Tirzah occurs in the next chapter. Here their story begins to unfold in narrative form. Their story is within one of the censuses from which the book of Numbers takes its English title. God commissions the census in Numbers 26:1–4, commanding the counting of "the whole congregation of the Israelites, from twenty years old and upward, by their ancestral houses, everyone in Israel able to go to war." The context is the war against Midian (Num. 25). The "whole congregation" is a gender-inclusive expression, "Israelites," *beney yisrael*, that functions as an inclusive term when used for the whole people. Although those "able to go to war" has traditionally been understood to refer to males because of the amount of time that females of child-bearing age spent pregnant and

---

26. See Carol Meyers's essay "Everyday Life," in Carol A. Newsom and Sharon H. Ringe, *Women's Bible Commentary* (Louisville, KY: Westminster John Knox Press, 1992).

nursing, there are accounts of individual female combatants such as Deborah, Jael, and Judith. At the end of chapter 26, the text shifts from the war. God tells Moses to use the census to apportion land according to the number of names in the census (26:53) and according to paternal tribal affiliation, *matoth-avotam* (26:55).

The conflation of the military muster with the apportionment plan meant that only males were entitled to inherit the inhabited Canaanite land that God had promised the Israelites under this schema. The land was not given just to males of war-fighting age or to every family represented in the muster census. Instead, only patriarchal households counted, while excluding Mahlah, Noah, Hoglah, Milcah, and Tirzah and, likely, an unknown and unacknowledged number of others. Patriarchal households[27] headed by a male, *av* ("father"), were not the only type of Israelite household; Israel's ancestral matriarch Milcah, the mother of Bethuel and grandmother of Rebekah, was head of her own household as an *em* ("mother").[28] There is no accounting of the number of *beyt emoth* ("mother's households") in ancient Israel at any time. But more germane to the text at hand, men died and left women as the heads of households, no matter how the family unit was previously structured and without regard to the preferred structure in that culture, legislature around levirate practices notwithstanding.

The disenfranchisement of women from inheriting land was particular to Israel in the ancient world. Just as Israel was relatively isolated in largely restricting women from public and professional religious roles, they were also virtually alone in legislating women's exclusion from property law. Women throughout the ancient Near East, from Egypt to Mesopotamia broadly, and specifically in places like Sumer, Ugarit, and Elam, owned and inherited property for more than a thousand years before the codification of Israelite law. The codes of Hammurabi and Israel's Hittite neighbors also legally enfranchised the property rights of women.[29]

Mahlah, Noah, Hoglah, Milcah, and Tirzah were specifically excluded from the census because they were manless. Their father was dead, they were unmarried, and they had no brothers. There was no male relative close enough to them in the patriarchal system of kinship that Moses was using

27. Here I am simply referring to the attribute of male-headed households.

28. See Gen. 24:28 for Rebekah's matriarchal household; see also Song 8:2 for another and 2 Sam. 2:18 for David's sister Zeruiah, whose sons bore her name, as Bethuel bore his mother's.

29. For a sampling of cotemporal legal codes, see Victor Harold Matthews and Don C. Benjamin, *Old Testament Parallels: Laws and Stories from the Ancient Near East*, 4th ed. (New York: Paulist Press, 2016). See also the excursus on "The Inheritance Rights of Daughters" in the JPS Torah Commentary on Numbers.

whose allocation of land would extend to them. In the time accounted for in the thirty-two verses in Numbers 26:33–65, Mahlah, Noah, Hoglah, Milcah, and Tirzah analyze and respond to the inequity of the land distribution system. The Torah does not reflect on their deliberations, presenting their response in word and deed as seemingly spontaneous.

The first word of the Numbers 27 account of their story is a declaration of the women's agency: *vatiqravnah*, "they-(women)-came-near." Next comes their patrimony: they, the daughters of a man whose genealogy is traced for five generations, came forward. Then their names are introduced with *v'-'elleh shemoth*, "these are the names," reproducing the first words of the book of Exodus. That Exodus list is all male; this one is all female. The form is used some two dozen times in the canon, including twice for these women, to introduce genealogies and lists of personal names.

The articulation of the women's agency continues in verse 2, *v'-ta'amodnah*, "they-(women)-stood." They stood before God—symbolized by the tent of meeting, the leading men in their community, and all of their people. The five of them stood together, perhaps in a line, perhaps in a wedge, perhaps in a clump. Their timing, according to the narrative, at the end of the land distribution but before dispersal of the leaders, is propitious and hardly coincidental. The assembly had not been formally closed; there may well have been other complainants waiting in the wings. Mahlah, Noah, Hoglah, Milcah, and Tirzah stationed themselves between the temporary abode of their God and their people, their bodies taking the intermediary position so frequently inhabited by Moses. In verse 4 they tell Moses—they don't ask for a thing—they tell him, "Give us the land!" As they make their argument, the emphasize their father's lack of male offspring and clear his name of any association with the infamous rebels whose descendants would not be looked on favorably for bringing such an appeal.

Their demand in verse 4 is delivered in the imperative (command) form: "Give to us a possession among our father's brothers." Moses, who had no trouble deciding on his own (according to the preserved narrative) the fate of Midianite women to execution, rapine, and forced pregnancy, appears unable to render a just judgment in this case. To his credit he appeals to God, rather than dismissing them out of hand. God vindicates Mahlah, Noah, Hoglah, Milcah, and Tirzah in strong terms: "The daughters of Zelophehad are right in their speaking." While *ken* means "yes" in Modern Hebrew, its semantic range in Biblical Hebrew is somewhat broader, including "just so," "right," "correct," "honest," and "righteous." It is a powerful affirmation, without peer in the canon for women or men. To be sure, God pronounces other people, predominantly men, "righteous" using other terms, but no one else using the language in this verse. The women's assertiveness is matched by

God's response but undermined by the passive NRSV translation of verse 7, "Let them possess. . . ." The text says, "You shall surely give to them a possession." "To them" is common plural (or masculine), *lahem*, and not feminine plural, *lahen*, a reminder that women are not exclusively represented in feminine forms; the so-called masculine form is an inclusive, common plural form and must be considered so, unless conclusively demonstrated otherwise.

Then God reveals new *torah* for Mahlah, Noah, Hoglah, Milcah, and Tirzah, a distinction not lost on the rabbis (see *b. Bava Batra* 119a–b; *Sanhedrin* 8a). The addition to the *torah* was that women would now be eligible to inherit land in limited circumstances if they lack brothers (v. 7). *Midrash Rabbah BaMidbar* 21:12 suggests that the inheritance *torah* was hidden from Moses; the rabbis say throughout the tradition that the *torah* was revealed to the women because of their merit or worth. In *b. Bava Batra* 119b, Mahlah, Noah, Hoglah, Milcah, and Tirzah are righteous (*tzqnywth*) exegetes (*drshnywth*) and sages (*chmnywth*).

Mahlah, Tirzah, Hoglah, Milcah, and Noah (in a new sequence) reappear in Numbers 36. The passage is silent on what happens with them in the intervening chapters. The text does not say that Moses has failed to obey the command of God and has not given Mahlah, Tirzah, Hoglah, Milcah, and Noah an inheritance in the promised land. (The text will never admit this, but it will become clear in Joshua 17.) Instead, the text turns to ritual matters (Num. 28–30); the war on the women, children, and men of Midian (Num. 31); the choice of the women and men of Gad and Reuben to forgo their unseen inheritance in the promised land (Num. 32); preparations to enter the land (Num. 33–34); and provisions for the Levites (Num. 35). The allocation of towns and grazing lands, along with cities of refuge so that those who commit unintentional homicides can escape blood vengeance, marks a return to the inheritance narrative of Mahlah, Tirzah, Hoglah, Milcah, and Noah in Numbers 36.

There is an inversion of Numbers 27 in Numbers 36: In 27:1 the women come forward, *vatiqravnah*; in 36:1 the male heads of the patriarchal households of Gilead and Machir come forward using the same verb, *vayiqrevu*. The men come forward in the presence of the leader of the community just as the women do. They are related to the women through their common ancestors Asenath and Joseph, sharing Manassite tribal heritage. However, the text does not place the men in front of or even near the sanctuary (or God). Moreover, Mahlah, Tirzah, Hoglah, Milcah, and Noah are no longer subjects with agency but objects of dispute. They are not even mentioned by their own names until verse 11.

While the topic of discussion, the women do not appear in the text. If they are present, they have been rendered invisible and silent. The male leaders object to God's judgment through Moses to allow the women and other women in the same circumstances to inherit. As was the case with the presentation of the women in chapter 27, the men appear with their case suddenly, seemingly spontaneously, with no attention to their deliberation or strategizing. The objection of the men is that the daughters of Zelophehad might marry outside of their father's tribe and one tribe would get more land than another. Then everybody would go around marrying fatherless daughters to get their land. They do not call the women by name. Then Moses speaks, *al-piy YHWH*, at the command—literally "mouth"—of God, according to the narrative.

However, Moses does not actually consult God as he did before. Moses takes the words of the divine judgment for Mahlah, Tirzah, Hoglah, Milcah, and Noah and changes them. First, he applies them to the men who object to the inheritance God has given the women: "The descendants of the tribe of Yosef are right (*ken*) in their speaking." Next, Moses makes his fulfillment of God's command conditional: if the women marry within their tribe, they will be able to receive the inheritance. Moses also makes the requirement statutory for other women who share their circumstances.

In verses 10–12, the women's agency returns in stages. At the end of verse 10 they do as commanded. However, the command, now attributed to YHWH, is the focus of the verse; their action is secondary. After their compliance they are named individually and open verse 11 with a verb, *vatihyeynah*, that expresses their "becoming" (women/wives of their cousins), rather than their *doing*, as in chapter 27. The men whom Mahlah, Noah, Hoglah, Milcah, and Tirzah take as husbands are never named in the text. In verse 12 the women's agency slips away: "Among the families of the descendants of Manasseh ben Yosef they [common plural] became wives and their inheritance was among the tribe of their father's clan." But where among their father's clan was their inheritance? In whose control? Not theirs. Moses still did not obey the command of God, even after tailoring it to suit the patriarchal concerns of his constituents.

The canon is silent on Mahlah, Noah, Hoglah, Milcah, and Tirzah (back in their initial order) until Joshua 17. The space between Numbers 36 and Joshua 17 is significant because of what does and does not transpire. What transpires is the death of Moses and elevation of Yehoshua ben Nun (Joshua, son of Nun) in his stead; what does not transpire is Moses' obedience to God's command, since he never gives Mahlah, Noah, Hoglah, Milcah, and Tirzah their inheritance. For reasons not addressed by the text, Moses returns to his work preparing (the rest of) the people for their inheritances and ignoring the women and God's instructions.

In Deuteronomy, Moses reflects on the people's journey with God to this point, including the apportionment of the promised land. He mentions the (sub)tribe of Manasseh and their land four times, but does not mention Mahlah, Noah, Hoglah, Milcah, and Tirzah or God's commandment regarding them (see Deut. 3:13; 29:8; 33:17; 34:2). In Deuteronomy 3:12 Moses even says that he—not God—gave Manasseh their land. And when God prepares Moses for his own death, God permits him to see the land that he will never enter (Deut. 3:26–27). Among the tribal allotments, God shows Moses the land of Manasseh in which the women were to have had their inheritance (Deut. 34:1–2). Neither God nor Moses mentions his failure to give them the land.

The Torah is conflicted on why Moses was barred from the promised land. According to Exodus 17:6, Moses provides water for the people at God's command by striking a rock as he is told. In another version of the story in Numbers 20:8ff., God tells Moses to command the rock, but he disobeys and strikes the rock. In the Numbers account God then bans Moses from the promised land: "Because you did not trust in me, to show my holiness before the eyes of the Israelites, therefore you shall not bring this assembly into the land that I have given them." God's rebuke does not mention the water or the rock, and could well refer to Moses' disobedience with regard to Mahlah, Noah, Hoglah, Milcah, and Tirzah. That is my preferred reading as a womanist.

For many womanist and feminist readers and hearers of the Scriptures, the saga of Mahlah, Noah, Hoglah, Milcah, and Tirzah, the daughters of Zelophehad, is an empowering text, demonstrating women's agency in confronting sexism and other forms of injustice in one's own cultural and religious community. In a truly rare move in the Scriptures, their story is an explicit affirmation of women's agency and resistance to patriarchy by God. But there is more to this story.

I am particularly interested in what Mahlah, Noah, Hoglah, Milcah, and Tirzah reveal about Moses, the larger-than-life charismatic religious leader. Moses' intractability marks a nadir in his relationship with women in the canon. Moses' life is saved as an infant because of the actions of a group of women and a little girl: his mother Jochebed, the midwives Shiphrah and Puah, the daughter of the pharaoh, and his sister Miriam (Exod. 2:1–10). He takes a considerable risk to help seven Midianite sister shepherds when he is on the run after killing an Egyptian man (Exod. 2:11–22). Moses' choice to go to his death without obeying God in the matter of the daughters of Zelophehad surprises me, in light of his earlier history. Yet read in light of his role in the attempted Midianite genocide, his obstinacy is part of a larger pattern of troubled relationships with women that emerges with the dissolution of his first marriage.

Moses' use of his power and authority to disenfranchise women in his community identifies him as one of the male religious leaders in virtually every religious tradition of which I have ever heard whose response to women's demands for equality—even a small amount of parity—is, "Over my dead body." As a womanist I think of leaders of the civil rights and black power movements who kept women in their place and of those male pastors who exclude women from leadership in the black church, notably from ordination and, in some cases, from other institutional leadership. Like Moses, they are famous for fighting for the freedom of their people, whom they largely conceive of as men; however, that freedom comes with constraints. To borrow an infamous quote from a different context in American public discourse, Moses went to his grave holding the women's piece of the promised land clutched in his cold, dead hand, even though it may have cost him his place in the promised land.[30]

Though the Torah ends with God's promise to Mahlah, Noah, Hoglah, Milcah, and Tirzah unfulfilled, that is not the end of their story. After Moses is dead and buried, Mahlah, Noah, Hoglah, Milcah, and Tirzah take their case to Joshua, Moses' successor. The speed of Joshua's response to their case stands in sharp contrast to Moses' refusal to grant them their (literally) God-given inheritance.

In Joshua 17, Mahlah, Noah, Hoglah, Milcah, and Tirzah make another demand for their inheritance rights. So much time has passed, and given that the scroll of Joshua was not physically attached to the Torah, the narrator feels the need to remind the reader/hearer that there was a man named Zelophehad who did not have any sons and had daughters named Mahlah, Noah, Hoglah, Milcah, and Tirzah. Then, the saga appears to repeat itself. The women draw near (*vatiqravnah* again) before Eleazar the priest (again), before Joshua ben Nun (instead of Moses) and before the leaders (again) in verse 3. They say, "The HOLY ONE commanded Moshe to give us an inheritance along with our male-kin." They do not say, "*Moshe failed to obey God and died.*" There is no need. The implication is clear.

Again, the women do not ask for their land—they simply affirmatively assert their rights. The location of their demand is not disclosed in the unit. Given the many parallels with their first claim, it is not unreasonable that they were again in front of the sacred space, as suggested by the presence of Eleazar the priest. Here is where the parallels end. Joshua does not consult God; he does not consult Eleazar or the elders who were present when God

30. In 2000 at the annual convention of the National Rifle Association in Charlotte, NC, renowned actor Charlton Heston responded to Vice President Al Gore's gun-control proposal with the words "As we set out this year to defeat the divisive forces that would take freedom away, I want to say those fighting words for everyone within the sound of my voice to hear and to heed, and especially for you, Mr. Gore: 'From my cold, dead hands!'"

commanded Moses to give Mahlah, Noah, Hoglah, Milcah, and Tirzah their inheritance.

Joshua does give them the land, immediately. The speed of his compliance stands in marked contrast with Moses' defiance. In the same verse that the women present their case, Joshua complies: "And he gave to them according to the mouth of the HOLY ONE an inheritance among the male-kin of their father." The tribal allotment is restated, and the inheritance of the women as daughters of Manasseh is repeated.

The final passage in which Mahlah, Noah, Hoglah, Milcah, and Tirzah appear is 1 Chronicles 7 in a Manassite genealogy. First Chronicles 7:15 mentions casually, "Zelophehad had daughters." With all the references to Mahlah, Noah, Hoglah, Milcah, and Tirzah, there is no mention of them having children with the husbands forced on them by Moses.[31] Moses' delay has consequences, whether intended or not. The line of Zelophehad appears to die out with his daughters or is subsumed into the lines of their husbands. Yet their names live on in the Scriptures of their people.

SERACH BAT ASHER

Numbers 26:46 And the name of the daughter of Asher was Serach.

Serach bat Asher appears three times in the Scriptures. In addition to Numbers, she is visible in Genesis 46:17 and 1 Chronicles 7:30. In each case she is named along with her brothers. I do not suppose that Serach was Asher's only daughter or that his siblings did not also have daughters. But Serach bat Asher was significant enough to be included in the canon three times. Unlike her relatives Mahlah, Noah, Hoglah, Milcah, and Tirzah (see "Mahlah, Noah, Hoglah, Milcah and Tirzah, the Daughters of Zelophehad"), there is no narrative in the Scriptures explaining her significance.

Fortunately the Hebrew Scriptures are not the end of sacred literature in either Jewish or Christian traditions. Rabbinic exegesis offers continuing insights into biblical texts and the prominence of Serach bat Asher. According to this tradition, it was the voice of Serach, preserved for centuries, that led Moses to the bones of Joseph and made it possible for Israel to be redeemed from Egypt. The rabbis give her a voice. In order to do so, they turn to the larger exodus narrative with their comments on Exodus 13:19. In the *Midrash*

---

31. This observation comes in personal communication from Kimberly Russaw, whose dissertation addressed them at some length: "Daddy's Little Girl? An Examination of Daughters in the Hebrew Bible" (PhD dissertation, Vanderbilt University, 2016).

Shemot Rabbah 20:19, the commentary on Exodus, the rabbis ask and answer, "How did Moshe know where Yosef was buried? Some opine that Serach the daughter of Asher showed him the place in the Nile where he was buried." Beneath this one line is the tradition that Serach bat Asher lived hundreds of years like the ancestors of old as the keeper of the secret of Yosef's watery grave. The story is continued in *Devarim Rabbah* 11:7, the commentary on Deuteronomy:

> After Moshe had tired himself out, a certain Segula (an alternate name for Serach) met him and observing that he was weary from his efforts she said to him: "My lord Moshe, why are you tired?" He replied: "For three days and three nights I have been going round the city to find Yosef's coffin and I cannot find it." Said she to him: "Come with me and I will show you where it is." She took him to the river and said to him: "In this place have the magicians and astrologers made for him a coffin of five hundred talents in weight and cast it into the river, and thus have they spoken to Pharaoh: 'If it is your wish that this people should never leave this place, then as long as they will not find the bones of Joseph, so long will they be unable to leave.'" Immediately Moshe placed himself by the bank of the river and called out: "Yosef, Yosef, you know how you have adjured Israel, 'God will surely remember you'; give honor to the God of Israel and do not hold up the redemption of Israel; you have good deeds to your credit. Intercede then with your Creator and come up from the depths." Whereupon immediately Yosef's coffin began to break through the waters and to rise from the depths like a stick. Moshe took it and placed it upon his shoulder and carried it, and all Israel followed him. And whilst Israel carried the silver and gold that they had taken away from Egypt, Moshe was carrying Yosef's coffin. God said to him: "Moshe, you say that you have done a small thing; by your life, this act of kindness is a great thing; since as you ignored silver and gold, I too will do unto you this kindness in that I will busy myself with your burial."

These classic *midrashim* offer readings to explain why Serach bat Asher was prominent enough to be named in three different biblical books, even though no details are given about her other than the names of her father and brothers. I am interested in what is *not* said about Serach; she is not described as a wife or mother in the biblical text. Somehow she made a name for herself apart from the social roles that dominate the portrayals of women in the Scriptures.

WOMEN OF GAD AND REUBEN

> Numbers 32:25 Then said the descendants of Gad and the descendants of Re'uven (Reuben) to Moshe (Moses), "Your servants will do as my lord commands. 26Our little ones, our women, our livestock,

and all our animals shall remain there in the cities of Gilead; [27]but your servants will cross over, each one combat-ready before the HOLY ONE OF OLD, to do battle just as my lord speaks."

Just after the Midianite war, as Moses is handing out pieces of the promised land to everyone but women in their own households—even when commanded to do so by God—two groups of Israelites decline the inheritance that Moses offers them (see the previous entries "Women of Midian" and "Mahlah, Noah, Hoglah, Milcah, and Tirzah, the Daughters of Zelophehad"). The descendants of Leah's sons Gad and Reuben decide that they like the looks of the land that they are passing through right now, thank you very much. They would prefer not to see what is behind door number two.

The two tribes present their intentions to Moses as a united front. The text uses a singular verb, literally "he said," with a double plural subject, "the descendants of Gad and the descendants of Reuben." This grammatical configuration suggests unanimous support for their petition to Moses. The women and men of Gad and Reuben are in agreement. They have found their promised land on *this* side of the Jordan. The Gadites and Reubenites present their case as follows: They have a lot of cattle. The grassland that is before them would be good for cattle. They want that land. That's it. The narrative is placed after that of the Midianite war, suggesting that the land is newly available (subdued by God in v. 4) as a result of dispossessing and nearly annihilating the Midianites. The land that the Gadites and Reubenites want is on the east side of the Jordan, whereas the other tribes will settle on the west side.[32]

The text acknowledges that the Gadites and Reubenites have a great many cattle. However, it does not say if they have more than other tribes or, if so, how this occurred. The juxtaposition of this unit with the Midianite war makes it possible to read that the two tribes were enriched as a result of that war in which 675,000 sheep, 72,000 oxen, and 61,000 donkeys were taken captive, according to Numbers 31:32–34. The reason for the two tribes having received more of the spoils of war, if this is indeed the case (however one understands the numbers), than the others is not explained.

The Midianite war also yielded a great harvest of sexually inexperienced girl's bodies as the spoils of war. According to Numbers 31:35, some 32,000

32. The Israelite journey has not taken them from west to east, to the closer West Bank of the Jordan River. Rather, they have circled the Sinai Peninsula one or more times, crossed into the Arabian Penninsula where the eastern fork of the Sea of Reeds (Red Sea) is bordered by modern-day Egypt, Israel, and Jordan, and eventually entered Canaan somewhere north of the Dead Sea. This meant that the Israelites crossed the Jordan from east to west under Joshua.

girls were captured. When the Gadites and Reubenites say that they and "their women and little ones" will stay on the Gilead side of Jordan, they are speaking for their share of the captured Midianite girls, as well as the women of their own people. Indeed, the Midianite girls are in the process of becoming the women of Gad and Reuben, as they are in the other tribes where they have been taken captive.

Ultimately, the people of Gad and Reuben win the day by promising to cross the Jordan in times of war and come to Israel's defense, but in Judges 4 and 5 they do not keep their promise. In Joshua 22:10ff. the Gadites and Reubenites make their own altar, further isolating themselves from the rest of Israel, which nearly leads to civil war. The two tribes and their people become marginalized in the rest of the Scriptures. The tribe of Reuben, Leah and Jacob's firstborn, disappears altogether.

As an American reader with ancestral roots in the cattle-grazing lands of Texas, I see the women of Gad and Reuben through the lens of frontierswomen. And as an African American woman, I also see the presence of the Midianite girls as an enslaved population, subject to sexual use, as were African women in the Americas during (and after) American chattel slavery. In my family's ancestral stories, some black folk and white folk found ways to live and work together within complicated and occasionally flexible hierarchies in the absence of slavery but in its shadow. Following the sequence of the overarching narrative, I imagine equally complicated relationships among the women of Gad and Reuben, their share of the captive Midianite women and girls, and the older and disabled men of their people who could not go to war.

In Numbers 32:16 the fighting men of Gad and Reuben leave their newly claimed land to help the other tribes conquer and settle Canaan. The men say that they will build "sheepfolds and towns," then accompany (or follow) their kin to Canaan. If we take seriously the narrative framework, it is not reasonable to suppose that all of the necessary buildings and structures were constructed, given the urgency of the muster. Rather, I read that the men folk threw together rudimentary shelters and sketched out the perimeters of their holdings, leaving the bulk of the work to those they were leaving behind. The absence of every able-bodied war-fighting man means that the Israelite women, their daughters, their very young sons, the elderly, and disabled men settled their piece of the promised land along with the transplanted women and girls of Midian. These women, children, and elder men bought, built, and bartered homesteads on their own; planted, tended, and harvested fields on their own; raised and grazed, mated and milked, sheared and slaughtered their livestock on their own; hunted, killed, skinned, butchered, quartered, and preserved meat on their own; spun and wove cloth; ground and milled wheat and barley; and made everything they couldn't buy.

Without their able-bodied fighting men, there would have been a significant population gap, a significant space in childbearing. The captive women
and girls would have been relatively free of the sexual abuse and forced pregnancy that characterized the lives of the enslaved. How might the free and
enslaved women have cooperated and strategized to survive together? It is
important to consider that none of these lands was vacant, even with the deci-
mation of the Midianites. How did the women of Gad and Reuben interact
with the Canaanite women and men around them? Did they form economic
and other alliances? Was their settlement vulnerable to attack once it became
known there were no warriors with them?

Their story continues in Joshua when after an indeterminate number of
years (Josh. 22:3–9) the men of these three communities return to their side
of the Jordan to join their women and children. There could have been a rude
awakening when their menfolk came home from the war. What was that rein-
tegration like? What were the consequences of the return of the able-bodied
men for the Midianite women and girls? That the whole community fades
from the pages of Scripture invites midrash. In my womanist imagination, I
consider how the women of Gad and Reuben saw themselves in relationship
to the land they settled and to their distant kin across the Jordan.

> *Grandmother, who are those men, and why are they yelling at father? Why
> is mother crying? Why is everyone so angry?*
>
> *Ah, child, Devorah, the great leader of our people across the river has
> called your father and all of the men to war with the Canaanites on the far
> side of the river. Folk are arguing about whether or not they should go.*
>
> *But Grandmother, how can those people be our people. I've never seen any
> of them before. They dress funny and they talk funny. I can't understand half
> of what they say.*
>
> *Child, you know the stories, how the great One God led us out of slavery
> to freedom, giving us this good land for our cattle and our people. Well, they
> tell different stories. They say that God called us all to live beyond the river
> and that we wouldn't go. They say we built our altar without their permis-
> sion. They say they let us keep it only because we promised never to use it.
> They say we broke our word, but they're willing to overlook it if we fight
> with them. Now they say that we are one people with one enemy. But they
> also say that not all of us are their people. They complain that too many have
> married the people around us and that we're more Canaanite than Israelite.*
>
> *Grandmother, what does that mean?*
>
> *It means they need us. And that they hate the fact that they need us.
> Child, we are the people of this land. We have traveled a long way to get
> here. We have married and buried here. We have kin-ties with all the*

peoples around us. They are us, and we are them. We are all Father Avraham's children. The children of our Great Mothers Hagar, Sarah, and Qeturah live at peace here. We won't go to war against each other.

So everything will be all right?

Yes, child, everything will be all right. They may tell different stories or cut us out of their stories altogether. But we have our own stories. And the God of our ancestors who gave us this land and brought us through blood and battle from slavery and death is here with us in our promised land.

5

Deuteronomy: Torah Reenvisioned

The book of Deuteronomy is a reiteration of Mosaic Torah in condensed form. It is arguably midrash, nearly in its entirety, including some variances from the earlier accounts of events that it reframes. The canonization of these plural narratives is part of the richness of the biblical literary tradition and a warning against literalist fixations on single narratives or single accounts of narratives. As a sanctioned and authorized restatement of Torah, Deuteronomy models the relationship between midrash and Scripture. It is by no means a womanist midrash; yet as midrash it invites continued reinterpretation.

Without referencing Genesis—which seems to have circulated independently as an after-the-fact prologue to the Torah—Deuteronomy presents itself as a lengthy farewell address by Moses, some thirty chapters in a single sermonic utterance (Deut. 1–30), followed by putting his affairs in order (Deut. 31), final words of blessing (Deut. 32–33), and his death (Deut. 34). Deuteronomy also serves as a theological and ideological bridge between the Torah and the Deuteronomistic History (DH) in Joshua, Judges, Samuel, Kings, and portions of Isaiah. In specific *toroth* and once, in the case of the prophet Miriam, by name, Deuteronomy addresses women as part of the community of Israel submerged in *beney yisrael*, "descendants of Israel." Deuteronomy also targets non-Israelite women as a specific and continuing threat to Israelite women and men and their occupation of the land. In this culmination of the Torah, women and girls are daughters, sisters, wives, mothers, mothers-in-law, female slaves, war captives, and victims of ethnic cleansings.

CAPTIVE WOMEN

Deuteronomy 21:10 When you go out to war against your enemies, and the HOLY ONE your God will place them in your hand and you will take them captive—[11]you may see among the captives a woman beautiful in form, whom you desire and want to take as your woman/wife. [12]You shall bring her home to your house; she shall shave her head and do the same to her nails. [13]Strip the garments of her captivity from her, and she shall remain in your house a full month, mourning for her father and mother; after that you may penetrate her and marry/rule over her, and she shall be your woman/wife. [14]But if you take no delight in her, you shall release her person and under no circumstances shall you sell her for money. You must not shackle her as a slave, since you have violated her.

Deuteronomy standardizes the practice of abducting women as spoils of war into forced marriages and, usually, pregnancies. It makes a few changes to the *toroth* articulated in Numbers 31:

1. The women of any group designated as "the enemy" are now available for forced conjugal cohabitation; previously only Midianite women were specified for forced unions (Num. 31:17–18).
2. The Israelite men may choose women for conjugal relations based on their appearance, "a woman beautiful in form whom you desire" (Deut. 21:11). The male desire is articulated with *ch-sh-q*, the verb used in Genesis 34:8 to describe Shechem's desire for Dinah, which led him to rape her. Curiously, Deuteronomy uses the same verb to describe God's love for the Israelites (Deut. 7:7; 10:15; 21:11).
3. The targeted women are no longer required to be sexually uninitiated or virgin girls, as they were in the Midianite war as recorded in Numbers.
4. The Israelites have developed a protocol for breaking in their new war-trophy women. The humiliation-based breaking-in process consists of shaving the woman's head, cutting her nails,[1] and stripping her, indicated by the usage of the Hiphil of *s-w-r*; no mention is made of clothing her. The traumatized woman is to be given a month to mourn her mother and father—the text specifies both parents—and to accept her new situation. Then, whether she is ready or not, the male Israelite who chose her because he desired her is given divine/Mosaic authority—the two voices are presented as one—to penetrate her, literally to come upon and enter her, presumably holding her down if necessary. The male Israelite is to "husband" and/or "master" his new woman; *b-'-l* means both.
5. Lastly, Deuteronomy extends to the captive women the *toroth* in Exodus 21, which had previously applied only to Israelite women and girls sold into slavery by their fathers. Israelite men are not permitted (perhaps that

---

1. The nail cutting may also be a practical, protective step on the part of the rapist-husband.

should read "no longer permitted") to use the captive women sexually and then sell them. Sexual intercourse, even under these circumstances, has consequences. For the Israelites, those consequences are expressed statutorily. To use the woman and then sell her is categorized as a violation, using the same term ('-n-h) that describes the Egyptian oppression of the Israelites in Exodus 1:11 and Sarai's abuse of Hagar in Genesis 16:6. However, the text does not see the abduction of women into forced unions and subsequent impregnation as violations. Nor does the text see raping or using the woman sexually and then freeing her from bondage as a violation (Deut. 21:14); the text prevents only selling her after using her.

Immediately after the verses that deal with taking women as war captives comes a passage addressing male responsibility toward women and their children when he has more than one and loves one but hates the other.[2] The *torah* prevents the man from inheriting the son of the loved woman over the son of the hated woman where the child of the hated woman is the firstborn. This attempt to require primogeniture is surprising, given Israel's disregard of primogeniture in the stories of its patriarchs. Esau loses his standing to Jacob. Malachi 1:2, using the same vocabulary as Deuteronomy 21:15, parodies this verse by proclaiming divine love for Jacob but hatred for Esau. Reuben never enjoys the status of the firstborn among the sons and tribes of Israel, and Simeon does not get to take his place as second-born. Jacob perpetuates the practice of upending birth order by blessing Joseph's sons out of order.

Yet this text does serve to protect the interests of a child who otherwise might be vulnerable. Through that child, who is most likely a son, because there is no evidence that primogeniture applied to female children, his mother would benefit from his inheritance. The sequence of these texts seems to be an attempt to protect the children of captive women and an acknowledgment of how hated they and their children were, even as the practices of abduction and forced marriage and impregnation continued. The relationship of this unit to the one before suggests a pattern of men raping women whom they found desirable and then selling them, leading to the provisions in verse 14. Perhaps without the availability of a monetary incentive, retaining the captured women was perceived as more advantageous than simply releasing them. In any case, the women remained in Israelite communities, resulting in pregnancies and internal strife, all of which likely occasioned the statutory revision in verses 15–17. Curiously, no attention is given to the religious practices of the women: They are not expressly forbidden their own religion; neither are they

2. NRSV and JPS soften Deut. 21:15 by translating that the woman is "disliked" and "unloved," rather than "the-hated-woman," *hashenuah*. The passage uses passive participles for both "hated" and "loved."

described as being forced to assimilate Israelite religion. Arguably, there was some degree of interreligious exchange and subsequent syncretism.

STUBBORN AND REBELLIOUS DAUGHTER

> Suppose someone has a stubborn and rebellious daughter who will neither obey her mother nor her father, and they discipline her, but she does not listen to them. Then her mother and her father shall seize her and bring her out to the elders of her city at the gate of that place. They shall say to the elders of her city, "This daughter of ours is stubborn and rebellious. She will not obey us. She is a glutton and a drunkard." Then they shall stone her, all the women of the city, to death. So you shall purge the evil from your midst; and all Israel will hear, and be afraid (see Deut. 21:18–21).

This *torah* does not exist, not exactly. There is a corresponding *torah* dealing with a stubborn and rebellious son in Deuteronomy 21:18–21, who is to be stoned by the men of the city. But curiously there is no corresponding *torah* for daughters. It is not difficult to imagine a biblical death sentence being imposed on women in a comparable situation. But was there (or was there imagined to be) a comparable situation? The young man in the original *torah* is accused of being a glutton and a drunkard. Were these the only manifestations of what is called here *rebellion*? Were women not equally subject to gastronomic and alcoholic excess? Or was the perception of rebellion so gendered that women displaying the same behaviors were simply not seen as rebellious?[3] As is the case with many *toroth*, what is easily read as a brutal legislation is somewhat ameliorated by context—how much, is left to the reader to determine. The requirement that parents bring their rebellious child to the elders of the city and testify that they have attempted to discipline the child prevents parents from outright killing their child on their own and provides some form of due process.

The provocation for the trial and execution is rebellion. Taking seriously the characterization of rebellion as gluttony and drunkenness, I am considering this text as referring to the disruptive behaviors of a person in the throes of an addiction. Obviously, the text represents a time with no understanding of the phenomenology of addiction, when it was believed that a person chose to drink and chose their subsequent behavior. The intractability of addiction was perceived but attributed to stubbornness. Therefore, the addict was con-

---

3. Deut. 22:13ff. will prescribe the death penalty for women who cannot prove that they were virgins on their wedding night; however, the word "rebellion" is not used in the passage.

demned to death, in part because of the high regard for mothers and fathers in Israelite culture. The Israelite esteem for parents is fairly egalitarian, with both parents specified in about ninety individual *toroth*, although the male parent is always listed first.

It is important to note that classical rabbinic Judaism does apply this text literally. Midrashic wrestling with this text delineated so many prerequisites and exclusions as to make it virtually impossible for people to execute their children (see *b. Sanhedrin* 71a and *Mishnah Sanhedrin* 8:1–7), truly ameliorating the text. In a similar approach, ancestral African American exegesis explicitly and articulately rejects the authority of passages pertaining to slavery and resists the authority of other texts by failing to proclaim them as normative or authoritative. While there is a tradition of violent rhetoric in some families in the African diaspora, reflecting these verses—for example, a parent, especially a mother, saying, "I brought you into this world and I'll take you out of it," as a form of scolding—most black families deny the scripturality of this text by failing to conform to it.[4] Those few families in which corporal punishment takes lethal form are held up as objects of horror. A womanist midrash of this text shares with the rabbinic midrash the complete rejection of the violence called for in these verses as an appropriate model of ethical parenting.

SLANDERED CHASTE WOMAN

Deuteronomy 22:13 It may be that a man takes a woman-as-a-wife, and after penetrating her, he hates her. [14]Then he places charges against her, giving her a bad name, sending it out saying, "This woman I took-as-wife and when I approached her, I did not find evidence of her virginity." [15]The mother of the girl and her father shall then submit the evidence of the girl's virginity to the elders of the city at the gate. [16]The father of the young woman shall say to the elders, "My daughter I gave to this man as a wife, but he hates her. [17]Look! He has placed charges against her saying, 'I did not find evidence of your daughter's virginity.' Yet here is the evidence of my daughter's virginity." Then they shall spread out the garment before the elders of the town. [18]The elders of that town shall take the man and chastise him. [19]They shall fine him one hundred shekels of silver that they shall give to the girl's father because he slandered the name of a virgin of Israel. She shall remain his wife; he shall not be permitted to divorce her all his days.

4. However, other texts, such as Prov. 12:34 ("Those who spare the rod hate their children") and Prov. 23:13 ("Do not withhold discipline from your children; if you beat them with a rod, they will not die"), calling for parental violence are taken literally by many in Afro-diasporic communities.

Perhaps there are no more patriarchal texts in the Hebrew Scriptures than those that regulate women's sexual activity, often with lethal consequences, with few parallels so constraining male sexual behavior. This passage, which requires a woman's parents to prove her virginity publicly and in which a falsely accused woman's *father* is compensated for the shame-injury due *him*, is one in a series. While there are other texts in which women are subjects with agency, power, and authority, this is not one. The bride and her mother are objects, props, and acquisitions here. This passage and those that immediately follow, which clearly articulate differing sociocultural religious standards for female and male sexuality, are enshrined in the Torah as Scripture. Unmarried girls and women are expected to be sexually chaste and virginal, and they can be executed if they are found to be sexually active or if they cannot successfully defend themselves against a false charge of being a sexually experienced unmarried woman. Married men can have sex with prostitutes, slaves, foreign women, and likely widows and divorced women.

Virginity, here the plural *betulim* ("evidence-of-virginity"), means the blood evidence proving that the girl's hymen was intact. There is no corollary for men or boys. The only form of this evidence acknowledged in the text is postcoital blood. Virginity testing, compulsory gynecological examination made infamous in contemporary shame-honor societies, seems to have been unknown or unpracticed. There is no mention in the biblical narrative of a midwife, for example, certifying that a woman has an intact hymen, which is surprising, considering how easily blood evidence could be falsified. Given that a woman's life will hang in the balance, these passages are shockingly inexact.

The passage describes a system under which families have to be proactive against false charges of sexually experienced women masquerading as virgins to deceive their marriage partners. Under this system, women made sure their daughters had the requisite proof as a matter of course. In the scenario envisioned by the text, the girl and her mother obtain and provide a bloody cloth (literally, "garment") as the acceptable affirmation of virginity. This is stored until it is needed and presented publically as statutory evidence. This passage raises the question as to what women's conversation occurred preparing a girl for both her first sexual experience and the need to present blood evidence accompanying her initial penetration. Was there a form of a sex talk between Israelite mothers and daughters that explained the mechanics of sexual intercourse, along with the need to secure evidence of virginity?

The penalty for false accusation is an unspecified "punishment," "chastisement," or "rebuke"—all translations of *y-s-r*. In a few cases, it consists of a stern talking to, such as hearing the divine voice in Deuteronomy 4:36 and God's warning in Isaiah 8:11; in other cases, it is mere "instruction" (Isa.

28:26; Ps. 16:7). In any case, the false accuser's punishment is fleeting, having no enduring effect on his well-being or status in the community. The man is fined and required to stay married to the woman he slandered until her death—no matter what.[5]

The requirement that the false accuser stay married to the slandered chaste woman is intended to protect her and her family's name. The text imagines that otherwise she would be socially and therefore financially vulnerable, with a cloud over her name and reputation. The text does not consider what a bride might endure at the hands of a man who "hates" her but is forced to remain married to her. The biblical texts do not attend to spousal battery. The following unit makes it clear that it is far better to be *falsely* accused of unchastity than to be *truthfully* accused of unchastity. A final technical observation is that the age of the girl in question is difficult to ascertain. Throughout these *toroth*, she is referred to as a *na'arah*, "girl." (Actually, the text uses the masculine singular *na'ar*, "boy" or "youth," and Masoretic rabbis who standardized the Hebrew text between 1004 and 1008 CE supplied the feminine ending.) Girls and boys in this category are generally pubescent and adolescent teenagers.

This unit rests on many false and troubling assumptions. They include that sexual activity is the only way a hymen can be broken and that all virgins bleed during their first sexual experience. The text is written from the perspective of trying to protect a woman, her name, and her family from false accusation. But it really is about male honor, maintained through the control of female sexuality. According to the text's logic, a mean-spirited false accuser opens himself up to rebuke and/or chastisement, in addition to a fine, by making his unsubstantiated allegations public. In the opening discourse, the man who makes a public false accusation is said to be motivated by hate (*s-n-'*), illustrating how vulnerable a girl's reputation—and therefore her life—was. It is certainly possible that if the allegation was not made public, a quiet divorce could be obtained. However, as a woman or girl who was neither virgin nor widow, her marriage options would be severely reduced, and some measure of shame might attach to the family. This text seeks to make girls and women slightly less vulnerable to execution on a vicious whim. It is also possible that a man might keep his suspicions to himself or, when not motivated by "hate," not be concerned at all with evidence of virginity. Indeed, it is impossible to know whether this *torah* reflects actual social practice or is articulating desired social practice from the perspective of the reformers. Did this *torah* arise because of a common or regularly occurring problem? Was there a particularly notorious case that gave rise to this legislation? Or is this jurisprudence simply a

---

5. Her options for "no matter what" are circumscribed by the adultery statutes. She cannot have sex with other men without lethal consequences.

reflection of (some) male fixation with female sexuality? There is evidence that other *toroth* are, in fact, not practiced normally by the Israelites; for example, Passover observances are instituted *after* the discovery of portions of Deuteronomy in an early form in 2 Kings 22, with no evidence Passover was observed prior to Josiah's seventh-century reign.

THE LAST WORD OF TORAH

The first word of Torah is *bereshit*, "beginning." The last word of Torah is *Yisrael*, Israel. The Torah is the story of the journey from the beginning of creation to the formation of the people named Israel. Women and girls travel that journey, often invisible, silenced, and overlooked. But they are there. Their people, their journey, and their Scriptures, their Torah, cannot exist without them.

RESOURCES ON TORAH

Allen, James. *Without Sanctuary: Lynching Photography in America*. Santa Fe, NM: Twin Palms, 2000.

Anderson, Cheryl B. *Ancient Laws and Contemporary Controversies: The Need for Inclusive Biblical Interpretation*. Oxford: Oxford University Press, 2009.

Bailey, Randall C. *Yet with a Steady Beat: Contemporary U.S. Afrocentric Biblical Interpretation*. Atlanta: Society of Biblical Literature, 2003.

Bellis, Alice Ogden, and Joel S. Kaminsky. *Jews, Christians, and the Theology of the Hebrew Scriptures*. Atlanta: Society of Biblical Literature, 2000.

Benjamin, Don C., and Victor H. Matthews. *Old Testament Parallels: Laws and Stories from the Ancient Near East*, 3rd ed. Mahwah, NJ: Paulist Press, 2007.

Bird, Phyllis A. "The End of the Male Cult Prostitute: A Literary-Historical and Sociological Analysis of Hebrew *Qādēš-Qĕdēšîm*." In *Congress Volume: Cambridge 1995*, Vetus Testamentum Supplement, edited by John A. Emerton, 37–80. Leiden: E. J. Brill, 1997.

Brenner, Athalya. *Exodus to Deuteronomy*, Feminist Companion to the Bible (Second Series). Sheffield, England: Sheffield Academic Press, 2000.

———. *A Feminist Companion to Exodus to Deuteronomy*. Sheffield, England: Sheffield Academic Press, 1994.

———, and Gale A. Yee. *Exodus and Deuteronomy*. Minneapolis: Fortress Press, 2012.

Brooten, Bernadette J. *Love between Women: Early Christian Responses to Female Homoeroticism*. Chicago: University of Chicago Press, 1996.

Carasik, Michael. *The Commentators' Bible: The JPS Miqra'ot Gedolot (Leviticus)*. Philadelphia: Jewish Publication Society, 2009.

Copher, Charles B. "The Black Presence in the Old Testament." In *Stony the Road We Trod*, 146–64. Minneapolis: Fortress Press, 1991.

Drinkwater, Gregg, Joshua Lesser, and David Shneer. *Torah Queeries: Weekly Commentaries on the Hebrew Bible*. New York: New York University Press, 2009.

Dube Shomanah, Musa W. *Postcolonial Feminist Interpretation of the Bible*. St. Louis: Chalice Press, 2000.

Eskenazi, Tamara Cohn, and Andrea L. Weiss. *The Torah: A Women's Commentary*. New York: Women of Reform Judaism, Federation of Temple Sisterhood, 2008.

Fisher, Eugene J. "Cultic Prostitution in the Ancient Near East: A Reassessment." *Biblical Theology Bulletin* 6 (1976): 225–36.

Gafney, Wilda C. *Daughters of Miriam: Women Prophets in Ancient Israel*. Minneapolis: Fortress Press, 2008.

Gafney, Wil. "A Queer Womanist Midrashic Reading of Numbers 25:1–18." In Athalya Brenner and Archie Chi Chung Lee, *Leviticus and Numbers*. Minneapolis: Fortress Press, 2013.

Goldstein, Elyse. *The Women's Torah Commentary: New Insights from Women Rabbis on the 54 Weekly Torah Portions*. Woodstock, VT: Jewish Lights Publishing, 2000.

Goss, Robert, and Mona West. *Take Back the Word: A Queer Reading of the Bible*. Cleveland: Pilgrim Press, 2000.

Henshaw, Richard A. *Female and Male: The Cultic Personnel: the Bible and the Rest of the Ancient Near East*. Allison Park, PA: Pickwick Publications, 1994.

Hurston, Zora Neal. *Moses, Man of the Mountain*. New York: HarperPerennial, 1991.

Meyers, Carol. *Discovering Eve: Ancient Israelite Women in Context*. New York: Oxford University Press, 1991.

Meyers, Carol L. "Miriam, Music, and Miracles." In *Mariam, the Magdalen, and the Mother*, 27–48. Bloomington: Indiana University Press, 2005.

———. "Mother to Muse: An Archaeomusicological Study of Women's Performance in Ancient Israel." In *Recycling Biblical Figures*, 50–77. Leiden: Deo, 1999.

———. "Procreation, Production, and Protection: Male-Female Balance in Early Israel." *Journal of the American Academy of Religion* 51, no. 4 (December 1, 1983): 569–93.

Nash, Peter T. *Reading Race, Reading the Bible*. Minneapolis: Fortress Press, 2003.

Nasr, Seyyed Hossein, Caner K. Dagli, Maria Massi, Dakake Joseph, E. B. Lumbard, Mohammed Rustom, and Maria Massi Dakake. *The Study Quran: A New Translation with Notes and Commentary*. San Francisco: HarperOne, 2015.

Newsom, Carol A., and Sharon H. Ringe. *Women's Bible Commentary*. Louisville, KY: Westminster John Knox Press, 1998.

Nissinen, Martti. *Homoeroticism in the Biblical World: A Historical Perspective*. Minneapolis: Fortress Press, 1998.

Page, Hugh R., and Randall C. Bailey. *The Africana Bible: Reading Israel's Scriptures from Africa and the African Diaspora*. Minneapolis: Fortress Press, 2010.

Rashkow, Ilona N. *Taboo or Not Taboo: Sexuality and Family in the Hebrew Bible*. Minneapolis: Fortress Press, 2000.

Rice, Gene. "Africans and the Origin of the Worship of Yahw*h." *Journal of Religious Thought* 50, no. 1/2 (Spring 1993): 27.

Russaw, Kimberly. "'Daddy's Little Girl?': An Examination of Daughters in the Hebrew Bible," PhD diss., Vanderbilt University, 2016.

Sadler, Rodney Steven. *Can a Cushite Change His Skin?: An Examination of Race, Ethnicity, and Othering in the Hebrew Bible*. New York: T. & T. Clark, 2005.

Sarna, Nahum M. *Shemot: the Traditional Hebrew Text with the New JPS Translation*. JPS Torah Commentary. Philadelphia: Jewish Publication Society, 1991.

Scholz, Susanne. *Biblical Studies Alternatively: An Introductory Reader*. Upper Saddle River, NJ: Prentice-Hall, 2003.

Segovia, Fernando F., and Mary Ann Tolbert. *Reading from This Place*. Minneapolis: Fortress Press, 1995.

Segovia, Fernando F. *Decolonizing Biblical Studies: A View from the Margins*. Maryknoll, NY: Orbis Books, 2000.

Sugirtharajah, R. S. *Voices from the Margin: Interpreting the Bible in the Third World*. Maryknoll, NY: Orbis Books, 1991.

———. *Voices from the Margin: Interpreting the Bible in the Third World*. Revised and expanded. Maryknoll, NY: Orbis Books, 2006.

Tigay, Jeffrey H. *Deuteronomy*. JPS Torah Commentary. New York: Jewish Publication Society, 1996.

van Wijk-Bos, Johanna W. H. *Making Wise the Simple: The Torah in Christian Faith and Practice*. Grand Rapids: Eerdmans, 2005.

———. "Writing on Water: The Ineffable Name of God." In *Jews, Christians, and the Theology of the Hebrew Scriptures*, edited by Alice O. Bellis and Joel S. Kaminsky. Atlanta: Society of Biblical Literature, 2000.

Walker, Alice. *In Search of Our Mothers' Gardens: Womanist Prose*. San Diego: Harcourt Brace Jovanovich, 1983.

Walsh, Jerome T. "Lev. 18:22 and 20:13: Who Is Doing What to Whom?" *Journal of Biblical Literature* 129 (2001): 201–9.

Warrior, Robert Allen. "Canaanites, Cowboys, and Indians." *Union Seminary Quarterly Review* 59, nos. 1–2 (January 1, 2005): 1–8.

Westenholz, Joan. "Tamar, Qĕdēšā, Qadištu, and Sacred Prostitution in Mesopotamia," *Harvard Theological Review* 82 (1989): 245–65.

Williams, Delores S. *Sisters in the Wilderness: The Challenge of Womanist God-Talk*. Maryknoll, NY: Orbis Books, 1993.

Wright, David P. "'She Shall Not Go Free As Male Slaves Do': Developing Views about Slavery and Gender in the Laws of the Hebrew Bible." In Bernadette J. Brooten and Jacqueline L. Hazelton, *Beyond Slavery: Overcoming Its Religious and Sexual Legacies*. New York: Palgrave Macmillan, 2010.

TRANSLATIONS OF THE BIBLE

Attridge, Harold W., Wayne A. Meeks, and Jouette M. Bassler. *The HarperCollins Study Bible: New Revised Standard Version, Including the Apocryphal/Deuterocanonical Books with Concordance*. San Francisco: HarperSanFrancisco, 2006.

Bail, Ulrike. *Bibel in gerechter Sprache*. Gütersloh: Gütersloher Verl.-Haus, 2006.

DeYoung, Curtiss Paul, et al. *The Peoples' Bible: New Revised Standard Version with the Apocrypha*. Minneapolis: Fortress Press, 2009.

Fox, Everett. *The Five Books of Moses: Genesis, Exodus, Leviticus, Numbers, Deuteronomy; A New Translation with Introductions, Commentary, and Notes*. The Schocken Bible, vol. 1. New York: Schocken Books, 1995.

Jewish Publication Society. *Tanakh: A New Translation of the Holy Scriptures according to the Traditional Hebrew Text*. Philadelphia: Jewish Publication Society, 1985.

Priests for Equality. *The Inclusive Bible: The First Egalitarian Translation*. Lanham, MD: Rowman & Littlefield, 2007.

Stein, David E. *The Contemporary Torah: A Gender-Sensitive Adaptation of the JPS Translation*. Philadelphia: Jewish Publication Society, 2006.

PART II

Womanist Midrash on Women of the Throne

6

Chapter Counting Queens

The book called "Kings" could be translated "Monarchs" or even "Queens-and-Kings." *Malakim* is a common plural, and the double book chronicles female and male royal persons. There is a surprising number of women in the books of Kings and Chronicles. I focus on the royal women of Israel and Judah, most of whom are least known, even among those who read and study the Scriptures. Bathsheba and Jezebel are perhaps most commonly known. Some might name Esther, though she did not rule in Israel or Judah.

Monarchy in ancient Israel is regularly erroneously configured as an exclusively male occupation. Many textbooks offer lists of "kings" in Israel, in spite of the fact that not all of the monarchs they list are in fact male. Athaliah is regularly classified as a king, rather than as a queen, in textbooks and resources for scholarly and lay readers. This tradition in biblical scholarship is based on the understood differences between female and male royal persons in ancient Israel, as embodied in the terms "king" and "queen"; that is, the primary governing royal ruler is a king. The roles of Israelite and Judean royal women were as varied as the differing Hebrew vocabulary used to portray them (that variety will be addressed below). The Scriptures preserve the names of some twenty royal women in the genealogies of the monarchs of Israel and Judah. In addition to their names, many of these royal women are preserved with geographical data.

I use the expression "royal women" because the title "queen" is a bit of a misnomer in Israelite/Judean monarchy. Most Americans or other Westerners hear the title "queen" tend to imagine the wife of a monarch. However, in biblical Israel the woman called queen in many translations is the mother of the reigning monarch, or the widow of the previous king. In most cases, she is named and introduced for the first time in association with her son's ascent to the throne. The wives of monarchs in Israel and Judah were not called queens (see the chart below). In addition, *malkah*, the feminine noun corresponding to the Hebrew word for king, *melek*, with which it shares its root *m-l-k*, is rarely used in the Scriptures, except for queens outside of Israel. The non-Israelite women described as *malkah*, a female monarch, include the queen of Sheba, Queen Vashti, sixty queens of an unknown provenance (Song 6:8), the queen of heaven, and a Babylonian queen. Finally, in Ezekiel 16, God describes Jerusalem as a girl child who grows up worthy of a queendom.

The same root, *m-l-k*, is also regularly translated in verbal form as "reign." As a rule, I prefer to use the same word to translate Hebrew roots in all their forms, for example, *prophets*, *prophesy*, and *prophecies*. This can be surprisingly difficult with royal families. Not only are "king" and "queen" completely different words in English; they don't work well as verbs. The word "queen" in the NRSV is a translation of different Hebrew words and groups together royal women who have different social roles and standing:

Vocabulary	Gloss	References
malkah	female monarch	1 Kgs. 10:1, 4, 10, 13; 2 Chr. 9:1, 3, 9, 12; Esther;* Jer. 7:18; 44:17
malka	female monarch	Dan. 5:10 (Aramaic)
timlok	be-queen	Esth. 2:4
yamlikah	made-her-queen	Esth. 2:17
m'lukah	queendom	Ezek. 16:13
gevirah	great lady	1 Kgs. 11:19; 15:13; 2 Kgs. 10:13; 2 Chr. 15:16; Jer. 13:18; 29:2
shegal	royal consort	Neh. 2:6; Ps. 45:9
bat-nadiv	noble daughter	Song 7:1
sarah	princess	Jdg. 5:29 (omitted); 1 Kgs. 11:3; Isa. 49:23; Lam. 1:1; Esth. 1:18

*Used exclusively in Esther, more than two dozen times.

The only woman whose Israelite or Judean royal office is identified with *m-l-k* is Athaliah, the female monarch who ruled Judah for seven prosperous years. Her reign was longer than a number of her male predecessors and successors.[1] It might be argued that Athaliah was a king, that is, the ruling monarch—rather than a queen-partner and/or a parent—because of the way in which monarchy functioned in Israel and Judah. That is how she is often listed in reference works.

The title *gevirah* means "Great Lady" and is most commonly translated as "Queen Mother"; it is the title for the senior royal woman in Judah. The root, *g-v-r*, means greatness or power rooted in strength, for example, a warrior's or hunter's prowess.[2] The title is specifically used for the mothers of Judean monarchs Asa and Jeconiah, in addition to the Egyptian queen Taphanes.[3] Generally, outside of the annals of the Israelite and Judean monarchs, *gevirah* means mistress of slaves, as in Sarah's status over Hagar (Gen. 16:4, 8) and a foreign commander's wife over her slave as in 2 Kings 5:3 (see also Ps. 123:2; Prov. 30:23; Isa. 47:7). Modern Hebrew has transformed *gevirah* to *geveret* to refer to every married woman or serve as polite address for an unknown woman.

The comparative number of queen mothers is one major characteristic distinguishing the portrayal of the southern monarchy (Judah) from the northern (Israel). The royal résumés in the books of Kings and Chronicles name the mothers of the Judean monarchs as a matter of course, whereas the Israelite royal mothers go largely unnamed. The pattern holds for both monarchies in both sets of texts. The import of the *geviroth* is illustrated in their numbers and names preserved in the Scriptures: four named Israelite queens and sixteen named Judean queens.[4] Virtually all of the queen mother citations follow the same form, introducing the reign of the monarch or death and the succession. A number of *geviroth* functioned as regents when their sons ascended the throne as young children. There are also other royal wives who

1. Her description as *moleketh*, "she who reigns," in 2 Kgs. 11:3 (duplicated in 2 Chr. 22:12) is the same form as the promise of a son of David to rule on his throne in Jer. 33:21, a Qal active participle.

2. The masculine form, *gibor*, means "warrior" by default and suggests all the characteristics of a manly man in Israelite culture.

3. Identifying royal persons in the text is made more difficult by recurring names; for example, both Israel and Judah have monarchs named Ahaziah and Jerhoram, also called Joram. Maacah (the most common woman's name in the Hebrew Bible) is the name of one of David's wives, a later queen mother who served twice, and of one of David's granddaughters. Additionally, some names occur in both genders; a king's mother and a male prophet are both named Micaiah. Lastly, that all Judean mothers of kings are not called queen mothers may be an artifact of the way in which their brief mentions occur, just as male monarchs are not called king in each text in which they occur.

4. All but one occur in Kings (Saul's wife is in Samuel); many are duplicated in Chronicles, and one in Jeremiah.

gave birth to royal children but do not become queen mothers; for example, David fathered children with perhaps a dozen women.

The books of Samuel, Kings/Chronicles, and Jeremiah show bitter competition for power between the royal sons and some administrative officials and military leaders, but the queen mothers rarely made naked power grabs and are never shown to compete with each other for power. When royal women do take the throne by force, as do Jezebel and Athaliah, they take it from men. There are no narratives of royal women competing with other royal women for power or in order to place their children on the throne. For example, when Bathsheba works with Nathan to enthrone Solomon, she is not struggling against Haggith and Maacah, the mothers of Adonijah and Absalom, his chief competitors.[5] Despite the lack of documentation of conflict among the royal women, it stands to reason that there were vicious battles behind the scenes to gain and secure power for and through their sons. Also, it is probable that there were deep ties of friendship and kinship and practical alliances between some royal women. Those stories are missing from the Bible, as are the stories of the royal daughters for the most part. The biblical text completely neglects the knowledge passed down from royal mother to royal daughter—woman's wisdom, learned at the feet of their mothers. Royal mothers and daughters, like their narratives, are literary props for male characters.

Most queen mothers exist in the Scriptures as part of a naming formula for their sons. Few have any agency or life in the Scriptures. Furthermore, the Bible provides few or no clues about how or even how long these women lived or under what circumstances they died, with the exception of Jezebel's assassination and Athaliah's execution. Nehusta, the last queen mother, was surrendered by her own son to the Babylonians as Judah fell, without any mention in Scripture of her ultimate fate. Two, Maacah and Hamutal, were queen mother twice. One, Maacah, was fired. Strikingly, Scriptures do not report that any queen mothers died in childbirth, a common occurrence in the ancient Near East. Nor are there stories of their deaths during the formative years of their children. The Israelite and Judean kings die in battle, from disease, or from old age. Those who die in their prime may well be survived by their mothers, who in most cases are not seen in the text again. What happens to the queen mothers when their grandsons or usurpers take the throne? I imagine they live on, perhaps in seclusion, perhaps in confinement until the day of their own death. Remarkably, the Scriptures do not record the death

---

5. In contrast, the Torah has a number of stories of fierce conflict between women married to the same man: Hagar and Sarah, Rachel and Leah; and in the Prophets we find Hannah and Penninah.

of a single queen mother.[6] Therefore, I am treating the queen mothers as though they live through the events that unfold around the mentions of their names.

In this volume I list the royal women independently of their spouses and children. So many women in the Scriptures are reduced to incubators. The preservation of the royal women's names is important. Because barely a tithe[7] of women have their names preserved in the biblical text, it matters to call these women by name as a womanist practice. And because many readers will not know who they are without reference to the men in their lives, I have grudgingly listed the royal women I will discuss in sections like "Overshadowed by Saul" and "Dominated by David." The irony of needing, in a feminist and womanist work, to identify women in relationship to men is not lost on me. So I invite the reader to say the names of the royal women, however unfamiliar they may be. We call your names. *Ashé.*

MAJOR ROYAL WOMEN OF ISRAEL

1. Ahinoam bat Ahimaaz, origins unknown
2. Bathsheba, Hittite
3. Zeruah, Ephraimite
4. Jezebel bat Ethbaal, Sidonian

MAJOR ROYAL WOMEN OF JUDAH

1. Naamah the Ammonite
2. Micaiah bat Uriel, Gibeah in Benjamin
3. Maacah bat Absalom, Jerusalem (twice)
4. Azubah bat Shilhi, origins unknown
5. Athaliah bat Omri, Israelite
6. Zibiah of Beer-sheba, Israelite
7. Jehoaddin of Jerusalem
8. Jecoliah of Jerusalem
9. Jerusha/h bat Zadok, origins unknown
10. Abi/Abijah bat Zechariah, origins unknown

6. The death of Athaliah is not an exception. Athaliah died as the sovereign of Judah, functionally as its king, and it is as a ruling sovereign that her death and the ascent of her successor are recorded.

7. Just about 9 percent of the personal names in the Hebrew Bible are women's names according to Carol Meyers, "Everyday Life: Women in the Period of the Hebrew Bible," in *Women's Bible Commentary*, ed. Carol Ann Newsome and Sharon H. Ringe (Louisville, KY: Westminster/John Knox Press, 1992), 252.

11. Hephzibah, origins unknown
12. Meshullemeth bat Haruz, Israelite
13. Jedidah bat Adaiah, Israelite
14. Hamutal bat Jeremiah, Israelite (twice)
15. Zebidah bat Pedaiah, Israelite
16. Nehushta bat Elnathan, Jerusalem

In contrast to the four named Israelite queens, there are sixteen named queens in Judah. One of those may be a duplicate, albeit with a different name and provenance; that is a difficult determination to make.[8] As queen mothers, they seem to exercise influence primarily with their sons, particularly after the deaths of their spouses, the previous monarch. The queen mother's throne that Solomon constructed for Bathsheba (1 Kgs. 2:19) may have been passed down from each queen mother to her daughter-in-law, who succeeds her figuratively if not literally. I write about each queen mother passing down the *giverah*-throne to the next, not articulating a historic claim that the women were alive or that there was even such an enthronement ritual, but as a way of linking the generations and illustrating the continuity of the tradition. It does seem likely that the queen mothers had a role in choosing their successors, women who would make appropriate mates for their sons. The hymn in praise of the warrior-hearted woman of Proverbs 31 is the composition of an unknown non-Israelite queen mother describing the kind of daughter-in-law she seeks for her son.[9]

8. Some royal women are clearly missing; the text lists no women/wives for the following Judean monarchs: Abijah, Jehoram, Jotham, Jehoahaz, Jehoiachin, and Zedekiah.
9. See my *Daughters of Miriam: Women Prophets in Ancient Israel* (Minneapolis: Fortress Press, 2008) for translation of and commentary on Prov. 31.

7

Overshadowed by Saul

AHINOAM BAT AHIMAAZ, SAUL'S WIFE

1 Samuel 14:49 Now the sons of Sha'ul (Saul) were Yonathan (Jonathan), Yishvi (Ishvi), and Malchi-shua; and the names of his two
daughters were these: the name of the firstborn was Merav (Merab),
and the name of the younger, Michal. [50]The name of Sha'ul's (Saul's)
wife was Ahinoam bat Ahimaaz.

Ahinoam bat Ahimaaz is the first royal woman in Israel named in the Bible.
She was Saul's primary wife. Ahinoam is also the mother of Saul's children
listed in 1 Samuel 14:49. Based on their ordering in the biblical text, we find
Jonathan, their oldest son; then two more sons, Ishvi (who is not mentioned in
the later genealogies and may have died in his youth) and Malchi-shua; then
their daughters, Merab, the firstborn, and Michal, their younger daughter.
The sequence in the verse suggests to some that Jonathan is the eldest child
and not just the eldest son. However, the term "firstborn" is not attached to
him or any of his brothers but rather, only in feminine form, to Merab. So I
read her not as the firstborn daughter but as the firstborn child.

Ahinoam enters the text seemingly as an afterthought.[1] Saul has been proclaimed monarch (1 Sam. 10:1) and is fighting the enemies of Israel (1 Sam.
11:11–14; 13:2–4, etc.). In 1 Samuel 13:16, her son Jonathan is at his father's
side in battle, indicating that she and Saul have been married and parents for
quite some time before Saul's elevation, according to the internal chronology

---

1. The genealogy is not necessarily tied to the unit in which it appears and makes no
claim as to Ahinoam's life or death, beyond having given birth five times.

of the passage. Even if Jonathan is just on the cusp of manhood, twelve or thirteen, that is potentially thirteen or fourteen years of marriage in addition to an unknown number of years between him and Michal (and Merab, if she too was older than Jonathan).

So arguably Ahinoam is at Saul's side literarily during the portions of his narrative where she is neither named nor referenced. Ahinoam is there before, during, or after the moments when Saul is chosen by God (1 Sam. 9:15–16) and anointed by Samuel (1 Sam. 10:1). She is there when her husband is rejected by God (1 Sam. 15:10–11), if not at that moment, then surely afterward when he goes mad (1 Sam. 18:10). Ahinoam is there and surely has something to say when Saul betroths their daughter Merab to David (v. 17). I imagine she has something else to say when Saul breaks off that engagement (v. 19). Surely Ahinoam is present when Saul marries their daughter Michal to David (v. 20). She is there when her husband and king is superseded by and struggling with David (1 Sam. 19). And Ahinoam is there when Saul breaks up Michal's and David's marriage (1 Sam. 25:44). In my reading, Ahinoam survives Saul when their sons Jonathan and Malchi-shua die (1 Sam. 31:2), along with another of Saul's sons, Abinadab.[2] She survives Saul, who kills himself (1 Sam. 31:4). And she is there when David takes her daughter Michal back, only to abandon and/or imprison her (2 Sam. 2:14–16).

Saul speaks of Ahinoam only once. He seemingly curses her and their son Jonathan: "Then Sha'ul's rage burned against Yonathan. He said to him, 'You son of a twisted, rebellious woman! Do I not know that you have chosen the son of Yishai [Jesse, David's father] to your own shame, and to the shame of your mother's nakedness?'" (1 Sam. 20:30). Saul is doing something similar to the contemporary practice of calling a person an SOB. While that epithet may be directed primarily toward the person to whom it is being addressed, it is at the same time a slur on the person's mother. In Biblical Hebrew an idiom description of someone as a person (daughter/son/woman/man) of X is generally a comment on just that person. Yet it is difficult with modern ears not to hear Saul calling Ahinoam a twisted, rebellious, and/or perverse woman.[3] This is sort of a chicken-and-egg curse. Saul is cursing Jonathan, and Ahinoam is collateral damage.

Saul is credited with four more sons in subsequent genealogies, Abinadab and Eshbaal (1 Chr. 8:33–40; 9:39–44) and Armoni and Mephibosheth (2 Sam. 21:8). The text does not name Ahinoam for the first of these, Abinadab and Eshbaal; they appear to have been born to someone other than Ahinoam. It is clear that Ahinoam is not Saul's only woman; Saul's last two

2. Abinadab's mother is never identified.
3. The KJV, JPS, and NRSV choose those translations respectively.

sons acknowledged in the canon, Armoni and Mephibosheth, are the sons of a secondary wife, Rizpah bat Aiah.[4] Lastly, according to 2 Samuel 12:8, Saul has an unknown number of other women whom David eventually inherits.

Having erased so many other women's names, the Scriptures formally present Ahinoam bat Ahimaaz as the wife of Saul, mother of his children, and the daughter of her parent (otherwise unknown). Yet she does not speak and is not described as doing anything other than giving birth. Her inclusion in the royal genealogy may well have set the pattern in the records of the monarchy of Judah, in which the names of royal women are preserved more often than not. Each of Ahinoam's daughters has her own name and a portion of her story preserved in the Scripture, which is highly unusual for two generations of women and likely due to their proximity to David.

MERAV (MERAB) BAT AHINOAM, SAUL'S DAUGHTER

> 1 Samuel 18:17 Sha'ul (Saul) said to David, "Here is my elder daugh-
> ter Merav (Merab); her I will give to you as a wife; only be a warrior
> for me and fight the HOLY ONE's battles." . . . [19]Then at the time when
> Merav bat Sha'ul (Merab, Saul's daughter) should have been given to
> David, she was given to Adriel the Meholathite as a wife.

Merab (Merav) is the eldest child of Ahinoam bat Ahimaaz and Sha'ul ben Kish. She is a patriarchal pawn in her father's games, primarily with David. Merab has a name but no agency. She is promised by her father to David in a transaction between men. Later she is given away by her father to a different man than promised. Almost as soon as she is introduced, Merab begins to fade—to be erased—from the Scriptures. English readers will find her mentioned in 2 Samuel 21:8 as the mother of five murdered sons, handed over by David to their deaths.[5]

The sum of Merab's recorded life is that she is engaged to David, taken back from David, given in marriage to a man she may have neither chosen nor consented to, spent years of her life birthing and raising five sons, only to

---

4. Rizpah is well-known in many African American preaching contexts for shaming David into giving Saul, Jonathan, and Merab's five sons a decent burial after he handed them over to be impaled (2 Sam 21:7–14).

5. The MT identifies Michal as the mother of the lynched (hung and impaled) men, as does the LXX. However, since the text names their father as Adriel, the man to whom Saul gave Merab instead of David, most commentators read Michal's name as a scribal error, as do I. Indeed, the Targum harmonizes the traditions by saying that Merab gave birth to them and Michal raised them. In either case, Merab disappears whether into her own fog or that of her sister.

see them murdered by David, using the Gibeonites as his proxy. Since she is not slaughtered with her sons, she may have lived to grieve them and perhaps curse David and her father until she died.

MICHAL BAT AHINOAM

1 Samuel 18:20 Now Michal bat Sha'ul (Saul) loved David, so Sha'ul (Saul) was told, and the thing was right in his eyes.

Michal bat Ahinoam has a larger footprint in the Scriptures than her elder sister or mother. Her name appears eighteen times versus three for her elder sister Merab and a single reference for their mother.[6] Unlike her mother and sister, Michal exercises a great deal of agency in the Scriptures: she loves; she speaks; she conspires; she lies; she moves; she looks; she despises; she criticizes. David is the object of most of her agency. And like the other women she is the object of patriarchal actions: she is given away (1 Sam. 25:44); she is likely imprisoned and made barren[7] (2 Sam. 6:23). Michal has a life, thoughts, and feelings. She loves David.[8] Michal makes decisions and acts on her feelings. She resists the patriarchal authority of her father and husband and pays the price.

After Jonathan declares his love for David and with tears enters into an unprecedented covenant with him (1 Sam. 18:1–6), the narrator proclaims Michal's love for David, repeatedly in 1 Samuel 19. It is striking, because she is the only woman in all of the Scriptures who is said to love a man—and that love will not be returned. Michal's father uses her love for David to ensnare him. Saul waives a traditional bride-price (*mohar*) to make sure David has no excuse for declining the offer. Instead, he requires of David a mere one hundred Philistine foreskins (1 Sam 18:25).[9] Marital practices in ancient Israel were culturally codified rather than legally stipulated. Arranged marriages

6. There is another Ahinoam in Samuel, one of David's women, but she is not bat Ahimaaz.

7. Michal's barrenness appears to be the result of abandonment of the marriage bed by David. Having been returned to David's royal household, without marital intimacy with him or the possibility with anyone else, she was in a virtual prison, even if she was not physically confined.

8. The idiom "fall in love" does not exist in Biblical Hebrew, although English readers will find it in some translations of the Scriptures.

9. The concept of dowries—in the Bible and elsewhere—is tricky; the translation "bride-price" and the exchange of currency or other valuable objects makes it seem that women were simply bought and sold. This is an oversimplification. Very few texts mention the practice at all, possibly because it was as commonplace in ancient Israel as it was in the ancient Near East. The term *mohar*, "dowry," occurs only in Gen. 34:12; Exod. 22:17; and 1 Sam. 18:25.

were common, perhaps normative, but are not frequently described in the text. How a couple married is regularly less important to the authors than that they did and produced whatever child is essential to the narrative.

Michal becomes aware of her father's plans to kill David (1 Sam. 19:11). Saul's plans may have been widely known, at least within his palace and household, or perhaps Michal had her own networks of information. Taking initiative, Michal warns David about the plot against his life. Then she physically helps him to escape. Describing this action, 1 Samuel 19:11 reports that she lets[10] him down from the window, conjuring up an image of her securing a hastily made rope of bedclothes and anchoring it with the strength of her arms and body. After the escape, Michal conceals David's whereabouts by lying to her father's men.

Michal's agency becomes more pronounced. She covers for David's absence by placing a *teraphim*-image[11] on the bed with goat hair to pass for David, presumably from afar. It is not clear whether Michal and David live in Saul's family compound or at some distance, whether the image is her own, part of her own religious identity and practice, or shared by Saul and his family at large. There is also no way to know how widespread was the practice of worshiping with images; it certainly occurs frequently enough to be regularly condemned by prophets. It is also not clear whether Michal understood her image to be of the God of Israel, as did Micah's mother in Judges 17:3, or if she is worshiping other, household gods, like Rachel in Genesis 31:19. As in Genesis 31:34, when Rachel steals her father's *teraphim*, it is clear that the actual religious practices described in the text do not conform to those exhorted by the text.[12]

Michal remains while David flees. When her father's messengers come for David, she lies, saying that he is ill (1 Sam. 19:14). Her deception is initially successful. Between verses 14 and 15, the messengers return to Saul without David, repeating that he is sick. In verse 15 Saul sends them back and tells them to bring the whole bed with the sick David in it, so that he might kill him with his own hands. Again, reading between the lines between the verses, the messengers bring the bed with the image and the goat hair to Saul, and Michal goes with them; whether voluntarily or not is not disclosed.

Even though Saul knows that Michal loves her husband, he is surprised and outraged that she has chosen David, whom he refers to as his enemy, over her own father. Michal lies again; in verse 15 she says that David threatened

10. In the Hiphil, *vatored*, "causing him to descend," placing the agency and physical labor on Michal.

11. *Teraphim* are images of gods worshiped by individual households. Their presence in Saul's home is no doubt intended to further discredit the failed monarch.

12. They also serve as a reminder that monotheism was a development in Israel's theology over time.

to kill her. Are Michal's lies motivated by her love for David or her fear of her father, or both? That episode ends abruptly with no response from Saul. The reader is left to wonder whether he said or did anything to his daughter. David has escaped from Saul and abandoned the one woman who loves him; this will not be said of any of his other many, many women. While David is on the run, he seeks out Michal's brother Jonathan—but not Michal—in 1 Samuel 20. The story shifts to the reciprocal love between David and Jonathan, which stands in stark contrast to Michal's one-sided love for David.

While David is inscribing his love for and with Jonathan in a covenant, Michal is forgotten and neglected by him, her father, and the text. Then David moves on to other women. David takes two women, Abigail and Ahinoam (1 Sam. 25:40–43). As an afterthought to David's new marriages, the narrator mentions that Saul has nullified Michal's marriage to David, giving her away to another man. There is neither precedent nor allowance for this in the Torah or in Israelite culture.

Michal, the only woman in the Scriptures said to love a man, is recycled and reissued. It is not just David who thinks that the love of women is insignificant; the text and its narrative have no regard for Michal's love or the lies it has birthed to save David's life. Jonathan and David share a number of tender scenes around their deceit to save David's life, and they share kisses and a tearful goodbye.[13] In contrast, Michal seems to be a fool for risking her privilege, status, and relationship with her father—if she ever had one—for a man who does not love, want, value, or miss her.

Saul gives Michal to Palti (sometimes Paltiel) ben Laish from Gallim. The report accompanies the announcement of two of David's marriages. The sequence may indicate Saul's response to David's new wives, or it may be that the report of David's most recent conjugal unions has jogged the narrator's mind, recalling Michal. The brief report in 1 Samuel 25:44 removes all of Michal's agency; she is the object of Saul's verb giving her to Palti. Afterwards, the narrative ignores Michal and focuses on David and his exploits. She reappears in 2 Samuel 3:13 when David demands her return. In the intervening passage, Saul dies (1 Sam. 31:4); his cousin Abner (Avner) places Saul's son Ishba'al[14] on the throne (2 Sam. 2:10), and David struggles to take the monarchy from the formidable warrior Abner, who rules by proxy. Abner and

13. See 1 Sam. 20 for the lengthy—forty-two-verse—treatment of the relationship between David and Jonathan.

14. Saul's son is named Ishba'al and called Ishbosheth. Saul's family has several members named for Ba'al—a Canaanite deity *and* a title used for Israel's God (Hosea, in Hos. 2:16, famously tells the people to stop calling their God Ba'al). A biblical editor replaced the name "Ba'al" with the word for shame, *boshet*, but the older form survives in some manuscripts.

David agree that Abner will transfer the monarchy to David and return his woman.

> 2 Samuel 3:12 Avner (Abner) sent messengers to David at Hebron, saying, "Whose land is this? Inscribe your covenant with me. And look! My hand will be with you to bring all Israel around to you." [13]David said, "Good. I myself will inscribe covenant with you. But one thing I ask of you: you will not see my face or be in my presence unless you bring Michal bat Sha'ul (Saul) when you come to see me." [14]Then David sent messengers to Ishba'al ben Sha'ul (Saul) saying, "Give me my woman Michal, whom I betrothed for one hundred Philistine foreskins." [15]So Ishba'al sent and took Michal from her husband Paltiel ben Laish. [16]And her husband went with her, weeping as he walked behind her all the way to Bahurim. So Avner (Abner) said to him, "Go on! Turn-back-around!" Then he turned-back-around.

Since seeing David two years prior, Michal has lived with and been loved by another man. Since her return the relationship between Michal and David is unclear. After their reunion, David begins to acquire women and children at a frenetic pace. Second Samuel 5:13 reports that David took an unknown number of women as primary and secondary wives, fathering some number of daughters and sons. Eleven names are given in 2 Samuel 5:13, but it is not clear if this is the total or just the sons or just the firstborn son with each woman, as in 2 Samuel 3:2–5.[15] Since the text aims to show David's virility, and Michal is not identified as a barren woman, the implication is that David does not have sex with her ever again.[16]

After assuring the reader of David's potency, Michal returns to the narrative:

> 2 Samuel 6:16 As the ark of the HOLY ONE OF OLD came into the city of David, Michal bat Sha'ul (Saul) looked out of the window, and saw King David leaping and dancing before the HOLY ONE; and she despised him in her heart.

JPS adds "for it," at the end of verse 16, indicating that Michal despised David for his worshipful dance. This is certainly how I have heard the passage interpreted in the African American community. However, the Hebrew verse does

---

15. See "Daughters of David" and "Granddaughters of David" in chapter 8 for discussion of David's female offspring.

16. It is possible that David abandons Michal's bed because she has had another husband with whom she has presumably been having sex, in order to avoid paternity confusion. David will not always be that finicky about having sex with other men's women, to wit, his marriage to Abigail and rape of Bathsheba.

not include "for it." I believe that the reason Michal despises David is that, after all she has done for him, after taking and using her love to escape from and ultimately succeed her father on the throne, he has abandoned her. David has moved on to other women and other children. He will not return to her bed; he will not father children with her. She is a living widow[17] watching him woo, seduce, and impregnate women all around her. Michal, who has used her agency in the narrative to defy and deceive her father, has lost that agency. She has been passed from man to man and now finds herself retrieved like property, but not rescued to the loving embrace of the man she once loved. Michal uses her voice for the last time in the Scriptures to tell David about himself in 2 Samuel 6:20: "How the king of Israel honored himself today, stripping today before the eyes of the slave-girls of his slaves, as any empty fellow might strip, uncovering himself."

David's response does not acknowledge her feelings for him, her actions on his behalf, her suffering on his behalf, any indebtedness to or care for her at all. Instead, he taunts her with his theology that it was God who elevated him at her father's expense—somewhat inverting the narrative, in which he descends through a window with her help. And about those slave-girls enslaved to his slaves, the lowest of the low, especially compared to a king's daughter, David says to Michal in verse 22, "I will make myself yet more accursed than this, and I will be degraded in my own eyes and with the slave-girls of whom you speak, with them I shall be honored."

In other words, "I have yet to begin to debase myself. I'll do so with whomever I choose—anyone but you. And they—slaves of slaves—those girls are just my speed. No matter what I do, they'll cheer me on, and they'll like it." David and the text turn from Michal, her living widowhood inscribed for perpetuity in verse 23: "And Michal bat Sha'ul did not have a child to the day of her death."

Ahinoam bat Ahimaaz and her daughters Merav (Merab) bat Ahimaaz and Michal bat Ahimaaz have passed from the gaze of the biblical editors; they are no longer of interest to those whose focus is on David as the anointed-messiah[18] king of Israel. But they are still of interest to me. Contemplating

---

17. I draw the notion of a living widowhood from the fate of David's anonymous women in 2 Sam. 20:3: "They remained confined until the day they died, a living widowhood."

18. The Hebrew Bible uses the word *meshiach*, from which the word "messiah" is derived, to describe David and Cyrus of Persia. In the New Testament, the term will be translated by the Greek word *christos*, as David and Cyrus are *christos* in the LXX. Most Bibles use the literal "anointed" to translate *meshiach*, reserving "Messiah/Christ" for Jesus in the NT. This leaves the erroneous perception that the title was used only of Jesus.

the relationships between Ahinoam and her daughters Merab and Michal fires my midrashic womanist imagination. How did this seasoned royal woman prepare her daughters for their roles as royal women—first as daughters and then wives? What did Ahinoam think of the young David, as fiancé to both of her daughters, of Michal's love for him? Could her mother's eye see the selfishness underneath the beauty of David? How does she respond to Saul's changing moods, rages, threats, and curses? Was she able to remain in her daughters' lives after their marriages? Was she there for Merab after David had her children and Ahinoam's grandchildren murdered? Was she there for Michal when David replaced and abandoned her? I believe Ahinoam had her own well of wisdom and experience in sharing a king with other women. She shared Saul with Rizpah bat Aiah (2 Sam. 3:6–11; 21:8–15), and there were other women.[19] Surely Ahinoam shared her mother wit, her womanist ways, with her daughters.

I offer a midrash on Ahinoam, Merab, and Michal:

> *Michal sobs inconsolably; only tears have bathed her face in recent days. Her hair hasn't been oiled or twisted. Such sleep as she has had has been from exhaustion, fitful, fleeting. At other times she falls deathly silent, staring at something no one can see. Then she talks to herself, or someone else. The servants make the sign of the evil eye behind her back. They say she is as mad as her father, that David is better off without her.*
>
> *The only one who can calm her, feed her, bathe her, hold her is her mother. There are no "I told you so's." Even though she did tell her that something about that boy just wasn't right. Pretty is as pretty does. And God don't like ugly. Now there was just "Hush, baby, mama's here." Her arthritis-swollen fingers untangling the tightly wound coils of her daughter's hair, as she had when she was a child cradled between her thighs. How she wished she were as active as she was then! She had to cross her ankles around her to hold her still to finish her hair. Her beautiful hair. She had been tearing it out, since they had taken her scissors and knives, after she had cut it and more that last time. Best not to think about that.*
>
> *Having soothed Michal, Ahinoam goes to Merav's room. She had come home to Mama after David manipulated the Gibeonites into killing her babies—all of them. Merav couldn't stay in that house after that. Her husband used to come regularly, coaxing her to return. But we haven't seen him around here in a while now. Merav is on the terrace, pulling up flowers*

---

19. See 2 Sam. 2:8, where God through Nathan acknowledges giving David "his master's women," as though that should have kept him from having Bathsheba abducted so that he could rape her.

and weeds together. Tearing at their leaves and petals and flinging them as
far away as she can. Ahinoam sits wincing and waits. She aches to take her
firstborn in her arms, but this child of hers can no longer stand to be touched
and will not even meet her eyes. So she waits, wondering who will mother
these daughters that David has broken after her death.

RIZPAH, SAUL'S SECONDARY WIFE

2 Samuel 21:8 The king, David, took the two sons of Rizpah bat Aiah,
whom she gave birth to for Sha'ul (Saul)—Armoni and Mephiba'al;
and the five children of Merav bat Sha'ul (Saul), whom she gave birth
to for Adriel ben Barzillai the Meholathite. ⁹David gave them into the
hands of the Gibeonites, and they hung them on the mountain before
the HOLY ONE OF OLD. The seven of them fell together. They were
put to death in the first days of harvest, at the beginning of barley
harvest.

Rizpah is the last of Saul's royal women whose name is preserved in the
Scriptures. She is the mother of his sons Armoni and Mephiba'al (called
Mephibosheth). She is the daughter of Aiah, who is not otherwise known.[20]
Rizpah is a secondary or low-status wife, a *pilegesh* (*piylegesh*). The term is
usually mistranslated a "concubine," which denotes a female sexual partner to
whom a man has no legal ties. As wives with lower status than primary wives
(*isshah/nashiym*) their children were legitimate, the men were called husbands,
and their parents were called in-laws, all signaling a legitimate marriage. Ultimately secondary marriage meant that children, while legitimate, were not
entitled to an inheritance.

Rizpah's body becomes a site of contestation for the monarchy after Saul's
death. Only Judah swears fealty to the young David, while the bulk of Israel
follows Saul's son Ishba'al (Ishboshet) ben Ahinoam. Ahinoam's youngest
son is on the throne; therefore, as the queen mother, she and her daughters
would have been protected from those seeking revenge on the house of Saul.
But Rizpah is accessible and vulnerable; her secondary status translates into

---

20. Aiah is treated as a male in commentaries such as Stephen Dempster's "Aiah"
in *AYBD* 1:130, but since there is no verb attached to the name, it is impossible to
determine gender. Israelite identity can be reckoned matrilineally, e.g., Bethuel ben
Milcah, or patrilineally, e.g., Rivqah (Rebekah) bat Bethuel. While the name has a
traditional feminine suffix, as in Sarah, Leah, Shoshonah, etc., some males, e.g., Jonah
and Elkanah, have names with the same form. In addition, women and men shared
some names, such as Gomer, Shelomith, and Micaiah. With no other evidence available, Aiah can be the mother or the father of Rizpah.

a lack of financial and other insulating resources. Rizpah's children, along with Merab's children, are superfluous and dangerous as potential claimants to the throne. Ahinoam, Merab, and Michal are apparently unavailable to those struggling for the kingdom of their father and husband.[21] Sexual access to a royal woman is a claim on the throne and underlies David's demand for Michal's return, even though he does not return to the marriage bed. David's son Absalom rapes David's women, using this logic as part of his attempted coup in 2 Samuel 16:20–23. Further, Solomon will have his brother Adonijah killed for asking for David's last royal woman, Abishag, in 2 Kings 2:13–25.

During the two years that David struggles to seize the monarchy after the deaths of Saul and his beloved Jonathan, Saul's nephew and the former commander of his army, Abner, wields power behind and through his cousin Ishba'al/Ishboshet, whom he crowned (2 Sam. 2:8–10). Abner is the one who offers the united Israel to David, turning against the house of Saul and returning Michal to David. And when Abner is accused of raping Rizpah, he does not deny it:

> 2 Samuel 3:6 While there was war between the house of Sha'ul (Saul) and the house of David, Avner (Abner) strengthened himself in the house of Sha'ul. ⁷Now Sha'ul had a wife-of-lesser-status whose name was Rizpah bat Aiah. And Ishba'al said to Avner, "Why have you gone in to my father's low-wife?" ⁸And Avner was furious, very much so, on account of the words of Ishba'al; he said, "Am I a dog's head for Yehudah (Judah)? This day I show fidelity to the house of your father Sha'ul, to his kin, and to his friends, and have not let you be found in the hand of David; and you assess against me a crime concerning this woman this day! ⁹So may God do to Avner and so may God add to it, just as the HOLY ONE has sworn to David, that will I do for him: ¹⁰To transfer the monarchy from the house of Sha'ul, and set up the throne of David over Israel and over Yehudah, from Dan to Beersheba." ¹¹And Ishba'al could not answer Abner another word, because he feared him.

Abner's response to the claim that he raped Rizpah was to rage about the accusation, list his past support for the house of Saul, and to promise to help God keep a divine oath to elevate David. He never denied raping Rizpah. She was a casualty to the messy, bloody business of kingmaking. It is rape in my reading, because there would have been no possibility of consent for the unprotected woman of the former, now dead, king from the commander of the nation's army and kingmaker. Abner could not have her husband's throne,

---

21. After David's death and the division of the monarchy, his granddaughters will be sought after as marriage partners to strengthen claims on his throne.

but he could have *her*. His scheme was not to put himself on the throne but to make himself indispensible to the inevitable monarch. By declaring for David, he identifies as a garden-variety rapist, not a throne-usurping rapist. He is given a pass. The rape of Rizpah is unavenged.

Rizpah is more than one more raped, used, and discarded woman in the Scriptures. In 2 Samuel 21:1–14, her sons will be offered up as human sacrifices to end the famine plaguing David's newly united monarchy. When David asks about the three-year famine in the land, God tells him that bloodguilt endures on the surviving members of Saul's house for an extermination campaign against Gibeon. Yet annihilating one's enemies was standard fare in the ancient Near East as it is in the biblical text, often at the command of God.

It is ironic that Saul and his house are faulted for doing what every Israelite leader from Joshua to David also does. God does not tell David specifically how the bloodguilt is connected to the famine or how to relieve it; so David asks the offended Gibeonites what they want in order to bless God's people and end the famine. They ask for seven of Saul's sons/children/descendants.

The editors of the Bible are not at all disturbed by the magical[22] influence the non-Israelite Gibeonites have over Israel's fertility and fecundity, nor by the human sacrifice required to purchase their blessing, nor even the notion that God withholds blessing from Israel because of the Gibeonite grudge. As David chooses sacrificial victims from Saul's offspring, he protects the son of his beloved Jonathan and condemns both of Rizpah's sons to death, along with those of Merab, Saul's older daughter. The Gibeonites lynch[23] Saul's sons and grandsons in the presence of God at a local shrine, the Hill of God (*Gibeath-Elohim*, 1 Sam. 10:5). Rizpah, who never speaks in the Scriptures, is the passive victim of Abner's assault and the passive topic of Ishba'al's accusation. She asserts herself for the only time in the text to protect the bodies of her sons in death, as she could not in life: "Then Rizpah bat Aiah took sackcloth, and spread it on a rock for herself, from the beginning of harvest until rain fell on them from the heavens; she did not allow the birds of the air to come on the bodies by day, or the wild animals by night" (2 Sam. 21:10).

Rizpah bat Aiah watches the corpses of her sons stiffen, soften, swell, and sink into the stench of decay. Apparently she is denied permission to bury

---

22. While magic often has a negative valence for Christian interpreters, it was regarded as a normative part of the ancient world. Some magic is condemned in the Hebrew Bible, e.g., witchcraft or sorcery (see Lev. 19:26 and Deut. 18:10). However, note that only female sorcerers are subject to the death penalty (Exod. 22:18). Other forms of magic are used normatively without sanction, such as Jacob's use of rods to increase his flocks at his father-in-law's expense (Gen. 30:37–42) and Joseph's practice of divination (Gen. 44:5, 15).

23. The verb *y-q-'* means "hang," "dislocate," and/or "impale."

her dead. Denial of proper funerary rites was a common means of cursing and punishing an enemy and their people in and beyond death in the ancient Near East. Rizpah fights with winged, clawed, and toothed scavengers night and day. She is there from the spring harvest until the fall rains, as many as six months from Nissan (March/April) to Tishrei (September/October), sleeping, eating, toileting, protecting, and bearing witness.

Moved by her actions, David retrieves the unburied bones of Saul and Jonathan—whom David loved as his own soul and more than women but couldn't be bothered to bury—from the people who took them when they had been left to rot. He gives them a proper burial, along with the sons of Rizpah bat Aiah and the sons of Merab bat Ahinoam. Then, and only then, does God break the famine. There was no need of a Gibeonite blessing after all. Perhaps David misunderstood the divine message; perhaps he used the occasion to rid himself of potential competitors. In either case, lynching Rizpah's and Merab's sons did not heal the land or the people. Doing right by a multiply wronged woman did. Sermons about Rizpah are not unheard of in black churches; she has a following among womanist preachers, who remember, lament, and are strengthened by her strength.

David's lament for Saul and Jonathan in 2 Samuel 1:24 exhorts the daughters of Israel to "weep over Saul who clothed you with crimson, in luxury, who put ornaments of gold on your apparel." I say that the daughters of Israel should have wept for Ahinoam bat Ahimaaz, her daughters Merab and Michal banoth Ahinoam, and her sister-wife Rizpah bat Aiah. Although they may have been clothed in luxury, they were stripped of those they loved most dearly. In spite of their differing status, Rizpah and Ahinoam and her daughters suffered as much at the hands of the man who lamented their shared Saul and Jonathan as they suffered at the hands of those that killed them.

8

Dominated by David

There is a perception among my students that David had a couple of wives, but certainly not a couple dozen, and that Solomon's legendary marriage volume is de novo and not a generational pattern. These commonly held assumptions do not hold up under close reading of the biblical text. There are ten named individual women to whom David is either engaged or married or with whom he fathers children—in addition to at least two different groups of women whose numbers and names go unrecorded. These numbers regularly come as a shock to students and congregants. Most are aware of David's notorious transgression with and against Bathsheba but are not familiar with the extent to which the Bible chronicles his womanizing. Table 1 on the next page is a quick and dirty list of David's women.

The collective categories "Saul's former wives" and "other primary wives and secondary wives taken in Jerusalem" could have included a handful, dozens, or hundreds of women on a Solomonic scale. There is simply no way to know how many marriage and sexual partners David had. I have discussed the royal women who overlapped Saul and David: Ahinonam bat Ahimaaz and her daughters with Saul, Merab and Michal, and Saul's low-status wife, Rizpah, above. I address the rest of this great constellation of royal women here in the sequence in which they are presented in the Scriptures.

AVIGAYIL (ABIGAIL)

1 Samuel 25:2 There was a man in Maon, whose work was in Carmel. The man was exceedingly rich: he had three thousand sheep and a thousand goats. And he happened to be shearing his sheep in Carmel.

David's Women	Description of Women	Scripture Reference
Merab bat Ahinoam	Saul's oldest daughter, given to another instead of David	1 Sam. 18:17, 19
Michal bat Ahinoam	Saul's daughter, given to another after her marriage, living widow	1 Sam. 18:20–22; 19:11–13; 25:44; 2 Sam. 3:14–16; 6:16–23
Abigail	wife of an inhospitable drunk Calebite, Nabal, after whose death David sends for her; mother of David's second son, Chileab/Daniel (likely died)	1 Sam. 25:1–42
Ahinoam of Jezreel	married on the way home from marrying Abigail; mother of David's first son, Amnon	1 Sam. 25:43
Maacah bat Talmai	daughter of King Talmai of Geshur; mother of David's third son, Absalom, and daughter Tamar	2 Sam. 3:3
Haggith	otherwise unknown mother of David's fourth son, Adonijah	2 Sam. 3:4
Abital	otherwise unknown mother of David's fifth son, Shephatiah	2 Sam. 3:4
Eglah	otherwise unknown mother of David's sixth son, Ithream	2 Sam. 3:5
Bathsheba bat Eliam	wife of the murdered Uriah; mother of Solomon, Shammua (Shimea), Shobab, Nathan	2 Sam. 11–12; 1 Chr. 3:5
Saul's former wives		2 Sam. 12:8
Abishag of Shunem	in David's last, impotent days	1 Kgs. 1:1–4
other primary and secondary wives	taken in Jerusalem, mothers of Ibhar, Elishua, Nepheg, Japhia, Elishama, Eliada, Eliphelet, Jerimoth	2 Sam. 5:13–14; 2 Chr. 11:18

1 Samuel 25:3 The name of the man was Naval (Nabal), and the name of his woman was Avigayil (Abigail). The woman was of good understanding and beautiful of form, while the man was coarse and evil in deeds.

Avigayil (Abigail) is a beloved character in the biblical text and later rabbinic and Christian interpretive literature. She is portrayed as a beautiful and wise woman, married to a drunken, boorish, likely abusive husband, who is swept off her feet by David, who marries her after her divinely orchestrated widowhood. That David and Abigail's relationship is consummated only after their marriage, following the death of her husband from natural causes, stands in sharp contrast to David's eventual relationship with Bathsheba. Although often taught as a romantic tale in congregations and other contexts, there is no talk of love, and there are many indications of multiple motives, including mercenary ones, on and below the surface of this story.

After the introduction of beautiful, shapely Abigail and horrible Nabal, the young, handsome, dashing David appears in 1 Samuel 25:2. He identifies Nabal as a prospective patron because of his great wealth. Nabal is also a fellow Judahite.[1] No geographical or genealogical information is provided for Abigail. Pointing out that he could have taken what he wanted, David asks Nabal for food for himself and his men (1 Sam. 25:5–8). Seeing no reason to share his wealth with a boy who looks more like a runaway servant than a warrior-king, Nabal declines and insults David (1 Sam. 25:10–11). While readers and hearers of Scripture have been trained to identify with David as God's anointed and rightful king of Israel, there is no obvious mechanism by which Nabal and Abigail would have come by this knowledge. Indeed, David is on the run from the legitimate king, Saul.

David's request is not a request at all. In response to being denied free provisions and insulted, he prepares to wage war against Nabal for refusing to share his goods. Even though Nabal has violated the cultural code of hospitality, David's response is inexplicably violent. When one of the servants tells Abigail what has happened, the story takes a new direction. Abigail nurtures the ambitions of the young would-be monarch at the expense of her husband and behind his back, feeding David and his men out of her husband's wealth.

Abigail rides to David in secret and throws herself at his feet, abasing herself, calling David her lord (*adoni*) twelve times in 1 Samuel 25:24–31. She refers to herself as his "slave-woman" six times in the passage—*amah* in verses

1. Nabal's hometown, Maon, is in the tribe of Judah, some twenty miles south of David's family home in Bethlehem. The action of the story takes place on the other side of Israel, one hundred miles to the northwest, in Carmel.

24 (twice), 25, and 28, and *shiphchah* in verses 27 and 31. Given the near ubiquity of sexual exploitation of enslaved women, there is an inevitable sexual undercurrent to that language. Abigail even asks him in verse 28 to forgive her (but not her husband) for an undisclosed transgression. She also asks that the iniquity—presumably her husband's refusing to extend hospitality—and any bloodguilt be on her, and she offers David a blessing of foodstuff for him and his men. Lastly, Abigail prophesies to David in verses 29–30 specifically that he will be *nagid*,[2] "prince," over Israel.[3] In response, David blesses Abigail and her discernment in 1 Samuel 25:33. David credits her with saving her own life and that of every male in her husband's service, using colorful language in verse 34: "Surely as the HOLY ONE, the God of Israel lives, who has restrained me from doing evil to you—had you not hurried and come to meet me, truly by morning there would not have been left to Naval a single man to piss on a wall."[4]

It is chilling as a modern woman to hear the beloved David of Scripture prepare to blame Abigail and God for the lethal violence he would have inflicted upon her in mere moments if she had not the God-given sense to hurry to him with gifts and obeisance. As a womanist, I am reminded of the ways in which batterers blame their victims for their assaults, sometimes invoking religious justifications. Abigail is not a romantic. The valorization of Abigail's buying her life and those of the servants and/or slaves on her husband's estate with her self-abasement and his pilfered goods overlooks her vulnerability to David. The union of Abigail and David is no more romantic than those of battered women who do and say anything to calm their abusers in the hope of preventing today's beating. Abigail's generosity and submission is a last-ditch, desperate gamble masked in charm.

Abigail may have learned how to negotiate with a violent man in her own home. When she returns home after being dismissed by David, she finds her drunken husband partying away. She wisely waits until the morning, when he is no longer intoxicated, to tell him what has transpired. The spouses and children of alcoholics know to avoid the drunken person in their home. Her betrayal seems to have sent her husband into an early grave—or God struck him down, or both. Once she is a respectable and available widow, David sends for her. But how respectable was it for Abigail to marry so soon after her husband had died? Although neither her mourning period nor even a funeral is reported, a reader can infer only the former.

2. *Nagid*, literally "front-man," "ruler," was the title used most for Saul and by David in first-person accounts; see 1 Sam. 9:16; 10:1; 13:14; 25:30; 2 Sam. 5:2; 6:21; 7:8; 1 Kgs. 1:35.

3. In Jewish tradition Abigail is recognized as a prophet; see *b. Megillah* 14a (in the Babylonian Talmud).

4. David's image has been partially rehabilitated by contemporary translations like the NRSV, CEB, and JPS, which clean up his language. The KJV preserves the quote.

The woman who showed so much strength shows none now. She tells the messengers she will be David's slave/servant and theirs as well, positioning herself as the lowest of the low (1 Sam. 25:41). Perhaps this is all shrewd rhetoric. She does take five of her own women-servants with her; she is not quite destitute and alone. Perhaps Abigail has correctly sized up David and determined flattery, compliance, and self-abasement are the keys to surviving him. Abigail and David ride off into the sunset—in my imagination—and then come to a thudding halt.

David and Abigail are riding off into what I had always hoped was more of a partnership between equals than one regularly finds in the sacred pages. She is clever and savvy and knows her way around a power-hungry man's ego. He is violent and ambitious, self-centered, and really good at conquering, leading, and inspiring people. They each have their respective gifts of God. And then, before they arrive at their destination, David stops one verse later, seemingly on the side of the road, and picks up another woman.

David's honeymoon with Abigail has now turned into a threesome. In fact, it is not clear[5] that David consummates his union with Abigail—which may explain his desire for another wife. Curiously, the text continues to identify Abigail as the wife of Nabal. From this point forward Abigail will appear only in the company of one or more of David's other wives and women. Her story continues within the story of David's next wife.

Abigail has been married, perhaps unhappily so, been widowed, remarried, pioneered a settlement, been abducted, been rescued, gives birth to a son for the legendary king David, and perhaps watches that child die in infancy. Since no other children are credited to her, it is possible that David abandons her the way he abandons Michal. It is also possible that she dies. Another possibility is that once David has impregnated a woman, he moves on.[6]

AHINOAM OF JEZREEL

1 Samuel 25:42 Avigayil (Abigail) hurried and got up and mounted a donkey. Her five serving girls went with her to tend her. She went after the messengers of David and she became his wife. [43]David also took Ahinoam of Jezreel; both of them became his wives.

5. Abigail does not give birth until after Ahinoam, suggesting that David did not sleep with her until she was sure she was not pregnant with Nabal's child.
6. This possibility is suggested by the pattern in the list of David's children born at Hebron and their mothers. Shimon Bar Efrat's commentary on the Davidic genealogy in Samuel in the *Jewish Study Bible* suggests the list may acknowledge only the first-born child of each woman, opening up the possibility that David had many children with each.

> 1 Samuel 27:3 And David dwelled with Achish at Gath, he and his men, every man with his household, and David with his two wives, Ahinoam the Jezreelite, and Avigayil of Carmel, Nabal's widow.

> 1 Samuel 30:5 The two wives of David had been taken captive: Ahinoam the Jezreelite, and Avigayil the wife of Nabal the Carmelite.

David has a new wife, Ahinoam. Nothing of their courtship, ceremony, or celebration is preserved. She appears as a footnote to his marriage to Abigail; 1 Samuel 25:43 simply records Ahinoam of Jezreel also became David's wife. But she doesn't even get her own sentence; the verse continues by announcing "the two of them" as his wives. Though the text doesn't name Abigail here, she is present but secondary, as she will be in every place Ahinoam is named.[7] There is no story to go with Ahinoam's marriage to David. She is not identified as having significant family or political connections. She is not even described as beautiful or in any way attractive. The passage in 1 Samuel 25:43 simply says he "took" her.[8] Was David's action motivated by anything other than Ahinoam's gender and apparent availability?

Ahinoam is from Jezreel. There are two cities by that name. One is less than fifteen miles from Carmel, where David met and married Abigail; the other is somewhere in the tribal lands of Judah. Most scholars believe Ahinoam was from the northern city and that David traveled through it with his new bride Abigail and saw and married Ahinoam there. The narrative gives no indication of time, making it possible to read the marriages as virtually simultaneous. The immediacy of David's marriage to Ahinoam further dispels any romantic notions about his union to Abigail.

No retinue is described as accompanying Ahinoam, whereas Abigail is accompanied by her five serving-women. At the same time Ahinoam has nothing in the text, no wealth or possessions, while David and Abigail likely transported all of her late husband's wealth in flocks and servants. Even though Ahinoam may have had or found at least one woman-servant of her own, she is surrounded by Abigail's servants, whose first loyalty is not to Ahinoam.

Ahinoam and Abigail begin their shared marriage on the road; they will travel together without a permanent home until David settles in Hebron, where he will be anointed (again) and enthroned (2 Sam. 1:1–4). David and his two wives spend their corporate honeymoon fleeing from Jezreel to the Philistine city of Gath, more than one hundred miles to the south. Ahinoam,

---

7. Ahinoam is always named with reference to her home city, Jezreel, and with, but before, Abigail (1 Sam. 25:43; 27:3; 30:5; 2 Sam. 2:2; 3:2; 1 Chr. 3:1).

8. The verb *l-q-h* means "take" in any context and is also the normative verb for what is contemporarily called "marriage"—hence the NRSV's use of "married." The comparison is inexact. "Taking" in marriage in the Scriptures is hierarchal and patriarchal. Men take women as wives; women do not take men as husbands.

Abigail, and David eventually live together with his six hundred troops and their families for sixteen months in a Philistine city, Ziklag, that becomes a perpetual Israelite holding and is eventually incorporated into the territory of Judah (1 Sam. 27:2–6). While David is raiding and killing every woman and man among the non-Israelite peoples he raids, Abigail and Ahinoam are living separately or together as cowives. The text is not interested in their experience or relationship.

Ahinoam and Abigail and the women of David's troops, six hundred or more if each man has at least one woman of his own, have to make a life for themselves, their children, and their menfolk in the city they have been assigned. The women have to do the work of establishing their homes without their men, who are mercenaries in the service of the Philistine monarch. For Abigail, who left a wealthy estate, it is like starting all over again. We have no way of knowing how different the present circumstances are for Ahinoam, or how difficult she and Abigail find them.

While David and his warriors are away, the Amalekite kin of people that David and his troops have exterminated (1 Sam. 27:8) come seeking vengeance. However, unlike David they do not kill the women and children:

> 1 Samuel 30:3 When David and his men came to the city, look! It was burned with fire! Their women and sons and daughters, they were taken captive. ⁴Then David and the people who were with him raised their voices and wept, until there was no longer strength within them to weep. ⁵David's two wives also had been taken captive, Ahinoam the Jezreelite, and Avigayil (Abigail) the wife of Naval (Nabal) the Carmelite.

Although David's tears could signify his care and concern for his two women, they could also be tears of rage. In 1 Samuel 30:17–19, David recovers his women, the families of his men, and all of their livestock and possessions. He also takes the livestock and possessions of the Amalekites who had seized them. The adventures of Ahinoam and Abigail with their shared husband, David, continue in the Scriptures. In 2 Samuel 2:2–4 Ahinoam and Abigail travel with David to Hebron, where they must settle anew, making yet another new life for themselves. Here David is anointed king over Judah, but not yet all Israel. They are officially royal women now. And they have a royal task: produce an heir and a spare.

Ahinoam becomes pregnant and delivers her child before Abigail conceives sometime later. Ahinoam's child is David's firstborn son, Amnon, who figures prominently in the Scriptures for raping David's daughter Tamar (by another mother). Next, Abigail gives birth to a son, Chileab, who likely dies in infancy, since there are no stories about him, and he does not figure at all in the fight among David's sons for his throne. Ahinoam and Abigail fade from the account in Samuel; they are included in the longer genealogy of David and his children in 1 Chronicles 3.

Ahinoam is plucked from obscurity, brought into a plural marriage in which one wife (Michal) has been abandoned. She travels, lives, works, is abducted, and then is rescued with another wife, who preceded her temporally by a relatively short period. Yet Ahinoam eclipses David's other wives by giving birth to the new king's coveted firstborn son.

MAACAH, HAGGITH, ABITAL, EGLAH

2 Samuel 3:2 Children were born to David at Hebron: his firstborn was Amnon, to Ahinoam the Jezreelite. [3]His second was Chileav (Chileab), to Avigayil (Abigail) the wife of Naval (Nabal) the Carmelite. The third was Avshalom ben Maacah, daughter of King Talmai of Geshur. [4]The fourth was Adoniyah (Adonijah) ben Haggith. The fifth was Shephatiah ben Avital (Abital). [5]And the sixth was Ithream, to David's wife Eglah. These were born to David in Hebron,

2 Samuel 5:13 In Jerusalem, after he came from Hebron, David took more secondary and primary wives; and more sons and daughters were born to David. [14]These are the names of those who were born to him in Jerusalem: Shammua, Shobab, Nathan, Shlomo (Solomon), [15]Ibhar, Elishua, Nepheg, Japhia, [16]Elishama, Eliada, and Eliphelet.

The next pool of women who share David are given short shrift. Maacah bat Talmai is the daughter of Talmai, monarch of the tiny principality of Geshur, which bordered the tribal lands of Manasseh and was eventually folded into Israel during Solomon's rule. Maacah was the mother of Absalom (Avshalom) who rebelled against his father David and nearly took the throne from him. She is also Tamar's mother. The Scripture makes a point of David's silence in response to his son Amnon raping his daughter Tamar—because he was his firstborn and he loved him.[9] But the text does not acknowledge that Tamar has a mother or how she responds to her daughter's assault. Her son Absalom runs to his maternal grandfather's territory after he kills his half-brother Amnon for raping Tamar. Perhaps she helps her son escape to her people. The Scriptures erase Maacah from Absalom's long struggle with David for the crown, and she is nowhere to be seen when Absalom is executed, lamented, and buried. David's grief, however, plays center stage in the stories the Scriptures choose to tell. The Scriptures portray Maacah and

9. This explanation, that David's silence was a result of his love for his firstborn son, is preserved in 2 Sam. 13:21 in the Qumran texts (1QSam^a) and LXX but not the MT.

Bathsheba as the only women who give birth to more than one of David's children.

Haggith, Abital (Avital), and Eglah are treated as little more than named wombs in the story of David. Abigail, Ahinoam, Maacah, Haggith, Abital, and Eglah are mentioned again in the genealogy in 1 Chronicles 3:1–9, in which David's subsequent children with Bathsheba are also named (see the next section, "Bathsheba"). There is also a list of names of other children born to unnamed women for David. The Chronicles genealogy provides a time frame of seven years and six months for David's procreation in Hebron (1 Chr. 3:4). In 2 Samuel 5:13, David takes an unknown number of unnamed secondary wives in Jerusalem and fathers more children with them. Daughters and sons are acknowledged, and a list of names follows, which the reader/translator must gender on her or his own: Shammua, Shobab, Nathan, Solomon, Ibhar, Elishua, Nepheg, Japhia, Elishama, Eliada, and Eliphelet.[10]

That Maacah, Haggith, Abital, and Eglah join Abigail and Ahinoam, marry David, and give birth to his children at Hebron means David has at least six wives with whom he is living, sleeping, and making babies before he ever lays eyes on Bathsheba; this is in addition to his banished but still legal and accessible wife, Michal. What was life like for all of them?

BATHSHEBA

2 Samuel 11:2 And it happened, at evening time, that David rose from his lying-place and went walking about on the roof of the king's house, that he saw a woman bathing from the roof; the woman was extraordinarily beautiful in appearance. [3]David sent someone to inquire about the woman. It was reported, "Is not this Bat-Sheva bat Eliam, the wife of Uriah the Hittite?" [4]And David sent messengers and he took her, and she came to him, and he lay with her. And she had purified herself after her defilement. Then she returned to her house. [5]The woman conceived. And she sent and had someone tell David, "I am pregnant."

2 Samuel 11:26 When the wife of Uriah heard that Uriah her husband was dead, she lamented over her lord-husband.

10. Most translators presume them all to be male, with the names of David's daughters unrecorded. However, since there are no verbs attached to any of these names, their gender cannot be determined with complete certainty. Many of these names occur in other narratives for male characters; other names do not reoccur. While it is possible that the list is intended to identify David's first male offspring with each unnamed mother, that does not account for the introduction specifying that "daughters" were born to David. (See also sections later in this chapter, "Mother and Sisters" and "Daughters of David.")

Bathsheba bat Eliam, mother of Solomon, victim, then wife, then survivor of David, is named Bat-Sheva, "daughter of an oath." She is a promise kept. The nature of the promise is not revealed; she may have been the answer to the prayer of a couple who struggled to conceive. She is the ninth individual woman linked intimately to David. Bathsheba is a beautiful woman. This is not a neutral statement or entirely in praise of her and her beauty. While David will be held accountable for his sin with against her, the text insinuates that her beauty is partially to blame. More of Bathsheba's beauty than could normally be seen is visible because she is bathing. The verb *r-ch-tz* could indicate a regular hygienic bath or a Torah-prescribed cleansing in response to menstrual or other state that required ritual ablution.[11] I am inclined to read the bathing in 2 Samuel 11:2 as a basic bath, because there is no identification of a condition for which she would be required to purify herself at this point. The passage portrays the rooftop location as neutral. It is neither salacious nor condemned. David's ability to view her body is attributed to the size and position of the royal residence and not to any temptation or solicitation on her part. Bathsheba is the object of David's vision, his interest, his curiosity, and his lust to acquire and dominate. Rape is not about sexual desire. (Subsequently I delineate the reasons for reading the encounter as rape.)

Bathsheba is introduced patriarchally as a daughter and wife, named with regard to the men in her life, her father Eliam and her husband Uriah the Hittite. Her naming formula communicates and emphasizes she is not sexually available. According to the Torah any man other than her husband who has sexual contact with her is guilty of a crime against her husband, whether adultery or rape. If she were unmarried, the crime would be against her father. Her naming and presentation also identify her in relation to the Hittite people. Bathsheba's husband and father raise the question of her ethnicity. The text does not reveal the ethnic origin of Bathsheba or her father, but identifying her husband Uriah as a Hittite raises the possibility that her father, and hence she, is a Hittite as well.[12] There is no tribal affiliation or city of residence given for Eliam, which is counterindicative of Israelite ancestry. Further, a Hittite identity for her father would account for her Hittite husband. While regularly denounced, intermarriage did occur with some frequency; however, the most

11. See the discussion on the terms *tamei* and *tahor* in the entry on "Women Who Give Birth," in the chapter on Leviticus.

12. Israelites reckoned lineage paternally; even if her unknown mother is an Israelite, she would be a Hittite if her father is a Hittite. This is the case even if the Hittites have a different understanding of identity; it is the Israelite understanding that functions in the Scriptures. Maternal lineage will become essential in rabbinic Judaism at some distance from ancient Israelite religion.

common form was Israelite men with non-Israelite women to secure Israelite offspring.[13] If Eliam were a Hittite, his daughter's marriage to another Hittite would be unremarkable as the marriage is presented. The marriage of an Israelite woman to a Hittite man could be expected to raise eyebrows and generate commentary; however, neither commentary nor concern is articulated. One reason for silence around Bathsheba's and her father's origin would be to obscure the non-Israelite origins of Bathsheba, her son Solomon, and his descendants.

It is also possible that Bathsheba and her father are Israelites. There is an argument that Bathsheba's father is not only an Israelite but one who is so well known that his genealogical and geographical description is superfluous, accounting for their absence. In this line of thought, her father's name occurs in addition to her husband's to signal the importance and renown of her father and her family. Scholars who hold to this position identify Bathsheba's father Eliam with Eliam ben Ahitophel of Gilo in Judah (2 Sam. 23:34). Eliam ben Ahitophel was one of David's elite warrior corps.[14] Ahitophel, who would have been Bathsheba's grandfather in this genealogy, was one of David's primary advisors (2 Sam. 15:12).[15] In support of an Israelite identity for Bathsheba and her father are their Semitic[16] names and Bathsheba's apparent observance of Torah-based customs around hygiene and purity.

Even if Hittite ancestry is not evoked for Bathsheba by the disclosure of her husband's ethnicity, the inclusion of the Hittites in Israel's story at this point is significant. The Hittites were a formidable empire in Anatolia (modern Turkey) and had settled Canaan before Abraham's journey, such that when he sought burial grounds for Sarah, he purchased land from them (Gen. 23:3–9). Esau marries two Hittite women, Judith (Yehudit) bat Beeri and Basemath bat Elon (Gen. 26:34), with no suggestion that he traveled to Anatolia to find them. The Hittites remain in Canaan after the Israelite arrival (Judg. 3:5),

13. Intermarriage was regularly practiced among ancient Israel's significant figures, including David's grandmother Ruth the Moabite and ancestral figures such as Joseph, who with Asenath the Egyptian produced the (half) tribes of Ephraim and Manasseh; Judah and the Canaanite Tamar; Simeon and his Canaanite wife; and Moses with the Midianite Zipporah and an unnamed Nubian wife.

14. These warriors were called "mighty men" in the KJV; that language is familiar to many womanist readers and hearers of the text.

15. Randall Bailey traces the relationship between David, Eliam, and Ahitophel to the beginning of his reign in Hebron, seven years earlier in *David in Love and War: The Pursuit of Power in 2 Samuel 10–12* (Sheffield: JSOT Press, 1990), 87.

16. Hebrew in all its forms (i.e., biblical, rabbinic, medieval, and modern) is a Semitic language. Semitic languages are part of the Afro-Asiatic family, along with the people who speak them. Hittite is an Indo-European language from a completely different language family.

in spite of assurances of their divine removal.[17] Uriah and Abimelech (and potentially Eliam) are Hittite mercenaries serving under David's command (1 Sam. 26:6). Later, the Hittites within Israel would be pressed into forced labor on Solomon's building projects (1 Kgs. 9:20). Then Solomon turned to them for some of his wives (1 Kgs. 11:1). The Hittites were key coalition partners for David and later Solomon. As mercenaries they invested blood and sweat equity into the fledgling monarchy. By seizing the wife of one of his Hittite strike-force officers, David is acting against his own strategic interests, in addition to violating the standards of his community and his God.

I have consistently referred to the violation of Bathsheba's body as a rape, even though the vocabulary of the biblical text is frustratingly ambiguous about whether the sex act between David and Bathsheba is consensual. The passage does not say that David uses force against Bathsheba, as it does in other accounts of rape.[18] For what David does to Bathsheba, the passage does not use any of the words that signal rape in other cases.[19] Despite the absence of these terms, I read the encounter as rape.

David inquires about Bathsheba and sends someone to determine who she is. That unnamed person returns and reports to him. There is a space of time when Bathsheba has presumably finished bathing and returned to her home, while David is discussing her and her particulars, unbeknownst to her in (2 Sam. 11:3). Knowing full well that she is married to one of his officers, David then sends a group of men to take her and bring her to him. There is a terrible irony in that the verb *l-q-ch*, "take," normally indicates marriage when a woman is its object; here it signifies the violation of marriage.

When David sends for Bathsheba, she does not have the option to refuse his invitation; nor do his men have the option to refuse to bring her. The description of her going with the messengers may suggest to some readers that she complies or participates willingly. However, the absolute power of an ancient Near Eastern monarch combined with the absence of her husband's protection greatly reduce Bathsheba's ability to consent to the sexual encounter. That she "came to him," conjoined with "he sent messengers to take her" in 2 Samuel 11:4, simply suggests that she walks along with the messengers rather than that she is stuffed in a sack or carried aloft to be brought to him. To come when beckoned by the king does not imply consent.

---

17. See Exod. 23:23, 28; 33:2; 34:11; Deut. 7:1; 20:17; Josh. 3:10.

18. The use of force accompanies the accounts of the rape of Dinah and those in the Torah's statutes (Gen. 34:2; Deut. 22:25, 28).

19. The verb *a-n-h*, "oppress," "humiliate," describes rape in the case of the Levite's wife Tamar and others (Judg. 20:5; 2 Sam. 13:22, 32; Lam. 5:11). *Sh-g-l* describes rape in Zech. 14:2.

I argue that Bathsheba's going with David's soldiers on her own two feet should in no way be read as consent, but rather as holding on to a shred of dignity by not being dragged or carried out. Yet commentators from rabbinic and Christian fathers to contemporary interlocutors describe the event as "adultery," signifying consent on Bathsheba's part.[20] Rape is an abuse of power that can include relational and positional power, in addition to physical power. The power dynamic here is clear: David uses the power and authority of his office to wield lethal violence to keep her. He sees her, sends for her, and has sex with her without her consent. He rapes her. In the subsequent narrative, Nathan and God treat David as a rapist by condemning him but not imputing sin to Bathsheba as a complicit, consenting person. Their treatment of her is consistent with the treatment of women who are raped in the Torah statutes.

After the rape, Bathsheba purifies herself from defilement. Some interpreters[21] regard this as a reiteration of the earlier bath in 2 Samuel 11:2, in order to explain that only David could be the father of Bathsheba's child because she has just completed her menstrual cycle. However, it makes sense to read this act of cleansing sequentially as a second act. Even if Bathsheba's earlier ablutions were ritual purification after completion of her menses, she would need to purify herself again as a Torah-observant woman because of the sexual encounter, whether consensual or not. That Bathsheba is apparently Torah-observant might seem to indicate she could be the daughter of a Hittite man and an Israelite mother who taught her those traditions. It is also possible that she washes herself after the violation like many raped women, to cleanse herself from the touch of her violator. The place of her ablutions is not disclosed. Did she wash his touch off of her skin as soon as he finished using her? Did she return to the home that was no longer safe for her to bathe in her own space? The passage also neglects to tell us how she made her way home. Was she under guard or left to find her way on her own? There is no mention of servants in her home; they may simply be invisible to the text. Even were there no servants in her own household, surely her trip to the palace under guard did not go unnoticed by her neighbors.

20. The Zohar refers repeatedly to David's sin with Bathsheba (Zohar B 107a, C 23b). Among the church fathers who call Bathsheba an adulterer are Chrysostom (*Homilies on Repentance and Almsgiving* 2.2.4–7) and Augustine, who calls it a "seduction" (Letter 82). Contemporarily, in the *Jewish Study Bible* Shimon Bar-Efrat subtitles the relevant section as "Adultery and Murder" and claims in the note on 2 Sam. 11:3, "David commits adultery with Bathsheba," implicating her as a participant, not victim.

21. See P. Kyle McCarter, "II Samuel," in *Anchor Yale Bible* (New Haven, CT: Yale University Press, 1974), 286, and Shimon Bar-Efrat's commentary on 2 Sam. 11:4 in the *Jewish Study Bible*.

There is no way to know how much time passes between David's rape of Bathsheba and her discovery of her pregnancy. The verb *h-r-h*, "conceive," in 2 Samuel 11:5 includes the word *har*, "mountain," evoking the possibility that women could not be certain they were pregnant until they were showing. Weeks, perhaps months, pass. Bathsheba is home without her husband and has to find a way to inform David of the consequences of his actions. She is no longer in contact with him and may have not seen him since the attack. She finds someone to take a message. How hard, how humiliating, it must be to say the words out loud and acknowledge the rape and her pregnancy? It is doubtful any messenger she is able to secure is able to go straight to the king. Instead, her messenger may have to approach the main gate and relay her message to the first guard she encounters. The messenger would likely be passed along to a bureaucrat or household manager. There may be a discussion as to whether or not the messenger should be admitted to David's presence. It's possible that the messenger has to tell many people that David has gotten Bathsheba pregnant before the message reaches him. There is no record of a response. Bathsheba must wait to see what, if anything, David will do. Simultaneously, she waits for her husband to return, not knowing which will happen first. What will she tell Uriah about how this child was conceived? Will he know it isn't his? And how will he respond?

The story leaves the reader to construct a life for Bathsheba before and after her assault by David, particularly as she waits for David to respond to her message. Curiously the text does not say that Bathsheba and Uriah do not have children; this child will not be identified as Bathsheba's firstborn.[22] With no children present in the narrative and her husband away, there is little to distract from her situation or occupy her days, even with whatever labor her household requires. In response to this sketch of a woman, a womanist reading constructs Bathsheba as a full, three-dimensional character, not the two-dimensional prop used in the Scriptures. Who and where are the women in her life? To whom can she and does she turn? Where is her own mother? Does Bathsheba consider terminating the pregnancy?[23] It is not difficult to imagine that Bathsheba is traumatized and seeking refuge, as not even her own home is safe.

Another anonymous messenger appears and informs Bathsheba that her husband Uriah is dead. She knows he is a warrior and may have lived with

22. If there were children in the home, it is hard to imagine that the text would not add depriving children of their father to David's account.
23. What might be the only use of an abortifacient in the canon is the potion a woman suspected of adultery is forced to drink in Num. 5:21–31, which, if she has transgressed, supposedly will make her innards, including the fruit of a forbidden union, fall out. It is possible midwives also provided abortion services.

this fear/expectation. Does she know or suspect initially that David has had Uriah killed? When does Bathsheba come to know the truth? The narrator's knowledge of David's crime may reflect wider common knowledge, especially given David's publication of penitent psalms. Second Samuel 11:26 repeatedly emphasizes Bathsheba's marriage as she mourns her husband Uriah: she is "the (*issah*) wife/woman of Uriah," and he is "Uriah her (*ish*) husband/man"; lastly, he is her *ba'al*, her only legitimate "lord," "master," or "husband." The lamentation Bathsheba makes for her husband will include a traditional period of mourning, perhaps seven to forty days, during which her pregnancy will only become more pronounced. As soon as the mourning period is over, David again sends men to take her; this time the verb is '-*s-ph*, "gather." Bathsheba is simply collected like a possession; there is no entreaty, no proposal, and, arguably, no consent.

A pregnant Bathsheba enters the home that David shares with six other women (Abigail, Ahinoam, Maacah, Haggith, Abital, Eglah) and their children. Somewhere Michal, a seventh woman, is locked away. Unlike Abigail, Bathsheba does not have serving women from her former life to accompany her. Other women are there, at the very least, serving women and midwives. Does Bathsheba have someone she considers a friend? How much interaction does she have with David's other women? What is that interaction like? Soon after her arrival, Bathsheba gives birth to a son who struggles for his first breath. When he dies, his death is placed squarely on David's shoulders, as a penalty for his sin against God. The text never claims a sin against Bathsheba. That too is in keeping with the Torah, in which a crime is against a father or husband but not the woman. Bathsheba isn't even a person in Nathan's famous accusatory rhetoric: she is a farm animal.

In 2 Samuel 12:1–6 the prophet Nathan crafts a parable to confront David about his sin. To represent Bathsheba, Nathan famously uses a lamb beloved as though she were a daughter. Nathan's rhetoric raises the following questions: Does Nathan (or God) view Bathsheba as property? Or are those the only terms by which he can reach David, because *David* considers women property? There is some irony in David's being moved by the story of a man's love for a substitute daughter, given his lack of response when his own daughter is raped in the next chapter. David's punishment decreed by Nathan is asymmetrical. David will not have to bear the consequences of his action in his own body; no one will lay a hand on him. Because David has taken and raped someone else's wife, his wives will be taken and raped (2 Sam. 12:11; 16:22).

The punishment makes sense according to the shame/honor dynamic operative in the ancient Near East, but it is indefensible to many contemporary readers and hearers of the biblical text engaging it as Scripture. Even within the context of the Scriptures, the severity of this punishment is mitigated by

David's ability to replace women whom he deems unsuitable for whatever reason. Even upon his death at a ripe old age, David has yet another woman in his impotent embrace (1 Kgs. 1:1–4). Similarly as it pertains to Uriah's murder, David remains untouched. He will not suffer any physical injury; instead, there will be perpetual violence in his house or dynasty.[24]

David's crime against Bathsheba is ignored, denied, or glossed over. Bathsheba is an object to David, Nathan, and the text. David's sins against God and Uriah, and to some degree Eliam, Bathsheba's father, are lamented. But Bathsheba's experience and articulation of her rape, like her name, are missing from the judgment against David. When God kills her child to punish David, the text does not use Bathsheba's name; she is still "the wife of Uriah" (2 Sam. 12:15). Neither does Nathan mention her name, calling her "the wife of Uriah" in 2 Samuel 12:9–10. Bathsheba will also be the wife of Uriah in Jesus' genealogy in Matthew 1:6. Bathsheba has a brief moment of subjectivity when the text gestures at her grief and records David's consolation of her in 2 Samuel 12:24, but that grief is for the loss of the child conceived through rape, not for the rape itself. If David's comfort included any words, they go unrecorded. Instead, the text focuses on their sexual intimacy, which produces Solomon. The comfort is that David does not abandon Bathsheba to starvation or to survival in sex-work—possible outcomes for a widow, especially one without children. Bathsheba will remain a royal woman, sheltered, clothed, and fed; but the text will never acknowledge that a crime has been committed against *her*.

The biblical text does not directly address the notion of consent within the bounds of marriage. It is difficult to imagine, let alone characterize, the nature of Bathsheba's subsequent intimate life with David. Bathsheba may well have wanted a child with David in order to secure her future. Yet as a modern woman I have great difficulty imagining her in that marriage, continuing to live and sleep with David and giving birth to four more children for him. As a womanist I want to hear Bathsheba's voice. I want to hear why she makes the choices she makes—if indeed she had choices to make.

Using my sanctified, womanist imagination, I hear Bathsheba confronting David and demanding the respect that she is due. I hear her speak:

> *You are not going to shut me away as you did your first wife, Michal. You stole the life I had with my husband in the sight of God, the man I love, the husband I chose to live with. You stole our future and you stole our children. I can't get that back, but I can have your children and the security that comes with them. I will be the mother of kings.*

24. The same word, *bayit*, means both "house" and "dynasty."

Bathsheba disappears during Solomon's childhood. Her subsequent birthing and mothering are compressed into a single verse in 1 Chronicles 3:5, in which her name is misspelled "Bath-shua,"[25] while the corresponding passage in 2 Samuel 5:14 omits her name. Bathsheba gives birth to at least four more children for David: Shammua/Shimea, Shobab, Nathan, and Solomon. The sequence is surprising, because Solomon is their fourth child according to the Chronicler, and not the second, as it might appear. And, since the genealogy seems only to name David's male offspring, it is entirely possible that Bathsheba also gave birth to daughters for David. Bathsheba remains obscured, as the story focuses on David's reign and, at the end of his life, the conflict between David and Absalom, who seeks his father's throne. At the end of David's reign, when the narrative returns to Bathsheba, the thirty-three years that David reigned in Jerusalem have passed, and David is in his last days. What, other than raising her children, has Bathsheba been doing for the past three decades? What is her relationship with David like? Who are her friends, conversation partners, confidants?

In 1 Kings 1:11 the prophet Nathan returns Bathsheba to the biblical narrative. He is concerned about the succession after David's imminently approaching death. That Nathan emerges as a conversation partner for Bathsheba may be surprising for some readers. I believe that in the intervening thirty-plus years, Nathan became a friend, advisor, and perhaps a father figure to Bathsheba. The naming of one of her children after him may reflect her own relationship with him. The succession crisis develops because David is clearly dying and has never designated a crown prince. He has many surviving sons, one of whom, Adonijah, has already proclaimed himself king while David is yet alive.

In 1 Kings 1:11–14 Nathan wants to save Bathsheba's life and the life of her son Solomon; it would not be unexpected for an insecure monarch to kill off his siblings and any perceived rivals. Nathan seems to have predetermined that Solomon is the best choice to succeed as king. He does not say that God has spoken to him or that he is trying to get the rightful king on the throne. His strategy may have been to gain Bathsheba as an ally, since the account reads more like partnership than pandering. Nathan seems genuinely to care for Bathsheba. Nathan works with Bathsheba to make sure that Solomon inherits the throne—not Adonijah, David's oldest surviving son, who is publicly claiming the throne (1 Kgs. 1:5). In their work together Bathsheba comes fully into her own, displaying more agency than simply repeating Nathan's words. This sets the pattern for her final scenes in the Scriptures.

---

25. The letter *vav*, which makes both the consonantal *v/w* sound and the vowel sound *u*, replaces the letter *bet*, which makes *b* and *v* sounds.

Confronted with the possibility of losing her life and that of her son because of David's lack of planning and political impotence, Bathsheba agrees to partner with the prophet Nathan and takes her own life and fate and that of Solomon into her own hands. That she has a choice here is crucial. Bathsheba is masterful; she plays to David's ego, calling him "my lord" repeatedly. She bows down before him, the man who raped her and murdered her husband. Following Nathan's advice, Bathsheba asks David why he is going back on his word to make Solomon king after him (1 Kgs. 1:13). Curiously, the Bible does not record David ever making that commitment. There is a tradition in rabbinic scholarship, the classical exegesis of Rabbi David Kimkhi,[26] that the way in which David comforts Bathsheba after the death of their first child is to make this promise. I prefer a reading in which Nathan makes the decision himself and goes to Bathsheba to help make sure it happens. Bathsheba takes Nathan's plan in 1 Kings 1:13–14 and makes it her own in verse 21. She supplies her own dialogue, including the text of the vow that David supposedly made to her in the Most Holy Name of God, so that she cannot be contradicted. She is not a puppet reciting a script. She is a partner, improvising as necessary.

Bathsheba and Nathan tag-team David. As though it were by chance, but fully orchestrated, Nathan enters and takes up the case as Bathsheba leaves. David lies dying with his professional and personal impotence on display.[27] Bathsheba's speech hinges on the vow she claims David made to her, even though there is no record of it. When Nathan continues the conversation, he repeats Bathsheba's words about the royal celebration Adonijah is throwing. Nathan adds the question as to whether David planned this all along and simply did not tell him. Nathan appears to have been dismissed without an answer to his question, but he will be recalled later, in verse 32.

Their plan works. The first thing David says is, "Bring Bathsheba back to me." He doesn't even answer Nathan's question about the succession. When Bathsheba reappears before David, she stands in his presence (1 Kgs. 1:28). The power of the throne shifts from David to Solomon through Bathsheba and her unbent spine at that very moment. Then, after he does what she wants, Bathsheba bows to David one last time, again her choice. When Solomon is anointed as king over Israel, Bathsheba is not mentioned (1 Kgs.

---

26. Kimkhi (alternately spelled Kimchi) wrote commentary on the text of the Bible published within traditional Jewish Bibles called *Miqra'oth Gedeloth*, "Great Bibles." The twelfth-century scholar is also known by an acronym of his initials, Radak.

27. First Kgs. 1:4 can be understood to mean that David was sexually impotent at this juncture and the whole court knew it.

1:38–40). After all of her hard work to get him on the throne, after the price that she paid for his life and his crown, surely she was present. Bathsheba is similarly excluded from David's death scene in 1 Kings 2:1–10. Her absence seems fitting, though she may have truly mourned him, having found some manner of life with him as the father of her children.

Bathsheba is at her most powerful in her final appearance in the Scriptures. In 1 Kings 2:19, Solomon gets up off of his throne, bows to Bathsheba, and enthrones her in majesty as his right-hand woman. She becomes the first of the queen mothers, a tradition that will live in the Judean monarchy until its end. In this her closing scene, a desperate, grasping Adonijah asks Bathsheba to intercede with Solomon for him. He makes a grand speech about relinquishing his claim to the throne. He then asks for the last woman David lay with, Abishag from Shunem (1 Kgs. 1:1–4). Of course, the claim on a royal woman is tantamount to a claim on the throne. But Adonijah underestimates Bathsheba. He does not know that she is the one who placed Solomon on the throne. Bathsheba promises to take the matter to Solomon and keeps her word. She does not have to tell Solomon how to respond to this request. She simply repeats it, knowing what the outcome will be. As her son and the son of the shrewd David, Solomon recognizes the threat and executes Adonijah. Bathsheba has now secured her son's reign. Bathsheba then fades from the Scriptures. She is no longer an abducted and raped wife, soon to be widowed. She is now the queen mother of the united monarchy of Israel.

ANONYMOUS WOMEN

A single verse recounts the fate of some of David's women:

> 2 Samuel 20:3 David went to his house in Jerusalem, and the king took ten secondary wives he had left to watch the house and put them in a house under guard, provided for them, and he did not come to them. They remained confined until the day they died, a living widowhood.

David had previously left these ten women behind in Jerusalem while he ran away from his own son, Absalom, who was making claims on the throne (2 Sam. 15:16). Absalom raped some or all of those women in public, laying claim to the throne of Israel through the bodies of the royal women of Israel (2 Sam. 16:22). In response, David abandoned them again, this time to a living death. They would be fed, housed, and clothed, but would never again be part of his life.

AVISHAG (ABISHAG) THE SHUNAMITE

1 Kings 1:1 Now the king, David, had become old, advanced in years; and while they covered him with clothes, he could not get warm. [2]So his servants said to him, "Let a virgin girl be sought for my lord the king, and let her stand before the king, and let her be his caretaker; let her lie in your bosom and warm my lord the king." [3]So they searched for a beautiful girl in all the territory of Israel, and they found Avishag (Abishag) the Shunamite, and brought her to the king. [4]The girl was beautiful, exceedingly so. She became the king's caretaker and served him, but the king did not know her sexually.

Avishag (Abishag) is the last individual woman—if indeed she is a woman and not a girl—with whom David is associated in the Scriptures. She is young, unmarried, and sexually inexperienced, all of which suggest that she is just at the age of sexual maturity, perhaps thirteen to sixteen. David's servants acquire her before she can be married to someone else. David, on the other hand, is at the end of his life and his forty-year reign, placing him anywhere from his sixties to early seventies.

Abishag's story does not have a glorious ending in spite of its promising beginning. There appears to have been quite a search throughout the territories of Israel to find a girl who would stimulate David. The search seems similar to the one to procure Hadassah to meet the sexual needs of Xerxes.[28] In contrast with Esther, Abishag does not have a relative or legal guardian pimping her out, as Mordecai did to Esther. When David's son Adonijah falls for Abishag, he asks Bathsheba to exercise her influence over Solomon and give her to him. Bathsheba passes on the message, and Solomon interprets the request as keeping one foot in the palace door for a possible claim on the throne. Solomon has Adonijah killed, and Abishag disappears. She may have been killed along with him.

I can imagine whole volumes of midrash exploring the lives and relationships of David's women. Only Bathsheba survives him in the Scriptures. What happens to the rest? I don't imagine that David's other women were actually killed, as they were neither plotting to seize the throne nor part of the machinations of others. There is certainly no record of Solomon killing any more of his siblings; it is unlikely that he did any harm to their mothers. It is most likely that they lived out their lives in isolation from intrigue (and the opportunity to foment trouble). Perhaps they joined Michal and the anonymous royal wives of 2 Samuel 20:3 in confinement. The constellation

---

28. Hadassah's name is changed to Esther, and Xerxes is called Ahasuerus in the Hebrew Bible.

of David's intimate partners is simply erased with his death and burial, since he, the reason they are in the Scriptures, no longer exists.

MOTHER AND SISTERS (ZERUIAH AND ABIGAIL) OF DAVID

1 Samuel 22:1 David went from there, Gath, and escaped to the cave of Adullam. When his sisters-and-brothers and all his father's house heard, they went down there to him. ²Everyone who was in distress, and everyone who was in debt, and everyone who was embittered gathered themselves to him. He became a leader over them; there were with him about four hundred individuals. ³David went from there to Mizpeh of Moab. He said to the king of Moab, "Please let my mother and father come to you, until I know what God will do for me." ⁴And he led them before the king of Moab, and they stayed with him all the time that David was in the stronghold.

1 Chronicles 2:13 Yissai (Jesse) became the father of his firstborn, Eliav (Eliab), then Avinadav (Abinadab) the second, then Shimea the third. ¹⁴Nethanel the fourth, Raddai the fifth. ¹⁵Ozem the sixth, David the seventh. ¹⁶Now their sisters were Zeruyah (Zeruiah) and Avigayil (Abigail). The sons of Zeruyah (Zeruiah) were: Avishai (Abishai), Yoav (Joab), and Asahel, three. ¹⁷Avigayil (Abigail) birthed Amasa; the father of Amasa was Yether (Jether) the Ishmaelite.

The women in David's life include his mother, sisters, daughters, and grand-daughters, in addition to his many intimate partners. During the time that David runs from Saul, his mother, father, siblings, and everyone else in his father's household, along with a number of malcontents, join him in his most recent place of retreat. David does not send for them. They show up on their own. He then takes his family to their Moabite relatives, the kin of his great-grandmother Ruth.

The text does not preserve his mother's name. That omission is all the more striking because the names of David's sisters, brothers, father, at least one daughter, sons, several granddaughters, one grandson, and generations of (mostly male) descendants are preserved. The mention of David's mother here raises a number of questions: Where has she been during the rest of the story, particularly the parts that revolve around her family? Why is the name of David's mother erased when the names of so many royal women are preserved?²⁹ The rabbis correct this oversight, providing both name and

29. While the office of the queen mother is a uniquely Judean office, the Judean context of scripturalization and canonization led to the names of significant Israelite

lineage for David's mother in the Babylonian Talmud,[30] Nizbeth bat Adael, evoking strength and standing. I will use that name for her.[31]

Nizbeth has been erased from the earlier narratives featuring her family. She and her daughters, Abigail (Avigayil) and Zeruiah (Zeruyah), were completely excluded from the account of the festal meal Samuel shared with her husband and sons, his inspection of their sons and brothers, and his ultimate selection of her baby boy, David, as the messiah-king in 1 Samuel 16. In stark contrast to the tender portrait of Hannah sending her son Samuel to Eli and visiting him repeatedly, Nizbeth is not there to kiss her child good-bye when Saul sends to Jesse to take her youngest son to play the lyre and calm his raging madness. Nizbeth is not depicted as being present when David marries one of the king's daughters. However, when his life is in danger, and by extension the lives of his parents, David's mother comes into the narrative in 1 Samuel 22:3. David's banditry has endangered her life, so he takes direct action to preserve her life with that of his kin.

David's mother and father, unspecified siblings, and all his father's household flee to join him in 1 Samuel 22. Grammatically, those siblings, *echayv*, can be all male or a mixed-gender group. The genealogy in 1 Chronicles 2:13–16 names David's sisters and brothers, making it possible all of them are intended in 1 Samuel 22:1. If his sisters have now married and are part of their husbands' households, they might be excluded from David's father's household in verse 1. However, if the point of the narrative is to portray David as protector, it does not make sense to exclude them, especially since they also could be targets for retaliation and are easily accounted for in the plural form. That is why I have chosen to make them explicitly present in the translation. In addition, their sons become David's most elite warriors, suggesting strong familial ties. Thus, when their mother runs to be with them all, it is more than plausible that they do as well.

David has two sisters, Zeruiah and Abigail. The Bible mentions Zeruiah (or her name as part of her sons' names) more than two dozen times.[32] Many

---

royal women being preserved. For example, the text names Zeruah, the mother of Jeroboam, the first king of Israel after the division of the monarchy, and identifies her as a widow in 1 Kgs. 11:26. (This may not be her actual name but a slur, "diseased woman," i.e., source of a rotten son.)

30. *b. Baba Bathra* 91a.

31. Her rabbinic name, *ntzbt*, is derived from the stem *n-tz-b*. In Aramaic it conveys "strength" (e.g., *nitzbeta'*, Dan. 2:41), and in Hebrew evokes "standing" (e.g., *nitzevet*, 1 Sam. 1:26). Her midrashic genealogy, bat Adael, seems to be formed from "congregation," *'ad'* and "God," *'el.*"

32. 1 Sam. 26:6; 2 Sam. 2:13, 18; 3:39; 8:16; 14:1; 16:9–10; 17:25; 18:2; 19:21–22; 21:17; 23:18, 37; 1 Kgs. 1:7; 2:5, 22; 1 Chr. 2:16; 11:6, 39; 18:12, 15; 26:28; 27:24.

readers might conclude that the Zeruiah named in the formula "son(s) of Zeruiah" is their father; they would be wrong. While most Israelite genealogies are indeed patrilineal, this is not the case for all, as we have seen with Bethuel ben Milcah in Genesis 24:24. The form of Zeruiah's name may also lead some readers to assume Zeruiah is male—it is the same form as the names of Isaiah, Jeremiah, and many other men in the canon. Further, her name ends in the Divine Name "Yah," which functions as grammatically masculine[33] but has no meaning in regards to the gender of the person so named. The "Yah" suffix is attested in a number of women's names.[34]

Zeruiah's sons are David's inner circle and premiere warriors, playing prominent parts in his narrative. The text does not identify the man with whom Zeruiah had children. His absence is striking since his sons are so prominent. David is their most famous relative; it is curious that they are not identified as David's nephews, as the sons of the king's sister. But they are called by the name of their mother, and the reader/hearer is expected to know who she is.

Zeruiah and Abigail are older than David. Their sons are his companions and may have been age-mates, possibly growing up together. On the other hand, they could have been many more years older than David, especially if the age gap between David and his sisters is large. It is difficult to imagine that the youngest of David's nephews could be much younger than he and still be counted among his warriors, let alone his chief warriors. That Zeruiah is listed first may indicate she is the eldest. Zeruiah has three sons, Abishai (Avishai), Joab (Yoav), and Asahel; Abigail has one son, Amasa. Neither sister is credited with daughters. The father of Abigail's son is identified, unlike the father of Zeruiah's sons; he is Jether (Yether), an Ishmaelite.

The verse that identifies Amasa as the son of Yether also identifies his mother Abigail as the daughter of Nahash (2 Sam. 17:26). Since Abigail is David's sister, her parents are presumably his parents. There are at least two feasible possibilities for this discrepancy: the presence of the name Nahash in verse 26 is a textual corruption; the name of the Ammonite king Nahash was mistakenly duplicated from the following verse.[35] The minority position is

33. In actuality the name "Yah" is grammatically feminine because of the *mapiq*, a small dot in the final letter. In some contemporary Jewish practice, "Yah" is used as a feminine name for God.

34. E.g., Queen Athaliah in 2 Kgs. 11:1 (whose name also appears with the masculine suffix *hu* in 2 Kgs. 8:26); Micaiah, used for a woman and a man (2 Chr. 13:2; 1 Kgs. 22:8); Zibiah in 2 Kgs. 12:1; Jecoliah in 2 Kgs. 15:2; Bithiah in 1 Chr. 4:17; and Noadiah in Neh. 6:14.

35. Shimon Bar-Efrat's commentary in the *Jewish Study Bible* is representative of this position.

that David's mother remarried at some point—widowhood would be the most palatable option culturally; Nahash would have then been Nizbeth's first husband. In support of this, a family relationship between David and the king of Ammon would account for the surprisingly amicable relationship between the two (2 Sam. 10:2).[36]

David's habit of referring to his nephews by their mother's name, "You sons of Zeruiah,"[37] preserves David's relationship with his sister and may say something about her. People who knew them all may have recognized her strength in her sons. By contrast, David does not call his other nephew, Amasa, the son of his sister Abigail. There is something about Zeruiah and her sons that they are remembered the way they are. That something is now lost to us.

DAUGHTERS OF DAVID

> 2 Samuel 5:13 David took more primary and secondary wives from Jerusalem after he came from Hebron, and more daughters and sons were born to David.

David has an unknown number of daughters. Second Samuel 13:18 explains that virgin daughters of monarchs wore a particular type of clothing, which indicated that they were all afforded some degree of royal privilege. Practically speaking, they would be valuable marital assets for forming alliances. David has one daughter whose name is preserved, Tamar bat Maacah. Tamar's name is included because of the events that happened to her and because of her: her rape by her half-brother Amnon and Amnon's subsequent execution by her brother Absalom (see the next section, "Tamar bat David"). But what about the rest of David's daughters? How many were they?

Among David's twenty named children, it is difficult to account for his daughters. A number of the names listed in 1 Chronicles 3:6–9 are impossible to gender: Ibhar, Elishama, Eliphelet, Nogah, Nepheg, Japhia, Elishama, Eliada, and Eliphelet. Most likely, they are all male, representing a first son with a series of unnamed royal women. With nineteen sons, David could have a dozen or more daughters. There is really no way of knowing. David's daughters are not considered important to the story, especially if they are successfully and appropriately married off.

---

36. Richard D. Nelson offers this possibility in the entry on Nahash in the *Anchor Yale Bible Dictionary*, 4:996.
37. See 2 Sam. 3:39; 16:10; 19:22.

It is unfortunate that only rape and incest bring a royal daughter out of David's family closet. Using my sanctified womanist imagination, I see Bathsheba's daughters and all she had to teach them. I imagine Tamar's sisters trying to comfort her after her rape. I imagine royal daughters, loyal to their mothers, sometimes in conflict with other royal women, all competing for David's time and attention. I don't have to imagine the people jockeying to get a place in David's family, using his daughters' bodies as their bridge.

TAMAR BAT DAVID

2 Samuel 13:1 This happened later: Avshalom (Absalom), David's son, had a beautiful sister and her name was Tamar; Amnon, David's son, loved her. ²Amnon was distressed; he made himself sick on account of Tamar his sister, for she was a virgin and it would take a miracle in Amnon's perspective to do anything to her. . . . ¹²She said to him, "Don't, my brother! Do not abuse me; for it is not done thus in Israel! Do not do this depraved thing! ¹³As for me, where would I take my shame? And you, you would be as one of the despicable in Israel. Now then, speak—please!—to the king, for he will not withhold me from you." ¹⁴But he was not willing to do what she said. He was stronger than she, so he violated her, laying her down.

Tamar bat David is one of three women named Tamar in the Hebrew Scriptures. The first Tamar is the Canaanite daughter-in-law of Judah the patriarch. Judah impregnates Tamar, making her the mother of the tribe of Judah in Genesis 38. It is in the name of the first Tamar that Boaz is blessed on the occasion of his marriage to Ruth: "May your house be like the house of Perez, whom Tamar gave birth to for Judah."[38] David's daughter is the second Tamar; her brother Absalom's daughter, named in her honor, will be the third. Tamar bat David is also Tamar bat Maacah. As the daughter of a king, Maacah bat Talmai was already a royal woman when she married David. She came from Geshur, bordering the territory of Manasseh. Tamar's mother Maacah is also the mother of Absalom. The narrative does not indicate which is the elder, or if they have other siblings.

The passage describes Tamar's beauty and her half-brother Amnon's love for her. "Love" ('-h-v) is a challenging word here because of its incompatibility with rape in the minds of many readers and hearers. This Hebrew word is used for the love that Isaac has for Rebekah, Jacob for Rachel, Elkanah for

---

38. "Your house" in Ruth 4:12 is masculine singular, indicating that the blessing is directed toward Boaz and not Ruth.

Hannah, and Shechem for Dinah, whom he also raped. Samson loves Deli-
lah; Michal loves David, but David loves Jonathan. Solomon loves many foreign women (and his God). Rehoboam loves (another) Maacah more than
any of his other women, just as the Persian king loves Esther more than any
of his other women. The God of Israel loves the people of Israel and particular individuals like Solomon. In each of these accounts the verb '-*h*-*v*
expresses love, including twice the love of a rapist for his victim. The verb
also expresses parental love and other affections, such as love for a particular
food.[39] Amnon's love in 2 Samuel 13:1 is articulated along with his desire to
"do something (anything) to her" in verse 2. This may be why JPS chooses
"infatuated" instead of "love." The NRSV's translation of "fall in love" here
and other places is not helpful; the notion of "falling in love" is a postbiblical
construct. The simple truth is that there are some people who rape the persons they profess to love. There is no reason to change the verb. The reader
must wrestle with its dissonance.

Amnon plots with his cousin Jonadab (Yonadav), David's nephew, to gain
access to Tamar, so that he may rape her. The need for the plot suggests
something about the life of Tamar and other royal women. They are apparently not normally alone with men, even relatives—most likely to protect
their virtue, honor, and physical person. Jonadab is wise (*chakam*) like a sage.
However, *chakam* is translated as "crafty," "clever," "subtle," and "worldly-
wise" in the NRSV, JPS, KJV, and Fox, as translators balk at attributing the
usual meaning of the stem to the man with this plan. This description, combined with the verb *ph-l-*', meaning "to work wonders," as in the miracles
God performs, suggests just how inspired Amnon thinks Jonadab's plan is
and how twisted it is to the narrator and intended audience. Amnon thinks
it would take a miracle to gain access to his sister, and his friend and cousin
was wise enough to craft a plan that fit the bill. The specter of a family member enabling the sexual abuse of a relative is unfortunately a well-known and
enduring phenomenon.

David plays the role scripted for him. He goes to see his son, who is feign-
ing illness.[40] David sends a message to Tamar—the most interaction he will
have with her in the whole sordid story—telling her to go to Amnon's house.
The plan concocted by Jonadab leaves Tamar alone with Amnon in his home

39. See Gen. 24:67; 25:28; 29:18; 34:3; 37:3; Judg. 16:4; 1 Sam. 1:5; 16:21; 18:1;
20:17; 2 Sam. 12:24; 1 Kgs. 3:3; 11:1.
40. Second Sam. 13:7 suggests that each royal may have had his or her own house.
Given the number of David's offspring, such an arrangement would mean dozens, if
not scores, of princely households. It is also possible that marriageable daughters lived
with their mothers.

for an extended period of time. She prepares and cooks food for him, physical tasks that enable him to watch her and the movement of her body as the initial phase of his assault. His control of her, his surveillance of her, and her submission to his bidding are part of what gratifies him. Since they are not alone, he orders everyone else out of the house in verse 9. He has her bring the food to him in his room, manipulating her into entering the most private recess of his home. Manipulating her is part of the exercise of power over and against her that makes up this attack. He makes her come to him. He asks her to have sex with him, and she refuses, horrified by the request. Tamar's voice is powerful but ultimately ineffective in the Scriptures.

Tamar's response is "Don't!" The verbal negation *al*, rather than the negative particle *lo'* ("No!"), suggests that Tamar knows Amnon is not really asking for consent but stating his intent. Her response is, "Do not do what you are thinking; don't make me do this." In 2 Samuel 13:12 she gives him reason after reason: she doesn't want to; he would be forcing her; what he's asking is depraved and completely unacceptable in their culture. When it becomes clear that her wishes are irrelevant and that he is not asking her consent, she focuses on what this would mean for him and for his reputation (v. 13). Lastly, in what seems like a desperate last-ditch effort to get away from him, Tamar suggests he ask their father for permission to marry her. I think they both know that permission would not be forthcoming. Amnon does not listen to her.[41] Her words have no meaning. Amnon no longer pretends to be infirm. Now that he has her where he wants her, Amnon uses his physical strength against his sister Tamar and rapes her. The text emphasizes her helplessness by stating, "He lay her," not "He lay *with* her," omitting the preposition in describing the rape. Tamar is the physical and grammatical object of his rapine.

The truth about Amnon's "love" now reveals itself. Once he has finished raping her, he discovers that he hates his sister Tamar more than he ever loved her (2 Sam. 13:15).[42] He discards her by telling her to get out. Again, Tamar refuses. Amnon overpowers her once more through a surrogate. Unashamed that his rape of her is obvious, Amnon calls a servant to put her out (v. 17). Tamar, citing Torah and tradition in verse 16, would stay with him as his wife. Rape-marriage was legal in two forms: (1) the abduction of enemy girls and women as slaves and brides,[43] and (2) marriage as the penalty for a rapist

---

41. The expression *s-m-'b'qol* means "obey" and "hearken," as well as "hear." Amnon completely disregards Tamar's words.

42. NRSV translates this perverted love as "lust," while JPS calls it "passion."

43. See Num. 31:18; Judg. 21:12, 20–21.

to appease the honor of his victim's father and family.[44] But Amnon scorns Torah and tradition as much as he scorns Tamar. The servant locks the door behind her after forcibly putting her out, a second and third assault.

In the aftermath of the assault, Tamar continues to use her voice, her agency, what is left of her power. She does not hide her assault or own its shame as her own. In 2 Samuel 13:19, Tamar proclaims it publicly so that it may be Amnon's shame and ultimately his death sentence. But she will have to wait years to see justice done. Tamar rips open her royal dress just as her body was ripped open, using that sartorial wound to make visible her vaginal wounds and those of her soul. She cries, not silent tears but a cry (z-$'$-q) loud as the cries heard in battle, the cries of women in labor, and the cries of desperate people to their God (e.g., Exod. 2:23; 1 Sam. 14:20; Isa. 26:17). Tamar's cry holds Amnon accountable—even when their father does not.

One revelation of the narrative is that Amnon can count on his father David to come and see about him when he is or pretends to be sick, but Tamar cannot count on her father to come to her when she has been devastatingly violated. Nor can she count on him to avenge her or in any way punish, rebuke, or hold Amnon accountable for his actions. Her brother Absalom would avenge her, although apparently with his own motive and perhaps with some complicity.

Where Tamar goes as she weeps, cries, and even screams is unknown. She finds ashes along the way and places them on her head as a public sign of mourning. Tamar will not be shut away with her brother's shame imposed on and in her body. The text offers a final vivid, poignant detail, Tamar's hand laid on her head as she walks away. It is not clear if Tamar has a destination in mind, if she intentionally seeks out her brother Absalom, or whether he comes to her when he hears her screams or hears about her. Her actions, though, cause some people to run to see what is going on and others to tell the tale.

Absalom's response is chilling and suspicious. He doesn't ask Tamar what has happened to her, why she is crying, why her clothes are torn, what she is mourning with the traditional sign of ashes on her head. Instead, he asks if her brother Amnon has "been with" her (2 Sam. 13:20). Does he know she was being set up? Does he know and hold back so that he can use the crime to advance his own claim to David's throne? I'd like to believe that he did not know how far it would go and that had he known, he would have intervened. Nonetheless, Absalom bears the taint of complicity that cannot be easily erased. What the text does say in verse 21 is that he tells her to be quiet and not to take (literally "place") this matter to heart, because Amnon

44. See Deut. 22:28–29.

is her brother. Absalom becomes a surrogate father to Tamar, opening his home to her for what looks like the rest of her life. Now that she is no longer marriageable and likely "ruined," David may not provide for the daughter he can no longer barter in marriage. She is useless to him.

Tamar is completely devastated. With this description Tamar exits the Scripture as an active subject. She is the object of all subsequent references to her. David is told what has happened in 2 Samuel 13:21. Either he is so isolated that it takes a while for the news to get to him, or his underlings are afraid to bring the news to him. He does not come to see the screaming Tamar as he has the scheming Amnon. He is angry. But he does nothing and says nothing. Is David angry about what has happened to him, which is how the Scriptures understand rape, as a crime against a father? The Qumran manuscript 4QSam[a] continues in verse 21 beyond the MT: "and David would not grieve the spirit of his son Amnon, because he loved him, for he was his firstborn." David's reluctance to punish Amnon is better understood as reluctance to do anything that would upset Amnon.[45] David's concern for his son's well-being is not simply placed above his concern for his daughter; he has *no* concern for his daughter's well-being. Before Tamar returns as even an object, the object of provocation, two years pass.

David's anger seems to dissipate and disappear. Absalom hoards his anger, stoking it and nurturing it for two whole years until it is time to release it. Absalom is something less than an avenging angel. Absalom charms David into sending all of his siblings, or at least all of his male siblings, to him for a feast in honor of the annual sheep shearing (2 Sam. 13:23–29). He arranges for his servants to execute Amnon while he is more than just a little bit drunk. Thinking all of his sons have been killed, David collapses to the floor in a display of grief that he does not offer on behalf of his ravaged daughter. The same Jonadab, David's nephew, who devised the rape scheme, tells David that only Amnon was killed and Absalom had been planning to kill him from the moment of the rape—it was inevitable. This is supposed to mitigate David's grief and anger. Jonadab's cavalier words sound much like Absalom's to Tamar after the assault.

The execution is done in Tamar's name. However, given Absalom's subsequent attempts to seize the throne by any means—including raping David's wives himself (2 Sam. 16:22)—he is something less than the blood avenger envisioned by the Torah.[46] Tamar's name lives on in the generation that follows her, because her imperfect avenger, Absalom, with all of his mixed

---

45. The expression here, "grieve his spirit," is the same as in Isa. 54:6 and 63:10.

46. However, those statutes apply to murder exclusively, not rape. See Num. 35:16–21.

motives, names his own daughter for her (2 Sam. 14:27). Amnon's name is cut off in his generation with his death. That is a profound measure of justice in the biblical world.

Feminist readings of the rape of Tamar and its aftermath are plentiful.[47] *The Tamar Campaign*,[48] an African Bible study that explores the roles of women and men in this text, in conversation with domestic and sexual violence in their own contexts, uses both feminist and womanist approaches. Specifically, *The Tamar Campaign* provides a framework for women to talk about sexual violence, using its inclusion in the Scriptures as authority to discuss it in their own communities.[49] My womanist reading of this passage centers on the interrelatedness of Tamar, Amnon, Jonadab, Absalom, and David. They are family. They are a family in which sexual violence becomes habitual and generational. They are a family in which some of the men conspire together to rape and commit incest with one of their relatives. They are a family and community of men who object—to differing degrees—to the rape of women to whom they are close but who rape the women of other men and those in their families when it serves their interests.

Much of the public discourse around sexual violence against women and children centers on "stranger danger," unknown sexual predators, and to some degree date rape by current and prospective intimate partners. Meanwhile, the role of family members in these crimes has been more likely to be addressed on TV talk shows and crime dramas than sermons or congregational education programs. But there are perpetrators in all of our communities; they are in neighborhoods, schools, churches, synagogues, mosques, community programs, and families. Most often perpetrators of sexual violence prey on the trust and bodies of their own family members and friends.

Sexual offenders are not all lone wolves. As the biblical account of Jonadab's collaboration illustrates, there are other family members, adults, who know that a child or woman or man is being abused. They say nothing—or worse, they even participate. They exist and operate in a broader society that sexualizes women and girls, particularly black and brown women and girls.

47. See Pamela Cooper-White, *The Cry of Tamar: Violence against Women and the Church's Response* (Minneapolis: Fortress Press, 1995); and Phyllis Trible, *Texts of Terror: Literary-Feminist Readings of Biblical Narratives* (Philadelphia: Fortress Press, 1984).

48. Fred Nyabera and Taryn Montgomery, eds., *The Tamar Campaign* (Nairobi: The Fellowship of Christian Councils and Churches in the Great Lakes and the Horn of Africa [FECCLAHA], 2007).

49. Gerald O. West and Phumzile Zondi-Mabizela, "The Bible Story That Became a Campaign: The Tamar Campaign in South Africa (and Beyond)," *Ministerial Formation* 103 (July 2004): 4–12.

In addition to rape culture, black women and girls are subject to *misogynoir*, unflinching hatred directed toward black women that is racist, misogynistic, and usually expressed in sexually explicit terms.[50] While the term *misogynoir* is new, it describes a long-standing institutionalized set of demeaning and degrading practices in the West targeting black girls and women. Those practices include denigration of the black female body on film and in larger pop culture, the impetus for coining the word *misogynoir*. These phenomena are particularly prevalent in the Americas and other former slave-holding nations. The combination of rape culture and misogynoir produces a portrait of black girls and women as sexually voracious and promiscuous. That characterization has meant that black women in the United States were not deemed to be "rapeable"—that is, they could not be raped because they were perpetually available, incapable of withholding consent.[51] The legacy of that ideology has meant that the testimony of black girls and women who have been raped is regularly and repeatedly disregarded by family, friends, the legal system, and the wider society. Many religious communities and institutions participate in rape culture by disbelieving women and girls, ostracizing them if they report, and blaming them for their assaults, often while embracing accused and repeat offenders in their midst. The prevalence of rape, antagonistic treatment of victims and survivors by police and judicial systems, low levels of convictions, and brevity of sentences when convicted combine to shape the contours of a rape culture that is not limited to the United States.[52] The conspiracy to set Tamar up to be raped with impunity is a scriptural mirror illuminating acts of complicity in our own communities.

Jonadab's complicity also points to institutional complicity in covering up sexual abuse. He is an official and agent of the king. Jonadab knows the system and David's predictable behavior well enough to know that Amnon does not

---

50. Moya Bailey crafted the word "misogynoir" in a blog post entitled "They Aren't Talking About Me . . ." on *The Crunk Feminist Collective*, March 14, 2010. She defined it as describing "the particular brand of hatred directed at black women in American visual & popular culture." The original post can be accessed at http://www.crunk feministcollective.com/2010/03/14/they-arent-talking-about-me/.

51. The belief that black women could not be raped, promulgated during the slave-holding era, was legally codified, famously citing black women's lack of chastity. See Karen J. Maschke, *Feminist Legal Theories* (New York: Garland Pub., 1997), 41–44.

52. A rape culture is one that enables and normalizes rape and other forms of sexual violence against women. For more on rape culture, see Jennifer B. Wriggins, "Rape, Racism, and the Law," *Harvard Women's Law Journal* 6 (1983): 117–23; Emilie Buchwald, Pamela R. Fletcher, and Martha Roth, *Transforming a Rape Culture* (Minneapolis: Milkweed Editions, 2005); and Kate Harding, *Asking for It: The Alarming Rise of Rape Culture—and What We Can Do About It* (Boston: Da Capo Press, 2015).

have to fear punishment from his father. Indeed, once he gets Tamar where he wants her, Amnon does nothing to quiet her screams or hide his actions. Not only does he not threaten her into silence; with no concern about retribution, he calls a servant in to see the aftermath of the rape.

My womanist midrash is about those with the spirit of Jonadab, who are intentionally complicit and facilitate the sexual abuse and exploitation of women and girls in their own communities, in their own homes and families. Jonadab symbolizes for me all of those persons who know, could know, or should know about the sexual abuse of children in their environments but do not. He portrays those who are complicit in their abuse through their actions and their silences. Jonadab embodies officials and institutions who cover up for sexual predators among their clergy, employees, youth workers, and camp and scout leaders. He represents the women who deny the reports of their own children who are being raped, molested, and abused. The denial enables predation by men whom mothers have brought into the lives and homes of their children and/or by the brothers, uncles, cousins, granduncles, and fathers of their children. Like the biblical Jonadab, these facilitators frequently elude punishment, even when their complicity is known. However, while they may evade the legal systems of this world, the sudden disappearance of Jonadab from the story of David suggests ultimate justice.

Jonadab disappears from the text immediately after telling David that Absalom's killing of Amnon was inevitable and had been in the works since the rape. While Absalom sends his servant to kill his brother, a son of the king, I imagine that he kills Jonadab, the king's nephew, himself. Like Amnon, Jonadab has neither spouse nor heirs in the Bible. Had he had them, I believe that Absalom would have killed them all to avenge his sister, killing them as surrogates for Amnon, whom he couldn't touch directly. In either case, using my sanctified imagination, I see Absalom (Avshalom) venting his barbarous Iron Age rage on Jonadab (Yonadav), inflicting on him all the savagery he could muster, since Amnon's kill had to be a relatively clean execution:

> *Avshalom made Yonadav suffer as Tamar suffered. He made him scream as Tamar screamed. Avshalom left what was left of Yonadav in a pile of torn and tattered flesh, shredded like the remains of Tamar's royal dress, and walked away. Someone else would have to clean that mess up.*

I give Tamar the final word, a prayer and prophetic curse:[53]

---

53. This malediction draws on the covenant curses in Deut. 27–38 and Deborah's curse in Judg. 5:23.

Cursed be Amnon who lay with his sister, who ravaged her, the daughter of his father. Let heaven and earth bear witness of what you have done to me. Cursed shall you be in the city, and cursed shall you be in the field. Cursed shall be your basket and your kneading bowl. Cursed shall be the seed of your loins, the fruit of your ground, the increase of your cattle, and the issue of your flock. Cursed shall you be when you come in, and cursed shall you be when you go out. Now, therefore, you are cursed, cursed bitterly, because you ravaged and savaged your sister. Therefore, all women will turn from you, and men will play you false until you pay for your crime against me and against God, with your blood poured onto the earth to satisfy the blood of my virginity. I curse you with a curse, and you are accursed.

There is no record of Amnon marrying or fathering children during the two years between his rape of his sister Tamar and his assassination by their brother. Absalom's daughter Tamar becomes Tamar bat David's legacy as her namesake: "There were born to Absalom three sons and one daughter; her name was Tamar. She was a woman beautiful in appearance" (1 Sam. 14:27). According to the LXX, she married Solomon's son Rehoboam, making her the last queen of the united monarchy (2 Reigns 14:27 = 2 Sam 14:27). Subsequently Absalom fathered another daughter, Maacah (2 Chr. 11:20). Tamar lives the remainder of her life surrounded by family and generations of children.

GRANDDAUGHTERS OF DAVID

The text preserves the names of four of David's granddaughters: Maacah bat Absalom and Mahalath bat Jerimoth in 2 Chronicles 11:18–20, and Taphath bat Solomon and Basemath bat Solomon in 1 Kings 4:7–19. His granddaughters would be highly sought as marriage partners. It is in that capacity, as wives, that their names are preserved. Rehoboam, Solomon's son, married a number of David's relatives: David's granddaughters Maacah and Mahalath, and David's niece, Abihail (Avihail), daughter of his oldest brother. Rehoboam chose them likely to strengthen his claim to the throne, as the monarchy was coming apart under him.

The daughters of Solomon appear in a passage discussing his administration of the monarchy. He has twelve officials among whom he divides the responsibility to provision the royal household. To two of these men Solomon granted his daughters Taphath and Basemath in marriage. In total, we find here the names of David's two sisters, one daughter (but not the other daughter or daughters), four granddaughters, and a niece, along with his many wives—but not his mother. The preservation of their names is significant, because as few as 9 percent of all names in the Hebrew Bible belong to women.[54] It is one of David's most unexpected legacies, for their preservation results from his preeminence.

54. Carol Meyers, "Everyday Life: Women in the Period of the Hebrew Bible," in *Women's Bible Commentary*, ed. Carol Ann Newsome and Sharon H. Ringe (Louisville, KY: Westminster/John Knox Press, 1992), 252.

9

Israel's Maligned Queens

ZERUAH

1 Kings 11:26 Yarov'am ben Nevat (Jeroboam, son of Nebat), an Ephraimite of Zeredah, a servant of Solomon, whose mother's name was Zeruah, a widow woman, raised his hand against the king.

Zeruah means "Leprous Woman." This name given to Jeroboam's mother was most likely not her given name but one left for her because her son was blamed for the schism that broke the nation of Israel into two monarchies. That she is called a diseased woman likely reveals more about the contempt in which her son was held than anything about her. Likewise that she is called a prostitute, *gynē pornē*, in the LXX account in 3 Reigns 12:24b (roughly parallel to the MT account in 1 Kgs. 11:26–28) is not likely credible. Jeroboam, who rejected the sovereignty of the house of David, was in the eyes of the framers of the canon the son of a diseased whore.

The one piece of her introduction that may have represented the real woman underneath the vitriol is the disclosure of her widowhood. The text does not tell us whether Nebat died while Jeroboam was still a child—and truthfully it doesn't care. That it heaps such infamy on his mother suggests that his father was long dead and unavailable for such character assassination. His father's name, Nevat/Nebat, meaning "to bring to light" or "look over," is not defamed or distorted. Because she is alive and associated with his reign, her name becomes infamous along with his.

As for her actual name, one possibility is that her name and the pseudonym by which her memory was both sullied and preserved shared the same letters, distorting her name. She could have been named Zeruiah (Zeruyah) like David's sister (1 Chr. 2:16). She could have shared her name with the place names Zorah (Josh. 15:33) or Zererah (Judg. 7:22), which have feminine forms.[1] Instead, I would like to offer the name Zuryah, "the Holy One is my rock." The slur would be formed by switching the middle letters. As a result, the writers pen a name that deforms and ultimately desecrates her name and memory.

Despite the name-calling, this first queen mother of the new Israel is simply a woman who raised a son to heed the word of the Holy One of Old and to stand up for what he believed, no matter the cost: When the prophet Ahijah proclaims the word of God to him, that God has given him the lion's share of the monarchy, ten of the twelve tribes, Jeroboam accepts the mantle of monarchy (1 Kgs. 11:26–40). Through Ahijah, God declares that Solomon's son has forsaken God, choosing the gods of his women. As Nathan anointed David during Saul's reign, so Ahijah anoints Jeroboam during Rehoboam's reign—both at the call of God. Both David and Jeroboam are considered usurpers by the reigning monarch. David outlives the charge. Jeroboam does not escape the indictment. His mother bears the weight of the censure on her name.

Jeroboam is no usurper. The text reiterates the legitimacy of Ahijah's prophecy in 2 Kings 12:15. He and his mother are, however, on the losing side of history—in that the Judeans wrote the story of Israel. The northern nation of Israel is dispersed and disappears into the Assyrian Empire after its fall in 720 BCE, leaving the southern nation to produce the bulk of the Hebrew Bible and edit the whole. Zeruah and her son are also on the wrong side of the economic, political, and ideological forces that advocate for worship in Jerusalem and only Jerusalem. When the temple in Jerusalem is closed to him and his people, Jeroboam returns to the shrines of Samuel at Shiloh, Bethel, and Gilgal. These places were where God met God's people, heard their prayers, and responded to their needs throughout their history. Jeroboam is condemned for constructing calves that were regarded blasphemously (1 Kgs. 12:28–30), even though Judah had its own sculpted images, the cherubim. Also, he is accused of worshiping in Bethel and Dan instead of Jerusalem and of consecrating illegitimate priests (1 Kgs. 12:31–33; 13:33–34). In perpetuity, Jeroboam is associated with the fragmentation of the monarchy from which it would never recover; his mother's name and memory are perpetually cursed with his.

There is another royal woman in Jeroboam's life, his wife. Jeroboam's unnamed wife goes to the prophet Ahijah in disguise in 1 Kings 14:1–17 when their son falls ill. Her act evokes the wise woman of 2 Samuel 14:1–20 who

1. Cities and towns in the Hebrew Scriptures received their names from the names of women as well as those of men.

goes to David in disguise at Joab's urging. This time God reveals the deception; she becomes the bearer of a prophetic word against her husband and her
own house. Jeroboam's wife even becomes the harbinger of the death of her
own son—as soon as her feet touch her doorstep, her child will die; she will
never be a queen mother; and it is so. I wonder that she went home at all.

As a womanist, I see the queen mothers through the paradigm of the strong
black woman. The notion of the strong black woman is a blessing and a curse
in womanist discourse.[2] It has been a blessing, highlighting the strength of
black women to survive all that has been deployed against us, particularly
in the American context. The curse includes caricatures of black women as
domineering and as emasculating matriarchs, who represent demonized black
communities. Zuryah is also a single mother. Single motherhood has been
constructed as a pathological characteristic of the black family, especially since
the 1965 Moynihan report.[3] In much of U.S. culture, single motherhood is
portrayed as the promiscuous procreation of the unwed. This construction
fulfills stereotypes of sexual deviance on the part of black people, especially
women. The experiences of widows like Zeruah are rarely considered in dia-
tribes against single motherhood. Nor are the circumstances of women who
adopt, foster, or become the guardians of children in their families or wider
community accounted for when folk bemoan the state of single mothers or
households headed by women in the black community.

Zeruah and her son can be read as pawns of God and of the text, choosing
neither widowhood and fatherlessness nor the crown. Like so many black
women, she had to make do with her circumstances. Rising to the highest
office in the land was no guarantee of acceptance or even stability. Plenty of
black women have made their mark in corporate and academic worlds and
found that race and gender shape how they are perceived and treated. First
Kings 13:34 proclaims the erasure of the house of Jeroboam from the face of
the earth, but his mother's memory lives in the Scriptures that defame them
both.

IZEVEL (JEZEBEL)

1 Kings 16:31 And as if it had been a trifling thing for him to walk in
the sins of Yarov'am (Jeroboam) ben Nebat, Ahav (Ahab) took as his

---

2. See Chanequa Walker-Barnes's recent articulation of the strength mythos in *Too
Heavy a Yoke: Black Women and the Burden of Strength* (Eugene, OR: Cascade Books,
2014), 3–4, 14–39.

3. Office of Policy Planning and Research, United States Department of Labor, *The
Negro Family: The Case for National Action* (Washington, DC: U.S. Govt. Print. Off.,
1965).

woman Izevel (Jezebel) bat Ethbaal, king of the Sidonians, and went and served Ba'al, and worshiped him. . . .

2 Kings 9:30 Yehu (Jehu) came to Jezreel. When Izevel heard of it, she painted her eyes with mineral-powder, made her head pleasing, and looked out of the window. [31]As Yehu entered the gate, she said, "Is it peace, Zimri,[4] who killed his lord?" [32]He lifted up his face to the window and said, "Who is with me? Who?" Two or three eunuchs looked down on him. [33]He said, "Drop her." So they dropped her. Then her blood spattered on the wall and on the horses, and Yehu trampled her. [34]Thereupon he went in and ate and drank and he said, "Now, tend to that accursed woman and bury her, for she is a king's daughter." [35]They went to bury her, and they did not find of her more than the skull and the feet and the palms of her hands.

Jezebel is perhaps the most infamous Israelite queen. Her name—if Jezebel is her name—is a cross between a taunt and a slur. The name Jezebel shares the same consonants as what may be her original name, *Izevul*. If this theory is correct, her name could have meant "Ba'al Exalts"[5] but was transformed into "Lacking Nobility" and "Fecal Matter."[6] Jezebel's biblical name has become a byword for women of a certain type: assertive, aggressive, sexualized, allegedly promiscuous. In some contexts, her name is synonymous with women who wear makeup, red lipstick, red anything. Black women have been regularly constructed as Jezebels and castigated for that construction, the elements of which have very little to do with the biblical narrative.[7] Jezebel's story extends from 1 Kings 16:31 to 2 Kings 9:37, though some of that real estate is taken up by the Elijah story. She is archived anonymously in Psalm 45, and her name is a slur in Revelation 2:20. Her name and memory have given birth to extensive scholarship, including a feminist midrashic epistolary memoir.[8]

At least two traditions prevail about Jezebel in the Scriptures. The primary one is that Jezebel is a zealous worshiper of Ba'al, which is enough to condemn her in the eyes of the text. That is the root of the animus extending far beyond the Scriptures. Jezebel's Ba'al worship becomes a framework for critiquing and controlling women's behavior, particularly black women's behav-

---

4. Roughly a decade previously, Zimri, a military commander in Israel assassinated his king, Elah, and reigned for seven days before taking his own life.

5. For the range of possible meanings, see the corresponding entries in *HALOT* 39 and BDB 33.

6. See Gale Yee's entry on "Jezebel," *AYBD* 3:848.

7. For a recent exploration of the Jezebel trope applied to black women, see Melissa Harris-Perry, *Sister Citizen: Shame, Stereotypes, and Black Women in America* (New Haven, CT: Yale University Press, 2011).

8. Eleanor Ferris Beach, *The Jezebel Letters: Religion and Politics in Ninth-Century Israel* (Minneapolis: Fortress Press, 2005).

ior, by making Jezebel the archetypal bad woman. Her worship of Asherah is complicated, because it is shared by many in Israel, certainly opposed by the framers of the Bible, but tolerated on some level by many prophets, including Elijah, who slaughters the prophets of Ba'al but not those of Asherah (see the next section, the excursus "Asherah").

A secondary tradition is the description of Jezebel's wedding day submerged in Psalm 45. It is a love song for a human king and not addressed to God.[9] Psalm 45 is also in part a wedding psalm for a princess from the coastal city of Tyre in Phoenicia who is marrying one of the kings of Israel. Her name is not given in the psalm, but Jezebel is the infamous Phoenician princess who marries into Israel; no other qualifying union is disclosed in the Scriptures. The bride in this psalm is called the "daughter of Tyre" in verse 12 (v. 13 in the MT), but the NRSV transforms her into the whole "people" of Tyre. JPS preserves her as a "lass"; LXX has "daughters." Verse 9 describes her and her attendants to the king, verses 10–12 are addressed to her, and verses 13–14 describe her:

> [9]Daughters of monarchs are among your ladies of honor; at your right hand stands the queen in gold of Ophir.
> [10]Hear, O daughter, pay attention, daughter, and incline your ear; forget your people and your father's house. [11]The king will desire your beauty, daughter; since the king is your lord, bow to him. [12]Daughter of Tyre, the richest of the people will seek your favor with gifts.
> [13]With every kind of treasure the king's daughter is set like a jewel in cloth of gold; [14]in brilliant embroidered robes she is presented to the king; after her the young women follow, her companions come to her.

If Jezebel is the bride, then Psalm 45 preserves an unfamiliar, salutary, hopeful portrait of Jezebel before her name becomes a curse. Her wedding is not universally opposed. Jezebel joins a long line of foreign brides, from the time of the patriarchs through Moses himself to the golden era of David and Solomon and beyond. David is never critiqued for his foreign marriages; Solomon is critiqued for their number and aftereffects, but not their initiation.

Of course Jezebel ignores the psalmist's advice. Nothing on earth could get her to forget, abandon, or betray her identity and culture. In hip-hop womanist parlance, she stays true to her set, her 'hood, or her colors. Jezebel is a straight gangsta, ride-or-die Ba'al worshiper. When Jezebel dies, she dies with her face made up and hair done (some womanists would say "with her hair did"). When Jezebel dies, she dies having remained faithful to her gods

---

9. See vv. 1–5, 7–9, and 17, in which the psalmist promises to venerate the king's name, not God's, for all time.

unto death. It is a painful irony that the biblical authors castigate the Israelites for failing to model this kind of fidelity.

Furthermore, there is the possibility that Jezebel's marriage is less than voluntary. The "queen" in Psalm 45:9 is a *shegal*. The Hebrew word means "a seized and raped woman" in Deuteronomy 28:30, Isaiah 13:16, and Zechariah 14:2, and "a royal consort" in Daniel 5:2–3, 23 and Nehemiah 2:6. Since so many royal marriages were arranged for political reasons, royal daughters likely could not refuse arranged marriages, while other women in the canon could decline. If Jezebel's marriage is more compulsory than customary or she is styled as royal hostage, then that certainly mitigates against any loyalty to Israel and its God.

First Kings 16:31 criticizes Ahab's selection of Jezebel as his bride because she is foreign and she and her people worship Ba'al along with Asherah. Jezebel is not the only foreign woman married to an Israelite or Judean monarch to maintain fidelity to her religion and culture of origin, yet clearly she is among the most, if not *the* most despised. It is probable that Jezebel's religious devotion is embarrassing for the biblical editors. Her faith was a nonnegotiable, in spite of living in a foreign land and being married to someone with a different, intolerant religion. On the other hand, the Israelites seem to have never met another deity that they wouldn't try out for a while. Their love affair with Ba'al in particular—that junior deity with the bad habit of trying to kill off the father god, El, with whom YHWH has self-identified—was a serious problem. Jezebel is a model of religious fidelity; she is faithful to her gods until the moment of her death.

Jezebel appears next in 1 Kings 18:4, killing off the prophets who do not serve her gods. Her decision to persecute and execute the indigenous prophets in the land to which she has come as a foreign bride is extraordinary. In addition to keeping faith with her gods, she is eradicating a significant component of the local religion. Though described as a colonized woman, a *shegal*, Jezebel is colonizing the religious landscape around her. She is something of a fundamentalist; her support of her own prophets on an industrial scale can be read as evangelical missionary work. Jezebel uses the considerable resources at her disposal to support the religious institutions of her people in her new land. She feeds eight hundred fifty prophets of Ba'al and Asherah out of the royal treasury, figuratively "her table" (1 Kgs. 18:19).

Jezebel is the power *of* the throne; she is not the power *behind* the throne. So when the story of Elijah butchering her prophets makes its way to the palace, the king's immediate response is to tell Jezebel (1 Kgs. 19:1). Jezebel has not usurped Ahab's authority; he has yielded it to her. That is their arrangement. Constructing their marriage on their own terms, choosing their own power dynamics and gender roles, sounds more like a contemporary feminist union than an Iron Age one in the ancient Near East. In 1 Kings 19:2, Jezebel, not Ahab, sends Elijah a message promising to slaughter him within the next twenty-four hours, just as he has slaughtered her prophets. At this point even Ahab knows he is an ornamental, not functional, "king."[10] Emphasizing that the power of the throne is in her name, the LXX has Jezebel say, "As surely as I am Iezabel/Jezebel and you are Eliou/Elijah. . . ."[11] When Elijah hears that she has put a hit out on him for killing some of her prophets, he runs away to cower in a cave. His fear is real, because her power is real.

Jezebel is at the height of her power in 1 Kings 21, when she arranges for a man to be falsely accused of blasphemy and executed for a piece of property her husband desires (to the point of sulking in v. 4). This indicates that Jezebel is not entirely heartless. She cares for her husband. Whether she agreed to this marriage or not, she is in it with him. When Ahab explains why he has taken to his bed and refuses to eat, in verse 7 Jezebel reminds him who is actually in charge: "You, now you govern Israel? Get up, eat something, and cheer up; I, I will give to you the vineyard of Navoth the Jezreelite." Jezebel exercises what has come to be called the "divine right of kings." She takes what she wants and uses the Torah statutes as cover. While it is not clear whether there is a written Torah scroll available, her instruction to make sure the unfortunate man is condemned by two witnesses fulfills the evidentiary requirement articulated in Deuteronomy 17:6 and 19:15. While cursing the reigning monarch was a crime in virtually every ancient monarchy,[12] charging him with cursing God reflects Jezebel's awareness of Israelite culture and knowledge of the Torah prohibitions (now located in Exod. 22:27 and Lev. 24:15–16). Jezebel does all of this on behalf of her husband, the nominal king. Her actions can be construed as marital fidelity. Not only is Jezebel faithful to her gods; she is faithful and attentive to her husband.

Remarkably, Jezebel is literate and writes the letters necessary to exercise her will (1 Kgs. 21:9–10). A ninth-century-BCE seal widely believed to be Jezebel's survives, indicating Jezebel had her own correspondence, apart from that issued with the king's seal.[13] No other women in the Scriptures are described as writing. Overall, literacy in the ancient Near East is rare and

10. The functional/ornamental language comes from the ABC television series *Scandal*, created and written by Shonda Rhimes, in which the fictional adulterous president tells the First Lady that she is an ornamental but not functional wife (Season 1, Episode 8, "White Hats Off," 2012).

11. The Greek spellings of their names differ from those in Hebrew.

12. See the execution of David's antagonist Sheba on the order of a woman for cursing David in 2 Sam. 20:1–22.

13. See Nahman Avigad, "The Seal of Jezebel," *Israel Exploration Journal* 14, no. 4 (1964): 274–76.

usually associated with monarchy. In addition to the monarchy, other literate women in the ancient Near East include scribes. Hennie Marsman details some thirty Hebrew and Aramaic seals and seal impressions (bullae) belonging to women in the archaeological record.[14] It appears that in upper-class settings, in royal households, and in those of bureaucrats and administrators, women's literacy was common if not normative.

Jezebel is not portrayed like other royal women. There is something almost unnatural about her presentation as a woman in the text. There is no description of her in the primary role for a biblical woman, birthing and mothering the next generation. Altogether Ahab has some seventy sons with an unknown number of unidentified women (2 Kgs. 10:1); only Joram, also called Jehoram,[15] is identified as Jezebel's son. That there is no depiction of any of Jezebel's children being hunted down after her death may indicate that Joram/Jehoram was her only surviving child. Unlike other queen mothers, Jezebel is not identified in her son's ascension genealogy (2 Kgs. 3:1). This is in sharp opposition to the eighteen queen mothers who are listed in their sons' genealogies, some recorded multiple times.[16] Jezebel's maternity is established only a few verses before her death. She is identified as Joram's[17] mother in 2 Kings 9:23; in the same verse Jezebel is called a whore, for the first and only time in the Scripture.

In 2 Kings 9:22 Jehu[18] the soon-to-be-usurper asks Joram about his mother Jezebel's "whoredoms and sorceries." The authors of the Hebrew Bible typically use the charge of whoredom to indicate infidelity to the God of Israel and to label women as bad, whether or not they have transgressed sexually. Whore language is often tied to the metaphor in which worship of other gods is considered marital infidelity and typically described as whoredom. Ironically, Jezebel is never in relationship with the God of Israel, and therefore she has not broken any actual or metaphorical vows. Further, there is no indication that women who marry into Israel are expected to convert; even when intermarriages are critiqued, the foreign spouses are not pressured to embrace

14. See Hennie J. Marsman, *Women in Ugarit and Israel: Their Social and Religious Position in the Context of the Ancient Near East* (Leiden: Brill, 2003), 643–58.

15. There are multiple monarchs named Joram/Jehoram in Judah and Israel. Both spellings are used for each. The phenomenon is similar to the James/Jim naming pattern and occurs for a number of names.

16. 1 Kgs. 11:26; 14:21, 31; 15:2, 10; 22:42; 2 Kgs. 8:26; 12:1; 14:2; 15:2, 33; 18:2; 21:1, 19; 22:1; 23:31, 36; 24:8, 18; 2 Chr. 12:13; 13:2; 20:31; 22:2; 24:1; 25:1; 26:3; 27:1; 29:1; Jer. 52:1.

17. *Jehoram* is an alternate spelling. Both *Joram* and *Jehoram* are used in Kings and Chronicles; see 2 Kgs. 1:17; 8:16; 2 Chr. 22:5–6.

18. Jehu was a military commander who would seize the throne of Israel after killing Joram/Jehoram, Jezebel's son.

the God of Israel. Jezebel has been faithful to her gods and to her husband. She does not use sex or sorcery to kill the Israelite prophets or take Naboth's land; she uses power and authority like any male monarch. Similarly, the charge of sorcery is bombast and may indicate how simply unacceptable it was that Jezebel, a foreign woman, was the de facto monarch of Israel.

After Ahab's death, the only influence Jezebel would have would be as queen mother. The image of Jezebel as queen mother must be pieced together. It is not clear how many children she has. The mother of Ahab's heir Ahaziah is never identified (1 Kgs. 22:40, 49, 51). Ahaziah conveniently falls out of a window before he is able to produce a son (2 Kgs. 1:2), putting Jezebel's one clearly identified son on the throne in 2 Kings 1:17–18. That Jezebel would ultimately be killed by being thrown out of a window may not be a coincidence. Did she push the son of her husband by another woman out of that window or have someone else do it in order that her son could become king?

Jezebel's death narrative is without peer in the Scriptures. It is an epic event told in four acts that take up thirty verses. In the first act God pronounces sentence on Ahab and Jezebel to Elijah (1 Kgs. 21:14–24). In the second act Ahab's death and aftermath fulfill God's prediction, foreshadowing Jezebel's looming fate (1 Kgs. 22:34–40). In the third act an anonymous young prophet reissues the judgment on Jezebel and the (remaining) house of Ahab (2 Kgs. 9:4–10). The fourth act is the narration of Jezebel's death in 2 Kings 9:30–37.

The accounts exemplify a prophecy-and-fulfillment rubric. Jezebel is an object lesson, along with Ahab to a lesser degree. Jezebel's violent death and the disposition of her corpse—a horrendous desecration by a profane animal—are a warning.[19] Her fate is a warning to women who would usurp power and to men who marry foreign women. To make its point, the overarching narrative emphasizes that the violently spilled blood of Ahab will not be covered by the earth but instead will be licked up by dogs (prediction in 1 Kgs. 21:19; fulfillment in 1 Kgs. 22:38). The LXX also predicts prostitutes will bathe in his blood in 1 Kings 20:19, fulfilled in 1 Kings 22:38, but without antecedent in the MT. Prediction-and-fulfillment accounts repeat that the flesh of Jezebel will be (and is) eaten by dogs. Lastly, the account of Jezebel's death includes the infamous scene in which she prepares for her death by putting on her makeup and doing her hair.

Why does Jezebel adorn herself for her death? Is this the ultimate use of feminine wiles to seduce her killer into changing his mind? No, the emphasis on Jezebel's appearance, even womanliness, is not about sex. Her executioners are eunuchs, men on whom seduction skills would be of no avail. Instead,

19. To get a sense of the Israelite disdain for dogs, see Exod. 22:31; 1 Sam. 17:43; 2 Sam. 16:9; Ps. 22:16; Prov. 26:11.

it is about her sense of self. Jezebel is a woman and a foreigner, doubly marginalized and doubly despised. As a woman, culturally constructed through the artifice of beauty, she will go to her death. She is a queen until the end, determined to go to her death on her own terms.

There is another aspect of Jezebel's death scene that merits comment. She is the mother of a murdered son. Her son will not be lamented in the world of the text. Some will not consider his death murder. Jehu the regicide, the king-slayer, is titularly head of state and understands himself to be acting on behalf of the state—and God. Jezebel and her son and their people are reviled in the text. Their lives don't matter to the framers of the text. As a womanist writing in the age of the Black Lives Matters movement, that gives me pause. Jezebel's preparations for her death are also preparation to join her son in death.

Jezebel is distinct from most other women in the canon because of the vast power she wields. Her only peer is Athaliah, an equally despised Israelite queen who becomes a Judean king. The biblical editors do not, cannot, deny Jezebel's agency. The text and generations of male-stream Christian and Jewish interpreters are critical of that agency. It is most unseemly for them, particularly because of her gender. Jezebel is critiqued in and beyond the canon for her agency, which is constructed as usurpation of God-given royal male privilege. As soon as Jezebel secures the vineyard her husband desires, her death is decreed. Jezebel is destined to be dog food,[20] a gruesome fate made more distasteful by the use of unclean animals. In comparison, her husband Ahab dies a warrior's death; dogs lick his spilled blood but do not defile his body (1 Kgs. 22:34–38). In the history of interpretation, Jezebel is reviled by rabbinic and patristic fathers alike. Ephrem the Syrian refers to her as "insane" and pronounces that her sins are many.[21] He also accuses her of trying to seduce Jehu.[22] According to Ambrose, Jezebel keeps Ahab from repenting.[23] Similarly, in the Babylonian Talmud the rabbis use Jezebel as the example for why men should not follow their wives' counsel; it will lead them to hell.[24]

I listen for Jezebel's voice in and between the lines of the Scriptures, and I don't hear a sound. Instead, I hear the words of the gospel hymn "May the Work I've Done Speak for Me."[25] Jezebel's final words are her beautifully

---

20. Her fate is prophesied repeatedly, in 1 Kgs. 21:23 and in 2 Kgs. 9:10, before being fulfilled in 2 Kgs. 9:35–37.

21. Ephrem the Syrian, *On the First Book of Kings* 19.2; 19.13.

22. Ephrem the Syrian, *On the Second Book of Kings* 9.30.

23. Ambrose, *On Naboth* 17.70–73.

24. *b. Baba Metzia* 59a.

25. Composed by Sullivan Pugh, recorded with Mahalia Jackson in 1960; the copyright is currently held by Excellence Music.

made-up face and her gorgeously arranged hair. She is the first woman to rule Israel. And she will not be the last. In her way, Jezebel paves the way for the last monarch of Israel, the beloved Jewish queen Alexandra Jannaea Salome, known as Shelamzion, the peace of Zion.[26]

EXCURSUS: ASHERAH

The Canaanite mother goddess Asherah plays an important if contested role in the Israelite Scriptures. She is present and worshiped, and then condemned and worshiped anyway. Based on the accounts in the books of Kings and Chronicles of her images, sacred poles, being alternately constructed and demolished, Raphael Patai[27] and later Ilona Rashkow[28] demonstrate that Asherah was worshiped in the Jerusalem temple along with YHWH for periods ranging from twenty-three to one hundred years. The sequence includes four periods of her presence in the temple: 35, 100, 78, and 23 years, until the day of the temple's destruction. The archaeological data reveals countless household images identified as Asherah in Canaan from before the arrival of the Israelites until after the fall of both monarchies. And there is the Kuntillet Ajrud inscription in the Sinai that blesses a petitioner in the names of YHWH and "his" Asherah together. The thinking is that since YHWH became identified with El, the spouse of Asherah, YHWH and Asherah were perceived and worshiped by some as a conjugal couple. Often English translations like the NRSV use "sacred pole" instead of Asherah's name.

In the Hebrew Bible, El is accepted as a normative name for YHWH, who says, "*Ani el*," "I am El," in Isaiah 43:12 and 45:21. That identification is also the root of the conflict with the Ba'al tradition; Ba'al was the patricidal offspring of El, with whom he was in perpetual conflict. This conflict is made more complicated by the fact that *ba'al* is a title in Biblical Hebrew meaning "lord" and "master." *Ba'al* is used to refer to human men as husbands and slave owners as well as to YHWH and the Canaanite deity Ba'al Haddu, who is eventually known as just Ba'al.[29]

---

26. Queen Alexandra inherited the throne from her husband Alexander Jannaeus and ruled Israel 67–76 BCE. She was the last of the Hasmoneans, the dynasty descended from the Maccabees. The contention between her sons led to Rome's intervention and culminated in the rule of Herod.

27. Raphael Patai, *The Hebrew Goddess* (Detroit: Wayne State University Press, 1990).

28. Ilona N. Rashkow, *Taboo or Not Taboo: Sexuality and Family in the Hebrew Bible* (Minneapolis: Fortress Press, 2000).

29. See Hos. 6:2 for one attempt to sort out the "ba'als" of Scripture.

The prophets vehemently prohibit the worship of other gods in general and Ba'al in particular, but surprisingly they name Asherah with much less frequency. Elijah's infamous contest with the prophets of Ba'al vividly illustrates this point. He challenges the prophets of Ba'al but not those of Asherah; yet both groups are present. In 1 Kings 18:19–40, the dramatic performance on Mount Carmel, Elijah ridicules the very notion that Ba'al is a god. But Elijah does not ridicule or challenge Asherah's divinity. When Ba'al fails Elijah's test, Elijah personally slaughters every one of the four hundred fifty prophets of Ba'al present, but he does not lay a hand on a single one of the four hundred prophets of Asherah. Many of the latter prophets avoid critiquing Asherah, while condemning Ba'al; for example, Jeremiah rails against Ba'al thirteen[30] times but mentions Asherah only once.[31] Hosea preaches against Ba'al six times but never mentions Asherah worship.[32] The prophets who do not condemn the worship of Asherah at all include Ezekiel, Joel, Amos, Obadiah, Jonah, Nahum, Habakkuk, Haggai, Zechariah, and Malachi.

The religious iconography of ancient Israel incorporated a number of elements sacred to Asherah, most notably the tree of life and lions. The basic element of Asherah's name, '-sh-r, is regularly associated with happiness, prosperity, fertility, and abundance through a number of different roots with the same spelling and is found in the name of the tribe of Asher. It may well be that some of the Israelites attributed this beneficence to Asherah or associated it with her.[33]

---

30. Jer. 2:8, 23; 7:9; 9:14; 11:13, 17; 12:16; 19:5; 23:13, 27; 32:29, 35.
31. Jer. 17:2.
32. Hos. 2:8, 13, 16–17; 11:2; 13:1.
33. See Gen. 30:13; Deut. 33:29; 1 Kgs. 10:8; Isa. 56:2; Mal. 3:12; Ps. 1:1; Job 5:17; Prov. 3:18.

10

Royal Women of Judah

NAAMAH THE AMMONITE

1 Kings 14:21 Now Rehav'am (Rehoboam) ben Shlomo (Solomon) reigned in Yehudah (Judah). Rehav'am was forty-one years old when he began to reign, and he reigned seventeen years in Yerushalayim (Jerusalem), the city that the HOLY ONE had chosen out of all the tribes of Israel, to put God's name there. His mother's name was Naamah the Ammonite.

Naamah the Ammonite is the last queen mother of a united Israel and the first queen mother of the new Judean monarchy. She is mentioned three times in the Scriptures: 1 Kings 14:21, 31; 2 Chronicles 12:13. In keeping with the prominence afforded her as a queen mother, Naamah is known as mother of a monarch rather than as the spouse of one. She is actually one of Solomon's many women. That she was from Ammon reinforces the understanding that Israelite identity is configured paternally in the Scriptures. In ancient Israel and surrounding nations, offspring shared their father's ethnic or national identity. This practice is what made rape a terribly effective and genocidal tool of war.[1] It is likely that David procured a bride from Ammon for his son to broker a treaty and provide a buffer between tiny Israel and larger encroaching ancient Near Eastern empires. The *torah* that no Ammonite

---

1. Bear in mind that the religion of ancient Israel is not the same as Judaism; the vast majority of Jews in modernity determine identity based on the mother's identity. Contemporarily some egalitarian branches of Judaism recognize both.

or Moabite should be admitted to the presence of YHWH (Deut. 23:3) has been disregarded—and not just on account of David's Moabite lineage—or deemed not to appy to offspring with Israelite paternity.

As queen mother, Naamah may have helped to select her successor, participating in the process of finding and vetting a suitable bride for her son. The famous poem in Proverbs 31 in praise of a worthy wife, literally a warrior (-hearted) woman, is an example of an otherwise unknown queen mother articulating the qualities she desires in a wife for her son Lemmuel. I imagine that some families in Jerusalem and among Israel's neighbors jockeyed to get their daughters noticed by Israel's kings and queen mothers, in hope of power and influence. The relatively smooth royal succession in Judah meant that each queen mother was succeeded by her daughter-in-law in most cases. In my reading, Judean queen mothers inherited the throne, *kisse'*, that Solomon had installed for Bathsheba, the first queen mother, in 1 Kings 2:19. *Kisse'* can mean "throne," "seat," or "chair"; as a sign of office, I translate it "throne." At some point *Giverah* Naamah, originally of Ammon, yielded her throne to her daughter-in-law Maacah. In the entries that follow I use the language of passing down the queen mother's throne figuratively, not making a historic claim for an enthronement ritual using the same throne but as a way of talking about the succession of queen mothers.

MICAIAH BAT URIEL

> 2 Chronicles 13:1 In the eighteenth year of King Yarov'am (Jeroboam), Aviyah (Abijah) began to reign over Yehudah (Judah). [2]He reigned for three years in Yerushalayim (Jerusalem). His mother's name was Micaiah bat Uriel of Gibeah.

According to Chronicles, Naamah's daughter-in-law and successor is a woman named Micaiah from Gibeah, Saul's ancestral land in Benjamin. Here in 1 Chronicles 13 she is the mother of King Abijah; however, later in 2 Chronicles 11:20 his mother is identified as Maacah bat Absalom, David's granddaughter. First Kings 15:2 also names Abijah's[2] mother as Maacah. The women's names are different enough in spelling that the confusion is not easily explained, further complicated by the significant difference in their stated paternity and ancestral homes. For reasons that are no longer clear, the name of Micaiah bat Uriel has been preserved in the royal Chronicles of Judah. Though we cannot be sure that she existed as more than a textual variant, I

---

2. Abijam, as he is called in 1 Kgs. 15:2, is an alternate version of Abijah.

call her name, honoring the decision of those who included and preserved her name in the Scriptures.

MAACAH BAT ABSALOM

1 Kings 15:2 Aviyam (Abijam) reigned for three years in Yerushalayim (Jerusalem). His mother's name was Maacah bat Avishalom (Abishalom).

2 Chronicles 11:18 Rehav'am (Rehoboam) took as his woman Mahalath bat Yerimoth (Jerimoth) ben David and Avihail bat Eliav ben Yissai (Abihail, daughter of Eliab son of Jesse). [19]She gave birth to children for him: Yeush (Jeush), Shemariah, and Zaham. [20]After her he took Maacah bat Avshalom, who gave birth to Aviyah (Abijah), Attai, Ziza, and Shelomith for him. [21]Rehav'am (Rehoboam) loved Maacah bat Avshalom (Absalom) more than all his other primary and secondary wives (he took eighteen primary wives and sixty secondary wives, and became the father of twenty-eight sons and sixty daughters).

There is some confusion about which of Naamah's daughters-in-law succeeded her as queen mother. First Kings 15:2 has Maacah bat Absalom (alternately spelled Abishalom), while 2 Chronicles 13:2 has Micaiah bat Uriel. The more detailed Chronicles account includes Maacah and other wives, declaring that Rehoboam loved her above all others; however, her status as David's granddaughter is a good reason for making her his senior wife and queen mother. Her status differs from his other women in another significant way: they are conquest-wives, acquired through abduction as signified by *n-s-'*, rather than the traditional *l-q-ch*.[3]

Maacah bat Absalom, David's granddaughter through his son and rival Absalom, becomes Rehoboam's most important wife. Rehoboam is Solomon's son, who presides over the remnant of Judah after the fracture of the monarchy. Rehoboam marries within his own family, targeting David's descendants, likely in an attempt to shore up his appeal as the legitimate heir to David. In addition to Maacah, he marries Mahalath, David's granddaughter through the otherwise unknown Jerimoth (Yerimoth). Mahalath is Rehoboam's first cousin, as is Maacah. Also, he marries Abihail (Avihail), another cousin, who is David's niece, the daughter of his oldest brother, Eliab (Eliav). Clearly taking

---

3. Other abducted brides in the canon famously include the prepubescent girls of Shiloh in Judg. 21:20–23; Ruth and Orpah in Ruth 1:4; a number seized by the exiles in Ezra 10:44; seventy-eight women seized by Rehoboam in 2 Chr. 11:21; fourteen seized by Abijah in 2 Chr. 24:3; and two by the regent Jehoiada in 2 Chr. 24:3.

after his father and grandfather, Rehoboam has another seventeen primary wives and sixty secondary wives. Among all of these wives, Maacah is never lost in the shuffle, as she is Rehoboam's favorite and most beloved. Rehoboam chooses Abijah (also known as Abijam),[4] his son with Maacah, as crown prince, although he is not the firstborn (2 Chr. 11:22). It appears that she follows in the footsteps of Bathsheba in getting her son placed on the throne; unlike Bathsheba, she did not need outside help.

Maacah becomes queen mother again. According to 1 Kings 15:10, "Asa reigned forty-one years in Yerushalayim. His mother's name was Maacah bat Abishalom." There is a problem with this claim. The previous verse, verse 9, says that Asa is Rehoboam's son, who ruled after him. Is Maacah the mother of Rehoboam *and* his son Asa?[5] It is difficult to believe the text would not address such an incestuous union. Is the character of Maacah hopelessly entangled with one or more women? Is she another woman named Maacah?[6] The name Maacah is the most common woman's name in the Hebrew Bible; there are more Maacahs than there are Miriams/Marys in the New Testament, and they are just as difficult to disentangle. Did Maacah function as queen mother for her grandson Asa? That is reasonable, given her tremendous influence as David's granddaughter and Rehoboam's favorite wife. Maacah will also be remembered for apostasy, making the confusion about her name all the more perplexing.

Maacah commissions an "abominable" or "horrible" object of some sort to the goddess Asherah (see the excursus "Asherah" in chapter 9). While the biblical text makes clear that Asherah worship flourished under some monarchs, Asa was not one of them. He purged the land of idols (1 Kgs. 15:12); the editors of the Hebrew Bible consistently laud monarchs who dismantle the infrastructure of Asherah's worship. Maacah's actions were in defiance of the king's reformation. It is not clear what sort of object she had constructed. It is clear that the object is not a sacred tree, pole, or sacred grove, a traditional Asherah image synonymous with the goddess herself. In 1 Kings 15:13 this object is called a *miphletzet*, a term that occurs only in this narrative and its duplicate in 2 Chronicles 15:16. The rare use of the word and its unspoken horror inspired rabbinic commentators and Jerome, who imagine the object to be some sort of

---

4. In 1 Kgs. 15:2 he is Abijam; in 2 Chr. 18:20 he is Abijah.

5. The LXX resolves the issue by calling Abijah's mother "Ana," making her a different person but still daughter of Absalom.

6. The Peshitta, an Aramaic version of the Scriptures, makes her a different Maacah and names her father Abed-shalom. I don't rule out that she is yet another Maacah based on my own family history: After my mother Louvenia's mother, also named Louvenia, died, my grandfather married another woman named Louvenia some years later.

dildo.[7] Contrary to rabbinic interpretations, it is unlikely that the object was some sort of monster phallus. The Vulgate and subsequently Wycliffe and Douay, likely influenced by rabbinic tradition, contend that she was removed from presiding over sacrifices to the Roman male god Priapus (*in sacris Priapi*), rather than removed from queenly authority. It is clear that the object was not the anachronistic Priapus or any of his parts. The real question is, what was the *miphletzet* and how was it different from an Asherah pole?

Given that Asherah worship was a significant and regular phenomenon in Israel and Judah, and that no other queen mothers or other officials have been recorded as officially sanctioned for that worship, I am not inclined to accept that Maacah's sanction was (simply) for Asherah worship. There is no Asherah object in the passage. We simply do not know what the *miphletzet* was and how it was different from an Asherah pole. Therefore I suggest that Maacah deviated to some significant degree from orthodox Asherah worship and was sanctioned for that heterodoxy.

It is unclear if someone stepped in as a surrogate for Maacah, if the position was left vacant, or if the mother of the crown prince served in some capacity during the vacancy. Eventually *Giverah* Maacah yielded her queen mother's throne to her daughter-in-law Azubah.

AZUBAH BAT SHILHI

> 1 Kings 22:42 Yehoshaphat (Jehoshaphat) was thirty-five years old when he began to reign, and he reigned twenty-five years in Yerush-alayim (Jerusalem). His mother's name was Azuvah (Azubah) bat Shilhi.

The provenance of Azubah (Azuvah) bat Shilhi is unknown. She is the mother of Jehoshaphat ben Asa and is mentioned in a single verse (repeated in 2 Chr. 20:31.) Shili cannot be further identified as the mother or father of Azubah without a verb to determine gender. How and why Azubah became queen mother is an unanswered question. Abijah married fourteen women who could have been contenders for the role of queen mother if one of their sons

---

7. Rashi teaches, "Our Rabbis stated: *miphletzet* is a combination of *maphle'* (wonderful) and *leitzuta'* (for scorn). It carried lasciviousness to an extreme. She made for it a phallic symbol, and she would copulate with it every day." This interpretation is repeated in the Talmud in *b. Avodah Zarah* 44a. The sexual charge is not easily comprehensible, given that *maphle'*, *ph-l-'*, means "wonderful," perhaps "wonderfully horrible" in this case. While derived from *l-y-tz*, "scorn," particularly scornful talk, *leitzuta'* shares some letters with *zenuth*, which does mean "prostitution or harlotry," but they are different words.

among his twenty-two were to be crowned (2 Chr. 13:21). Somehow Azubah and her son Jehoshaphat distinguished themselves and inherited the thrones.

Because Azubah bat Shilhi does not have an immediate successor acknowledged, the next recorded queen mother is her granddaughter-in-law, Athaliah. Azubah's grandson Jehoram[8] does not have a complete enthronement biography, and his mother is missing from the annals (1 Kgs. 22:50; 2 Kgs. 8:16–18; 2 Chr. 21:1–6). His introduction in Chronicles provides limited details: He was the firstborn of seven sons;[9] his father gave his brothers wealth and fortified cities; and his first act as monarch was to kill his brothers and some "officials of Israel."

It is not clear what Azubah's absence from her son's genealogies portends. Normally the king's mother would become queen mother. As the case of Maacah demonstrates, the familial relationship is not denied, even when sanctioned for apostasy. No malfeasance is alleged here. None of the genealogies identifies whether the queen mother is living or dead; it should not be presumed that her absence is indicative of death, natural or unnatural. Further, the text that discloses the king's fratricide would hardly be squeamish about matricide, had he killed her with the other officials. Her name has been forgotten, disremembered, erased.

Azubah passed her throne down to a woman whose name is no longer remembered. Then Jehoram married Athaliah bat Ahab,[10] who would inherit the *giverah*-throne.

> *My name is . . . well, it no longer matters. I was Levti, "my heart," to my mother; I was Eshti, "my wife," to my husband; Giverti, "my queen," to his people; and Emmi-li-li-li, "my mother, mine, mine, mine," to my son. I belonged to everyone but myself. And it turns out that I was entirely forgettable along with my name. Once I was chosen by and for a king. I had more than beauty to commend me: beauty will turn a king's head, but it will not sway his counselors, especially his mother. I had my good name, now forgotten, my family's good name, no longer remembered. And I had strength; strength to make kings and strength to guide kings, even when they thought they needed no guidance. I gave my husband a son, and he gave me a king, making me a queen. They may no longer say my name, but I live on in the gaps within the annals of Israel. You just have to know where to look.*

8. A popular and recurring name for monarchs in Israel and Judah, regularly shortened to Joram.

9. No mother is named for his brothers.

10. Athaliah is called bat Ahab here and elsewhere bat Omri. Since Ahab is the son of Omri, both are true if she is the daughter of Ahab and granddaughter of Omri.

ATHALIAH BAT OMRI, THE QUEEN-KING

2 Kings 8:26 Ahazyahu (Ahaziah)[11] was twenty-two years old when he began to reign; he reigned one year in Yerushalayim (Jerusalem). His mother's name was Athalyah bat Omri, King of Israel.

2 Kings 11:1 Athalyah, the mother of Ahazyahu (Ahaziah) saw her son was dead, then she arose and destroyed all the royal seed. [2]Yet Yehosheva (Jehosheba), King Joram's daughter, Ahazyah's (Ahaziah's) sister, took Joash ben Ahaziah, and stole him away from among the king's children who were to be killed; she put him and his milk-nurse in a bedroom. They hid him from Athalyah so that he was not killed. [3]He was with her six years, hidden in the house of the HOLY ONE, and Athalyah reigned over the land.

Athalyah Molekhet. Athaliah, She-Who-Reigns. Second Kings 11:3 describes the most powerful woman in ancient Israel with the language of kingship using a feminine participle. She ruled Judah for seven years. It would be another seven hundred years before another woman did the same. The infamy of Athaliah (Athalyah, occasionally Athalyahu)[12] bat Omri parallels that of Jezebel, and in the eyes of the biblical authors, exceeds it by a magnitude. They are linked in the text. Athaliah's story is intertwined with that of Jezebel and her killer, Jehu, and begins before Jezebel's assassination. Athaliah, a non-Judean, non-Davidic woman ruled Judah, the home of the temple and the home of God. Yet, because of her Israelite heritage, she is not a foreigner. She even has an orthodox name, previously given to men, that incorporates the Holy Name (1 Chr. 8:26; Ezra 8:7). Unlike so many other royal women, she is not called out of her name.[13] Her story begins in 2 Kings 8 and continues through chapter 11 (also 2 Chr. 22–24), where it intersects the story of the prophet Elisha.

Athaliah is *bat Omri*, a daughter or descendant of Omri. It is not clear whether Omri, the ninth-century dynastic monarch of Israel, is her father or grandfather. If Athaliah is the unnamed daughter of Ahab introduced as the wife of the new king Joram/Jehoram) in 2 Kings 8:18, this would make Omri, Ahab's father, Athaliah's grandfather. In that case, *bat Omri* in 2 Kings 8:26

11. Ahaziah is called both Ahazyah and Ahazyahu, sometimes in the same narrative.
12. Athaliah's name, like some others, occurs with a number of spellings in the Hebrew Bible. However, most contemporary translators default to a single dominant spelling of Athaliah. The LXX renders her name as "Gotholia" to approximate the hard guttural sound of the *ayin* in her name in antiquity; now the *ayin* is largely silent.
13. Names and naming hold significant value for womanists; defaming or distorting someone's name is therefore a grave offense. Many Afro-diasporic communities share that value. In African American contexts, calling someone out of their name is a violation of that principle.

means "descendant of" rather than actual "daughter of" Omri. To clarify, the NRSV adds the word "grandfather" to 2 Kings 8:26; it is absent in Hebrew. If Omri was Athaliah's grandfather, then her mother could have been Jezebel. However, the biblical text doesn't go quite that far and lump the two detested women in the same house or dynasty, *Athalyah bat Izevel*. As either Omri's daughter or granddaughter, Athaliah would have been cotemporal with Jezebel, well aware of the power she exercised and the circumstances of her death. They may have been close in age, because of long procreative periods. Also, many women gave birth for him, and therefore, Omri could have had daughters and granddaughters the same age or with inverse ages.

The house of Omri was a well-known political entity in the ancient Near East; its footprint in the historical record is in sharp distinction to its presentation in the biblical text. These rulers are named *ben Omri*; Omri is their most significant ancestor, whereas in the biblical text David is the venerated progenitor of Judah.[14] Omri is the first Israelite (or Judean) monarch's name to have been discovered in archaeological sources; he is preserved on the famous Moabite stele inscription,[15] and his successor kings on numerous Akkadian inscriptions.[16] Within the pages of the Bible, the house of Omri is held in low regard, and his reign is not discussed, generally an indication that an ill-favored monarch enjoyed military and economic success that the biblical editors did not wish to acknowledge. The choice of an Omride princess for the Judean monarch illustrates the renown of the family, in spite of the biblical tradents' opinion of them. Ahab (Omri's son) and Athaliah are the most significant and the most reviled Omride monarchs in the Bible.

The narrative introduces Athaliah by name as the queen mother; one of her sons, Ahaziah, is king in Judah. In 2 Kings 8:28 King Ahaziah of Judah

14. The Tel Dan Stele, another ninth-century-BCE text, names Joram—likely Jezebel's son—as "ben Ahab" and Ahaziah as "ben Jehoram" and "of the house of David." The stele is fragmentary and has been reconstructed. Compare the translations of Alan Millard in William W. Hallo and K. Lawson Younger Jr., eds., *Monumental Inscriptions from the Biblical World*, vol. 2 of *The Context of Scripture* (Leiden: Brill, 2003), 162; and Shmuel Ahituv, *Echoes from the Past: Hebrew and Cognate Inscriptions from the Biblical Period* (Jerusalem: Carta, 2008), 468.

15. King Mesha of Moab laments Omri's forty-year domination of his land and his eventual liberation of the disputed territory on the stele, which dates from 840–830 BCE (Hallo and Younger, *Monumental Inscriptions*, 2:137).

16. King Shalmaneser of Assyria lists tribute received from cowed Judean kings, including "Jehu ben Omri," on carved bulls and marble slabs in his administrative and royal cities Calah and Asshur (Hallo and Younger, *Monumental Inscriptions*, 2:267–68). Perhaps Shalmaneser's most significant monument is his Black Obelisk, on which Jehu's image is carved. It is the only surviving portrait of an Israelite or Judean monarch, and he is kneeling in submission (Hallo and Younger, *Monumental Inscriptions*, 2:269–70.

joins forces with the Israelite monarch Jehoram[17] to wage a military campaign against the Aramean monarch Hazael at Ramoth-Gilead, presumably leaving Athaliah to govern in his stead. In 2 Kings 9:24, the Judean monarch Ahaziah watches the killing of the Israelite monarch by his successor on the field of battle, Jehu having been anointed by Elisha and commissioned back in verse 7 to "strike down the house of [his] master Ahab." Jehu commands that Ahaziah of Judah be struck down, and in verse 27 he too dies at Megiddo with King Jehoram of Israel. Ahaziah's rule over Judah lasts barely a year. The story ignores Athaliah for several chapters, focusing on Jehu's assassination of Jezebel and destruction of the house of Ahab.

Athaliah's first action in the narrative (2 Kgs. 11:1) is to observe and assess the previous actions of Jehu. She sees (*ra'atah*), then she gets up (*v'taqom*), and gets to work. Immediately after he has Jezebel killed, Jehu solicits the murder of all of Ahab's children by their caretakers, then kills the killers, along with any of Ahab's nobles, friends, and priests that he can find (2 Kgs. 10:1–12, 17). Jehu also slaughters all of the worshipers of Ba'al that he can, but following the pattern of Elijah, he spares the worshipers of Asherah. The inclusion of the episode is meant to suggest Athaliah was faithless, but the text cannot make that claim directly. She never worships Ba'al or even Asherah. Athaliah is an orthodox, faithful Israelite.

Athaliah seizes the opportunity presented her and secures the throne after Jehu begins exterminating members of her family. Jehu has already killed most of the men who could compete with her for the throne. Athaliah finishes the task. The text blames Athaliah alone for the carnage, and yet it is not likely that she kills every heir and relative she can find with her own hands. Unmentioned are the assassins who follow her orders to secure her reign, and the men, soldiers, and bureaucrats who accept her rule. Athaliah commands loyalty. The text does not record any resistance to her rule from soldiers, bureaucrats, or the people.

Athaliah's slaughter takes a page from the book of Jehu—and that of virtually every other monarch in antiquity. Unlike Jehu, she is not praised for her actions. In 2 Kings 10:30 God tells Jehu that he has "done well in doing that which is right."[18] It is not clear whether Athaliah would have annihilated her own family for the throne if Jehu had not demonstrated that none of her

---

17. The Israelite Jehoram is different from the Judean Jehoram, Athaliah's late husband, with whom he overlaps; adding to the confusion, both men are also called "Joram" for short.

18. At another point the account that presents Jehu as following the prophetic command of Elijah accuses Jehu of treason, *q-sh-r*, but 2 Kgs. 9:14 translates it as "conspire." When Athaliah cries, "Treason! Treason!" with her last breath, accusing the priests who crowned her nephew in her stead, she uses the same verb (2 Kgs. 11:14).

children or grandchildren would be safe on the throne or as heirs to it, or if he had not already had the strongest contenders murdered. Athaliah does not see in Jehu God's obedient servant. Instead she sees a grasping, power-hungry king-slayer who has destabilized Israel and Judah, leaving them open to invasion. Indeed, Jehu has no claim of divine authorization to kill Ahaziah. He may well have thought to attempt to rule both nations. Athaliah would not allow that. Athaliah completes Jehu's liquidation. She targets all of her grandchildren, not just the males, as she knew better than anyone else that girl children were also potential threats.[19] She is also making sure that none of her kin can be used against her. Her reign will be vulnerable as long as there is a claimant to the throne with blood ties to David. It may also be that having seen what Jehu did to her family, Athaliah kills the remnant of her family so that no one else can.

Jehosheba (Yehoseheva), her husband's daughter, thwarts Athaliah by hiding her grandson J(eh)oash, along with his milk-nurse. The narrative does not identify Jehosheba's mother. It is possible that Athaliah is her mother, and the authors of the text do not want to credit any daughter of Athaliah and the house of Ahab and Omri. Unlike Ahab, who has seventy children with various birthing partners, Ahaziah and Jehosheba are Jehoram's only children in the canon, and Athaliah could have birthed both of them. Jehosheba is already at risk for having survived the massacre. She is a royal daughter. Her actions multiply the peril she faces. Yet 2 Kings 11:2 does not consider the threat to her life.

Jehosheba's agency is almost eclipsed in Athaliah's story. Jehosheba decides not to support the reign of her queen mother. Instead, she takes the role of monarch maker upon herself and chooses the infant[20] son of Tzivyah (Zibiah), Joash/Jehoash, as the next king from among Ahaziah's children. Her choice has the earmarks of prophetic privilege, as prophets are kingmakers. It is not clear whether Jehoash (also called Joash) is the youngest or how many children or sons she chooses among, or if she simply takes the first or only child she sees. Jehosheba puts Jehoash into hiding with his milk-nurse; she has saved both of their lives. Jehosheba's husband, Jehoiada (Yehoiada), hides him in the Jerusalem temple complex and is called his "advisor" (2 Chr. 24:1); however, "advising" a nursling means ruling in their stead. In making that choice, Jehoiada leaves an unknown number of children and other relatives to certain death. While the narrative does not name her at this point, Athali-

---

19. The expression "all the seed of the kingdom" in 2 Kings 11:1 makes clear that she targets everyone without regard to age or gender.

20. The child is a newborn; seven years later, at his coronation, he will be seven years old (2 Kgs. 11:21).

ah's daughter-in-law, Zibiah of Beer-sheba, becomes queen mother for the record,[21] whether or not she survives the purge. If the slaughter is restricted to the king's children, it does not include her, but killing women who could be or become pregnant is standard fare in Israelite practice.

Athaliah is the only woman described in the canon of Scripture as ruling Israel or Judah, using the verb *m-l-k*. Second Kings 11:4 asserts that "Athaliah reigned over the land." She is frequently placed on lists and charts of the "kings" of Israel and/or Judah. Biblical Hebrew simply does not have the language to name a ruling queen/female king. For that matter, neither does English; the word "queen" evokes a secondary or subordinate royalty unable to take the throne in many places, except when a male is unavailable.[22] Because her marriage previously brought a measure of peace between the sibling nations, Athaliah, as an Israelite ruling Judah, may have reunification of the monarchies as her goal.

The biblical writers are silent on the seven years of peace, stability, and prosperity during Athaliah's reign. One can easily imagine that they would trumpet any instability or political or national disaster as a sign of divine displeasure. They have nothing negative to say, so they say nothing. The fact that she, a non-Davidide, rules Judah longer than some who are more legitimate in the writers' eyes was unacceptable and undeniable. They cannot erase her from their archives, so they do not include the substance of her reign.

Ultimately Athaliah is undone by Jehosheba and her husband, Jehoiada, who arranges a coronation for the young Joash. The combination of his survival against the odds and his descent from the line of David—carefully reinforced by the use of David's own weapons (2 Kgs. 11:10)—was powerful theater. There was also a significant military presence, including fearsome mercenaries, the Carites. The description of Joash's coronation raises a few questions. What was Athalyah's coronation like, if she had one? If she did not have a formal coronation, did she have some other affirmation? Did she have religious support, censored from the Bible's account?

As did Jezebel before her, Athaliah goes to her death on her own terms. She pronounces the coronation an act of treason (2 Kgs. 11:14). The priest Jehoida commands that she not be killed in God's house. Athaliah is no longer afforded the dignity of king or queen mother. The captains of the army put their hands on her body and force her out of the temple and into the palace

21. Queen Mother Zibiah will be named in her son's formal genealogy in 2 Kgs. 12:1 and 2 Chr. 24:1.

22. In 2013 the Succession to the Crown Act in Great Britain made it possible for a firstborn female child to rule, even if she has brothers born after her. Previously, female monarchs like Elizabeth I and II ruled when male heirs were unavailable or disqualified.

through the stable entrance, evoking another comparison with Jezebel, whose body was trampled by horses. Jehoiada offers her followers an opportunity to go and die with her. None is recorded as taking him up on the offer. He has her put to death at the palace by the sword according to verse 20.

Posthumously, there is an attempt to tie Athaliah to Ba'al worship. A major Ba'al shrine is demolished after her death (2 Kgs. 11:18), but the text does not say that Athaliah had anything to do with it. In the Chronicler's account (2 Chr. 24:7), Athaliah's children, but not Athaliah herself, are accused of plundering the Jerusalem temple in order to supply the Ba'alist temple. The record of Athaliah's story bears witness to the axiom that the "pen is mightier than the sword." The pens of canon makers and shapers, rather than the sword in her hand or those at her command, have had the last word. Athaliah's epitaph is in 2 Chronicles 24:7, *mirsha'at*: "that wicked woman." But what would she say for herself? My womanist midrash gives Athaliah voice:

> *Why? No one would ask a man why. I was born to rule. Athalyah Molekhet, that is my name. Like Puabi of Ur, Makeda of Sheba, and Hatshepsut of Kemet, I was born to rule, and I did. If it were not so, I would not have succeeded. It was the will of the God of Israel, the God of my ancestors, the House of Omri. When the traitor Jehu killed my son, then hunted the rest of my family, my blood, I swore that I would kill them all myself before I would let them fall into his hands. I took my blood-soaked throne with my strong right arm. When I secured my throne, God blessed me. I fed my people and kept them safe. We prospered until I was betrayed from within my own house. Daughter-of-my-blood, I see you. I have taught you well. I live on in you. My name will live forever. I am Athalyah Molekhet.*

ZIBIAH OF BEER-SHEBA

2 Kings 12:1 In the seventh year of Yehu (Jehu), Yehoash (Jehoash) began to reign; he reigned forty years in Yerushalayim (Jerusalem). His mother's name was Tzivyah (Zibiah) of Beer-sheba.

Tzivyah, Zibiah, inherited the queen mother's throne abandoned by Athaliah, who exchanged it for the sovereign governing throne. The verse does not mention Zibiah's parentage; instead, it heralds her home: Beer-sheba, named for the well over which Abraham swore an oath according to tradition (Gen. 21:29–33). This time there would be no foreign influence on the future throne. Perhaps Athaliah chose Zibiah for her son as an act of statecraft while she was in power. It is not clear whether Zibiah survived the bloodbath that inaugurated Athaliah's reign. That her son is hidden away with a nursemaid in 2 Kings 11:3, with no mention of her, may indicate her long-term absence or death. It does not appear that she functioned as queen mother, perhaps due to the fear that she would follow in Athaliah's footsteps, particularly if she were perceived as Athaliah's choice and/or ally. Instead, the priest Jehoiada—conveniently the husband of her son's rescuer, Jehosheba—seems to function as regent for the child king and arranges his two marriages.[23] The names, ancestry, and cultural heritage of the new royal women are all omitted from the text. Zibiah's influence may have been virtually erased from her son's life, but her name was preserved in the annals of the mothers and monarchs. Neither he nor his people would forget her.

JEHOADDIN OF JERUSALEM

> 2 Kings 14:2 [Amaziah ben Yoash (Joash)] was twenty-five years old when he began to reign, and he reigned twenty-nine years in Yerushalayim (Jerusalem). His mother's name was Yehoaddin (Jehoaddin) of Yerushalayim (Jerusalem).

This single verse, without duplication in Chronicles, is all that bears witness directly to Jehoaddin (Yehoaddin). She and the two queen mothers who follow are named as Jerusalemites; the two who follow them likely are as well, having strong ties to temple and monarchy. Perhaps the fear of foreign women, stoked to a fevered pitch by Athaliah's rule, resulted in successive "pure" Judean women being chosen as the mothers of the kings of Judah. Their selection raises questions about the families brokering daughters for royal power and grooming them to survive and perhaps connive. When Jehoaddin received the queen mother's throne, it may well have been empty. Athaliah was its last known occupant, and the fate of her daughter-in-law Zibiah was far from certain. In contrast, Jehoaddin's *giverah*-throne was passed down to Jecoliah.

JECOLIAH OF JERUSALEM

> 2 Kings 15:2 [Azariah ben Amaziah] was sixteen years old when he began to reign, and he reigned fifty-two years in Yerushalayim. His mother's name was Yecoliah (Jecoliah) of Yerushalayim (Jerusalem).

---

23. The circumstances of those marriages are questionable; the verb *n-s-'* indicates abduction marriages; see Judg. 21:20–23.

This verse and its duplicate in 2 Chronicles 26:3, in which the monarch is named Uzziah, are the only mentions of Jecoliah (Yecoliah). The office of queen mother endures, signified by the naming of the king's mother in his formal biography. The second Jerusalemite queen mother in a sequence of three, Jecoliah's reign points to a consolidation of power in Jerusalem. Marrying into the royal family provides a path to power without fomenting revolt. Her selection as a royal bride opened the door to that power. The enthronement of her son over other competitors would have elevated the status of her entire family.

JERUSHA BAT ZADOK

2 Kings 15:33 [Yotham (Jotham) ben Uzziah] was twenty-five years old when he began to reign and reigned sixteen years in Yerushalayim (Jerusalem). His mother's name was Yerusha (Jerusha) bat Zadok.

The spelling of Jerusha's name is not certain. Kings (above) ends it with an *aleph*, while 2 Chronicles 27:1 uses a *heh*. Her name is not nearly as important as her pedigree. Jerusha (Yerusha) is *bat kohen*, specifically a Zadokite. She is descended from that line of priests whose ancestor Zadok had the good sense to choose Solomon over Adonijah when David's throne was up for grabs (1 Kgs. 1:38–39). As a *kohenet*, the rabbinic term for woman with priestly lineage, Jerusha was also *bat Elisheva*, daughter/descendant of Elisheba, who married Aaron, the mother of all Israelite priests.[24] As a womanist, I like to call the names of women ancestors whenever possible.

Jerusha's family lineage also stretched back through Perez—whose name became synonymous with blessing in Ruth—to Tamar and Judah, through Elisheba's father Amminadab (Aminadav). Jerusha shared that exalted lineage with Boaz, his son born of Ruth, Obed, and their grandson, David. Jotham's marriage to a Zadokite *kohenet* was politically, religiously, and likely financially advantageous. Her choice indicates a tolerance, and perhaps preference, for a strong queen mother. The text does not list a daughter-in-law to succeed Jerusha as queen mother. The woman who gave birth to her grandson Ahaz, the next ruling monarch, is unknown.

24. I am using the anachronistic rabbinic term *kohenet* because Biblical Hebrew does not have a specific term to designate women in the priestly lineage that does not relate them to men, e.g., daughter or wife of a priest.

INTERREGNUM: A MISSING QUEEN MOTHER

Selah.[25]

ABI/ABIJAH BAT ZECHARIAH

2 Kings 18:2 [Hezekiah ben Ahaz] was twenty-five years old when he began to reign; he reigned twenty-nine years in Yerushalayim (Jerusalem). His mother's name was Avi (Abi) bat Zecharyah (Zechariah).

Abi (Avi), the daughter/descendant of Zechariah (Zecharyah), is Aviyah, Abijah in 2 Chronicles 29:1. Her notable ancestor Zechariah, most likely her father, is arguably the prominent and trustworthy Zechariah whom God commends in Isaiah 8:2. Her son Hezekiah would be remembered as one of the greatest monarchs in Israel or Judah. She passed her queen mother's throne down to her daughter-in-law, Hephzibah.

HEPHZIBAH

2 Kings 21:1 Manasseh was twelve years old when he began to reign; he reigned fifty-five years in Yerushalayim (Jerusalem). His mother's name was Hephzibah.

In contrast with her mother-in-law, from whom she inherited the queen mother's throne, Hephzibah gave birth to one of the most maligned monarchs in Israelite or Judean history, Manasseh. She appears only in 2 Kings 21:1. The *giverah*-throne passed down from her to her daughter-in-law Meshullemeth.

MESHULLEMETH BAT HARUZ OF JOTBAH

2 Kings 21:19 Amon was twenty-two years old when he began to reign; he reigned two years in Yerushalayim (Jerusalem). His mother's name was Meshullemeth bat Haruz of Jotbah.

Meshullemeth bat Haruz of Jotbah, the mother of Amon, appears only in 2 Kings 21:9. Her ancestor Haruz cannot be gendered and does not appear

25. The original meaning of this term is unknown. It seems to mark an interlude in the performance of a psalm, perhaps a musical interlude or dynamic shift in music such as the clap of symbols. Here it marks the silence of the interregnum.

anywhere else in the canon. Her hometown, Jotbah, is in the north, in the tribal lands of Zebulon, which may signal an attempt to strengthen ties between Judah and what remained of the fallen northern monarchy. There is a seal bearing the name of Meshullameth that cannot be dated with any certainty, so it can neither be identified as hers nor ruled out as hers.[26] However, she is the only person in the canon who bears her name.[27] Meshullameth passed her throne down to her daughter-in-law Jedidah (Yedidah).

JEDIDAH BAT ADAIAH

> 2 Kings 22:1 Yoshiyahu (Josiah) was eight years old when he began to reign; he reigned thirty-one years in Yerushalayim (Jerusalem). His mother's name was Yedidah (Jedidah) bat Adaiah of Bozkath.

Jedidah (Yedidah) is one of my favorite queen mothers; she was the daughter of the otherwise unknown Adaiah from Bozkath in Judah. Whether Adaiah is her mother or father is indeterminable from the citation, since some Israelites have maternal name formulae while others have paternal ones. Given that Josiah (Yoshiyahu) was only eight when he ascended the throne and no other regent is named, Jedidah no doubt served as his regent until he reached the age of majority.

It appears that she had the confidence and respect of the people—unlike her husband, who was murdered by his own subjects. By killing the king, the people essentially handed the reins of day-to-day governance over to Jedidah because of Josiah's minor status. That the people made no attempt on her life and trusted her to guide the child king speak volumes about the regard in which they held her. She and the prophet Huldah deserve the credit for raising the eight-year-old Josiah to be the man he becomes after his father's death. Josiah is one of the three most beloved kings in the biblical canon, and the great reformer of the first temple. While Jedidah would hand her throne down to her daughter-in-law Hamutal bat Jeremiah, its occupation after her

---

26. The seal has no title and does not bear her full name, daughter of Haruz. However, it is difficult to imagine that the queen mother's seal would need any information other than her name (Hennie J. Marsman, *Women in Ugarit and Israel: Their Social and Religious Position in the Context of the Ancient Near East* [Leiden: Brill, 2003], 658). The Jezebel seal does not further identify the monarch beyond her name.

27. Another Meshullameth is mentioned on a potsherd analyzed by Robert Deutsch and Michael Heltzer, *New Epigraphic Evidence from the Biblical Period* (Tel Aviv–Jaffa: Archaeological Center Publication, 1995), 86–88. This woman is identified as Meshullameth daughter of *'lkn*, a person, place, or other name that does not correspond to any in the Hebrew Bible.

would become as tenuous as that of the ruling monarch's throne. The Babylonians, with the help of Egypt, were slowly crushing the Judean monarchy to death.

HAMUTAL BAT JEREMIAH

2 Kings 23:31 Yehoahaz (Jehoahaz) was twenty-three years old when he began to reign; he reigned three months in Yerushalayim (Jerusalem). His mother's name was Hamutal bat Yirmeyahu (Jeremiah) of Libnah.

Hamutal bat Yirmeyahu (Jeremiah)[28] of Libnah in Judah served as queen mother twice; she gave birth to two future monarchs during the death throes of the Judean monarchy: Jehoahaz, born Shallum, and Zedekiah, born Mattaniah. After Pharaoh Neco killed Josiah in battle at Megiddo, the people placed Jehoahaz, Josiah's son with Hamutal, on the throne (2 Kgs. 23:31). The choice of Jehoahaz is interesting. He is the youngest of Josiah's four sons, according to 1 Chronicles 3:15, where he is called by his birth name, Shallum. As the youngest, he was unlikely to have ascended the throne on his own and may have been expected to be grateful and compliant. Three months into his reign, the pharaoh stages an elaborate display of submission. First he imposes a fine on him (2 Kgs. 23:33), the equivalent of renting his throne from Egypt, forcing him to travel as his vassal to demonstrate his fealty. When the humbled monarch complies, the pharaoh takes him hostage.

It is unlikely that the queen mother traveled with Jehoahaz to Riblah in Syria, so she likely escaped her son's fate. If she had gone with Jehoahaz, the narrative would have acknowledged her capture, as it would do for Queen Mother Nehushta when she was held by the Babylonians (2 Kgs. 24:12). I read then that Hamutal remained in Jerusalem. Inevitably the news would have reached her that a trouble-making and ill-named prophet, Jeremiah of Anathoth, was prophesying about her and her son. Here I have joined together two fragments of Jeremiah, 13:18[29] and 22:10–11, in a single utterance, since the text of Jeremiah is notoriously asynchronous:

> Say to the king and the queen mother;
> "Abase yourselves and sit-down-low,
> for your crown of glory has come down from your head."
> . . . .

28. Her father should not be confused with the prophet Jeremiah.
29. The identity of the queen mother here is not certain. This first passage may well refer to Nehusta.

Do not weep for the dead, and do not mourn him.
You should all weep—weep!—for the wayfarer,
for he shall never again return and see the land, the land of his birth.
For so says the HOLY ONE OF OLD concerning Shallum ben Yoshiahu,
    King of Yehudah,
the one who reigned in place of Yoshiahu (Josiah) his father, and who
    went out from this place:
He shall never again return there.
For in the place where they have exiled him, there shall he die,
and this land he shall never see again.

The news did not bode well. As Jeremiah prophesied, Jehoahaz never returned from his humiliating encounter with the pharaoh. Neco exiled him to Egypt and imprisoned him there until the day he died (2 Kgs. 23:34). Exercising his sovereignty over Judah, Neco selected as monarch in his stead another of Josiah's sons, by another woman: Jehoiakim, born Eliakim, of Zebidah (v. 36). By selecting a new king, the pharaoh selects a new queen mother (see the next section, "Zebidah bat Pedaiah"). Given that he did not kill the king, there is no reason to believe that the pharaoh killed Hamutal. It is possible that she lived in seclusion or even under house arrest while another woman and her son reigned. The successors to the thrones do not triumph with the deposing of Hamutal and her son. The days of the queen mother's throne being passed down from mother-in-law to daughter-in-law were seemingly over.

ZEBIDAH BAT PEDAIAH

2 Kings 23:36 Yehoiakim (Jehoiakim) was twenty-five years old when he began to reign; he reigned eleven years in Yerushalayim (Jerusalem). His mother's name was Zebidah bat Pedaiah of Rumah.

Zebidah (or Zebudah according to the scribal emendation) bat Pedaiah of Rumah becomes queen mother as a result of the Egyptian Pharaoh Neco's micromanaging his recently reacquired holdings in Canaan, the monarchy-in-name-only of Judah. Having deposed one monarch and his queen mother, he selects another, bypassing Josiah's firstborn son, who, it might be argued, had a right to the throne and would not feel beholden to him. Neco chooses Josiah's second son, Eliakim, and renames him Yehoiakim, Jehoiakim. That his mother is *not* the former queen mother may be a bonus; there would be no entrenched power that was not beholden to Egypt. The new queen mother was not a Judean like the last two queen mothers; she was from Zebulon in the north. She does not have a Jerusalem power base, another desirable characteristic. Jehoiakim successfully taxed Judah for the pharaoh (2 Kgs. 23:35).

Then he was essentially passed in servitude to Nebuchadnezzar of Babylon after Babylon's defeat of Egypt in 605 BCE (2 Kgs. 24:1). It is unlikely that Zebidah exercised any real authority during her son's reign, given Judah's vassalage to Egypt and then to Babylon. However, she may have picked or had a hand in picking his wife, Nehushta, the mother of her grandson, who would inherit his father's throne.

NEHUSHTA BAT ELNATHAN

> 2 Kings 24:8 Yehoiachin (Jehoiachin) was eighteen years old when he began to reign; he reigned three months in Yerushalayim (Jerusalem). His mother's name was Nehushta bat Elnathan of Yerushalayim. . . . ¹²King Yehoiachin of Yehudah surrendered to the king of Babylon himself and his mother, his servants, his military leaders, and his palace officials. . . . ¹⁵He deported Yehoiachin to Babylon; and the king's women and officers and the notables of the land were brought as exiles from Yerushalayim to Babylon.

Judah, the last remnant of Israel, with its tradition of queen mothers serving with their reigning sons, is no longer self-governing. The choice of Nehushta as a bride may represent an attempt to buttress the insecure throne with tethers to the noble families of Jerusalem. Nehushta's father, Elnathan, is likely Elnathan ben Achbor, who served her father-in-law King Josiah and her husband, Jehoiakim (2 Kgs. 22:11–20; Jer. 26:22; 36:12).

Nehusta and her son serve a scant three months before Nebuchadnezzar besieges Jerusalem. The Bible offers two chronologies of those last days. In the Kings chronology, Jehoiachin is eighteen when he ascends the throne, rules for three months, is besieged for an undisclosed period, and then surrenders (2 Kings 24:8–12). In his capitulation, Jehoiachin hands over the queen mother immediately after himself, then his servants, his soldiers, and his bureaucrats. In the Chronicles account, Jehoiachin is eight when he begins his reign, rules for three months and ten days, and is taken into Nebuchadnezzar's custody (2 Chr. 36:9). In both accounts the monarch is condemned for doing "evil in the sight of YHWH," a characterization tolerable for an eighteen-year-old but incomprehensible for an eight-year-old. Neither text specifies any action that merits this judgment; it just may be the conclusion drawn from the fall of Judah on his watch. If Jehoiachin were only a little boy during his brief reign, then Nehushta would have been the effective monarch. She may have had the support of her highly connected family, making it that much more important that she be handed over to Nebuchadnezzar.

Nehushta is never heard from again. Some time later, the prophet Jeremiah sends a letter to the elders of the exiles in Babylon; its introduction begins with the memory of the leaders of Judah and Jerusalem being taken into exile; her title is after the king's (Jer. 29:2).[30] Nebuchadnezzar returned to the storied lineage of Josiah to appoint the last king and queen mother of Judah: Mattaniah, the third of Josiah's four sons, and Nehushta, a seasoned queen mother. Nehushta and her predecessor (once removed) Hamutal, who is also her successor, are the last of the queen mothers. They are a sorrowful sisterhood of sisters-in-law and mothers of at least three of the sons of the great king Josiah (and grandmother of one of his grandsons) who fleetingly occupied the tottering Judean throne. In many ways, the fall of Jerusalem is written on the body of Nehusta: traded by her son in a futile attempt to save his own life, carried off into exile with all the other treasures of the nation, and later replaced by Hamutal's return as queen mother. Though she is not named, Nehusta is an ancestor of Jesus of Nazareth, whose genealogy passes through her womb with her son Jehoiachin, called Jeconiah in Matthew 1:11.

HAMUTAL, REDUX

Although Hamutal had lost her queen mother's throne to the imperial machinations of Egypt two queen mothers ago, Nebuchadnezzar's appointment of her son Mattaniah (whom he renamed Zedekiah) to the now largely ceremonial throne made her queen mother for the second time. In between her reigns, Zebidah bat Pedaiah passed the *gevirah*-throne to her daughter-in-law Nehusta bat Elnathan. Hamutal's ultimate fate is unclear. When Jerusalem fell, she may have come to a horrific end along with her son, or she may have been exiled to Babylon with the rest of the royal women in 2 Kings 24:15; that is my preferred reading.[31]

After an attempted rebellion (2 Kgs. 24:20), Zedekiah abandons Jerusalem by night and is captured by the Babylonians. Had Hamutal remained in Jerusalem with him, he would have abandoned her to Nebuchadnezzar along with everyone else, as he tried and failed to slink away in the night (2 Kgs. 25:5). Captured, Zedekiah is taken to Riblah in Syria, where Pharaoh Neco deposed his youngest brother Jehoahaz for his immediate older brother Jehoiakim. His sons—but not his daughters (see the next section, "The Last Princesses

---

30. Jeremiah consistently calls Jehoiachin "Jeconiah" (Jer. 24:1; 27:20; 28:4; 29:2) or "Coniah" (Jer. 22:24, 28; 37:1), never "Jehoiachin."

31. NB: The queen mother in that verse is Nehushta. Hammutal could have easily been among the king's "women," inclusive of "wives" and other assorted royal women.

of Judah")—were slaughtered in his sight. So the image of his sons' deaths would be his last sight; Nebuchadnezzar had Zedekiah blinded before imprisoning him for the rest of his life.[32] The text does not say whether Hamutal saw her grandsons butchered and her son blinded; it is not concerned with her experience of or feelings about the downfall of her nation or the deaths of her grandsons. If there was a physical queen mother's throne, Nebuchadnezzar may have carried it off with "all the treasures of the king's house" after the ravishment of Jerusalem's temple and palaces (2 Kgs. 24:13).

The province of Yehud, as the remnant of Judah would be known, would have a number of male leaders, some of whom would bear the title *pachat*, governor, among them Nehemiah, Gedaliah, and Zerubbabel. No women are named in the tradition of the queen mother associated with these men in the biblical text (Neh. 5:14; Jer. 40:5; Hag. 1:1). However, the archeological record suggests that there was at least one woman associated with the office of the governor who served in the administration of the province. Zerubbabel's apparent successor Elnathan was assisted by a woman named Shelomith, identified as the *amat*, woman-servant of the governor Elnathan, on her mid-sixth-century-BCE seal.[33] A second seal bearing just the name Shelomith has also been found.[34] Shelomith is identified in 2 Chronicles 3:19 as the daughter of Zerubbabel, which would make Elnathan her husband and *amat* an honorific, not an indication she was enslaved.

THE LAST QUEEN MOTHER: A REQUIEM

Ultimately, Hamutal's once-fruitful womb had been exhausted. There were no more monarchs to be birthed, raised, and enthroned from the line of David and Josiah. From his exile in Babylon, Ezekiel gave voice to a lamentation for the fallen princes of Judah (called Israel). It is also a lamentation for Hamutal, crediting her, rather than Nebuchadnezzar, with choosing Zedekiah as the last king of Israel in Ezekiel 19:

---

32. The text records Zedekiah's end in synoptic passion narratives in 2 Kgs. 25:1–21; Jer. 39:1–10; 52:1–27; and 2 Chr. 36:11–21.

33. Nahman Avigad, *Bullae and Seals From a Post-Exilic Judean Archive* (Jerusalem: Hebrew University Institute of Archaeology, 1976), 11–13.

34. See Eric Meyers's very helpful assessment of the Shelomith seal, "The Shelomith Seal and the Judean Restoration: Some Additional Considerations," in *Eretz-Israel: Archaeological, Historical, and Geographical Studies* (Jerusalem: Israel Exploration Society, in cooperation with the Hebrew Union College/Jewish Institute of Religion, 1985), 33–38.

[2]. . . What is your mother? A lioness among lions;
she lay down among young lions nurturing her cubs.
[3]She raised up one of her cubs, he became a young lion;
and he learned to prey on the prey; he devoured human beings. . . .
[5]When she saw that she was hindered, that her hope was lost,
she took another of her cubs and she made him a young lion. . . .
[10]Your mother was like a vine in your blood, transplanted by the waters,
she was fruitful and she was full of branches from abundant water. . . .
[14]Fire has gone out from her staff, has devoured her branches and fruit.
No longer is there a strong staff in her, a scepter for ruling.
This is a lamentation, and it is used as a lamentation.

LAST PRINCESSES OF JUDAH

Jeremiah 41:10 Then Yishmael (Ishmael) took captive all the remnant of the people who were in Mizpah: the daughters of the king and all the people who were left in Mizpah, whom Nebuzaradan, the officer of the guard, had committed to Gedaliah ben Ahikam. Yishmael (Ishmael) ben Nethaniah took them captive and set out to cross over to the Ammonites.

Jeremiah 43:5 Yochanan (Johanan) ben Kareah and all the commanders of the army took all the remnant of Yehudah (Judah) who had returned to settle in the land of Yehudah (Judah) from all the nations to which they had been driven: [6]the men, the women, the children, the daughters of the king, and every soul whom Nebuzaradan the captain of the guard had left with Gedaliah ben Ahikam ben Shaphan, including the prophet Jeremiah and Baruch ben Neriah. [7]So they came into the land of Egypt, for they did not obey the voice of the HOLY ONE; they arrived at Tahpanhes.

It appears the last king of Judah, Zedekiah ben Hamutal, Josiah's son, has an unknown number of daughters whom the text does not name. It is also possible they include the daughters of one or more of the last kings of Judah. It is not clear whether the princesses are adults, children, or a mixture of both. Jeremiah 41:16 identifies a group of women and children along with eunuchs, the traditional attendants for royal families. If they are Zedekiah's daughters, then some or all may be the granddaughters of Hamutal bat Jeremiah, the last queen mother of Judah, and they watch their home, city, and temple be sacked and demolished by the Babylonians. They escape the fate of their brothers, who are butchered before the eyes of their deposed father shortly before his blinding in 2 Kings 25:7 (repeated in Jer. 39:6 and 52:10). They are surely traumatized by the sights, sounds, and smells of pitched battle in and around their home. They would have been understandably terrified of what the Babylonians might have in store for them.

Their father was afraid, but more so of his own people than of the Babylonians. In Jeremiah 38:19 Zedekiah confided in the prophet, "I am afraid of the Judeans who have deserted to the Chaldeans, for I might be handed over to them and they would abuse me."[35] Zedekiah's fear of his own people was prescient, and like him, the princesses also had every reason to fear. Jeremiah had prophesied the fate of Zedekiah and his family. He promised Zedekiah that he would survive his encounter with the Babylonians (and the collaborators among his people) and that "it would go well with him" (Jer. 38:20) if he surrendered, but Zedekiah did not. The Babylonians captured but did not kill the fleeing Zedekiah; they gouged his eyes out, which may not have counted as the abuse he feared. Jeremiah 52:11 claims Zedekiah was housed and fed until the day of his death. Jeremiah also prophesied that all of the royal women would fall into the hands of the Babylonians (38:22–23). The prophecy was an elaborate performance in which Jeremiah gave voice to a taunting song of lament that he prophesied Zedekiah's women folk would sing to him. If the princesses were aware of the prophecy, that would have added terror to the uncertainty surrounding their fate.

The royal daughters were left behind to a precarious, unpredictable future with some members of the royal household, while the rest of the dignitaries are deported. Nebuchadnezzar entrusted them to one of his officials, who placed them in the custody of Gedaliah, whom he had appointed to administer Judah (now the Babylonian province of Yehud). The princesses left their decimated homes in Jerusalem for Mizpah, which functioned as the new administrative capital (2 Kgs. 25:22; Jer. 40:7–8), with the larger group of captives. The journey from Jerusalem to Mizpah is only a few miles, but it landed them in an alternate reality, one in which they were prisoners. They were also still princesses of the house of David; in their wombs lay the hope and promise of the future monarchy. Jerusalem fell in the fifth month, Av (Ab); the story does not return to the royal daughters until the seventh month, Tishri.[36]

After two months (if not some years and two months), when their relative Ishmael ben Nethaniah ("of royal seed" in 2 Kgs. 25:25) came thundering up on horseback with his troops, they may have thought they were being rescued in Jeremiah 40:1. It is not difficult to imagine them waiting with bated breath while he dined and negotiated with the collaborator Gedaliah, who governed

---

35. The abuse Zedekiah fears is *hit'allelu-bi*. While in some passages the abuse represented by '-*l-l* is limited to mocking (Exod. 10:2; Num. 22:29; 1 Sam. 6:6; 31:4; 1 Chr. 10:4), in Judges 19:25 it describes the savage gang rape of the Levite's low-status wife.

36. John Berridge suggests in his *AYBD* entry (3:881) on Jochanon that the assassination could have happened one or more years later in the seventh month. This would mean that the assassination was timed or triggered by the anniversary of the fall of Jerusalem and that the princesses had some kind of stability while in Gedaliah's care, which was unexpectedly yanked away from them.

but did not rule while their father was imprisoned in Babylon. Then their cousin killed the man who dared try and replace God's anointed, their father, at the table (Jer. 40:2). The tension was palpable. After the assassination he began killing Judeans, likely those who supported Gedaliah (v. 3). But he did not rescue the princesses. Suddenly, it's the next day in the story; their captors were dead, but the princesses did not appear to be free. Even if they were free to travel, they had nowhere to go. A group of pilgrims appeared on their way to Mizpah to worship, and Ishmael, taking off after them, left the princesses behind. They are once again surrounded by the dead and the dying, their fate and future no more certain than at the momemt of their (first) abduction. Ishmael killed seventy of the eighty pilgrims, sparing those who had enough valuables to buy their lives (vv. 7–8). These despicable deeds reveal Ismael's character to the princesses and confirm it to the reader. After dumping the bodies of the pilgrims in a cistern, Ishmael returned to Mizpah, where the princesses had surely spent a sleepless night. What would he do with them, to them?

The text portrays Ishmael as their captor (Jer. 41:10), not their liberator. He put them on the road again for approximately forty miles, intending to hand them over to the Ammonites. Suddenly, the princesses found themselves in the midst of another pitched battle. In Jeremiah 41:11, a little-known Judean military officer, Johanan (Yochanan) ben Kareah, and his troops attacked Ishmael. Verse 13 says "all the people" held hostage by him began to cheer the assault, which would include the princesses. The former captives liberated themselves, running to Johanan and his troops only to be briefly abandoned again as the two forces clashed. Rescued again but still not free, the princesses found themselves in the custody of Johanan.

The royal women have been passed from hand to hand, from man to man, as the ultimate patriarchal props. They have been passed from their father's household to their conqueror's grasp and that of his designees, taken from them, and then taken again. The men who have held their lives in their hands include King Zedekiah of Judah, Nebuchadnezzar, his chief military officer Nabuzaradan, Gedaliah (a high-level Judean bureaucrat turned collaborator), Ishmael (their royal relative turned bandit), and a warrior whose loyalties shifted from their father to the collaborator who governed briefly in his stead. They—their bodies and specifically their wombs—were valuble commodities. Within them lay the promise or threat of the continued line of Josiah and David, a puppet for Nebuchadnezzar to control, a royal figurehead who could spark rebellion under the control of Judean nationalists. In either case, the monarch would be produced by impregnating a royal woman; her consent would not be required. A single pregnancy would not be sufficient given the high rates of child and maternal mortality. Every potentially fertile royal woman was potentially subject to rape (though Nebuchadnezzar may have preferred to keep them from conceiving). As a royal descendant himself, Ishmael's offspring with them would have that powerful Davidic heritage on both sides. The women could not be sure of the motives of any of their so-called rescuers.

Johanan put the princesses and their traveling court, including the survivors of the Mitzpah massacre, on the road to Tahpanes in Egypt, more than two hundred miles away (Jer. 43:5–7), picking up the prophet Jeremiah and his scribe Baruch against his will along the way. The account judges their rescuer harshly for taking them to Egypt, for Jeremiah had previously declared (42:7–17) that God's will for him and any surviving remnant was to stay in Judah and by no means to go to Egypt. Indeed after asking Jeremiah to ask God what they should do, the people, presumably including Johanon and the princesses, told him he was lying when he said God said, "Do not go back to Egypt." When Johanon took them all to Egypt, it is not clear if anyone other than Jeremiah objected or resisted.

The rescue and relocation of the last Judean princesses to Egypt contradicts Jeremiah's prophecy that all of the royal women would go into exile in Babylon (Jer. 38:22–23). Jeremiah's reluctant presence may have been little or no comfort to the royal daughters. They were on their own to make a home in the land that once had enslaved their ancestors and may have well been or thought themselves to have been enslaved. It cannot be known whether the royal women were liberated and repatriated with the rest of their people or were held in bondage. What is known is that the Judean footprint in Egypt grew into thriving colonies including in Alexandria and Elephantine; the former produced one of the great canons of Israelite Scripture, the Septuagint (LXX).

In Jeremiah 44:17, the Judeans in the Egyptian diaspora have moved from Tahpanes on the edge of the Sinai Penninsula south to Pathros. There they reject Jeremiah and his preaching, choosing to worship the Queen of Heaven, whose neglect they are certain resulted in the fall of Jerusalem and their present circumstances. The repeated mention of women and men (Jer. 44:15, 19–20) and royals (vv. 17, 21) may indicate the royal women were part of that community. If so, they show the only agency afforded to them in their narrative in choosing to worship on their own terms. For the editors of the biblical canon, their worship was idolatrous. The Queen of Heaven cannot be identified with certainty but is generally associated with Asherah, Anat, or Astarte. However, Teresa Ellis makes a compelling argument that the title generally translated as "Queen of Heaven" can be understood as "Sovereign of Heaven" and represents the women naming YHWH in feminine terms as do many contemporary womanists and feminists.[37] If so, they offer a powerful interpretation of the fall of Jerusalem, laying its destruction at the feet of patriarchal religion. They are never heard from again, and there are no descendants credited to them.

QUEENS TO THE END

Each royal woman of Israel and Judah has her own story and her own voice, compressed into the annals of the largely male-dominated monarchy. Each find herself in an extraordinary marriage, virtually destined to be accompanied by power and conflict on an international scale, and destined to end in widowhood, often violently. Many of these women are outsiders to the families into which they married, either from foreign lands or from the northern monarchy sent to the southern one. For those in the south, widowhood becomes the gateway to power: a Judean queen mother is by definition a widow and a single mother. The outsider and minority status of many of the queens and their eventual single motherhood invite womanist reflection. However, neither they nor those who look to them can be limited to that single circumstance.

There are many models among them: There are women who would do anything to anyone to wield power, including women who sacrifice and abandon their own children to get ahead. There are women who kill, including their own children. There are women who risk everything to protect the vulnerable among them. There are women who play politics, following the rules of the men who have excluded them, and there are women who beat the boys at their game. There are women who brush up against a pink glass ceiling and those who are not held back by it. There are stateswomen with international ambitions and women who use their bodies to get ahead. There are women who chose wifedom and motherhood as sole or primary vocation, women whose whole lives are dedicated to the lives of their children. In the north they are largely ornamental; in the south they are potential powerbrokers. They are also, in the narrative at least, women who mother sons while their daughters are rendered inconsequential and invisible. Although there are very few contemporary corollaries to their power and status, they are a reminder that biblical women, like other marginalized people, are not always at the bottom of every hierarchy.

37. Teresa Ann Ellis, "Jeremiah 44: What If 'The Queen of Heaven' Is YHWH?" *Journal for the Study of the Old Testament* 33, no. 4 (June 2009): 466–67.

The recording of so many royal women's names in the Scriptures is extraordinary. The small pieces of biographical information about them are all the more tantalizing because there is so very little we know about the day-to-day lives of the royal women. My sanctified imagination conjures a royal women's house in Jerusalem with separate quarters for the queen mother or mother of the crown prince. If the king has a favorite wife who is not the queen mother or mother of the crown prince, she may have her own quarters as well.[38] More than biological receptacles, pleasure givers, and incubators, these women are potential partners in statecraft: elder royal women who have watched kings birthed and buried for two or more generations, aging but still fertile women of the most recent monarch, looking for a place in the bed and affection of the newly anointed king, his own women carefully selected by advisors and chief among them, the queen mother, all living together. What wisdom did those older women, no longer seeking the queen mother's throne, pass down to those still in contention? What conflict and competition flourished and endured? I don't imagine a utopian womanist commune, but I do see a space for women to live their lives largely unseen and unrecorded, to craft, recite, and perhaps write their own stories that are now lost to us.

Monarchy returned to Israel with Hasmoneans, descended from the Maccabees. The last monarch of their line before the domination of Rome was Queen Salome Alexander. There is no straight line or genealogy between the queen mothers and Salome Alexander, but I believe their spirit was passed to her.

---

38. See 1 Kgs. 7:8, where Solomon builds a palace for the pharaoh's daughter he married.

Appendixes

Appendix A

David's Offspring

The birth order for David's first six sons is dually recorded in 2 Samuel 3:2–5; 5:13–16; and 1 Chronicles 3:1–4. Chronicles continues the list of presumably male offspring[1] in sequence:

David's Children	Mother	Fate
1– Amnon	Ahinoam	Killed by brother, Absalom, for raping sister, Tamar
2– Chileab/Daniel	Abigail	Unknown
3– Absalom	Maacah, Princess of Geshur	Killed by cousin, Joab
4– Adonijah	Haggith	Killed on Solomon's order
5– Shephatiah	Abital	Unknown
6– Ithream	Eglah	Unknown
7– Shimea	Bathsheba	Unknown
8– Shobab	Bathsheba	Unknown
9–Nathan	Bathsheba	Unknown

1. Some have names with feminine forms, a reminder that it is impossible to gender persons by name in Hebrew.

(continued)

David's Children	Mother	Fate
10-Solomon	Bathsheba	Succeeded to the throne
11- Ibhar	Unknown	Unknown
12- Elishama	Unknown	Unknown
13- Eliphelet	Unknown	Unknown
14- Nogah	Unknown	Unknown
15- Nepheg	Unknown	Unknown
16- Japhia	Unknown	Unknown
17- Elishama	Unknown	Unknown
18- Eliada	Unknown	Unknown
19- Eliphelet	Unknown	Unknown

Unknown Birth Order

*Tamar	Maacah, Princess of Geshur	Unknown
*Unknown number of daughters and sons	Primary and secondary wives	Unknown

Appendix B

A Note on Translating

Translation matters. Translation is the only means non-Hebrew readers have to access the Scriptures of Israel in their own tongues. Yet the act of translation and principles that govern an individual translation are frequently invisible to many readers, save for expressed preferences for one translation of the Bible over another. Even then, the preference is often based on nonscholarly criteria: what the text sounds like, how familiar it is, how it corresponds to cherished previously held beliefs about what the text ought to say, or even a belief that only one translation of the Bible is authoritative.[1]

POIESIS: THE ART AND SCIENCE OF TRANSLATION

Original biblical translation is a regularly occurring feature of biblical scholarship, but it frequently appears without any reflection (even when it appears with voluminous footnotes). Because translation is perhaps the first layer of biblical interpretation—though a similar argument could be made for text selection—frequently consumed without notice by the reader, I find it important to reflect on how and why I translate the way I do. My definition of translation is "art and science, the product of rendering words from one language

---

1. I have previously addressed these issues in my essay "Hearing the Word, Translation Matters: A Fem/Womanist Exploration of Translation Theory and Practice for Proclamation in Worship," in J. Harold Ellens, ed., *Text and Community: Essays in Memory of Bruce M. Metzger*, vol. 1 (Sheffield: Sheffield Phoenix Press, 2007).

into another." The choice of the word "rendering" in the definition is almost arbitrary. Indeed, how does one translate "translation"?

Let me instead offer some synonyms that fit the above definition: *render* (comes most immediately to my mind, but what does it really mean?), *construe, convert, decipher, decode, elucidate, explicate, put, reword, simplify, spell out, transcribe, transliterate, transpose,* or *turn.* I could also say *alter, change, explain, gloss, interpret, metamorphose, transfigure, transform, transmogrify,* or *transmute.* Both sets of options demonstrate the flexibility of the notion and process of translation. While it is possible and even tempting to delve into a semiotic discussion here—what does any word mean? how does it mean what it means? and to whom does it mean what?—this book is not a semiotic primer. This is a book on interpreting Scripture through a womanist midrashic lens, including my practice and praxis of translating Scripture.

The relationship between translation and interpretation is fraught, particularly when dealing with religious texts. As a contemporary scholar of biblical literature, I have been shaped by the Western scholarly academy, which often differentiates translation from interpretation, coding translation as simultaneously neutral, in that it does not change the meaning of the text, and (therefore) good, because it preserves the meaning of the text, unchanged, perhaps leading to authorial intent. The Western biblical scholarly enterprise has also often coded interpretation as negative, unduly shaped by the interpreter, clouding the original meaning of the text with contemporary concerns. It is as though translation is or should be a word-for-word process comparable to a mathematic equation, in which interpretation is the variable in the very different ways that people hear, read, and understand the Scriptures. The translation/interpretation binary presumes that texts have meaning apart from their readers and that it is possible to read without constructing meaning and that the reader has no impact on the text she is reading. Rather, I hold that interpretation and translation are not polar opposites but two sides of the same coin.

Translation and interpretation are closely interwoven in ancient as well as contemporary engagements with sacred and secular texts. Translation and interpretation are linked in one of the ancient scripture collections of Jewish tradition and history, the Targum, the rendering of the Hebrew Scriptures into Aramaic, in which translation and interpretation occur simultaneously. The Targum (Targumim, plural) is both a translation of the Hebrew Scriptures and interpretive commentary on them. The word "Targum" means "translate," as it is used in Ezra 4:7. This is the case for both Testaments; see Matthew 1:23 and Acts 13:8 in the Peshitta, Aramaic Scriptures of both Testaments (without the targumic interpretive material). Both passages use *mettargam* to account for translation. The Aramaic Scriptures use the noun form, *metaturgemin*, for translator-interpreters and prophets, whom they understand as translating/interpreting God's words, not simply repeating divine discourse, for example, Deuteronomy 27:8 in *Targum Neofiti*: "You shall write on the stones all the words of this Torah, written, inscribed, and explained well, so as to be read and translated into seventy languages."[2] Interpretation is a separate word, *p-r-sh*, in the Targums of Deuteronomy 27:8 and in the Water Gate scene of Nehemiah 8:1–8, in which the Torah is also read (in Hebrew), translated into Aramaic (in v. 7 the Levites "help the people understand"), and discoursed upon further (v. 8, "read with interpretation" and "gave the sense").

This notion of the translator-prophet who interprets the Divine resonates with my experience and understanding of teaching and preaching the Scriptures in black churches. Simply reading the biblical text—often presumed to be the literal word of God or even inerrant—is insufficient. The preacher must translate and interpret the word of God into words fit for the congregation. There is often little to no emphasis on translation from Hebrew to English (with the exception of the claim in some cases of sole authority for the King James Version of the Bible as the only appropriate translation). Even so, the preacher—often identified as functioning in a prophetic capacity—performs a role similar to that of a *metaturgemin*, as an interpreter and translator of the Divine.

In my practice, translation is the result of this mysterious and nearly indefinable process, which is both art and science. The science is linguistic: lexical, philological, taxonomic, syntactical, grammatical, euphemistic, and, more than occasionally, idiosyncratic. The art is what I and each translator bring to each project from our selves: subject-matter knowledge and culture—race/ethnicity, gender and its performance, religious and/or ideological identity and commitments, appreciation for and facility with language, and internal sense that something is or just sounds right, and perhaps unnamed and unknown personality traits.

I describe translation as an act of *poiesis*, using the word in its original Greek and contemporary biomedical senses to name the process as I understand and perform it. Most simply, poiesis is "creation," from the Greek verb *poiein*, "to make," originally the creation of poetry, subsequently the creation of cellular elements in the human body such as hematopoiesis, the creation of blood cells. The former represents the understanding that each translation is an act of creation, and the latter demonstrates that the new creation is not ex nihilo—the translator is not inventing a new text out of nothingness—but, rather, the translation is made of the elements of texts: communication,

2. Cf. Targumim *Onqelos* and *Pseudo-Jonathan*.

language, and ideas, just as blood cells are made of the elements of the body. "Texts" is plural here because the literary texts are part of a larger textual world, including the translator and all of her constituent elements. The translator is also a text.

WHO TRANSLATES GOD'S WORDS AND HOW?

Frequently overlooked in discussions around translation is the question of *who* translates. Men are still overwhelmingly responsible for major versions of the Bible used in congregations and classrooms, even when women are invited (note the passive) to participate: The inclusion on the New Revised Standard Version of the Bible translating committee of Phyllis A. Bird, J. Cheryl Exum, and Katharine D. Sakenfeld in the Hebrew Bible and Lucetta Mowry in the Christian Testament is significant. The NRSV project began in 1974 and continued until 1988; it was not until the 1980s that women were invited to participate (in part because there were so few women with PhDs in biblical studies who could have done the work).

The category of race in biblical translation is complicated (perhaps to the point of uselessness as a category), given the complexity of Jewish identity, which while collapsed into "white" in the popular imagination, nevertheless includes persons of African, Asian, and Latinx heritage. It bears repeating that the ancient Israelites were an Afro-Asiatic people. The question of identity and ethnicity in Judaism grows more nuanced when one includes converts and adoptees. In the Gentile world, Bible translators have been overwhelmingly white, as is our guild. This means that until very recently, the Bibles that hold authority in my religious and academic worlds were produced by scholars who do not look like me, do not share my culture, and are part of a culture that has been openly hostile to the scholastic capacity, literary achievements, and even moral agency of my people.

As a result of the demographics of the guild, the voice of authority in biblical translation has most often been a white (Gentile) male voice, particularly in Christian contexts where Jewish interpretation of the Hebrew Bible has not been regarded as authoritative. However, things are changing; the 2011 Common English Bible included a number of scholars of color among its translators, including Efrain Agosto, Emerson Powery, Abraham Smith, Thomas Slater, Hugh Page, and two women of color that I have been able to identify, Seung Ai Yang and Eunny Lee (though there are some twenty women among the fifty-plus translators).

In light of the exclusion of women of African descent from the ranks of Bible translators, an important aspect of this present work, which distinguishes it from other womanist and feminist treatments, is its attention to translating the words of Scripture themselves. Translation is one of the primary modes of biblical scholarship in which I engage and is the basis of my exegetical and midrashic work. I do this work as a womanist and feminist, as a black woman who treasures the literacy denied to so many of my ancestors. I am also keenly aware that I am translating a text that has been used to dehumanize, enslave, and subjugate my people, including me to some degree contemporarily, and to pathologize my gender and ethnicity.

I engage in a number of translation practices to make Hebrew linguistic issues accessible to readers who do not know Biblical Hebrew. I introduce the reader to issues in translation, including but not limited to grammatical gender, biological gender, gendered nonbiological characters, and the literary genders of God in the First Testament. (However, it is not always possible to identify a character's gender.) I have previously proposed a number of translation principles that I have modified for this project:[3]

1. I begin with the dominant Hebrew manuscript, the Masoretic Text (MT), in conversation with the Samaritan Pentateuch, texts from the Dead Sea Scrolls, the Targumim (Aramaic texts including interpretive material), Septuagint, and Peshitta. The sacred stories originated as plural oral narratives and were preserved in a variety of written forms; all of these manuscripts bear witness to the Scriptures as a diverse tradition. Starting with the MT acknowledges its preeminent place in biblical transmission.

2. I assign meanings based on lexical values, not on religious or contemporary cultural traditions, even when it results in a theologically undesirable or untenable outcome. This is critically important when socially constructed gender roles are applied to the Scriptures and subsequent religious claims about gender roles are made asserting biblical and divine support. For example, I read the common plural as an inclusive plural, addressing and including the women of Israel; so the biblical command to wear *tzit-tzit* (fringe at garment corners) applies to the women as well as men, contrary to later practice and interpretation.

3. I try to reproduce the oral quality of the Scriptures. I translate with hearers in mind, rather than (just for) readers, to preserve the original context of the sacred stories that became Scripture. My favorite example of this is the difference between "Peter the flute-player collects salad vegetables preserved in vinegar'" and "Peter Piper picked a peck of pickled peppers." I do my best to preserve puns and wordplay, assonance and alliteration, as in the prayer for the healing of the prophet Miriam in Numbers 12:13: *El na rapha na lah*. To evoke the "-ah" sound and suffix I offer, "Holy One, hear and heal her."

3. Gafney, "Hearing the Word," 57–63.

(Cf. NRSV, JPS, KJV, and Fox. I have found no translation that attempts to preserve the sound here.)

4. I translate the Divine Name reverently and contextually. I avoid "The Lord" because it is *not* the Divine Name. (In addition, the title "lord" is a human patriarchal and hierarchal one that imports these notions shared with human men into a construction of God. This is most evident in cultures where the title is still in use for men, e.g., "Lord Bishop.") "Lord" is the most common choice for rendering the sacred Four Letters (*Tetragrammaton*) YHWH in English because of rabbinic practice. These letters form an unpronounceable name, marked with the vowels from other words (usually *adonai*, occasionally *elohim*). The secondary word is what is read aloud (*qere*) versus what is written (*ketiv*), so that "Lord," *adonai*, is most often read aloud, resulting in its near-perpetual substitution for and identification with the Divine Name. Confusion about this practice led a number of medieval commentators to fuse the sacred letters with the secondary vowels, producing an entirely new form, "Jehovah," which even God had never heard before the Middle Ages. Twelfth-century forms appear to be the earliest, lacking the "J" and "v" owing to their lack in Latin and subsequently in English. Eventually later editions of the Tyndale and King James Bibles would use the form.

By translating the names reverently I mean that I do not insert vowels, and by translating contextually I mean that I use expressions conveying divinity and majesty to render the Divine Name that fit well within the context of the passage. I use large-and-small capital letters to indicate the Tetragrammaton, as do many contemporary translations. Among my most common choices are THE HOLY ONE OF OLD, FIRE OF SINAI, and GOD-WHOSE-NAME-IS-TOO-HOLY-TO-BE-PRONOUNCED. My primary inspirations in this practice are Joel Rosenberg's translations in *Kol Haneshamah*,[4] the *siddur* (prayerbook) of the Reconstructionist movement in Judaism, and the editorial options provided for reading the Divine Name in the German Bible, *Bibel in gerechter Sprache* (*BigS*).[5]

---

4. David A. Teutsch and Betsy Platkin Teutsch, *Kol Haneshamah: Shabbat Vehagim*, 3rd ed. (Wyncote, PA: Reconstructionist Press, 2001). Rosenberg's choices for the Most Holy Name include The Source of Being, The Incomparable, The Ineffable, The One, The Mysterious, The Eternal, Fountain of Light, and many more.

5. Ulrike Bail, *Bibel in gerechter Sprache Taschenausgabe*, 4th ed. (Gütersloh: Gütersloher Verl.-Haus, 2011). The translators choose from a variety of options printed in grey in the body of the text, with a panoply of other options (also in grey) in the headers of the text for the reader to choose among, including a number of (German) transliterations of Hebrew: *Adonaj* (Lord), *HaSchem* (the Name), *Ha Makom* (the Place), pronouns—I/You/She/He, *Shekhinah* (the Divine Presence, feminine), God, I AM, and, in masculine and feminine forms, the One, the Living One, the Holy One, the Eternal One.

5. I use gender-specific language, for example, "She, the Spirit," rather than the gender-inclusive or neutral "the Spirit." I have determined from my work pastoring, preaching, and presiding in (Christian) congregations and teaching in college, university, seminary, and divinity school classrooms that people tend to hear neutral or inclusive language through a masculine cultural filter, so that they hear "the Spirit" as "He," just as they hear "God" as "He," no matter what I write or say, unless I specify "She." More than that, I believe that the refusal of translators to use explicit feminine grammar in English to translate explicitly feminine grammar in the Scriptures contributes to an intentional construction of the Scriptures of Israel that is even more androcentric than they are in actuality. This is more of an issue in Christian contexts but less so in Jewish contexts, in which congregants have some degree of Hebrew literacy (not universally the case). The Scriptures are certainly androcentric; yet they also contain woman-centered texts, explicitly feminine God-language, and inclusive passages that all too often are lost or intentionally obscured in translation.

6. Using explicitly feminine language in translation, I identify women and girls hidden in the plural forms of Biblical Hebrew. In fact, unless there is information in the text limiting the makeup of a group to male members, I translate that group inclusively, for example, "the daughters and sons of Israel," "the whole community, women, men, children, and the aged." Because so many readers/hearers of the biblical texts hear and read neutral/inclusive language as exclusive, many find it hard (if not impossible) to see and hear women and girls in the text unless they are explicitly mentioned. It is, then, critically important for womanists and feminists to name women and their presence in the biblical text so that they cannot be readily overlooked by readers, hearers, and interpreters of the text—particularly religious readers, hearers, and interpreters seeking a scriptural Word for themselves and/or their community. In addition to identifying female characters in the text indicated by feminine grammatical forms, I will use gender-specific inclusive translations in places where female characters have previously been lost in translation.

For example, Exodus 1:8 reads in part, "The offspring of Israel are more numerous and more powerful than we." My translation would read, "The offspring of Israel, *women and men, boys and girls*, are more numerous and more powerful than we." To make it plain, the Israelites, *beney yisrael*, "children of Israel" or in older translation "sons of Israel," are not limited to male offspring; the daughters of Israel did not stay behind in Egypt while the sons of Israel left for the promised land. A similar issue exists in New Testament scholarship for the translation of *adelphoi*, "brothers," "brothers-and-sisters," "siblings," "close relatives or kinsfolk"; some translations use "believers." I will not always indicate where I have added clarifying language as in the previous examples, since it is my contention that these characters are present in the original text; I am just rendering them audible and visible in translation. I am also influenced here by the Targumim, in which original language and clarifying language are presented together as *Scripture*.

7. I transliterate (provide phonetic pronunciations of) the names of biblical characters directly from Hebrew, in addition to using the regularly European-derived names that are more familiar to most (Christian) readers, when there are significant differences between the Hebrew names and their English corollaries. That is because the names of Hebrew biblical characters are not the same as the names that appear in most English Bibles. Those Anglicized names are not Hebrew—neither direct translations nor transliterations. The names of the three major prophets begin with the letter *yud, y*: Yeshayahu, Yirmayahu. and Yechezqe'l. Yet in English, speakers and readers known them as Isaiah, Jeremiah, and Ezekiel as a result of Hebrew mediated through Latin, German, and Greek respectively. The familiar Solomon is closer to the Arabic *Suleiman* than the Hebrew *Shlomo*, owing to Greek variants. This is more of an issue in the Christian Testament, in which names are often stripped of Jewish identity, and is all the more obvious and problematic in a Bible with both Testaments: *Ya'aqov* becomes "Jacob" in the Hebrew Bible but is known as "James" in the Christian Testament—except for references to the former Testament, creating an illusion that the one name is two very different names. (Hebrew names involving the letter *qaf* are traditionally rendered with a *k* or even a hard *c*, instead of its phonetic equivalent *q*. As a rule I retain the *q* for consistency.)

Even though the transliterated names may be unfamiliar and difficult to read and pronounce, I find it important as a womanist to preserve, respect, and honor the cultural integrity of the Israelite Scriptures by preserving, respecting, and honoring the names of biblical characters as they are recorded in the text. Naming and name-calling—calling someone by her or his name—have a particular significance for womanists and other readers in the African diaspora, especially in contexts in which an enslaving and/or colonizing culture has imposed its names on people and places in place of the names given within a community for its people and places.

In the American slaveholding context, enslaved Africans and their descendants were renamed by their captors and those who purchased, held, and bred them. Retention of African names was normally forbidden and punishable through tortuous, if not fatal, means. The English names imposed were also humble and humbling names, frequently shared with dogs. In (so-called) Christian contexts, some clergy refused to baptize or christen children of African descent with some names if they, the white clergy, did not find them to be suitable for children of color (meaning too dignified). This practice continues into modernity in some allegedly postcolonial spaces in which African and Asian Christians are given formally or informally biblical—but usually Anglicanized—or English names in place of their own cultural and communal names.

Using the less familiar form of the name serves another purpose as well. It reminds the contemporary non-Jewish reader that we are at a great distance—geographically and temporally—from the original context of these Scriptures; we need to be wary of interpreting as though they were composed in our immediate context or their messages directed toward us.

GENDER ISSUES IN BIBLICAL HEBREW

Gender matters. Gender matters in the text, in the world, in the world of the text, and in the world of the translator. Gender matters to me and to countless numbers of women hearers and readers of the biblical text for whom it is *Scripture*. Gender matters significantly to those who have been and are marginalized because of gender, especially when it is done in the name of God, appealing to the Scriptures. And gender matters to men. Gender matters to hearers and readers of the Scriptures who are privileged to share the gender of the dominant portrayal of God, the majority of biblical characters, the majority of biblical characters who have speaking parts, the majority of translators of biblical texts, and the majority of interpreters of biblical texts.

Because Biblical Hebrew is a gendered language, translation of the Scriptures has feminist and womanist (and masculinist and androcentric) implications. This linguistic gendering means that every noun and adjective and the overwhelming majority of verb forms in Biblical Hebrew are either feminine or masculine. There are also common forms that include both genders; older grammatical references identify some of these as "masculine plural," leading to generations of gender-based translation distortion. It is quite common that groups of people are regularly described with a (common) plural form used for both all-male groups and mixed-gender groups. In addition, there is no neuter gender in Hebrew, as there is in Greek and in English.

GRAMMATICAL AND BIOLOGICAL GENDER

The relationship between grammatical gender and biological gender for human beings and animals is relatively straightforward. Feminine forms correspond with female humans and animals almost without exception, and masculine forms normally correspond with male humans and animals. There are exceptions. In Ruth 2:8, Naomi addresses her daughters-in-law twice with a masculine or common plural, rather than the available feminine plural: "May the HOLY ONE act with loving-kindness *imakhem*, 'toward you guys,' just as *'asitem*, 'you two guys have done,' toward the dead (men) and to me." In the Great Isaiah scroll from Qumran, the text uses the masculine singular form of *prophet*, *navi'*, for the female prophet with whom Isaiah fathers a child in 8:3, where the MT uses the feminine form, *neviah*.

Even though there is a high degree of correlation between grammatical and biological gender, it is simply impossible to know the gender of characters in the biblical text without a relational noun, for example, "daughter" or "son of," or a verb connected to that subject (since singular verb forms clearly reveal gender). This means that names in genealogies often cannot be gendered with any certainty, particularly in a string of unmodified names. Even so, there are some traditionally masculine proper names and traditionally feminine proper names. English readers may use a tool like a concordance or Bible dictionary, which identifies (or assigns) gender, but should be aware that some characters simply cannot be identified in terms of gender because there is not enough grammatical information present. Unfortunately many biblical resources designed for lay use, presuming and constructing an androcentric text, simply gender everyone in a genealogy male unless a feminine marker is present.

Adding to this complexity, some boys and men are given names with feminine grammatical forms, for example, Jonah, Micah, and Judah. The *–ah* suffix is the primary feminine ending for nouns and some other forms, for adjectives, and for some verb forms, and it occurs in names like Deborah, Rebekah, Leah, Hannah, Dinah, and Zipporah. Masculine, singular common and proper nouns are random collections of letters: David, Nathan, Samuel, Moses. Some names are given to both genders, like Shelomith (women in Lev. 24:11 and 1 Chr. 3:19; men in 1 Chr. 23:18 and Ezra 8:10, plus a Shelomith of indeterminable gender in 2 Chr. 11:20). There is the presumptively male Gomer in Genesis 10:2 versus the infamous female Gomer of Hosea.

Women and men alike bear theophoric names (including a portion of a divine name). For example, Isaiah is male; Zeruiah (David's sister 1 Chr. 2:16) is female; their names have the same form and suffix. This is true even when the third-person, masculine, singular, suffix pronoun *–hu*, "he," is part of the name. For example, Micaiah (*Mikayahu*) ben Imlah is a male prophet in 1 Kings 22; Micaiah bat Uriel in 2 Chronicles 13:2 is a woman; both have the masculine suffix *–hu*. Queen Athaliah's name occasionally appears in this form. The suffix *–yah* is a shortened form of the Divine Name, the first syllable of the Tetragrammaton, familiar to many from *halleluyah*. "Yah" also functions as a stand-alone name for God. Its form is feminine, though it takes masculine verbs in the Hebrew Bible. In some contemporary Jewish practices this form is assigned corresponding feminine verbs to craft prayers and liturgy using feminine language, instead of or alongside masculine ritual language. (The divine name *eloah* also has a feminine form and takes a masculine.)

The relationship between grammatical gender and divine gender is complex. Longstanding practice has been to gender God as male, in part because the overwhelming majority of divine names and gendered expressions are masculine, and in part as a buttress to patriarchal social, cultural, and religious structures. (Christians add to this the notion that God is the father of Jesus.) Masculine language is not the only language used for the divine in the Scriptures. The Spirit (of God) is feminine in form and function, taking feminine verbs exclusively in the Hebrew Bible. (It is neuter in Greek. Masculine translations of the Holy Spirit in the NT are postbiblical, stemming from the translation of the Bible into Latin in the fourth century.) There is a wealth of feminine metaphorical and descriptive language for God, much of it centered on birthing and mothering, for example, Deuteronomy 32:18 and Job 38:8, 29. The only reproductive organ ascribed to God in the biblical text is a womb. Often the love God feels for humanity is expressed as emanating from that womb, *rechem*, using the verb *r-ch-m*, unfortunately regularly translated "compassion": Deuteronomy 30:3; Isaiah 49:13, 15; Jeremiah 31:20. Feminine biblical God-language has not been historically cited or received as evidence that God is female in whole or in part. Not even biblical literalists seem to take it literally.

All of this has implications for how Biblical Hebrew is translated into other languages and varies according to the gendered patterns of the translation language, so these issues are not present in all languages into which the Scriptures are translated. Translators regularly make gendered choices, for example, when to use pronouns "he" or "she"; when or if to capitalize them if referring to God; when to use a proper noun "the Spirit" or "God" instead of a pronoun to help the reader sort out the flow of the narrative; when or if to use the neuter "it" rather than a pronoun—"she, the city" or "he, the day"—and many, many more. We make choices, gendered choices, that reflect our own understandings of gender in our world and in the world of the text, including the gender of God in and beyond the text.

So then, what does it mean that the Hebrew Bible uses feminine and masculine language for God, but not evenly balanced? Is God overwhelmingly masculine with a significant feminine side? Does the category of grammatical gender simply not correspond with the ontology of God? Does God transcend gender? Is gendered God-language simply an artifact of certain languages, without any religious meaning? How shall we translate it, and why? Should we tell the reader what the text says and why we translate the way we do?

My translations in this work and others are responses to those questions, as is this translator's preface-turned-appendix. Because readers using standard English translations such as the New Revised Standard Version (NRSV), Jewish Publication Society (JPS) *Tanakh*, New International Version (NIV), or King James Version (KJV) may have difficulty identifying these issues in translation or in the underlying biblical text, my aim in this project is honestly to articulate those choices and reflect on them and their implications for biblical interpretation.

References

Ackerman, Susan. "The Queen Mother and the Cult in Ancient Israel." *Journal Of Biblical Literature* 112, no. 3 (Fall 1993): 385.

———. "The Queen Mother and the Cult in the Ancient Near East." In *Women and Goddess Traditions*, edited by Karen King, 179–209. Minneapolis: Fortress Press, 1997.

———. *Warrior, Dancer, Seductress, Queen: Women in Judges and Biblical Israel*. New York: Doubleday, 1998.

———. *When Heroes Love: The Ambiguity of Eros in the Stories of Gilgamesh and David*. New York: Columbia University Press, 2005.

Allen, James. *Without Sanctuary: Lynching Photography in America*. Santa Fe: Twin Palms, 2000.

Anderson, Cheryl B. *Ancient Laws and Contemporary Controversies: The Need for Inclusive Biblical Interpretation*. Oxford: Oxford University Press, 2009.

Andreasen, Niels Erik A. "The Role of the Queen Mother in Israelite Society." *Catholic Biblical Quarterly* 45, no. 2 (April 1983): 179–94.

Attridge, Harold W., Wayne A. Meeks, and Jouette M. Bassler. *The HarperCollins Study Bible: New Revised Standard Version, Including the Apocryphal/Deuterocanonical Books with Concordance*. San Francisco: HarperSanFrancisco, 2006.

Bail, Ulrike. *Bibel in gerechter Sprache*. Gütersloh: Gütersloher Verl.-Haus, 2006.

Bailey, Randall C. *Yet with a Steady Beat: Contemporary U.S. Afrocentric Biblical Interpretation*. Atlanta: Society of Biblical Literature, 2003.

Bellis, Alice Ogden. *Helpmates, Harlots, and Heroes: Women's Stories in the Hebrew Bible*. Louisville, KY: Westminster John Knox Press, 2007.

———, and Joel S. Kaminsky. *Jews, Christians, and the Theology of the Hebrew Scriptures*. Atlanta: Society of Biblical Literature, 2000.

Ben-Barak, Zafrira. "The Status and Right of the Gĕbîrâ." *Journal of Biblical Literature* 110, no. 1 (March 1991): 23–34.

Berlin, Adele, Marc Zvi Brettler, and Michael A. Fishbane, eds. *The Jewish Study Bible*. Oxford: Oxford University Press, 2004.

Bird, Phyllis A. "The End of the Male Cult Prostitute: A Literary-Historical and Sociological Analysis of Hebrew *Qādēš-Qĕdēšîm*." In *Congress Volume: Cambridge*

1995, edited by John A. Emerton, 37–80. Vetus Testamentum Supplement. Leiden: E. J. Brill, 1997.

Bowen, Nancy R. "The Quest for the Historical Gebîrâ." *Catholic Biblical Quarterly* 63, no. 4 (October 2001): 597.

Brenner, Athalya. *Exodus to Deuteronomy*, Feminist Companion to the Bible (Second Series). Sheffield: Sheffield Academic Press, 2000.

———. *A Feminist Companion to Exodus to Deuteronomy*. Sheffield: Sheffield Academic Press, 1994.

Brooten, Bernadette J. *Love between Women: Early Christian Responses to Female Homoeroticism*. Chicago: University of Chicago Press, 1996.

Carasik, Michael. *The Commentators' Bible: The JPS Miqra'ot Gedolot (Leviticus)*. Philadelphia: Jewish Publication Society, 2009.

Coleman, Monica A. *Ain't I a Womanist, Too?: Third-Wave Womanist Religious Thought*. Minneapolis: Fortress Press, 2013.

Common English Bible: A Fresh Translation to Touch the Heart and Mind. Nashville: Common English Bible, 2011.

Copher, Charles B. "The Black Presence in the Old Testament." In *Stony the Road We Trod*, edited by Cain Hope Felder, 146–64. Minneapolis: Fortress Press, 1991.

Deutsch, Robert, and Michael Heltzer. *New Epigraphic Evidence from the Biblical Period*. Tel Aviv-Jaffa: Archaeological Center Publication, 1995.

DeYoung, Curtiss Paul, et al. *The Peoples' Bible: New Revised Standard Version with the Apocrypha*. Minneapolis: Fortress Press, 2009.

———. *The Peoples' Companion to the Bible*. Minneapolis: Fortress Press, 2010.

Drinkwater, Gregg, Joshua Lesser, and David Shneer. *Torah Queeries: Weekly Commentaries on the Hebrew Bible*. New York: New York University Press, 2009.

Dube Shomanah, Musa W. *Postcolonial Feminist Interpretation of the Bible*. St. Louis: Chalice Press, 2000.

Ellis, Teresa Ann. "Jeremiah 44: What If 'The Queen of Heaven' Is YHWH? *Journal for the Study of the Old Testament* 33, no. 4 (June 2009): 466–67.

Eskenazi, Tamara Cohn, and Andrea L. Weiss. *The Torah: A Women's Commentary*. New York: Women of Reform Judaism, Federation of Temple Sisterhood, 2008.

Federation of Reconstructionist Congregations and Havurot. *Kol ha-Neshamah: Shabat ve Hagim*. Wyncote, PA: Reconstructionist Press, 1994.

Fisher, Eugene J. "Cultic Prostitution in the Ancient Near East: A Reassessment." *Biblical Theology Bulletin* 6 (1976): 225–36.

Fox, Everett. *The Early Prophets: Joshua, Judges, Samuel, and Kings*. New York: Schocken Books, 2014.

———. *The Five Books of Moses: Genesis, Exodus, Leviticus, Numbers, Deuteronomy: A New Translation with Introductions, Commentary, and Notes*. Schocken Bible, vol. 1. New York: Schocken Books, 1995.

———. *Give Us a King! Samuel, Saul, and David: A New Translation of Samuel I and II*. New York: Schocken Books, 1999.

Fox, Nili Sacher. *In the Service of the King: Officialdom in Ancient Israel and Judah*. Cincinnati: Hebrew Union College Press, 2000.

Frankel, Ellen. *The Five Books of Miriam: A Woman's Commentary on the Torah*. New York: G. P. Putnam's Sons, 1996.

Gafney, Wilda C. *Daughters of Miriam: Women Prophets in Ancient Israel*. Minneapolis: Fortress Press, 2008.

Gafney, Wil. "A Queer Womanist Midrashic Reading of Numbers 25:1–18." In Athalya Brenner and Archie Chi Chung Lee, *Leviticus and Numbers*. Minneapolis: Fortress Press, 2013.

Gibran, Kahlil. *Jesus the Son of Man*. New York: A. A. Knopf, 1928.

Goldstein, Elyse. *The Women's Torah Commentary: New Insights from Women Rabbis on the 54 Weekly Torah Portions*. Woodstock, VT: Jewish Lights Publishing, 2000.

Goss, Robert, and Mona West. *Take Back the Word: A Queer Reading of the Bible*. Cleveland: Pilgrim Press, 2000.

Harris-Perry, Melissa V. *Sister Citizen: Shame, Stereotypes, and Black Women in America*. New Haven, CT: Yale University Press, 2011.

Henshaw, Richard A. *Female and Male: The Cultic Personnel: The Bible and the Rest of the Ancient Near East*. Allison Park, PA: Pickwick Publications, 1994.

Hurston, Zora Neal. *Moses, Man of the Mountain*. New York: Harper Perennial, 1991.

Jewish Publication Society. *Tanakh: A New Translation of the Holy Scriptures according to the Traditional Hebrew Text*. Philadelphia: Jewish Publication Society, 1985.

Laffey, Alice L. *An Introduction to the Old Testament: A Feminist Perspective*. Philadelphia: Fortress Press, 1988.

Lemaire, Andre. "Education." In *The Anchor Yale Bible Dictionary*, edited by David Noel Freedman. New Haven, CT: Yale University Press, 2008.

Marsman, Hennie J. *Women in Ugarit and Israel: Their Social and Religious Position in the Context of the Ancient Near East*. Leiden: Brill, 2003.

Meyers, Carol L. *Discovering Eve: Ancient Israelite Women in Context*. New York: Oxford University Press, 1991.

———. "Miriam, Music, and Miracles." In *Mariam, the Magdalen, and the Mother*, edited by Deirdre J. Good, 27–48. Bloomington: Indiana University Press, 2005.

———. "Mother to Muse: An Archaeomusicological Study of Women's Performance in Ancient Israel." In *Recycling Biblical Figures*, edited by Athalya Brenner and Jan Willem van Henten, 50–77. Leiden: Deo, 1999.

———. "Procreation, Production, and Protection: Male-Female Balance in Early Israel." *Journal of the American Academy of Religion* 51, no. 4 (December 1983): 569–93.

———, Toni Craven, and Ross Shepard Kraemer. *Women in Scripture: A Dictionary of Named and Unnamed Women in the Hebrew Bible, the Apocryphal/Deuterocanonical Books, and the New Testament*. Boston: Houghton Mifflin, 2000.

Meyers, Eric. "The Shelomith Seal and Aspects of the Judean Restoration: Some Additional Reconsiderations." *Eretz Israel* 17 (1985): 33–38.

Nash, Peter T. *Reading Race, Reading the Bible*. Minneapolis: Fortress Press, 2003.

Neusner, Jacob. *Introduction to Rabbinic Literature*. Anchor Bible Reference Library. New York: Doubleday, 1999.

Newsom, Carol A., and Sharon H. Ringe. *Women's Bible Commentary*. Louisville, KY: Westminster John Knox Press, 1998.

Nissinen, Martti. *Homoeroticism in the Biblical World: A Historical Perspective*. Minneapolis: Fortress Press, 1998.

Page, Hugh R. *Israel's Poetry of Resistance: Africana Perspectives on Early Hebrew Verse*. Minneapolis: Fortress Press, 2013.

———, and Randall C. Bailey. *The Africana Bible: Reading Israel's Scriptures from Africa and the African Diaspora*. Minneapolis: Fortress Press, 2010.

Patai, Raphael. *The Hebrew Goddess*. Detroit: Wayne State University Press, 1990.

Priests for Equality. *The Inclusive Bible: The First Egalitarian Translation*. Lanham, MD: Rowman & Littlefield Publishers, 2007.

Rashkow, Ilona N. *Taboo or Not Taboo: Sexuality and Family in the Hebrew Bible*. Minneapolis: Fortress Press, 2000.

Rice, Gene. "Africans and the Origin of the Worship of Yahweh." *Journal of Religious Thought* 50, no. 1/2 (1993): 27.

Sadler, Rodney Steven. *Can a Cushite Change His Skin? An Examination of Race, Ethnicity, and Othering in the Hebrew Bible*. New York: T. & T. Clark, 2005.

Sarna, Nahum M. *Shemot: The Traditional Hebrew Text with the New JPS Translation*. JPS Torah Commentary. Philadelphia: Jewish Publication Society, 1991.

Scholz, Susanne. *Biblical Studies Alternatively: An Introductory Reader*. Upper Saddle River, NJ: Prentice Hall, 2003.

Schüssler Fiorenza, Elisabeth. *Democratizing Biblical Studies: Toward an Emancipatory Educational Space*. Louisville, KY: Westminster John Knox Press, 2009.

Segovia, Fernando F. *Decolonizing Biblical Studies: A View from the Margins*. Maryknoll, NY: Orbis Books, 2000.

———, and Mary Ann Tolbert. *Reading from This Place*. Minneapolis: Fortress Press, 1995.

Spanier, Ktziah. "The Queen Mother in the Judaean Royal Court: Maacah—A Case Study." In *Feminist Companion to Samuel and Kings*, edited by Athalya Brenner, 186–95. Sheffield: Sheffield Academic Press, 1994.

Stein, David E. *The Contemporary Torah: A Gender-Sensitive Adaptation of the JPS Translation*. Philadelphia: Jewish Publication Society, 2006.

Sugirtharajah, R. S. *Voices from the Margin: Interpreting the Bible in the Third World*. Maryknoll, NY: Orbis Books, 1991.

———. *Voices from the Margin: Interpreting the Bible in the Third World*. Revised and Expanded. Maryknoll, NY: Orbis Books, 2006.

Tigay, Jeffrey H. *Deuteronomy*. JPS Torah Commentary. New York: Jewish Publication Society, 1996.

van Wijk-Bos, Johanna W. H. *Making Wise the Simple: The Torah in Christian Faith and Practice*. Grand Rapids: Eerdmans, 2005.

———. "Writing on Water: The Ineffable Name of God." In *Jews, Christians and the Theology of the Hebrew Scriptures*, edited by Alice O. Bellis and Joel S. Kaminsky. Atlanta: Society of Biblical Literature, 2000.

Walker, Alice. *In Search of Our Mothers' Gardens: Womanist Prose*. San Diego: Harcourt Brace Jovanovich, 1983.

Walker-Marnes, Chanequa. *Too Heavy a Yoke: Black Women and the Burden of Strength*. Eugene, OR: Cascade Books, 2014.

Walsh, Jerome T. "Lev. 18:22 and 20:13: Who Is Doing What to Whom?" *Journal of Biblical Literature* 129 (2001): 201–9.

Warrior, Robert Allen. "Canaanites, Cowboys, and Indians." *Union Seminary Quarterly Review* 59, no. 1–2 (January 1, 2005): 1–8.

Weems, Renita J. *Battered Love: Marriage, Sex, and Violence in the Hebrew Prophets*. Minneapolis: Fortress Press, 1995.

———. *I Asked for Intimacy: Stories of Blessings, Betrayals, and Birthings*. San Diego: LuraMedia, 1993.

———. *Listening for God: A Minister's Journey through Silence and Doubt*. New York: Simon & Schuster, 1999.

———. *Showing Mary: How Women Can Share Prayers, Wisdom, and the Blessings of God*. West Bloomfield, MI: Walk Worthy Press, 2002.

———. *What Matters Most: Ten Lessons in Living Passionately from the Song of Solomon.* West Bloomfield, MI: Walk Worthy Press, 2005.

Westenholz, Joan. "Tamar, Qĕdēšā, Qadištu, and Sacred Prostitution in Mesopotamia." *Harvard Theological Review* 82 (1989): 245–65.

Williams, Delores S. *Sisters in the Wilderness: The Challenge of Womanist God-Talk.* Maryknoll, NY: Orbis Books, 1993.

Wright, David P. "'She Shall Not Go Free As Male Slaves Do': Developing Views About Slavery and Gender in the Laws of the Hebrew Bible." In *Beyond Slavery: Overcoming Its Religious and Sexual Legacies*, edited by Bernadette J. Brooten and Jacqueline L. Hazelton. New York: Palgrave Macmillan, 2010.

Index of Ancient Sources

Index of Subjects

CPSIA information can be obtained
at www.ICGtesting.com
Printed in the USA
BVHW072227130519
548184BV00001B/11/P

9 780664 239039